In and Out of the Spotlight

The Ups and Downs of an Actress

by

Lesley Mackie

First published in Great Britain in 2023
by SNB Publishing Ltd.
57, Orrell Lane,
Liverpool L9 8BX

Acknowledgements

There are some people I would like to thank specifically, although most of them are mentioned inside the book, most notably my mum and dad who supported me in my ambitions from early childhood, when wanting to become an actress was definitely not the norm for a working class child. I also acknowledge my elocution teacher, Miss Cita Angus, who fed my desire to tread the boards from the age of five onwards, and pushed me into the limelight whenever she got the chance.

I've used an abundance of photographs and have tried to seek permission when possible. However, many of the photographers are no longer with us, or are untraceable now. Thanks to all those at D C Thomson and the Perthshire Advertiser, to Alex Coupar of Spanphoto, Eric Thorburn in Glasgow, John Paul Photography in Inverness, Tom Bader in Worcester, Louis Flood and Angus Findlay in Perth, and Jennie Scott in London. Also to Lara Haelterman who designed the cover for this book.

To Terry Wale, my husband of 44 years, whose love and belief in my talent resulted in a play written specially for me, which undoubtedly changed my life and has given me plenty to write about.

Thanks and love to my family, especially Katy, Ollie and Dickie for always being there for me.

To all those who have been part of my life and shared my journey, my fellow-actors and my dear friends; I thank you for your company and wish I could have mentioned you all.

Preface

On one of my regular trips back to Dundee in 1990, I took my three-year-old daughter, Katy, along with me to see my childhood home in Tait's Lane in the West End of the town. I'd heard that the tenement building in Speed's Terrace was to be demolished and I wanted to take one last sentimental look at it. As we climbed the circular outside steps and walked along the 'plettie' by the boarded-up windows, I was able to look down on the communal 'greenie', where the washing used to be hung out and where I'd played with the other children when I was about my daughter's age. Having her there with me, I was able to see it all through her eyes, much as I had once seen it myself. Of course, the air-raid shelters that we used to run across had gone and everything was smaller than I remembered it – Hawkhill Primary School was barely a hundred yards away but back then I had a child's perspective. It had seemed quite a trek at the time to the church, the local shops – and my two grannies. It had been a warm and friendly world and revisiting it was a nostalgic experience, tinged with sadness when I thought of it all being reduced to rubble.

When I finally moved back to Scotland with my family in 1993, shortly after the birth of my son, I was told that the tenement had been saved and was in the process of renovation. I remember vividly the day that I went back and climbed those stairs again. They were all spruced up now, and along the 'plettie', I was confronted by brand new front doors and sparkling windows. I had the effrontery to knock on the door of Number 10, now fully modernised, and was shown around my old home by a friendly young man. What delighted me most was that the old hadn't been swept aside to make way for the new; that the past and the present could exist all at once. And it was this sense of continuity that made me feel the need to get in touch with my own past.

Showing Katy number 8, Tait's Lane in 1990.

Shortly after the move, I was asked to give a thirty-minute talk to a group of local businesswomen about *My Life in the Spotlight*. I had reservations about doing it, but realised, now that I was back on home territory, that this was something I might be asked to do again, so decided to face the challenge. Although I can easily talk for hours on a one-to-one basis, I did not have the confidence to arrive unprepared and 'ad lib', or even to work from notes, so the speech involved a lot of preparation; I knew that I would feel happier with a script. I quickly changed the title to *In and Out of the Spotlight* and I tried to put something together that would give a flavour of what my life had been, and was, about. I found that I enjoyed the experience, both the writing and the delivery of the speech, but as far as the writing was concerned, I couldn't stop. I started to expand my thirty-minute effort, and it has grown into this epic. I hope that others enjoy reading it.

Number 8, Tait's Lane after renovation.

Looking forward to the past

So, to begin at the beginning...

I was born in Kings Cross Hospital in Dundee on June 10th, 1951, weighing in at just under eight pounds. My parents were Leslie and Violet Mackie. According to various sources, I talked before I could walk and showed early signs of 'the performer'. I will resist boring you with too many early recollections, or relating stories passed on to me about the funny things that I said or did, and will jump straight to the age of five when I started at Hawkhill Primary School and already had a baby brother called Grant Leonard. I don't think that I felt envious at the time about the middle name, although it has since struck me that a young couple, newly married and with all the names in the world to choose from, not only gave me the female spelling of my father's name but left it at that with nothing in the middle. Dad wasn't given a middle name either, but he said that was because they didn't think he would live, and to waste a name in those days clearly had some importance when you were handing out family names, but I don't think that's why I missed out! In later years I heard that dad wanted to call me Serena, but mum didn't fancy that, and no other name came to mind. Why on earth didn't they follow tradition and give me my mother's name in the middle, as I would certainly have been happy as Lesley Violet?

Grant Leonard was destined to be entertained mercilessly by me during his own formative years, and I hope he derived a little pleasure from it; I do recall that he was a very receptive audience. It must be difficult to live with a performing sibling and, for a time, Grant was fairly reticent when he had to 'do a turn' at family parties. However, he overcame that and by the age of 11 was giving a very passable rendition of *The Sair Finger,* by Walter Wingate.

It has been well chronicled in the *Dundee Courier*, the *Evening Telegraph* and *The People's Journal* that I was sent to elocution lessons at the age of five to slow me down because I spoke at about 500 words a minute. I still talk quickly so I'm not sure just how successful my teacher was in that department. I went to Miss Cita Angus at the Dundee School of Music in West Bell Street. Mum taught piano there and it was fortunate for me that she worked beside someone who was arguably the best in her field in the Dundee area. Miss Angus was a very eccentric woman, very much of the old school, or what we called the 'How Now Brown Cow' mould, but she was highly thought of in the '50s and '60s and will be fondly remembered for her big hats, her strange ways, but above all for her professionalism and her fine attention to detail. Woe betide any girl who dared to perform *Tam o' Shanter* in high heels, or anything but the sturdiest of brogues. I had lessons from Miss Angus for twelve years, and every week for twelve years she asked me how old I was.

She would often call me into her little room just before my lesson and ask me to perform for her other pupils, to show them 'the right way' to deliver *The Twa Corbies* or *The Whistle,* and I'm sure it must have got up a lot of pupils' noses – not to mention the mothers' noses – that she was so tactless. Many parents sent their children to elocution lessons in order to improve their speech, but a child who actually performed was much more unusual in the '50s than it is now. Very few of us had television sets back then and, even if we had access to one, our choice of viewing would have been limited to harmless fare like *Watch with Mother* with Andy Pandy on a Tuesday and Bill and Ben on a Wednesday – and after 1967, the 'Test Card' when there were no programmes on at all – hard to imagine. Now we have a non-stop barrage of reality television which, of course, gives people of all ages the desire to perform because we are encouraged to believe that anyone can achieve success. Audiences seem as happy to watch a family member, friend or neighbour 'doing a turn' as a professional entertainer, and the Scots have always loved being able to say, "Ah kent his faither." But back then, I was the exception and not the rule, and I didn't live in the fiercely competitive world that kids have to cope with today.

My love of performing was never forced upon me; it was there from a very young age. My earliest memory of this was when a family friend took me to some yard near the Sinderins where her father worked. They lifted me onto a box outside the works and I sang *A Gordon for Me* for the assembled workforce; I was three years old. For most of my childhood I was out with my mother in tow – or I should say that she had me in tow – on two or three nights a week, reciting and singing at hospitals, old folks' homes and at

King George VI Memorial Club and the *Fiveways Club*, usually as part of a concert party, alongside old-timers like Chrissie Rhynd, Margaret Pert, Ron Gonella and Roy McRae. Those folk were famous in Dundee and provided heart-warming entertainment for many. It was great fun and I loved doing it. Nobody had to push me, although my parents were always enthusiastic in their support of my childhood ambitions. Perhaps if they'd known a bit more about the precariousness of the acting profession they might have been a little less keen; not that it would have made any difference. I said at five years old that I wanted to be an actress, and apart from one brief spell when I had notions of becoming a missionary, I never wavered.

1957, Little Red Riding Hood with Rowena Cooper.

So there I was at six years old, as Little Little Red Riding Hood, walking onto the stage at the old Nicholl Street Rep in Dundee, clutching a huge apple, and reciting,

"I've got such a pain in my poor little tummy
And all that she said when I went and told mummy was:
"Run along child and stop all that crying,
The pain will get better, you're not really DYING ..."

I was entranced by the actresses in the dressing room – they were extrovert, flamboyant, affectionate, and I must have spoken of them a lot because my Aunt Harriet christened her first baby, Amanda – after actress Amanda Walker who eventually married Patrick Godfrey who had been the Big Bad Wolf – and my nanny Johnstone took in an actor as a lodger for a while.

I had made my pantomime début and now I read my first newspaper reviews ... *She's so tiny you feel like tying her on the Christmas tree... Little Lesley Mackie endeared herself to the audience when she was onstage, perhaps because she was the spirit of pantomime, a child enthralled by the footlights*; and, in truth, that's exactly what I was. I had a glimpse of another world and I wanted always to be part of it, so I was delighted to be asked back the following year to be Laetitia in Ali Baba and the Forty Thieves alongside actress Tsai Chin.

When I was about seven, we started to take our holidays in Carnoustie. It didn't seem at all peculiar that, year after year, we travelled 11 miles to stay in Mrs Aimer's boarding house for a week. It was the ideal resort and, of course, the Talent Contests beckoned. On Thursday evenings throughout the summer, I became well-known to Bill and Betty Cummings, as they did to me, and a prize of half-a-crown (12.5p) was well worth having. I entered for everything. I even dragged Grant into Brother and Sister contests, and if they were one short for any beach or paddling-pool activity, 'Uncle' Bill would just put out a call for me, and I would happily oblige; it didn't matter that sport was never my strong point.

I think I must have been rather bossy as a child. There were several children living in and around Speed's Terrace, and the 'greenie' was an ideal place to rehearse, so I took it upon myself to organise concerts for neighbours and friends. I formed a club which the other kids seemed happy enough to join, even if I did charge them a penny for the privilege of attending each meeting. I have to say, in my defence, that the money was put away for charity. We met weekly on the Middle Green and always opened the proceedings with a hymn. We also rehearsed for Hallowe'en, and there can't have been too many guisers as well drilled as the ones from Speed's Terrace. We were keen to give value for money so that anybody who invited us in got a good 15 minutes-worth of entertainment. If we'd

7

had a good business manager, he might have persuaded me to cut the programme in favour of getting round a few more houses! Still, we usually earned enough to buy our fireworks. The culmination of our efforts was a 'greenie' concert which was designed to raise money for Oxfam. We pinned notices around and rehearsed with gusto. On the appointed date the rain poured, so the concert was quickly re-located to 10, Speed's Terrace, where hordes of neighbours crammed into the back room. We sold tablet as well as tickets and everyone took part; even my cousin Joyce, who was visiting from the South gave us a rendering of *Maybe it's Because I'm a Londoner*, and Grant brought the house down by hiding behind Joyce and me in *Charlie Brown*, only popping his head out at the end of each verse to say: "Why is everybody always picking on me?" It was a great success, and we raised the princely sum of £1/17/6d (£1.87) for the charity; we even got a 'write-up' in the local paper.

My interest in singing developed towards the end of my schooling at Hawkhill Primary when I won the Leng Silver Medal Competition for the singing of a Scots Song. My teacher, Mr Thomas Clark, then persuaded me to enter for the annual Gold Medal Competition, which was open to all silver medal winners between the ages of 11 and 18 who had won within their own schools, and without giving it much thought I chose to sing *A Rosebud by My Early Walk*, an absurd choice for an 11-year-old. The range was vast and the breathing impossible but, despite Mr Clark's advice, I dug my heels in, and of course I came a cropper. I had to sit there and listen to the judge saying what a bad choice I had made, and that if I came back next year with a simpler song, I would stand a good chance of winning it. So I went back the following year and sang *The Rowan Tree* for which I was awarded the Gold Medal, but I could have kicked myself for letting Mr Clark down and throwing away the chance of winning it while still at primary school.

Many years ago I met a woman who had been in my class and she reminded me that Mr Clark would often cajole the other pupils to finish their work early by promising them that, if they did, Lesley Mackie would perform a monologue for them. She was able to name *Peter at The Pictures* and *Betty Entertains the Minister* as part of my repertoire.

I moved onto the Harris Academy, where I was immediately put in a different class from Moira Brown, who had been my best friend throughout primary school. It wasn't easy to spend any time together, but we were young and fickle and made new friends quickly. As well as all the real work, I started to play the oboe as well as the piano, which led to music camps each year at Aberfoyle. There were also annual festivals in Dundee, Arbroath and Edinburgh for singing and for elocution – a discipline which went out of fashion long ago – and charity concerts galore. I even played hockey and netball in House matches, although I am sure that Birnam House could have done without the handicap! I must have shown willing enough though, because I was appointed School Captain when I went into my sixth year, although it was touch and go for a while, as my best friend, Doreen, and I had committed a misdemeanour at Belmont School Camp, and I held my breath as my future hung in the balance. Our two 'boyfriends', Mike and Hilton, had planned to drive up from Dundee to meet us in the car park in the middle of the night. At the appointed time, we slipped out of our dormitory in our pyjamas and dressing gowns, clutching a hot water bottle and a flask of coffee. We had no sooner settled into the car, passing round the top of the flask, when a great beam of light fell on us. Behind the beam was Rosie, our music teacher, and we knew we were in deep trouble. We were summoned before Donald Stewart, the Head of the Music Department, and fortunately we managed to convince him that it was just an innocent adventure. Well, so it was! We got off the hook, my reputation survived, and I still gained the Captaincy.

Having taken most of my Highers in my fifth year, I had a wonderful sixth year devoted largely to debating and musical activities. My partner in the Inter-Schools English-Speaking Union Debating Competition was Donald Findlay, the Boys' Captain, and together we reached and won the final. My forte was in the delivery of the speech, but I needed a bit of help in putting it together, and I shall always remember, with gratitude, the support and the advice I was given by several people, including the Rev David Gray, minister of our family church. As I was only the 'Seconder', I was fortunate to have Donald answering all the impromptu questions from the floor. He went on to become a well-known QC, and many years ago, had I not been otherwise engaged, I would have found myself responding to his *Toast to the Lassies* at a Harris FP Burns Supper. I heard from the lady who took on the task that, having prepared a 'reply' which assumed that Donald would throw in a few compliments, she was faced with a barrage of misogynistic vitriol and had to re-write her speech on the spot. A lucky escape for me!

I left school in 1969, having considered going to university to give me 'something to fall back on', but my heart was set on one thing only – I wanted to go to Drama College. As well as all my school activities, including playing Dido in *Dido and Aeneas*, I also attended the Youth Theatre at Dundee Rep and, as a result, participated in a few professional productions, including *Wait until Dark*, starring Jill Gascoine, who went on to have a very successful career.

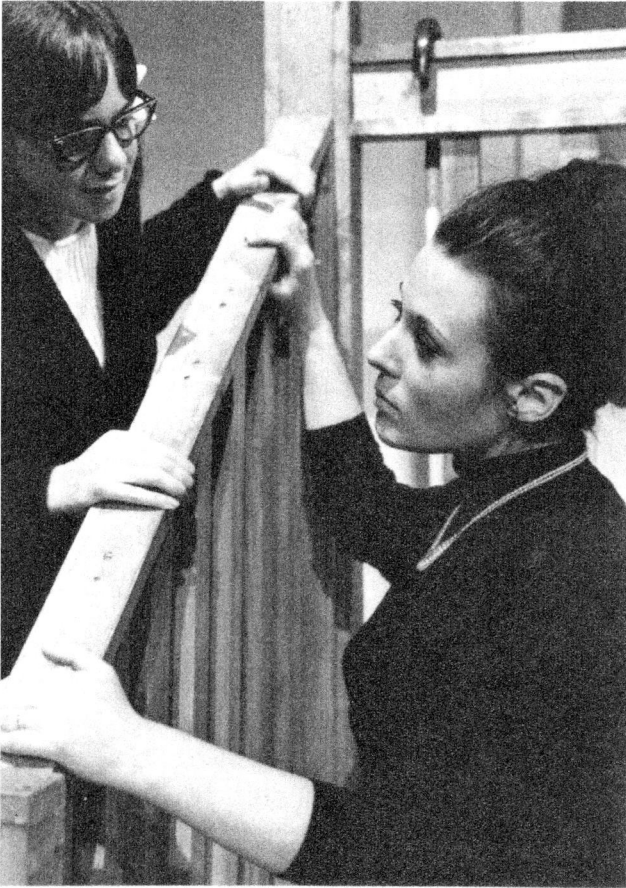

1968, Wait Until Dark – Dundee Rep with Jill Gascoine.

So, having prepared my two speeches with the help of Cita Angus and Donald Sartain, the then Associate Director at Dundee Rep, I headed with my family for Glasgow and the Royal Scottish Academy of Music and Drama (RSAMD). Had I known what was in store for me, I would have been even more nervous than I was. There were 70 female applicants for the three-year course, and only seven places on offer. The odds were pretty daunting (although nothing compared to today!), and so was the audition. I was ushered into the first room and, after a brief introduction, asked to do an improvisation, "Start as an old lady in a rocking chair", the examiner said, "then take us back through the ages and end up as a baby in the womb. Proceed when you are ready." Miss Cita Angus had never prepared me for anything like this, but I had no option. I'd been thrown in at the deep end, and it was a case of sink or swim. So, hurling caution to the winds, I crawled around the examiner's ankles, howling like a six-month-old babe and finally curled up into a foetal position at her feet. I went on to do a Highland Fling, danced with a chair, sang, read poetry, performed my two prepared speeches, and then went off to Butlin's Holiday Camp in Ayr with Doreen, wishing that I had applied for university. We were not going to Butlin's for a holiday, I hasten to add, but to work as waitresses for the summer – an exciting change, we hoped, from the Salvesen's 'Berry Belt' – but more of that anon!

We'd only been there for a couple of weeks when we managed to wangle a day off and hitch-hiked back to Dundee where my letter from Glasgow was awaiting me. I opened the envelope with some trepidation but, joy of joys, I had been offered a place; perhaps I wasn't so bad at improvisation after all. We had another reason for heading back; Michael Barry, who was involved with the Dundee Rep, was determined to launch us on a 'folk' career, and having taken publicity shots and christened us *The Mythic Sirens*, had found us a booking at the YMCA as a supporting act for the much-acclaimed singer, Archie Fisher. We probably sang very sweetly, and I am sure we looked charming in our crochet dresses – Doreen in pink and me in white – which had been made for us by Doreen's granny, but we never did get any more bookings. Maybe it was the ridiculous name that did it, but I still have that little white dress. I loved it.

We returned to Butlin's, where my news about the RSAMD helped to sustain me through the next four indescribably awful weeks. The wages, when they remembered to pay them, were appalling, and the hours were unsocial, to say the least. Nor was the camp the safest of places for young girls to be. We were usually allocated a night-watchman to walk us back to our chalet after the 3am shift, but we soon decided that we were safer walking back on our own! The chalets themselves were dingy and, according to Doreen, were decorated with the same wallpaper she remembered from an early childhood visit.

We worked in one of the 'restaurants', clearing away dishes, and occasionally serving up the burgers and chips. On one memorable occasion, I was on my way to deposit a tray of fresh food in front of an impatient queue of holidaymakers when I slid on something nasty and went flying, landing flat on my back in a sea of burgers and spaghetti! It was in my hair, it was everywhere, and I was so embarrassed that I refused to come out from under the counter until I was ordered to. I think this episode probably sums up my experience at Butlin's as well as anything. Hi-de-Hi!

I did, however, find a boyfriend in the camp. He was a dental student, employed as a wine waiter, which was a step up from us minions, and I thought at first I had hit the jackpot. He was certainly the first boyfriend I'd ever had with a flashy sports car, but it didn't last. I could certainly have used his expertise in the years to come when I had problems with my teeth! We finished our stint and went home where I prepared for my move to Glasgow and the RSAMD.

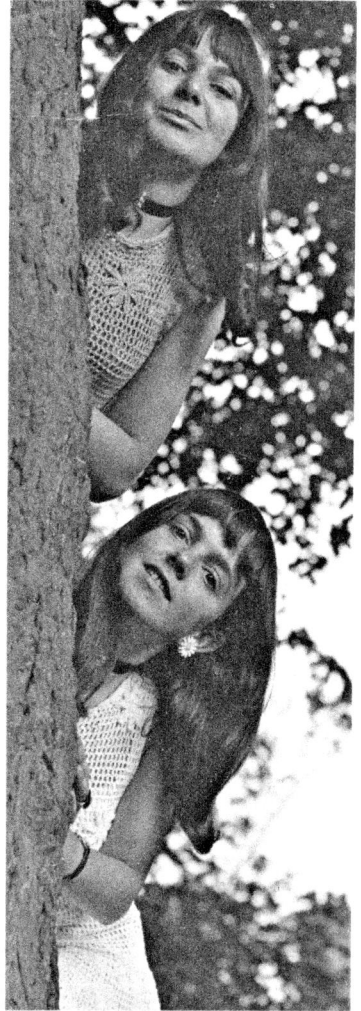

1968, Mythic Sirens.

12

One more step along the road

I was about to live away from home for the first time. I was one of three drama students who had found a place to stay in Gibson Hall, which was the Domestic Science Hall of Residence, and it was a great bonus to have found somewhere with meals provided; well, perhaps it wasn't that great, as the amount of food I was consuming undoubtedly affected my tiny frame! Although we often moaned about the rules and regulations, it was a good place to be in our first year at college.

The first six weeks were difficult, punctuated by many weepy calls home. Once I had settled in, however, I began to enjoy my time there and I finally realised what a worthwhile and enriching experience it was. Of course, it didn't help that the dreaded improvisation classes seemed to take up so much of our time in the early days. I remember *The Seven Deadly Sins* with great clarity. Seven of us were given slips of paper, each containing the name of one of the sins. The exercise was a silent one, and the rest of the students had to guess what sin we were trying to convey. I was 'Gluttony', and I had to go first. So I plunged in, trying to look piggish, opening invisible cupboards and stuffing huge amounts of imaginary food into my mouth. I was keenly anticipating the arrival of Sin Number Two because it meant that I would have somebody to act with, which I fondly imagined would make the exercise easier. I was a little startled when he arrived and began to take his clothes off. As he stripped down to the bare buff in a matter of seconds, I realised that he was 'Lust'; not only that, but he was looking in my direction! By this time all the girls were shrieking hysterically, the boys were urging him on, and the exercise ground to a halt. But it all came as a terrible shock to a wee lassie from Maryfield!

As I settled into my first year, my confidence grew, and I did all the things that students are supposed to do. I wore my granny's black, astrakhan coat which came down to my ankles, and purple lace-up boots. I wore hats and tammies of every description, and even crocheted myself a poncho with matching bag and tammy. Mum was persuaded to knit me a pair of knickerbockers, and I thought I was so 'with it'. When I see the photographs now, I can hardly believe that I went out looking like that. My father, of course, couldn't believe it at the time! I became very friendly with another drama student who was in the same hall of residence; Janis came from Cults, a posh suburb of Aberdeen, and she was also rather daunted by being away from home for the first time. It did not take long for us to adjust to the situation, and even break a few rules along the way; we had great fun sneaking our male friends in through the laundry window in the basement, up the back stairs and into our room for late night drinks and chat.

For me, the only fly in the ointment came in the shape of John Groves, the Vice-Principal. It was his job to develop our stagecraft, even to the extent of giving us kissing lessons: "Noses to the left, noses to the right" – and laughing lessons, although I never needed much training in that department. He also saw it as part of his function to prepare us for the tough world outside, and his methods were somewhat unorthodox. On one occasion, he chose a girl to sit out in front of the class while the rest of us were encouraged to comment on her looks and appearance. He turned to me, and said, "Ugly, isn't she? What do you think, Lesley?" I muttered something about not thinking she was ugly at all and tried to pick out a redeeming feature, but before I could get more than a few faltering words out, he exploded, "You're a liar! You're next. Right everyone, what do you think of Lesley? I'll tell you what I think. She'll play maids for the rest of her life!" I thought this a terrible insult at the time, but the irony of his remark struck me in later years when I discovered that some of the best parts are the scene-stealing maids.

Things never really improved with Mr Groves. I had hopes of continuing my oboe playing as it seemed such a shame to abandon it just because I had left school, but when I found that there might be an opening in the Music Academy Orchestra, John put his foot down, saying that I wouldn't have time for my own curriculum, never mind adding to it. I did indeed have a busy schedule, not to mention the many theatre productions we were expected to attend, but if he'd had a bit more foresight, he might have realised that an instrument would be a major asset in an over-crowded profession. Nowadays, they talk of a 'quadruple threat', when an actor can sing, dance, and play an instrument or two as well as act. John took every opportunity to exploit my trusting nature and my gullibility. One day during rehearsals for *Harlequinade*, which was our final production at the end of the year, he came in clutching a bottle of whisky. He said that it would be fun to use it in rehearsals, as they sold it in the joke shop, and it tasted exactly like the real thing. I had never tasted whisky before, but along with everyone else, I ventured to have a sip. I hated it, but others vouched for its authentic taste so I asked him where the joke shop was so that I could buy a bottle for my father's Christmas. Of course, it <u>was</u> whisky, and I never lived it down.

Towards the end of the year, a young man on the Teaching course, Doug Porteous, gathered a few of us together to form a little acting company. We started work on *The Bald Prima Donna* and an all-female version of *The Knack* (we were way ahead of our time!), which we planned to perform in repertoire at various small venues in and about Aberdeen during our summer holidays. We rehearsed in every spare moment, Doug directing as well as organising the summer season. At the end of term we all headed home to pack, and met a few days later at a cottage we were to share for the duration, which turned out to be brief. The whole thing was an unmitigated disaster. There had been no publicity – the best kept secret in Aberdeen. Only two tickets had been sold in advance, and we went into the streets before each performance trying to persuade people to come in, but after a few soul-destroying days we gave up. Having learned a lesson about shared responsibility and forward planning, we packed our bags and headed home.

Feeling a trifle deflated, I arrived back in Dundee to find my college report. Everything was in order except for the comments from John Groves. His advice was that I should change over to the Teaching Course because I did not have the necessary toughness to survive in the acting profession. The College Principal, Colin Chandler, wanted me to go through to Glasgow to discuss things, but ultimately it was to be my decision. I knew that if I chose to ignore John's advice, he would make my life hell for the next two years, but I had the summer to consider my options, so I put the dilemma to the back of my mind. I wanted to make the best of the rest of my long holidays, so went to work on the good old 'Berry Belt'. Dad was manager of the Christian Salvesen Cold Storage depot on the Kingsway, and Doreen and I always managed to find a summer job there. The raspberries moved along the conveyor belt, and we had to pick out the rotten ones. It was a boring job, but it was a great way of observing women at work, and observation being a vital part of the actor's stock-in-trade, I made the most of the opportunity. The conversation was often colourful and entertaining, and it certainly relieved the monotony. We also needed the money to subsidise our first holiday abroad.

We were to fly to Amsterdam, but from that point on it was to be a hitch-hiking holiday through Holland and Germany. Neither Doreen's parents nor mine were happy about this arrangement, and did their best to dissuade us, but as we had hitched so often in Scotland, and with great success, we were not going to be put off. The way things are now, I would sooner lock my daughter in her room and throw away the key, than allow her to go hitch-hiking. But times have changed, and it seemed to be a lot safer then, although it was not without its perils as we were to find out.

On arriving in Amsterdam we were horrified to discover that all the official Youth Hostels were full. A helpful passer-by directed us to a somewhat dubious-looking building by one of the canals, and as we approached the door we saw a rather large and obviously spaced-out woman slumped in front of it, chanting, "You want some dope? You want some hash?" We quickly side-stepped her, only to find our way blocked by an 'official' who stamped a large green letter 'H' on the back of our hands. It suddenly struck me that we were about to be admitted to a hippie hostel. It was still the early '70s, when drug-taking, flower-power, and 'love and peace, man' were almost obligatory, and particularly in Holland which had very relaxed laws on soft drugs. We must have seemed like creatures from another planet as we sat there in what was euphemistically known as the 'coffee bar' smoking our Consulates! There were notices on the walls about various 'missing' people, and photographs of a few who had died from drug overdoses. One in particular sticks in my mind about a boy who had jumped from a high window after taking LSD, believing that he could fly.

On venturing up to the dormitories, we were taken aback to find that they were mixed. Clutching our purses tightly and removing as few clothes as possible, we both slipped into a single bunk, hoping and praying that we would come through the night unscathed.

We should have known that the hippie culture was not a violent one and the only assault we suffered was on our ears, as we had to endure the strumming of guitars all night long. *Nights in White Satin* was all the rage at the time. The noise was augmented by the roaring of motorbikes outside as gangs of skinheads hung about, hoping to beat up a few hippies. It was an ominous start to our holiday, and we were stuck with the distinctive green 'H' on our hands for the rest of our trip. We enjoyed Amsterdam and did all the touristy things – like visiting the Red Light District, although I think that we expected something similar to the Blackpool Illuminations! We were agog at the sight of the whores of varying ages and attractions sitting in their windows waiting for customers. Some of the older ladies read books to pass the time, and others stood outside, shouting abuse at the sightseers and nosey on-lookers. We saw the occasional client enter then exit about 15 minutes later, putting a comb through his hair before disappearing into the night.

Before leaving Amsterdam, we did manage to spend one night in an accredited Youth Hostel, and the contrast was astounding – beautifully clean, and such lovely breakfasts. We headed for Zandvoort, desperate to use the tiny tent which Doreen had lugged along with her. We arrived at the campsite and gawped at all the fabulous tents. We erected our mini-version and as someone passed us and shouted "Hund-haus" (Dog kennel), we realised how ridiculous it was. We squeezed into it amidst great hysteria from our fellow campers, but we never managed to spend a single night in it because the rain came down and it collapsed on top of us in a tiny wet heap. Some kind people offered us the use of a spare tent which they erected alongside their own luxury one, but even the spare was a palace to us, and it saved us having to head off in the middle of a very wet night. We stuck to Youth Hostels after that.

We had two Golden Rules when it came to hitch-hiking: 1) Never accept a lift if there is more than one man in the car. 2) Never split up. On the two separate occasions we risked breaking the rules, we landed ourselves in very tricky situations. On our way to Koblenz, we flouted regulations by hitching on the autobahn, and when we were offered a lift by two young men, we debated at length before finally accepting; after all, they seemed quite nice. It was a big mistake of course, and my heart missed a beat when I saw a sign for Koblenz, and the driver went in the opposite direction. He suddenly took a turning, following a signpost which said, 'Zu den wäldern' (To the woods), and stopped the car in the middle of nowhere. What they had in mind was made clear and, as we trembled in the back of the car, in order to play for time we lit up our fags – something that was not frowned upon then. I ended up pleading with them in my halting German which, roughly translated, went something like this... "Please, we are young girls from the remote hills of Scotland. Our fathers wear skirts. They are very strict. We are not permitted to be alone with a man until we are promised in marriage!" I finally used what I believe was my trump card, by asking them what they would feel if their sister was in the same situation as we were. Somehow or other, it worked, but what they made of these two rigidly brought-up girls from the wilds of Scotland, hitch-hiking across Europe in their hot pants, and without a father in sight, I'll never know. We were just relieved to be dumped, albeit unceremoniously, back on the road to Koblenz.

For the most part, however, we were lucky with our lifts, and we got quite used to being chauffeured in luxurious Mercedes. In return, we would sometimes offer a driver a packet of fags, a modest but quite acceptable gift, but usually we sang to our drivers, a repertoire largely made up of Scottish folk songs, which they seemed to enjoy. At any rate, none of them stopped the car and asked us to get out.

It was time to head home, and it had started to rain. It rained and rained and as there seemed to be no end to it, we just kept going through Belgium without stopping. We left early in the morning for Köln Deutz and the police put us off the Autobahn on three separate occasions – we must have been pretty bold, not to mention reckless. My diary says, 'Pouring rain – hilarious!' It was certainly very kind of the drivers to pick up two very drowned rats with soggy backpacks, and I hope we were suitably appreciative – although I can't imagine that we were in *Mythic Sirens* mode by that point, so Scottish folk songs would have been off the menu. As we travelled for about 48 hours without any proper sleep we probably just dozed in the back of the big comfortable cars. After our speedy trip through Belgium, we jumped on the ferry to Dover, and it was back to the good old lorries – no more Mercedes for us! We hitched up to

London and after being deposited at a depôt just north of the capital, we faced the last lap.

Our lorry driver led us over to an empty lorry which belonged to one of his mates. He settled us in and went into the café to tell his friend that he now had a couple of girls to keep him company on the next leg of his journey, and they were already sitting in his cab. It was a bit of a cheek really, and we had an anxious wait, wondering how his mate would feel about his uninvited passengers. When the driver eventually emerged, he said he couldn't have someone sitting on the engine between the driver's seat and the passenger one, so one of us would have to transfer to another lorry. We had always travelled together in the front before, but it seemed like a reasonable request so, without too much debate, Doreen went into the front of a nearby cab which belonged to his pal. My driver said we could meet up at the next depôt. With the memory of Koblenz still strong we probably had nagging doubts, but here we were in the middle of nowhere in the middle of the night, so circumstances forced us to break our second Golden Rule.

All went well on the first leg of the journey with my driver generously sharing his sandwiches, and we had our pre-arranged stop for us girls to have a quick natter and confirm we were happy with the arrangement. When we set off again, Willie kept complaining that his 'load' was shifting, and he would have to stop to adjust it. He finally alighted from the cab, and I saw Doreen's lorry pass us by. I mentioned this, but he assured me that he would soon catch them up. Instead of climbing back into his own seat, he came round to the passenger side, and I suddenly had a little middle-aged man trying to cuddle in beside me. After a lot of pleading, I managed to ward him off but I counted the minutes until I was reunited with Doreen again outside Glasgow. She had encountered the same problem, so we had escaped by the skin of our teeth again.

Our luck, however, appeared to be running out as they dumped us in the early hours in some God-forsaken depôt with no apparent sign of life. A police car eventually appeared and, much to our surprise and relief, drove us to a better 'hitching' spot. When we arrived back in Dundee in the early hours of the morning, mum appeared at the window, and I recall her saying that at last she would be able to get a good night's sleep. It had been quite an adventure, and we must have remembered all the best bits, because the following year we were determined to head off again.

Into my second year! Gibson Hall had been lovely in many ways – no cleaning or cooking – and just <u>how</u> lovely we did not fully appreciate until we were later stuck in a cold and dingy flat, but we had begun to feel restrained with so many rules and regulations. Not only that but, because of all the cooked breakfasts and generous evening meals, I had put on over a stone, so although Janis and I could have stayed for another year we decided it was time to move on. I hoped that I would stand a good chance of losing a few pounds once I was fending for myself but, because I had always been slim until this point in time, I had no idea how to go about it. Over the next few years, endless attempts at dieting and endless binges became a source of worry and frustration, as the weight continued to pile on. Eight and a half stones doesn't sound very much, but at five feet nothing it was quite a lot. I admit to having stuffed my face, but my chubbiness may have also had something to do with my age and a kind of belated puppy fat, as eventually it all disappeared.

1972 - my first photoshoot

So at the start of the second year I moved into a flat with Janis. We quickly learned how much food and electricity cost as we stuffed coins into a hungry meter. We often sat around a one-bar electric fire wearing overcoats and thick socks, and it was dismal. The dreariness of the flat added to our misery about our weight, although I don't think it stopped us eating regular helpings of good old Scottish pie, beans and chips! Having spent our first year at an Annexe just off Byres Road, we moved into the main building in the town centre, so we were now part of college life in a much fuller sense. Peter d'Souza, one of our tutors who had joined the college at the same time as us, was a favourite of mine, and I was thrilled when he asked me to play First Fairy and Snug the Joiner in the final year production of *A Midsummer Night's Dream*. He directed me in comedic vein with pratfalls all over the place, so I had a ball, and was probably rather funny as a somewhat chubby wee fairy. It was exciting for two reasons, one being that I had been given this extra opportunity to perform before the public, but also because I was fairly obsessed with Mr Peter d'Souza. He was well aware of this and used to tease me mercilessly, which made me blush even more and rendered me a babbling wreck. In fact, the crush went on until my final year, when he was appointed as my private tutor. I had to 'come clean', as I was so self-conscious in front of him that the tutorials were a waste of time, but we chatted about it and I was allocated another tutor. Peter and I remained friends.

Apart from participating in 'The Dream', I was involved in productions with my own year group. I had a quaint part in *The Baikie Charivari* by James Bridie – a part which lingers in my mind as, for some reason or other, I made up half of my face as an old woman. I must have had a reason I suppose, but we were encouraged to be bold. As I had chosen not to take John Groves' advice to transfer to the Teaching Course, the first few months of my second year were punctuated by remarks like: "Oh, you're still here are you?" But at least I had the support of the rest of the staff, and my determination won through in the end. I was finally vindicated when, towards the end of my year, I had to face John Groves as our director on *Death Takes a Holiday*. One day, in front of the entire class, he made a public apology and admitted that he had made a mistake. I never knew what prompted this climbdown, and things never really changed, but perhaps he'd simply realised that my acting ability might just triumph over my lack of worldliness. And then again, perhaps I was just growing up.

On the domestic front, we had given up our drab and dreary flat at the end of the first term and, in desperation, Janis and I even attempted to get back into the hall of residence, but we had no joy there. Because of family church connections in Dundee, two elderly ladies, who lived in Stepps on the outskirts of Glasgow, offered to provide me with board and lodgings. Without other options, I accepted graciously, but living with them was tricky, although they probably had the same problem with me; it can't have been easy at their age to have a teenager invade their space, and I was not as considerate as I might have been – but they were very old-fashioned and told me off about the length of my nightie and various other things that I considered unimportant. They even had a 'visitors' cake box, which was banned to me, and a terrible torment when I was in bingeing mode. I think that I yielded to temptation on two occasions.

I started going to the local church to try and meet other people in the area and, lo and behold, the minister's daughter took me under her wing. Before long I had moved into the manse and was accepted as a fourth daughter. The Philps were very good people, and the light of that goodness seemed to shine from them. I was susceptible, and after a particularly moving talk from a visiting missionary, I felt that Jesus was trying to get through to me and, emotionally overcome, I rushed from the room, followed in close pursuit by Mrs Philp, who got down on her knees beside me and asked Jesus to come into my heart. At home in Dundee, I became an absolute pest, telling my mother that she was not a true Christian, because real Christians lived, breathed and slept with the word 'Jesus' on their lips. I gave them books to read; one I recall was titled *Christ died – Why?,* and this phase lasted until I left the manse at the end of my second year. Gradually, my fervour evaporated, and I returned to my semi-religious self. I realised that being a true Christian was hard work, and without the Evangelical forces around me, I did not have the necessary faith.

The summer holidays stretched ahead, and I had a lot of plans. I returned to Dundee and the 'Berry Belt' and it was around this time that I started driving lessons. I was not one of nature's drivers, as my father was constantly telling me, but I was keen to learn. However, the driving was put on hold, because Doreen and I were about to head off to Greece with our rucksacks on our backs. Our folks were not quite so anxious this time round, because it was a simpler proposition as we were only planning to 'hitch' between Dundee and London and had no intention of trying to get lifts in Greece. So we flew to Athens and booked into a Youth Hostel, not exactly in the league of the smart one in Amsterdam, but certainly not as bad as the hippie hostel. The facilities were not clean, with very basic shower and loo arrangements, and very poor security. We had items stolen from our rucksacks, a gorgeous purple choker and earrings that I had bought the previous year in Amsterdam, and which I still remember with fondness – and a couple of evening dresses. Taking long dresses on such a holiday seems crazy now, but it was the '70s, and they were *de rigueur*.

Although Doreen and I understood little of politics, we were aware that the atmosphere in Athens was not relaxed. The Colonels' regime was still very much in evidence, with soldiers patrolling the streets. We had been given a parcel to deliver to a lady friend of my Aunt Mina's, who was in the main hospital in the town, but it would have been easier to get into Fort Knox. Once inside, the décor was spartan, and there was no feeling of proper nursing care about the place. We handed over the parcel, and although we were only there for a short time, I felt that the doctor in attendance was very offhand; I even recall him smoking as he stood by her bedside. However, it was a brief visit, and we walked away and never saw the lady again. I have often wondered what happened to her and why she was in that hospital in the first place, but somehow never got around to asking. It was a relief to get out; a relief to escape to the searing heat of an August sun, compelling us to stop every hundred yards to buy iced cokes or lemonade to avoid total dehydration.

We trudged up to the Acropolis and saw all the wonderful ruins, but the heat was so debilitating that it was all we could do to stay on our feet. What fools we were to go to Greece in August. We both caught a tummy bug, which was a major problem because, at that time, you could walk for miles without finding a loo, and even if you did it was not likely to be a place you could linger. We didn't know about avoiding tap water, ice, or eating unwashed fruit – things that everyone knows nowadays – but travelling abroad was not quite so commonplace then, and mineral water wasn't readily available.

After a few days, we decided to head for a Greek island, where we hoped that the heat would be more bearable, so we made our way to Piraeus to wait for a sailing. We hadn't checked departure times and, as we hung about, we were approached and chatted up by two young Greek men. We had to make do with their few words of English and our non-existent Greek, but we weren't particularly enamoured with sitting overnight in the port until the morning boat, so we went with Dino and Alex to a rooftop discotheque. So daft were we, that the offer of a bed for the night from virtual strangers was preferable to hanging around in the port café until dawn, so after a drink or two, we headed for Dino's scruffy little bedsit, which was just a shed in the garden of a fairly imposing-looking building. He said that his family lived in the house, although why he was banished to an out-house was never explained. He generously offered us the single bed, but the night couldn't pass quickly enough. After a few sleepless hours, when they kept tickling our feet, the boys accompanied us back to the harbour for our early morning departure. Although we had made the mistake of disclosing when we were planning to return, we hoped that we had seen the back of them.

We loved the tiny island of Ios, which was totally untouched by tourism. Travel was by foot or by donkey, if you could bear to put the poor skinny creatures through the ordeal of carrying you up a very steep and rocky path when everywhere was accessible by foot. We sunbathed most of the time and met lots of students on the beach and in the little café at the top of the hill. There wasn't much else on the island, but we loved being in that tranquil and isolated little place. Most of the older women were dressed in black, and although the arrival of tourism must have been a tremendous shock for the older generation, it was a relief for the younger people, who had been burdened for too long with archaic laws and traditions. The moral code was very strict, particularly on the islands, and the sight of the scantily attired tourists must have caused a lot of discomfort for the natives. We heard that young girls were not allowed to go out with boys without a chaperone, and so I imagine that the young Greek men could not believe their luck to find this influx of young women, who seemed willing to chat and drink freely with them, not to mention other possibilities.

After a week of lazing around, we boarded a night boat, having paid the cheapest possible fare, which was Deck Class. We thought ourselves the lucky ones as we slipped into our sleeping bags and looked up at the stars. As we drifted off to sleep, we were rudely awakened by a monstrous wave which suddenly enveloped all the poor souls on the deck. The storm seemed to happen in an instant, and it was all we could do to gather up our bits and pieces and stay upright. We were in extreme danger of being thrown overboard in the lurching vessel, but somehow managed to struggle down onto a lower deck. We were just top deck paupers trying to save our souls, but so surly and officious were some of the crew that we felt they might actually block our way and send us back to face our fate. I have oft-times wondered how many people have gone missing in such circumstances, and if any effort would have been made to reach us should we have failed to get down to safety. It was odd to find ourselves sitting alongside women with live hens and other livestock on their laps. We arrived back in Piraeus at some unearthly hour of the morning in our sea-soaked garb and to our dismay we were greeted by the beaming faces of Dino and Alex.

We only had a few days left and most of the time seemed to be spent avoiding our two Greek admirers, but they did eventually get the message and we were left in peace for our last couple of days. There would be no holiday the following summer, but we had packed enough into the summers of 1970 and 1971 to keep us going for a few years. Despite all the 'incidents', I still remember them as halcyon days although I missed my stolen Dutch earrings and choker for a long time.

I returned to yet another spell at Salvesen's, and a few more driving lessons. The only other thing I remember vividly from that summer is that I lent my driving instructor the sum of £30. I didn't have any money beyond my student grant, but he was so persuasive in his appeal for the said amount to buy a car (was that possible?) so that he could teach privately, that I arranged to meet him near the Dundee Repertory Theatre on the Lochee Road to hand over the cash. Although mum was doubtful about it she came with me, so in a way she was as daft as I was. He disappeared shortly afterwards leaving a trail of debt behind him, and I discovered that quite a number of his pupils were owed money or had lent him things; one man had been into the driving school to ask about his Black and Decker drill. When I turned up on his doorstep to find out what he was playing at, I was greeted by a bedraggled looking creature with small children round her ankles, and it was obvious that she wasn't going to be able to help. I did not leave it there, however. When I returned to Glasgow, the college helped me find a solicitor, who traced him to Southampton. Under threat of court action he agreed to send the money, but I never received a penny, and we never saw or heard from him again; I can't even remember his name. All I ended up with was a bill for £6 from the solicitor which, at that time, I thought extortionate.

Into my third and final year. After the constant moving throughout the second, I was determined to find something more settled for my final one. I soon spotted an advert on the college notice board placed by a girl called Fiona Carmichael, looking for someone to share a flat in 34, Springhill Gardens opposite Queens Park on the south side of the city. She was a minister's daughter from the Dundee area. I moved in, and it was quite refreshing to have someone around who did not live and breathe the theatre. However, she was devastated when her boyfriend, who was a music student at the RSAMD, suddenly finished their relationship, and she decided to cut loose and get away from it all. The break-up of that relationship changed her life in a very dramatic way, because she moved to Switzerland to be a nanny, met a man called Hartwig Meins, got married, had two daughters, took on German as her first language and never came back, but we kept in touch.

After the Christmas break, my friend Janis moved in. It was a novelty to have a place of our own, we liked company, were very hospitable, and if anyone didn't feel like trailing home after an evening of socialising and boozing, we were happy to let folk stay. I enjoyed my last year, giving a few decent performances, the most popular being my 'Daisy' in the Christmas show. She was a little country flower, full of spoonerisms, awkward movement, and a little song, where I jumped and dropped octaves in comedic vein. Over the years, I often dragged out my moth-eaten Daisy hat and fading sheet of music to do my Daisy 'turn'.

I left college just before the end of term to start rehearsals for *The Great Northern Welly Boot Show* at the King's Theatre in

Glasgow, returning to the Athanæum building for the Final Showcase, where we all performed two speeches; I was awarded the Comedy Prize and, although I would have preferred the Gold Medal, I was glad to have won something. I was disappointed not to be able to go to London with the rest of the acting students to do our showcase for agents down there, but at least I had a job. On June 22nd, mum and dad came through for the last time for the Graduation Ceremony, when we were presented with our Diplomas. An era had come to an end, our college days were over, and a new part of my life had already begun.

THE GREAT NORTHERN WELLY-BOOT SHOW
by TOM BUCHAN & BILLY CONNOLLY
DIRECTOR ROBIN LEFEVRE

- 3 -

Making a splash

After three years as a student, I was suddenly an actress; a rather chubby actress it has to be said. I hadn't succeeded in any of my attempts to diet, and on my 21st birthday, my home-made card from Uncle Archie said: *RADA's BIGGEST STAR TO DATE IS 21 STONES OVERWEIGHT!* (RADA flowed better than RSAMD!) As far as work was concerned it didn't seem to be a problem and, in fact, once the weight dropped off, work was not quite so plentiful.

My part in the 'Welly Show' was Mary Hill from the Gorbals and my boyfriend, Big Jimmy, was to be played by Billy Connolly so, whatever else was in store, I was certainly assured of a few laughs. The cast was a rather uneasy mix of actors and variety artists; actors tend to abide by a fairly strict code, observing rules such as the 'half-hour call', which means that you have to be in the theatre thirty minutes before the 'Beginners Call', which is five minutes before curtain up.

I don't know many actors who will risk drinking alcohol before a performance, but with characters like Hamish Imlach, the well-known portly folk singer, in the cast, certain individuals turned up when they felt like it, and very often, straight from the pub. I had a few dialogue scenes with Billy, who often placed himself about six feet upstage of me. I don't think this was through any selfish desire to steal the limelight by forcing me to act with my back to the audience, but simply that his only stage experience at that time had been as a folk singer with *The Humblebums;* he had little basic stagecraft, but he was a lovely, funny bloke to have around. Little did any of us know that he was but a few years away from his rise to mega-stardom, and that one day he would play a leading acting role in a movie starring Dame Judi Dench, not to mention ending up as Sir William Connolly!

Billy was still with his first wife, Iris, and their two young children, Jamie and Cara, and I spent quite a few evenings back at their place after the show. Their flat was teeming with dogs, their labrador having just given birth to eight pups. In fact, I was all set to adopt one which I had already christened 'Oor Welly', when common sense prevailed and I realised how crazy it would be to trail an animal around from town to town, especially when you are living most of the time in 'digs'. One thing I did know was that dad wouldn't have given it house room, as he never liked animals in the home, our pets having been restricted to a rabbit, a mouse and a budgie!

1972, King's Theatre Glasgow – The Great Northern Welly Boot Show, about to get wed to Billy Connolly.

The show was loosely based on the Upper Clyde Shipbuilders' Work-In, and I do mean 'loosely'. An unusual element was introduced by the addition of a novelty act – a stripper, to be precise. Before rehearsals began, there had been a nationwide search for the right lady to fill this 'spot', and there was quite an outcry amongst the Scottish strippers when the part was finally offered to a Miss Brandy di Frank from Nottingham. She was only 22, although I felt like a child beside her. She had certainly been around, but had a steady boyfriend who looked after her interests and was often in evidence. Her 'act' consisted of a tasteful strip undertaken in the presence of two large cut-out heads of Harold Wilson and Edward Heath. She hung all her bits and pieces of discarded costume on their noses and ears until all she was left with was a shimmering G-string. The most controversial aspect of all this was which tune or song would accompany the strip, and the original idea was that she would do it to either *The Lord Is My Shepherd* or *Jerusalem*, but these were rejected for obvious reasons. What all this had to do with shipbuilders – or even welly boots – I can't recall, but Brandy's act to the strains of *Amazing Grace* was a highlight of the show and I seem to remember we played to bigger audiences than we might otherwise have expected.

Tony Palmer was our director, whose talents before and after our show were mainly channelled, very successfully, into the film world. It was generally thought that his rudeness and lack of social graces were a throwback to a time when he had been grossly overweight and somewhat bitter. Having lost most of the bulk that he had hated so much, he had never rediscovered how to relate to people. He seemed to have a soft spot for me, however, which was to have repercussions a few months hence.

After a short transition period, I moved into 291, Sauchiehall Street, which was quite a well-known address; over the years, many actors and theatre folk rented rooms there from Mrs Douglas, the Drama College secretary. Work was plentiful at this time, and I went straight from the 'Welly Show' into *The Calum Kennedy Show*, also at the King's Theatre, thereby missing out on doing the former at the Edinburgh Festival, although I did get another chance to repeat my Mary Hill a few months later! There were all sorts of variety acts in the show, including Scottish folk musician, Alistair MacDonald, and Calum's five daughters, who followed him onto the stage at the start of the show, singing: *I'm Following in Father's Footsteps*. Fiona, the eldest of the Kennedy girls, was the only one who went on to have a singing career. I had been hired as a comedy 'feed' for Jimmy Logan, and the next six weeks proved to be an excellent training ground for me. A feed's job is usually to deliver the straight lines so that the comic gets his laughs. To my delight I had one or two funny lines, but Jimmy made sure he had all the best ones!

I admired Jimmy and had a lot of respect for him, so when I was invited to join the Theatre in Education company at the Citizen's Theatre, I sought his advice. He was happy to give me the benefit of his wisdom and experience and invited me to go for a coffee at a local hotel after the show one evening. By the time he collected me in his smart Bentley, it seemed rather late to go to a hotel, so we drove back to his posh flat in Bearsden. It did not even occur to me to wonder how I was going to get home; maybe I assumed that he would give me a lift. At that time, he was married to his second wife, Gina Fratini, a successful British fashion designer, who came up from London for a long weekend each Thursday – but this was a Wednesday so, of course, the flat was empty, and had I known a bit more about naughty Mr Logan, I might have been a little more circumspect.

He produced a couple of steaks from his fridge and uncorked a bottle of red wine. After a quick sniff, he poured the entire bottle down the sink, and as I knew little about wine I was probably quite impressed. He was clearly used to entertaining and opened a second bottle which passed muster, and while I consumed a large glass of wine, he flamed the steaks in brandy. He gobbled his steak at an incredible rate and then moved in closer as I slowly devoured mine. It crossed my mind that he might kiss me, and I almost hoped that he would as he was still quite an attractive man in his mid-forties. He took hold of a pendant that I was wearing and spoke softly to it as if to a microphone, which was corny to say the least, but before I knew what had hit me, he picked me up, threw me over his shoulder, and strode through to the bedroom. I voiced a few ineffectual "No"s and prattled on nervously, but he clearly believed that 'No' meant 'Yes'. I suddenly blurted out that I wasn't on the pill, and those were the magic words that seemed to turn the whole thing on its head. He sat on the bed and proceeded to give me a lecture about the folly of being a young actress in the business and unprepared for such an eventuality as this. He gave me his private taxi number and a five-pound note to cover the cost of my taxi home. As he fell into a deep slumber, I awaited the arrival of the cab and slipped out of his flat like some little floozy and went back to number 291.

I felt a little awkward the following day, but as the taxi had only cost about £2.50 I felt obliged to give Jimmy his change. I popped into his dressing room just before the show and Gina was standing there, so I mumbled something about 'the change' from the bottle of whisky which he had asked me to buy for him the previous day, and scurried away. Later in the evening when we were standing in the wings, he thanked me for my tact, and the incident was never mentioned again. I thought that was quite gentlemanly of him, but it was indeed a different world from the one that young women inhabit now, I'm pleased to say. As far as I was concerned, it had become a good story to relate to a few select friends.

A few weeks later, however, I was walking along Byres Road on my way to see *A Clockwork Orange,* when a little disabled car pulled up beside me; it was Jimmy's old dad, Jack Short. At the tender age of 21, I thought he must be well over 80, but he was probably only about 76 at the time. In his younger days, he had been part of a vaudevillian act with his wife and family, and young Jimmy had been one of the child performers. Jack had a wooden leg, which I believe was the result of an injury during World War 1, but he was a feisty old guy who was often backstage at the King's. He opened his window and asked if I would like to join him for a bite to eat. I felt somewhat thwarted over my cinema trip, but I knew that I could go some other time, and Jack was an old man in need of company. So I went back with him to his little flat, and having put on a record of Jimmy singing Scots songs, he got on with the task of preparing the piece of liver he had lined up for his evening meal and was now planning to share with me. He offered me a whisky as an aperitif, something I have never had a taste for, but I tried to have a sip. The liver, a little undercooked, was placed before me with a little bit of tomato for garnish. I was about to sit down when he suddenly asked me to give him a cuddle. I gave him a hug, and then he uttered the immortal words, "Would you like to give an old man a wee sensation?"

Everything became clear, and I havered on about having a steady boyfriend. He said that he wasn't seeking a permanent relationship, but his wife had been dead for several years, and he had been on his own ever since; obviously one 'sensation' would be enough! I held my ground, and resolutely tried to make some inroads into the liver. He sat down beside me at the table, and my discomfort was interrupted by a phone call. I rushed to answer it, and it was Jimmy, who seemed a little surprised to find me alone with his dad, who he referred to as 'an old devil'. There was a second call from our mutual agent, Freddie Young, who wanted to speak to Jack. Before getting him to the phone, I chuntered on about needing to come round and see her, so I left the flat in great haste under the pretext of having been summoned by my agent. I had a great laugh with Freddie and her husband John, and for years after, John always greeted me with, "How about a wee sensation?" I don't suppose that anyone would laugh at this tale now, and probably consider it worthy of reporting to the MeToo movement; different times back then.

My diary was always full of aftershow parties and nights out with an assortment of folk. There was Billy and Jimmy, who were members of an Irish singing group on *The Calum Kennedy Show* – I still recall Billy's lovely rendition of *Help Me Make It Through the Night* as we all sat around relaxing in a hotel bar after the show one night – and folk musician Alistair Macdonald, who I went on to work with on future occasions. Drinking to excess was par for the course in the variety world, and with 'The Welly Show' and Calum's show, I had quite a baptism by fire in the professional theatre, and probably consumed far too much booze myself.

Before I finished my variety stint, I was already in rehearsals for my first big television play, *Just Your Luck* by Peter McDougall. They were looking for a skinny girl – and I was far from that – but I landed the part of Alison, a 16-year-old protestant girl who gets pregnant and has to marry a catholic sailor. We rehearsed in Kirkintilloch, filmed in Greenock and Glasgow, and recorded the interior scenes down in London. The play had a strong cast including Mary Riggans and Eileen McCallum, both of *Take the High Road* fame. Mary played my mother and Eileen my mother-in-law.

Just Your Luck had its funny moments as a play, but it did paint rather a bleak picture of life in Greenock, and the locals came out in force to voice their protests when we were filming. Even when we started at dawn, there was always a bunch of kids throwing stones, or women shouting at us. I particularly remember a loud and grating voice screaming, "Oor lassies dinnae get pregnant!" Our director, Mike Newell, who went on to climb the ladder of success, directing many films, including *Four Weddings and a Funeral*, marshalled a gang of local men to help us move the kids out of the way, but he made the fatal mistake of paying them for their services with bottles of wine. This had the effect of further aggravating the womenfolk who had enough to deal with without their men being plied with additional alcohol. A member of the crew actually added to a graffiti-filled wall by spraying the name of a local gang to give an authentic background for one of the scenes. Somehow the Press latched onto our problems, and we made the front pages for a few days, with headlines such as: *BBC GO HOME*!, but despite all the trouble, we managed to finish the filming and the locals even got involved in the 'wedding' scene. A crowd formed as the be-ribboned car approached the 'close', and as David Hayman and I emerged from it several women shouted, "Good luck hen", and one old biddy rushed across to David and gave him a big kiss. It seems that, no matter how tough people's lives are, there is something about a wedding that brings out the best in them, and the fact that it wasn't a real wedding didn't seem to matter at all.

Having made my theatrical and television débuts, my career in pictures was about to take off. They were looking for someone to play a twelve-year-old schoolgirl in a film called *The Wicker Man*. After strapping up my bust, I went to meet the director, Robin Hardy, and landed the fabulous part of Daisy, who had all of three lines to say. Oh well, maybe I wasn't destined to become a movie star just yet, but my week on *The Wicker Man* was to provide me with enough stories to keep me going for months. However, before my initiation into the glamorous world of movies, I still had the interior scenes of *Just Your Luck* to record down in London.

My diary entry for my day of departure reads: 'Train to London. Stayed with John. Slept on the floor – should have fixed up a hotel.' John was an old boyfriend who had lived a few doors away from us in Nairn Street and was now a 'roadie' with a rock band. I did eventually book into a hotel, but I led a somewhat haphazard existence at this time. Jean Faulds, one of the older actresses, did her best to keep an eye on me. I stayed on in London at the end of filming to catch up with a few friends and to try to find a London agent, although the one that had shown an interest in me after 'The Welly Show' was blacklisted shortly after I met him, so that wasn't too promising.

Between my return to 291, Sauchiehall Street and my week on *The Wicker Man*, I had to 'sign on' for the very first time. This was the start of a long relationship with the dole office, although I was fortunate in that it did not feature strongly in my early career.

I arrived in Newton Stewart full of anticipation. It was, after all, my movie début. The chaos that greeted me was something of a surprise. I discovered that I had been expected a little earlier to dance naked whilst leaping through a fire. Due to a mix-up, they hadn't put the 'fertility dance' in my contract, and I can't say that I was too disappointed about that. Strangely enough, the costume lady for *The Wicker Man*, Sue Yelland, was the same one I had just worked with on *The Great Northern Welly Boot Show,* and she and I kept in touch for some time.

I discovered that quite a few people had been sitting around for weeks waiting for the weather to change. My college friend, Barbara Ann Brown (now Barbara Rafferty), who had been hired to do just a few seconds filming, breastfeeding her baby amongst some ruins, had been there so long she was worried that Amy would be completely weaned before they got to her bit. I was staying in a nice hotel, which was just as well because I spent a lot of my week sitting there waiting to be called.

Newton Stewart had never seen anything like it. The once quiet little town had been invaded by hordes of actors and film crew. The entire membership of Scottish Equity seemed to be there, but only in the small parts. 'Stars' had been flown in from elsewhere to play the leading roles: Edward Woodward, Christopher Lee, Diane Cilento (ex-wife of Sean Connery and future wife of Anthony Shaffer who had written the screenplay), Britt Ekland and Ingrid Pitt headed the cast. Britt was playing a voluptuous Scottish wench, called Willow, and the reason behind this monumental piece of miscasting was that they needed a 'star name' for the American market. There were several vocal coaches on site to help the English and other foreigners master the dialect, and they even engaged my services a few weeks later to help Britt disguise her Swedish accent but, understandably, it was not an easy task. In the end a music student dubbed her song, Annie Ross dubbed her dialogue, and a stripper was engaged to stand in for a scene in which she was required to dance in the nude. Britt, having recently discovered that she was pregnant, wasn't happy about showing her bottom, although she did agree to exhibit her breasts. "I need more privacy", she said. "Everyone will be looking at me – and who can blame them?"

Lindsay Kemp played Britt's father, the landlord of *The Green Man* pub, and he was a bit of a loose cannon, causing quite a stir by disappearing with his partner for a few days in the middle of the filming. He had been banned from the local hotel because he poured a mug of beer down the front of the stripper's dress; what she did to offend him remained a mystery, but as he was in drag at the time it was all too much for the hotel management.

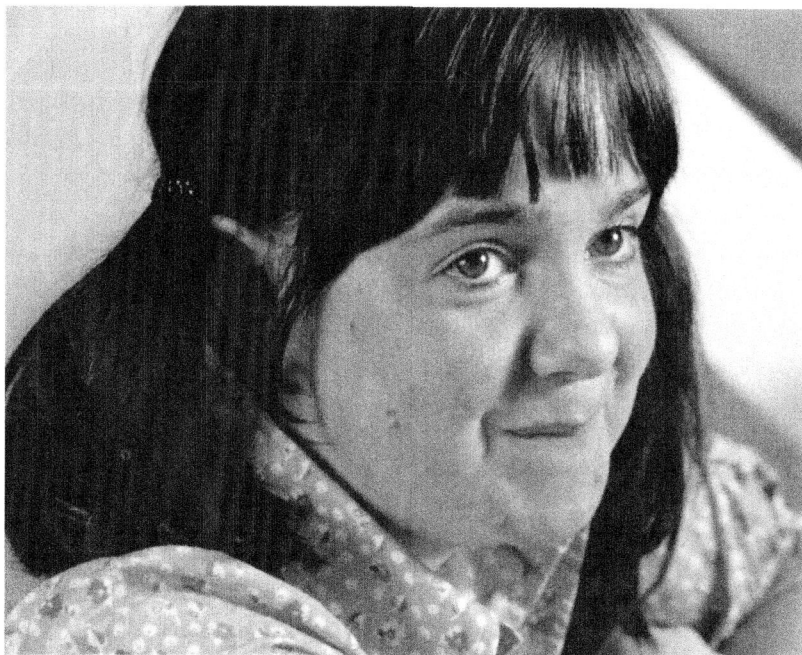

1973, The Wicker Man – Daisy

The Wicker Man was all about Pagan sacrificial rites; it was set on the fictitious Scottish island of Summerisle and many of the local people appeared as 'extras', often wearing animal heads, and I don't think they had much of a clue about what was going on. When they finally saw the film at its première in Stranraer, they realised that they had been playing ritual murderers and many were outraged by the storyline, not to mention its sexual content.

Although he had made a lot of commercials, Robin Hardy had little previous experience in feature films. He was terribly posh, and I was fascinated by this exciting and uninhibited new world – although horrified after a night out when I witnessed him peeing into a pot plant in the foyer of the hotel! One of the assistant directors, Mike Naylor, took a bit of a shine to me, and said that he planned to write a play for me. I liked the title – *A Postal Order from my Granny* – but he had serious drink problems, and I didn't think he'd have the tenacity and staying power required to get the play – starring Hattie Jacques and me – mounted in the West End of London, which was what he had in mind.

My one disappointment during the week was that I was unable to go to a dinner party which Britt and Diane hosted for all the actors involved in the filming. They went to tremendous trouble, preparing and serving it themselves; they even had wild rice flown in from Harrods, but I had made other plans and had to miss out on what I heard was a fun evening.

My contribution to the whole thing was minimal and, but for a happy accident, would have been limited to my one scene as 'Daisy', a little girl who enjoyed watching a beetle trap itself against a nail inside a school desk. I had a few lines of dialogue with Edward Woodward, and that was that.

At the end of the week there was a company 'get-together' in a local pub and, somehow, I ended up singing *Summertime* as a duet with Edward. This burst of exhibitionism resulted in an offer to sing a song in the film, a lovely Highland lament which was played over the opening title sequence.

Although *The Wicker Man* did not make much of an impact when it was first released, it enjoyed considerable success later when it won an award in France and went on to enjoy 'cult' status for a while during the '80s and beyond. As far as I was concerned, that one week reverberated and echoed through the coming years, and many people that I met on that film were to pop into my life again. I also had a fund of 'Wicker' stories which would keep me going for the rest of time.

As the filming had taken a little longer than planned, I was now heading straight to London for my next engagement, which was a reprise of 'The Welly Show' at the Young Vic. Bizarrely, when the film company heard that I was heading south, they asked if I would take the week's 'rushes' with me and deliver them to a studio in London as soon as I arrived. I still find it incredible that they would have trusted such a precious cargo to a fledgling actress they had known all of a week, and who had three lines in the film. They did, however, treat me to a sleeper, although I had to share with another lady, worrying all the while about the rather heavy priceless parcel on the floor beside my bunk bed. The following morning, I took a cab to the studios to deliver the package, but as my train arrived at 6am I had a long wait until opening time.

The 'Welly Show' had been well-received in Glasgow, but that's where it should really have stayed. Instead, four months later, London audiences were to have the privilege of seeing this uncompromisingly Glaswegian extravaganza. It was my first engagement in London, a three-week season at the Young Vic Theatre, a succession of drunken nights and lots of laughs. Well, we had to laugh, as the show was not exactly a smash hit. It must have been totally incomprehensible to the English who stayed away in their droves. We had all agreed to a profit-share contract and, as things turned out, we each made about £11 a week.

I stayed with our director, Tony Palmer, and his partner, novelist Angela Huth, who was none too pleased at my arrival as

Tony appeared to have taken a unilateral decision in offering to put me up. They lived in Eaton Terrace in a very smart area of London, and although I was grateful for such swanky accommodation, I have no idea why he was so magnanimous as he had not been asked to re-direct the London production. Perhaps he just wanted to vent his spleen and chose me to vent it on; it certainly seemed that way at times. He and Angela communicated much of the time by notes, which they left in prominent places. They usually related to money: 'You owe me 20p. Tony.' It didn't appear to be a happy relationship, aggravated by the presence of Angela's eight-year-old daughter Candida (from her marriage to Quentin Crewe), who Tony found irksome, always calling her 'stinky' or 'smelly'!

I had a lovely bedroom with an ensuite bathroom, and although the house and its location smacked of affluence, the Palmers clearly lived beyond their means – even the cleaning lady complained that she hadn't been paid for weeks. They had an 'au-pair' called Pascale, who often sat with me, gossiping and dishing the dirt on the Palmers and for that short time we became soulmates. It must have been a horrid existence to be young and French and working in such an unhappy household. One day, in a tremendous burst of generosity, Tony suggested that I invite a few chosen members of the company round for supper. Angela voiced strong objections, especially if there was any question of Brandy di Frank, the stripper, being included, and on the evening in question she decided to absent herself completely.

Tony decided that the bill of fare would be a beef stew and sent me to do the shopping, which I paid for, mentally adding it to the £1 he had already borrowed from me to pay his cleaning lady. The company were a little late in arriving after the show – probably sidetracked by the pub next door to the theatre – so Tony retired to his bed, reluctantly getting up to welcome them with a, "Where the hell have you lot been?" After some cajoling, he came downstairs to join the party and presented everyone with a can of beer to accompany the rather unappetising plate of stew, which was the beginning and end of his beneficence. At one point, he had the audacity to fetch a crate of wine from his cellar, but only to restock his wine rack, oblivious to the fact that his guests would have loved another drink. The 'Big Yin' made a few well-pointed remarks, even turning his empty can upside down, but our ex-director was nothing if not thick-skinned.

He made a big thing out of entertaining international stars. When I arrived back each night, he took great delight in slipping out of the lounge and telling me in hushed tones just who was in that night. It was Frank Zappa on one occasion, then the *Jackson Five* and *The Osmonds*. He even bought a candelabra for his piano when Liberace accepted an invitation although, much to Tony's chagrin, his illustrious guest could not be persuaded to 'tickle the ivories'. Curiously, throughout my entire stay, he never once invited me to meet any of his visitors, and I have since wondered if he told me about them just to make me feel excluded. But then, since I never set eyes on any of them, they might equally well have been a figment of his imagination. But if the goings-on in the Palmer household were peculiar to say the least, they were as nothing compared with the nightly shenanigans taking place at the Young Vic Theatre.

We had no sooner opened when Brandy informed us that she would have to miss the Saturday matinée due to a prior engagement at a working men's club. It wasn't easy to find a replacement at such short notice, but we managed to secure the services of a Miss Kissy Kichinski, an Amazonian creature with long dark hair and a deep husky voice. Despite being briefed on the tasteful nature of her 'spot' in the show, she came out with the immortal line: "Do you want the act with the champagne bottle or the one with the whips?" Fortunately she was prevailed upon to do neither and settled for a total strip with no 'props' and was plunged into blackout before she could do anything too alarming. I was a bit concerned because my Aunt Bessie was in that afternoon, but the show went smoothly, and I don't think Bessie even commented on the stripper.

Afterwards, while Kissy was sitting stark naked in the ladies' dressing-room, I took a deep breath and asked her how she managed to keep her breasts so firm. Without a moment's hesitation, she boomed: "It's the silicone darling!" When Brandy returned for the evening performance she could scarcely believe who we had found to replace her. It turned out that Kissy had only just completed, and was still recovering from, her recent sex-change operation. None of us had guessed, but it certainly explained the deep throaty voice.

The half-hour call was a mystery to many of the Welly crowd, and Billy used to have a member of stage management pop into the pub next door to give him his pre-show calls. I have an abiding memory of one evening when Billy was carried through the theatre foyer on a stretcher, apparently drunk, only five minutes before the show was due to start. He was shouting: "Where's ma dressing room?" Heaven knows what the audience made of it, and of course he was perfectly sober – well almost! It was just his crazy sense of humour; he was a 'one-off', as the world has since discovered.

Before the show ended, I asked Tony Palmer if there was anything he would like as a 'thank-you' gift, "A chandelier for the drawing-room", he said without hesitation, and he obviously meant it. Well, since I was only earning £11 a week, I had to search high and low for something within my price range, and I eventually found one in BHS for the princely sum of £6. Although I knew that it wasn't exactly what he had in mind, I almost gave it to him, but in the end I lost my nerve, gave him some booze and presented the chandelier to his appreciative cleaning lady.

On our last night at the end of the run, I was sitting in the pub with some of the cast, enjoying a few beverages before we went our various ways. Somehow, everyone disappeared, and I realised that I was alone and very drunk. I picked up my bag, which contained all the dressing room paraphernalia, including two pairs of wellies – white ones for the wedding and my favourite wee red ones for the scenes with comedic content – and headed in the direction of the Underground. Within a few yards, I succeeded in tripping over my large bag, ending up in a heap on the pavement. A lovely face appeared, the face of an angel, with long thick hair, who I vaguely recognised as someone who had been in to see the show a few times, and he manoeuvred me onto a train and guided me back to my 'digs'. Rummaging in my bag, I unearthed the key to the basement, which opened directly into Tony's studio full of valuable equipment. I staggered in, leaving my 'angel' to repack my bag and follow me upstairs to my luxury suite. It's all a bit hazy now, but the next thing I recall with any clarity is waking up early the following morning feeling as sick as a dog, and finding this rather pretty, young man with long hair and beads dangling round his neck lying next to me in the bed. He assured me that nothing had happened, which I did not doubt as I can't have been a very attractive proposition – and then I had to make a hasty exit in order to throw up in the loo!

I made a cup of coffee for him and thought it might be wise to try and sneak him out of the house before anyone else stirred. I discovered that Alan (for that was his name!) and his friend, Rab, were diehard Scottish 'Welly' fans. Rab had a yellow pushbike with a wee welly boot tied onto the front, which I had noticed near the Young Vic on a previous occasion. Alan left his address, and after walking a little way with him along the street, I returned to my quarters, in time to hear the phone ring on the landing. It was Angela, summoning me to come down and face the music. Somehow they knew that I'd had a visitor, and both she and Tony were livid; they virtually accused me of 'dragging back' a vagrant, and hard as I tried to explain that had it not been for Alan, I might have been left in the gutter in a pile of wellies, they remained stern and unforgiving.

On reflection, the Palmers were quite right to be mad; I was a silly young thing, and a guest in their home, but it was probably just as well it happened at the end of my stay as, judging by their reaction, they would probably have turfed me out anyway. I felt like a naughty child as I stood nervously facing them and apologised profusely, thanking my lucky stars that they did not seem to know that I had left the basement studio unlocked all night long (the consequences of which could have been disastrous), only remembering to lock it when I was showing Alan out a short time before. I left their study, feeling relieved that I was departing the next day. It was an unfortunate end to a very unusual three-week stay. I never saw or heard from them again, although Alan and Rab, who I got to know later, remained my good mates. Another adventure over.

As a postscript to this tale, I discovered years later, that Angela married again, had another daughter, and went on to have a successful career as a novelist. Candida Crewe also became a writer of some note.

4

Life upon the wicked stage

My first professional pantomime was *Mother Goose* in which I played Jeannie the Maid. It was directed by Phil McCall and took place in the little town of Motherwell. It was great fun most of the time, but I discovered how tricky it can be to work with 'comics'. My partner was a fellow who just suited himself. Every time I opened my mouth, he would say something like: "Just look at her – face like a nippy sweetie", and ruined my every line. I complained to the director, but to no avail. I probably over-reacted, but I was young and inexperienced, and didn't yet know how to handle people who didn't stick to the script.

The end of the panto saw me on my way back to London to meet up with all my friends. I always spread myself around on these trips and tried not to outstay my welcome anywhere. I was with Aunt Bessie for a while, then moved into Sue Yelland's house in Barnes. She had become quite a friend. I think she looked on me as a dizzy daughter and was trying to imbue me with a little sophistication, introducing me to wine, salad dressings and garlic bread. I also met some of the 'Wicker' crowd; I had long sessions with Gary Carpenter, the Assistant Musical Director, and we made a 'demo' of a couple of his own compositions. I had drinks galore with Mike Naylor, who was still in the process of writing the play for me, but the main purpose of my visit was to record some of the songs for the film. Paul Giovanni, the Musical Director, had written some very pretty songs, and they hoped to release a record of the film score to coincide with the film's release, but although we eventually recorded all the songs, the record never saw the light of day – well, not at that time. As the film gathered cult status over the years, the recordings were unearthed and put onto CD.

On the night before my attempt to teach Britt Ekland to speak Scots, I stayed with Robin Hardy and his wife Caroline. The Hardy family were terribly posh and seemed to me like creatures from another planet. As we waited for Caroline to serve the meal, her father started a risqué conversation which seemed to embarrass the entire family. He invited me to join him on an exotic holiday, and attempted to entice me by giving a rendition of *If You Were the Only Girl in the World*. As Caroline arrived with the food she trilled: "Shepherd's Pie", at which point, Robin hissed: "Oh, don't announce it darling, it's only shepherd's pie." He seemed to have little in common with his son, Jeremy, who was also present. I had a few outings with Jeremy, mainly to religious meetings at a house owned by Cliff Richard – or so I was told – where we took turns to read verses from the scriptures. It was an unusual relationship, which didn't really go anywhere. I do recall that he gave me a lovely book – *Jonathan Livingston Seagull* – before I returned home.

Our day with Britt was fun for me, if not for Robin. I think her contract specified that her own speaking voice was to be used, and *British Lion* were keen to make that work, as her song and body were no longer her own! I remember her as a friendly lady who was most curious to know how actors could live on the £20 per week they earned in the theatre. As the years went by, Britt proved to be something of a 'stayer' in the business and did pantomimes and other theatre work until she was well into her seventies. Despite her obvious glamour, Robin seemed much more attentive to me, but I read little into that at the time. 'Looping' was enjoyable; I had to 'lip sync' with her dialogue on film, and she then had to copy what I did. I said, "Good morning Sergeant", she would give her Swedish-Scottish version, and then say: "Does that sound Scots?" It was a tall order, although she seemed quite pleased with her efforts and said at the end of the day, "Now I'll be able to put on my Spotlight: *Speaks Scots*"! Maybe she had a sense of humour.

It was an exciting and busy period for me. I spent a lot of time that spring going up and down to London. I did a half hour BBC2 play on one trip, and on my last visit I recorded the opening song for the movie, the *Highland Lament*, down in Shepperton Studios, made even more enjoyable because I was so fond of Paul Giovanni, someone I would love to have gone on knowing; sadly, he died some years later when the AIDS epidemic struck. I returned to Glasgow to do an episode of *Sutherland's Law*. This memory is quite vivid for me, and only because three years at the RSAMD had instilled in me a determination to always create a character. I tried at every opportunity to use any accent but my own, and in this episode, when I was cast as a shoplifter, they agreed that I could do it with an Irish accent – which now makes me smile, although my training stood me in very good stead for my years in repertory theatre where versatility was much valued. I also did my one and only stint in Theatre in Education at the Citizens Theatre in Glasgow. If you want a tough initiation into acting, you couldn't find a tougher one than a job in some of the Glasgow schools; you get no compliments on your performance – in fact, the biggest compliment is if they listen at all.

As a working actress I knew that it was important to be able to drive, although I have never been asked to do so. As 1973 got under way, I decided it was time to get behind the wheel again. I was over my escapade with the conman driving instructor and as Mum and Grant had passed their tests under the expert tutelage of a retired army man, Major William (Bill) Stobie, I was happy to resume my lessons with him. I had no sooner mastered the hill start when my lessons had to be put on hold once more, as I was offered the part of Luisa in a charming and unusual musical by Harvey Schmidt and Tom Jones, called *The Fantasticks*.

Sir William Murray, a man in his mid-thirties, had long dreamt about opening a small theatre within the grounds of his family estate in Ochtertyre near Crieff, and our show was, in fact, his first production. It was exciting to be involved in something new, but it wasn't without its teething problems; publicity was chaotic, and the posters failed to explain that Ochtertyre was not actually in Crieff, but about two miles away; even if you managed to find it you then had to negotiate a mile and a half of driveway. So it was only the most stalwart and enthusiastic of playgoers plus a few friends and relatives who turned up. Sometimes we played to fewer than 20 people, which was sad because it was a lovely show; the original off-Broadway production ran for over 42 years, the world's longest running musical.

The cast of five lived in the mansion, and we were fed and cared for by a lovely lady who had been Sir Willie's nanny since his childhood. It was, in many ways, an idyllic time. The grounds were spacious and the surroundings delightful, although they played havoc with my hay fever. I was the only female member of the cast, playing opposite my rather dishy ex-movement teacher from college. We had three kisses onstage during the show, and on one occasion when the show was nearly cancelled, my first thought was the loss of my three kisses. I also spent a lot of time with Philip Guard, an older actor who, although very volatile and provocative on occasion, was erudite and interesting.

Sir Willie loved company, and on many a night after rehearsals or a performance we would all get together in his lounge, where he was more than generous with his booze. There were those who took advantage of Willie's generosity, but oh those Ochtertyre nights! He himself consumed a lot more than was prudent and, consequently, looked a good deal older than his 35 years. His marriage had broken down and he had a young son, who I don't recall ever seeing. He had a rather dotty girlfriend whom he'd met in a local bar, and although she lived in the mansion as a permanent guest, she seemed to be left to her own devices, as we rarely saw her out and about around the estate. We all suspected that her platinum blonde hair was a wig, and I had it confirmed one evening on my way to the loo when she staggered past me with her hair on back to front.

Sir Willie continued to produce plays and, over the next few years, not only increased the audience seating capacity, but also opened two bars and a spacious restaurant. People started to come in greater numbers, but in the end it was just too small a theatre to survive without subsidy. It was, of course, heavily subsidised by Sir Willie himself, and as he expanded his theatre complex his estate dwindled, finally passing into other hands. Despite his achievement, he ended up living in a wing of the mansion that his family had owned for generations. Some time afterwards we bumped into him as he was enjoying a night out in Perth, and only a week later we heard that he had shot himself. He was, I believe, a very lonely man and his theatrical venture was, at least in part, an attempt to keep that loneliness at bay. Whatever his motives, it was a very sad end for a man who had tried to do his bit for the theatre and lost everything in the process.

My involvement with the Greenock TV play, *Just Your Luck*, had created quite a lot of interest, and during the run of *The Fantasticks* I was asked to go into *Coronation Street*. I couldn't abandon the production of course, so I missed out on that chance, and on several others that came along about the same time. The trouble was, I had no one to advise me about managing my career. I didn't know, for instance, that when you play a significant role in a television play, it is wise to remain available in case other television offers come in. As it was, I gaily accepted every job that came my way and so I was usually in the back of beyond when the big opportunities presented themselves. I do believe that I would have had more of a television career had I been more available in the '70s, but there is no point in dwelling too long on lost chances or what might have been, because had I been guided differently at that time, I might have missed out on some of the most exciting theatrical experiences of a lifetime. The Edinburgh Festival of 1973 was not, I hasten to add, one of them, although it was memorable for a variety of other reasons.

I was already rehearsing in Edinburgh before Ochteryre was over. Those were the days when jobs sometimes overlapped and, although actors have never been well paid, you could make a living of sorts when the work was constant. I look with hindsight at one diary entry, 'Every actor I meet is mean'. I had no home, mortgage or commitments, had always been very good at managing my finances and I obviously had no idea what it meant to support a home and family on an actor's salary. Actors are not mean, just usually rather poor.

I should have realised that the combination of *Voyzeck* by George Büchner and a director by the name of Radu Peniciulescu did not hold too much promise in the way of fun, but it was to be my first time performing at the Edinburgh Festival, and I was looking forward to it. In his native Romania, Radu was used to long rehearsal periods, so we had the luxury of a full five weeks before opening the play at the Assembly Rooms. To my dismay, however, we spent the first half of this period doing improvisations. The idea was that Radu would observe us using our creative imaginations and, after getting to know us, he could then decide which parts we were to play. Unfortunately, the improvisations, exercises and games went on for so long that we began to wonder if there would be any time left to rehearse the play.

Day after day we sat around in circles, holding hands, and getting in touch with each other's auras. With our eyes shut, we groped our way around the room, trying to identify the features of anyone we happened to bump into, we stared into each other's faces, hoping to uncover the secrets hidden behind their eyes – and a whole lot more of what I considered to be pretentious nonsense. Having exhausted this exercise in time-wasting, and hoping that we might now be able to turn our attention to the script, Radu then exhorted us to 'experience the energy of the rehearsal room with all your senses.' We were to touch the walls, smell the curtains and taste the piano. This was bordering on lunacy but, being actors in an already overcrowded profession, nobody objected and we all wandered purposefully round the room trying to relate to the objects in our own individual ways. Having tasted the piano, I made my way to the curtains, barely able to suppress my mounting hysteria. One of my fellow-actors, Ron Bain, had his nose buried in them and, almost choking with laughter, I asked him to move over and give me a sniff. He hissed at me to clear off, as he was doing his best to take the whole thing seriously. His 'seriousness' paid off handsomely when he was given the leading role of *Voyzeck*, while my efforts were rewarded with the small part of Luisa, a giggling whore – which was, I have to say, no more than I deserved.

On top of all this, Radu's English was virtually non-existent and, once we eventually started rehearsals, communication became a major problem as he tried to convey his ideas to us. He would shout, "Don't pose", and actors thought they were being accused of narcissism when he had only wanted them to get a move on! "Don't pause!" One morning he informed me that, as I reminded him of a little mouse, he was going to put me in a cage which I would be required to share with two real mice. I breathed a sigh of relief when, along with other such brainwaves, he abandoned this idea. During the dress rehearsal, he suddenly felt that a particular scene would work better if all the girls stripped to the waist. None of us had a clue why, and nobody asked, but we all did as we were bid, and stood around in an embarrassed semi-naked huddle, while the men in the scene sniggered quietly. A few minutes later, Radu yelled out, "It not work!" and we all happily got dressed again, still none the wiser, but wondering if perhaps it was our fault that it hadn't worked!

In an effort to be friendly and hospitable, I invited Radu over to Ochtertyre to see *The Caretaker* with me one evening, and we both stayed overnight in the mansion. Perhaps I had been too friendly, but shortly afterwards he invited me round to his flat for coffee. As the evening wore on, it seemed sensible to accept his offer of a bed for the night as I didn't fancy trailing back in the dark to my own digs. He said "Goodnight" and left me with an invitation to visit him in his room. I knew that he was puzzled when I didn't accept as we clearly had a rapport, but it was not something I could contemplate. He even discussed the matter with another actress in the company and asked if she knew why I had resisted his charms. She was so moved by his plight that she 'did the honours' and seemed to quite enjoy the experience. She even received a gift; apparently he always gave a little memento to the ladies he made love to. Now, if I had known that...

Not only did we have the *Voyzeck* to contend with, but our entire company had also been roped in to swell the ranks of the crowd in the main production of the Festival, *The Thrie Estaites*. All we had to do was sit on the steps leading down from the acting area and watch the action unfolding before us, responding to it as the situation demanded. Each performance lasted nigh on three hours, and sitting there in the middle of a warm summer was no picnic. I rarely suffer from boredom, but this was excruciating. We were paid an extra £5 a week for taking part, but I couldn't name a figure that would have been high enough to make it bearable. We played *Voyzeck* in the afternoons and *The Thrie Estaites* in the evenings. Once both plays had settled into their runs, and unable to contemplate the many performances that loomed ahead, a few of us got together and worked out a rota system that would enable each of the professional actors in the crowd to have an occasional night off, which would make it a little less irksome. It seemed to work well, until it came to my turn.

Tom Fleming, who was playing the part of 'Divine Correction', used to walk amongst the crowd, stopping and blessing a few of us as he passed. Unfortunately, I was one of the more frequently 'blessed', and on the one evening I went absent, he noticed that my usually bowed head was missing, presumed that I must be ill, and went to the management to enquire after my well-being! The game was up, and I was severely, and quite rightly, reprimanded; it was, after all, extremely unprofessional behaviour – but I couldn't help feeling thoroughly aggrieved that I was the only one who was found out. Would that I could have borne my burden in the manner of Miss Elspet Cameron, a lady who had appeared as a crowd member in every production of *The Thrie Estaites* since the early'50s. In fact, she had a little party one day to celebrate her 100th performance, and I am sure that if ever her services had been required again, she would have been happy to join the throng, however old she had become.

I got to know Elspet over the years and she was greatly eccentric, always carrying a tin of cat food and a tin opener in her handbag, just in case she came across a stray. She travelled far and near to see her favourite actors in various productions. In her latter years she did a lot of 'extra' work, and took it as seriously as if she had been Dame Sybil Thorndike. She would often turn up at the end of a performance, armed with a selection of photographs so that I could help her choose a good one for *Spotlight* and she would let me know when she would be appearing on the telly and in what programme: "I'm the third patient from the end of the ward, Lesley", she would tell me on one of her regular and lengthy phone calls.

Although I remember another actor in our cast as being very talented, he was quite low-key, but Simon Callow was destined for a very starry future. Many years later, he reflected in his autobiography *Being an Actor* on this time in Edinburgh. It was saddening to read that he had lost his father on the first day of rehearsals and only coped because he barely knew him. He felt like an outsider in our Scots company where many of us already knew each other. Even if I'd known that, I'm not sure that he and I would have had much in common at this time in our lives. Our production of *Voyzeck* did not set the festival alight as it was just too *avant-garde*, and it's a wonder that the whole experience didn't put me off theatre for life. However I had a holiday planned so I put it all behind me as I headed off.

I'd arranged a few interviews in London followed by a week in Paris, with a final few days in Gloucestershire with Mike Naylor and his family, which was specifically to discuss *A Postal Order From My Granny,* the play that he had now finished writing for me – so it was a mixture of work and play. This would be my one and only holiday abroad on my own, and I still consider myself quite bold to have undertaken it. My old college pal, Jim McLure, had arranged for me to stay with a friend of his in Paris, a creative mime artist called Remy. I had met him once, so I wasn't exactly a stranger. He had a friend staying in his flat, and I was expected to muck in and take turns with the cooking. Being a very inexperienced cook, it was a challenge to shop for the food in a new country, although I think that my efforts were uninspired compared to the meals concocted by the two gay men. I recall watching Remy making soup from all the leftovers, and he was bunging in everything except the proverbial – even a couple of apple cores went into the pot – and although I was horrified it tasted delicious.

Remy had many interesting friends, and I met two American art students at his flat, Guy Bauman and Barbara Brink, who invited me to tag along with them on a couple of trips. They took me to the Louvre, but at that time it was rather wasted on me. I hate to confess it, but I found that wonderful art gallery pretty boring. My own artistic endeavours had always been marked as D minus at school, and I still have memories of attempting to draw a bus and the teacher holding my creation aloft whilst saying "Would you all look at Lesley's bus? Who would like to travel on this bus?" Totally humiliating, which may well have reinforced my belief that I was irredeemably useless at art.

During the days in Paris, I saw all the sights on my own, but I filled my evenings with Guy and Barbara. One evening when I was with them at a café theatre in Odéon, I glanced around and spotted the most divine-looking man. Just at that moment, someone behind him accidentally burnt a hole in his beautiful white sweater. I drew his attention to it, and we got chatting. His name was Yves, and when we left the café, he took the three of us for a coffee, dropping the others at their small hotel before taking me back home. He asked me if I would care to go back with him to his home or, if I preferred, to a hotel, but I was a lot more reticent than my personality might have led people to believe. I didn't want to jump in at the deep end with a virtual stranger, so I declined, but we arranged to meet the following evening at the same time, same place. I was quite excited at the prospect of having him all to myself.

I told Remy about it, and being a very liberated gay man he insisted that I prepare properly and take overnight things – a toothbrush for a start – and not let this exciting chance pass me by. I thought he might well be right; after all, I was on holiday, and perhaps I could risk a little more abandonment, so I left for Odéon with a great sense of anticipation. I waited in the café – and I waited

– and Yves did not turn up. Perhaps he sensed that I wasn't ready for this sort of brief encounter and that I might lose my nerve and back out at the last minute, or perhaps something had cropped up, but whatever the reason I was disappointed and felt that I couldn't go back to Remy's flat in case he had plans for his own evening. I ended up sharing Guy and Barbara's room for the night, which was fine, but not what fantasies are made of. I still have a pencil drawing that Remy did of me fast asleep in bed towards the end of my week's stay, and he had captioned it: 'Lesley after a night with Guy, Andrew, Yves…' – and I had actually spent a rather innocent week.

On my last evening, Remy, two of his friends and I had a meal at Joe Allen's restaurant, a lovely end to a very different holiday. Unfortunately, I woke up the next morning with the most appalling food poisoning. Remy had already left, but I managed to drag myself to a taxi rank and got to Orly airport. It was a ghastly flight, and I knew that I was in no fit state to head down to Gloucester, so I made my way to the people I had stayed with in London before I left for Paris and remained in bed until I felt well enough to move on.

I spent a few days with Mike Naylor, and it was more productive than usual because he didn't seem to drink so much when he was in his family home. We talked about his plans for the play, and his hopes of persuading Hattie Jacques to be in it. I was the main character, an intruder and a catalyst, arriving into a family situation and causing them tremendous upheaval and problems, while I waited for the postal order from my granny so that I could afford to go back home! It was set in the North of England, so the music was to have a brass band feel. The next step was to set up a meeting with the Musical Director, so things were in progress. Mike gave me a copy of the play, but I can't remember what I thought of it at that time; I was just thrilled to have a play written specially for me.

But other doors were opening and, having given up my bedsit in Sauchiehall Street, saving the princely sum of £4 per week, I returned to Dundee and the family home in Nairn Street which would turn out to be my base for some time; in fact, until I married in 1977. Not so much fresh fields and new horizons then, as familiar ground and old haunts, for I had just been invited to join the company at the Rep in Lochee Road, and I was looking forward to working in my home town.

5

A driving ambition

It was my first stint in repertory theatre, and after the fire in 1963, when the old Nicholl St theatre had been burned to the ground, the company had led a nomadic existence until it found a home in the converted former Dudhope church in Lochee Road, the one in which my parents were married back in 1950. I had been involved in various productions there when I was still at school, and had seen many shows, so was very familiar with the building. My first part was the title role in *A Day in the Death of Joe Egg*. Severe disability presents an enormous challenge, and I have always relished the opportunity to play parts which are a bit more demanding; playing 'the girl next door' has never been of much interest. My part consisted of noises, groans and a few fits. I was either confined to a wheelchair or lying on the sofa, apart from a brief fantasy sequence when I had a few seconds speaking and skipping like an able-bodied little girl.

1973, Dundee Rep – A Day in the Death of Joe Egg with Ursula Smith and Derrick Gilbert.

Before the season began, I managed to fit in a few radio broadcasts and even a *Songs of Scotland*. Over the years I did a few comedy spots in such programmes, and this was my first. I was a 'Tartan Waitress from the Highlands' called Teeny McSween, and it was written for me by Alex Mitchell, an elderly journalist who had written an article about me at the time of my *Play for Today*. He wrote many pantomimes, sketches and commercials, and became even more prolific when he retired. He sent me an early Christmas present that year, which consisted of a sketch called *The Small Big Drummer* and a load of old gags! I never found a use for the 'Drummer', but I strung together the best of the jokes and concocted a 'schoolgirl' spot which finished with my 'Daisy' song, a spot which served me well as time went by. I kept up with Alex for many years, and called him regularly when I was in Glasgow, sometimes meeting him in town, where he was often joined by colleagues from the world of journalism. He wrote wonderfully entertaining indiscreet letters full of showbiz gossip about all the comics of the time, but he gradually stopped socialising as his sight worsened, and I last spoke to him in 1987 when I was at the BBC for a radio recording just a few weeks before the birth of my first child. He sounded quite distant, and I think he had finally lost his great zest for life.

Dundee Rep was, in the main, a fairly happy experience. Unfortunately, the company were going through a tricky period when I arrived, and I only just about managed to stay out of it. Ursula Smith, a leading light in the company, had (allegedly) become difficult to work with, and I heard that several people had handed in their notice because of friction with this lady. I will never quite understand what she did to incur such dislike, but it was difficult to ignore the atmosphere in the dressing room. One evening, I was sitting with Ursula listening to the show relay over the tannoy, "Oh, she dried", yelled Ursula, as Xanthi paused for an inordinate length of time. "She fluffed" she added wickedly.

I witnessed a great deal of bitchiness during this season. Petty issues as to who had the best dress for the Christmas Revue were paramount, and the atmosphere was uncomfortable. Ursula used to cling onto the Director, Stephen MacDonald, as he put a comforting arm around her in the bar after the show. She would smirk over his shoulder and then disappear into the night with him, clutching a bottle of wine. Stephen appeared to be very much on her side despite the feelings of the company. One evening in the bar after the show,

Ursula was talking to me in a very loud voice. She'd had a few drinks and was telling me what I should do if 'the wee Arbroath man' bothered me in any way, "Tell him to piss off", she shrieked, "or, better still, tell him to fuck off." I noticed that the actor in question was within earshot, and after Ursula left, he cross-questioned me as to why his name had been projected round the bar. I gave an explanation of sorts and the following morning he went straight to Stephen's office with another grievance. I don't know exactly what was said, but Ursula was called into the office for her version of events, and in the dressing room that evening, her opening gambit was, "Well, I'll have to watch what I say in front of certain people in future." So, against my wishes, I became involved and had to be more careful after that.

Events came to a head at Christmas. I was the Pussycat in *The Owl and the Pussycat,* and we did most of the matinées while the other half of the company did a revue called *First Feet* in the evenings, in which I saw an ideal opportunity to try out my 'schoolgirl' spot. Stephen agreed to this, and I asked the company members if they minded if I used their names to make my jokes more personal. They all seemed happy to be included with one actor quite peeved that I didn't have a spare joke about him. I was a bit nervous of Ursula, so asked Stephen if I could use her name, but he said, "No", which was frustrating, as I liked the joke and I couldn't think of anyone else I could use instead. I boldly and a bit naughtily slipped the joke in at the technical rehearsal and was severely reprimanded by Stephen. I never used her name again, but managed to substitute another, so didn't lose the gag. It was petty, as the jokes were just silly. For the record, this was the offending joke, 'See thae actresses, they're that vain. I saw that Ursula Smith in the hairdresser's last week. She asked the fella to give her 'the Barbra Streisand look'. "Sure" he says, lifted his hairbrush and bashed her one on the nose!' Stephen was just being overprotective, and the result of all this was that he probably thought I had joined the band of Ursula's adversaries.

It was around this time that I did one of many newspaper interviews that had been part of my life since I was a child. It was a national newspaper, and although I didn't know it at the time, I was about to learn an early lesson about the power of the press. During our chat, the journalist made much of the fact that I was a television star now languishing in a local repertory theatre. It was a year since I had played Alison in *Just Your Luck*, but this play received such notoriety at the time that it kept me and the rest of the cast in the public eye for a bit longer than usual. I tried to enlighten him about the elusive nature of 'stardom', told him about the highs and lows of the last year and my disappointment at not being free for *Coronation Street* and other television work I had been offered. I went on to express my delight at being a member of the Dundee Rep company for the first time, giving me the opportunity to learn my craft and gain experience.

The headline, when it appeared in print, read: 'It's just my luck, says Lesley!' With a sense of foreboding, I went on to read the article, the gist of which was that I was now reduced to playing a pussycat in Dundee, which was 'hardly the fate anyone imagined after the plaudits she received for Peter McDougall's sensational television play!' I was shocked to say the least because, while I hadn't been misquoted, the newspaper had twisted what I had said in order to put its own views across, views that are just as prevalent today – namely, that you can't possibly be a 'star' unless you appear on the telly! To some extent it's true, but I had no wish to be associated with it and, deeply embarrassed, I found myself apologising to the management at the Rep for something I hadn't said, just in case they thought I was getting too big for my boots. Of course, if I had just ignored it, it would probably have passed by quite unnoticed.

This Christmas was significant for me in a personal sense, as it was in November 1973 that I first noticed my new next-door neighbour, Jack Bruce. He was the middle son of Jack and Alice Bruce, who had recently moved in. We hit it off at once and, although Jack eventually found it difficult to cope with dating a Thespian, we got on famously for a time, and I had a longer relationship with him than I ever had with anyone else, apart from my husband. We reached the stage of talking about an engagement, but he was a jealous Scorpio, and had we ever married, I think that he might have tried to persuade me to give up the business. But we had a lovely year together until we finally broke up in the spring of 1975.

In the midst of our two Christmas shows I was paid a visit by Mike Naylor and his Musical Director for *A Postal Order from My Granny;* Graham Collier was a brass band specialist, so the wheels were definitely moving. Mum agreed to put them both up – she had a lot to put up with back in those days – and they joined the family on their Hogmanay jaunt to the Dundee Rep. They wanted to hear me sing so that Graham could get some idea of my range, but my sweet 'pussy-cat' wasn't going to be very helpful in that department. I had my own plans for the rest of the evening, but managed to give them a rendition of *People* in the middle of the night before heading out to get on with my 'first footing'. Mum had made up beds for them, but the next morning we found them both slumped on chairs in the living room, still fast asleep and rather drunk. Drink was still a problem for Mike and would eventually sever our friendship, but at this stage we were getting along fine, and we had mutual high hopes for his play.

Being back at home for a few months presented me with the ideal opportunity to finally crack the driving, so I squeezed in a few more lessons and, on January 23rd, 1974, I failed my test. Having broken the news to me, the examiner cheekily asked if there was any chance of a couple of complimentary tickets for the current show at the theatre. I re-booked my test immediately and was given a date only four weeks ahead, so I enlisted Jack's help to get a bit of last-minute practice. He took me out a couple of times, but the day before my test he thought it would be a good idea to follow a 'test' car round Broughty Ferry, so that I could familiarise myself with the route. We were keeping what we thought was a close but discreet distance when, on turning a corner, we were waved down by a rather grumpy man who told us in no uncertain terms to stop tailing his car, as it was very distracting for the young bloke who was taking his test.

After mumbling our heartfelt apologies, we were just about to drive off, when the examiner came round to my side and, poking his head in, looked me straight in the eye and said: "And when is this young lady taking her test?" "Oh, not for ages yet", I muttered, and spent the rest of the day looking forward to the following morning with a sense of dread. To make matters worse, I had a call from Major Stobie, my instructor, to say that I would have to take the test in his new Mini, as he had just got rid of his Escort. I had an hour's practice in this unfamiliar car before heading off for the test centre, and when I entered the waiting-room I saw that there was only one other person there. Suddenly the door opened, and there was the grumpy examiner from the day before. He glanced down at the form in his hand, I held my breath and, after what seemed like an eternity, he called out the other girl's name. My relief was overwhelming as I waited for Examiner No. 2 – and consequently drove better than ever before and passed my test. Somewhat ironically, it was not the beginning of a life on the road, as I didn't own a car; in fact, I had to take a course of refresher lessons in 1995 – over 20 years later – so that I could finally take my place behind the wheel.

After a short break I was back at the rep for the spring season, and I had great fun playing Barbara in *Billy Liar*. This was followed by the rather thankless part of Dixie, the oldest of the children in Tennessee Williams' *Cat on a Hot Tin Roof* and I had the distinct feeling that I was there to act as chaperone for the two teams of younger children.

1974, Dundee Rep – Cat on a Hot Tin Roof. Martin Heller, Robert Robertson, Janet Michael, LM, Ursula Smith & Irene Sunters.

Janet Michael played the part of Mae, mother to the family of 'no-neck monsters', and it certainly never occurred to me at the time that not only would it be 23 years before I returned to work with the company in Dundee, but it would be to play Sister Mae in the 1997 production of *Cat on a Hot Tin Roof,* with Janet Michael as Big Mama. How quickly we all moved on a generation.

My final production was *The Chippit Chantie,* directed by Joan Knight, who was the resident artistic director at Perth Theatre, just 20 miles up the road. 'Chantie' was a hoot, but my most vivid memory is of one of the worst 'corpses' of my entire career. 'Corpsing' stories can leave a listener po-faced because they are usually caused by something which is inexplicably funny at the time, but only to the people concerned. On the night in question, we reached the courtroom scene, which was quite amusing in any case, but got out of control. Ursula Smith, playing Auld Brigie, suddenly grabbed the judge's long wig from its peg and plonked it on her own head. She looked hilarious, and virtually everyone onstage was rendered useless as hysteria took hold. The benches were shaking beneath us, and actors were trying to hide behind one another in desperation. Even Robert Robertson, playing the judge, was unable to utter, and when Brigie herself finally succumbed and joined the rest of us in this awful company 'corpse', we were suddenly sobered up by a very fierce, "Shut up the lot of you!" from one of Scotland's well-known actresses, Irene Sunters. We all thought she was a bit of a witch at the time, but if she had not barked at us at that moment, we might well have had to bring the curtain down. Just after she shouted, she lost her balance, fell right off the edge of the stage, twisted her ankle and had to use a walking stick for the rest of the run. A memorable 'corpse'!

From that first play together Joan took me under her wing, and in a way I became her prodigy. She was known for going out of her way to release actors to do the odd telly or radio broadcast, but that was just not Stephen's way, as I discovered when I was given the opportunity to go to Manchester to play a lovely role in *The Good Companions,* a production starring John Mills and Judi Dench, which was slated for London's West End. I'd auditioned down in London a few months previously and, although I knew I'd been short-listed, as time moved on I had put it behind me. Suddenly, the actress who had been cast as Susie Deans was not ideal and the company got in touch to find out if I was available. As we were still in the early stages of rehearsal, I went to see Stephen, just to find out if there was any chance of my going down to meet the director, Braham Murray, and the MD, André Previn, to see if the interview would result in a definite offer, but he just dismissed it out of hand. When Joan found out, she was horrified that I hadn't gone straight to her. She had come through the ranks of stage management and was aware how cruel the business can be, and how easily a career can be altered by one lost opportunity. However, it is rarely in our power to 'grasp the moment', and whether she could have persuaded Stephen remains a matter for conjecture – and my loss was Marti Webb's gain! My disappointment over *The Good Companions* was quickly eclipsed by an offer to join Miss Knight's company, and that first season of 1974 was to be the beginning of a long relationship, not to mention a very real love affair between myself and the Perth Repertory Theatre. Wherever I went in the future, I always seemed to gravitate back to 'The Fair City'.

As soon as 'Chippit Chantie' opened, I was commuting back and forth to Perth to rehearse for the first play in the Summer Season. We closed in Dundee and opened in Perth three days later; those were indeed the days. We rehearsed each play for nine days, had technical and dress rehearsals on a Monday and Tuesday, opened on the Tuesday evening, and somehow we made it. On this, my first outing in Perth, I discovered that Janet Michael and local actor, Martyn James, were already stalwarts at the theatre and they went on to become two of the longest-serving actors ever to work in Perth. They became something of an institution, and so familiar did they become that I recall a Scottish Theatre magazine which dared to suggest they had been there so long they were working on 'automatic pilot', but they were versatile performers and well-loved by local audiences.

As if to confirm the prediction of my old college adversary, John Groves, the first part I played at Perth was Susie the maid in an old Scots comedy called *Bachelors are Bold,* and with it came the absolute proof, as far as I was concerned, that those little maids are often the most rewarding, not to mention scene-stealing, parts!

'Bachelors' was one of three plays that made up the Summer Season of 1974 – the other two being *What Every Woman Knows*, and *Not Now, Darling* (No' the Noo Hen).

1974, Perth Rep – Bachelors Are Bold with Jay Smith.

As the season came to a close, the new company arrived to start rehearsals for *Joseph and the Amazing Technicolor Dreamcoat*. This was destined to be one of Perth's most successful and acclaimed productions and significant in a very personal sense because an actor called Terry Wale was in the cast – the man who would eventually become my husband. A lot of water was to flow under the bridge, however, before we finally married in October 1977.

I got on well with Terry from the very beginning. I recall looking across the stage on the first day of rehearsals and spotting this figure sporting a pink shirt and standing in a rather camp manner. He was attractive, probably gay I thought, and he looked like someone who could be a charming but safe escort. As I got to know him I discovered that he wasn't gay and I became a kind of confidante as his marriage was under severe strain. Constant separation causes many problems for actors, and Terry had recently returned from a lengthy engagement in Canada. Shortly afterwards he had to leave for Perth, soon to discover that his wife had started an affair. He didn't know what he wanted, but his instinct was to try and save his marriage. When he had any time off, he headed south to try and resolve the problems.

1974, Perth Rep – What Every Woman Knows with Janet Michael as Maggie Shand.

We all loved being part of 'Joseph', which was a sell-out. People who were unable to get tickets stood outside in Cutlog Vennel to hear the strains of the music. Although I was just one of the cogs in a very large wheel, I experienced for the first time the genuine thrill of a standing ovation. A production of *Twelfth Night* followed on, in which Terry played a very touching Sir Andrew Aguecheek, with me as Maria, yet another lovely 'maid'. It was this production which brought us into contact with Joan's assistant director, Andrew McKinnon, who became a friend for a good many years. At the end of the run Terry departed for London, but we were destined to work together occasionally over the next two years, and despite the transitory nature of our business our relationship developed.

In the meantime, I was gaining wonderful experience in a wide range of parts, getting a real taste of the rigours of fortnightly rep, and even managing to fit in the odd comedy spot at the BBC and Grampian Television. A new play opened every second Tuesday, and with rehearsals all day, performances at night, and learning lines on Sundays – sometimes into the early hours of the morning, there was little or no time for a social life of any kind. What <u>weekly</u> rep must have been like, I can only imagine. When I was young, lines seemed to sink in as if by magic. It almost happened by osmosis and caused very little angst. As we grew older and the parts got bigger, we could no longer depend on the magic of youth, and new, more considered tactics, had to come into being.

One of the plays was *Pygmalion* and Stephen MacDonald was playing Professor Higgins. I had the cameo role of Clara Eynsford-Hill, and as she was fond of me and extremely indulgent, Joan gaily released me to do a comedy spot on a BBC variety show. It meant missing two performances, and Maureen Beattie, who was playing Mrs Pearce, was asked to cover for me and play my part as well as her own. As it entailed a certain amount of extra company rehearsal, Stephen wasn't pleased and, in retrospect, I'm not at all surprised. Working in a repertory system was gruelling enough as most of the company were rehearsing during the days and playing in the evenings, and any extra rehearsal was bound to be unwelcome. My only excuse for my apparent selfishness was youth, and not knowing that it wasn't acceptable to disappear in the middle of a run. Joan was the director, Joan gave permission, what Joan said was law, and I didn't realise back then that being allowed to take on extra-curricular work was quite unusual, and I rarely came across it again. Looking back, I do not think that being given this kind of preferential treatment endeared me to Mr MacDonald.

During that autumn season I was given my first 'leading lady' in *My Fat Friend*. This play brought me face to face with one of the most difficult actors I have ever worked with. His name was Peter French, and he was playing the very camp leading role, and he was Camp with a capital C. It was quite something back in those days for a man to strut into the little circle bar clutching a dainty handbag.

Since my drama school days I have had an affinity with gay men, so I had no axe to grind, but he sensed my conventional background and went out of his way to embarrass me.

1974, Perth Rep – My Fat Friend with Peter French.

It seems naïve now, but I had developed a rapport with the local audiences and was concerned about the bad language in the play; even 'Jesus Christ' got a reaction back then – well, coming out of *my* mouth it did. If I could have flashed forward to 1984 and seen the tirade of four-letter words I would deliver with relish in *Piaf*, I don't think I would have believed it. But it was early days for me and swearing was not so prevalent onstage as it is now. One night after the performance, I made my way to the bar and was greeted by my Aunt Mina, who asked me if Peter was anything like his outrageous character in the play. I said that she would see for herself when he came up, but he was right behind me and hissed, "Why don't you tell her that I am a homosexual? You ought to be a schoolteacher in the Highlands!" That was me told. And the hissing went on for the rest of our time together.

It was panto time and *Dick Whittington* was upon us. I was Principal Girl (my one and only!) and Peter was giving his 'Dame'. We only had one duet, *I Wonder Why*, in which we also did a bit of 'tap'. Ironically, I was the one who showed great enthusiasm when the choreographer had suggested the routine, and Peter had been very reluctant. Thinking that he wasn't a confident dancer, I persuaded him that with a bit of practice we'd manage it; having agreed to do it he immediately launched into a rather intricate set of steps, his wicked face smirking in triumph as he saw me gawp; he was a real hoofer.

One evening, I noticed that nobody in the audience was looking at me during my solo bits, and as I glanced across I caught him mincing around, pushing up his padded bra, and just generally upstaging. This happened at every performance until I plucked up the courage to go to his dressing room before the show one night and knock tentatively on his door. I asked him if he had any idea why the audience were not looking at me and, without any hesitation, he glibly said he thought the lighting was too dim and I ought to have a word with Simon about getting a pink gel put in. I took a deep breath and blurted out that perhaps if he did a little less during the song the audience might notice that I was there, pink gel or no pink gel! He was livid, and ranted and raved before I made a hasty exit. When it came to our duet, he just stood there doing absolutely nothing. He held out his arm to me as if to say, "Take it away Lesley", and I had to sing and dance the entire number on my own. I felt so exposed and humiliated and was on the verge of tears when I went back to his dressing room where, still trying to avoid the issue, I explained that wasn't what I'd meant. His wrath was scary. He screeched at me that I would have to learn that the Dame is No 1 in a panto and he would do exactly what he liked and then, with a piercing, "Get out! Get out!", he slammed the door as I retreated, it caught my leg and I fell, landing in a writhing heap outside his door.

The drama was witnessed by a few members of the company, but none of them dared challenge Peter lest he take out his rage on someone else. I struggled through the rest of the show through a blur of tears, and it must have been apparent to some of the audience.

Clive Perry went to Peter's room afterwards and said (allegedly) that he had never witnessed anyone behaving so badly onstage. Unbeknownst to me, one of the company went to Joan Knight and reported the incident; she summoned Peter to her office and he was never invited back to Perth. He did sail into my dressing room the following day to deposit a bottle of placatory wine, but he hadn't expected to find me there. Taken by surprise, he plonked the bottle down, it fell over and rolled across the surface of the dressing table, and I literally had to grab it before it crashed to the floor. He exited with as much aplomb as he could muster, his black cloak flying behind him. Attached to the bottle was a note: 'This bloody panto will soon be over, and you won't have to put up with me any longer!' I felt quite sorry for him because I knew that he had recently broken up with his partner and was deeply unhappy.

Straight after panto, we had the pleasure of working with one of Peter's cronies and, although he wasn't in Peter's league of bitchiness, he could be very awkward. The play was *Busman's Honeymoon*, and he would oft-times cut screeds of dialogue on a whim. One night I was waiting to enter when I suddenly realised that he had cut my scene, so I didn't need to go on at all! We then did *Hay Fever,* and I only mention it because Jackie Coryton became one of my all-time favourite roles. It was directed by Clive Perry, and he was quite inspired on this play, the 'business' was complex and hilarious, and it was a joy to be in.

As time passed, I was beginning to feel the strain of fortnightly rep, so I approached Joan Knight and asked her if there was any chance of having a play out. True to form, she was very sympathetic, and said that I could opt out of *Mother Courage* if I really wanted to. On the other hand, the part she had in mind was mute and, with no lines to learn, maybe I wouldn't find it such a burden. She ran that theatre unchallenged with absolute authority for 25 years, and in a man's world she didn't achieve that without a measure of guile. I was aware, even then, that she was being devious as she knew that no young actress would turn her back on a part like Kattrin. I was seldom offstage and consequently called for rehearsals every day. So much for my play out – but I wouldn't have missed it for the world especially as Terry had been invited to join the company for that production.

Mother Courage turned out to be one of the highlights of my season. Apart from the challenge of playing a mute person, I also had to perform a rather daring stunt during a dramatic sequence towards the end of the play when Kattrin is shot. I had to execute a half turn and, with my back to the audience, somersault out of sight over the back of the set. I had the help of a stuntman during rehearsals and the comfort of a mattress to break my fall, but it is without doubt the most spectacular feat I have ever undertaken on any stage, and it is only in re-reading the review by Christopher Small in the Glasgow Herald that I can convince myself that I actually did it – and I'm glad that I did!

'There is a breathtaking moment at the end when dumb Kattrin is drumming to rouse the sleeping town. She defies them with a smile of beatific triumph, they fire, and without a sound, in one swift motion, she turns and falls off the roof, diving out of her life and theirs. How Lesley Mackie manages this without severe injury is a mystery, but it is the fitting climax to a beautiful performance, which, without a word spoken, puts dumb homely simple Kattrin with her grotesque gestures and her inarticulate animal cries, where she belongs, at the moral heart of the play, emblem of the real goodness that only speaks in deeds.'

Our only recreation came at the end of the evening show when we would all retire to the bar for a couple of drinks before heading back to our various digs and the learning of more lines. Apart from the stage and the auditorium, Perth Theatre has now been entirely renovated, leaving only fond memories of the tiny Circle Bar into which we all crammed after performances, and which was presided over by Liz Dewar, who also liked to reminisce about those far-off days once she moved up a tier and slaved over a hot computer as Box-Office Manageress.

I recall one evening after a performance of *Mother Courage* when I allowed myself to relax too much. Liz had persuaded me to try some *Southern Comfort*, an unfamiliar drink at that time. She poured it into a half-pint glass, and I remember thinking it was quite delicious. By the time I had finished it, however, I was on the point of collapse. I staggered from the bar to the mattress which was lying onstage behind the set and, once ensconced, Terry was unable to persuade me to budge. I was left in the locked and darkened theatre until I was rudely awakened at 6am the following morning by the arrival of the cleaning ladies. Despite an appalling hangover, I went on enjoying *Southern Comfort* for a long time afterwards, albeit in more moderate measures.

The success of the play gave me the necessary boost to battle on without a break until the end of the season, and by the time I had played Kay in the Gershwin musical, *Oh Kay*, I'd been going non-stop, day and night, for nine months. But, with the resilience of youth, I recovered quickly and headed off to appear in a couple of plays at the Traverse Theatre in Edinburgh. The lure of Perth must have been strong though, because I was delighted when Joan asked me to return for another four months, and even more delighted when I discovered that Terry had been asked back as well. Things were falling into place very nicely, or so it seemed...

1974, Perth – first day of rehearsals, when I first met Terry. LM front row second left. Terry Wale middle row fourth from left.

- 6 -

A pawn in knight's castle

At the end of the season, I made one brief trip to London before I headed back north to Edinburgh to start rehearsals at the Traverse Theatre, and Jack was there to help me move into a grotty little bedsit down Leith Walk, which must rate amongst the worst digs I have ever come across. I always think of this parting in Edinburgh as the one when we both knew it was all but over. He was a hairdresser when we met, joined the army in 1974, bought himself out a few years later, became a policeman, and then went on to own a very successful pub/eaterie in Roseangle. He married and divorced twice, eventually becoming a driving instructor and dog breeder, living happily ever after in Invergowrie with his third wife.

I was in two plays at The Traverse, and in the first one, *The Sunday Promenade*, I played a deaf mute. What with Joe in *A Day in the Death of Joe Egg*, Kattrin in *Mother Courage* and now Angelina all in a short space of time, I seemed to be specialising in such challenging roles, which, of course, would never happen now when an able-bodied actress would not be considered for these parts. I also had a lovely part in the second play *God Bless the Major*, so it was quite a stimulating time; in fact, I managed to add another Christopher Small review to my collection, 'A young actress of quite remarkable gifts.' When I left the Traverse, Mike Ockrent, the Director of the theatre, said that if I ever wanted a job, I only had to ask. He went on to achieve incredible success in the West End and Broadway but, although he endeavoured to get me into one of his big London productions, sad to say it didn't work out.

Another memory springs to mind. It was during my time there that television director Frank Cox got in touch to let me know that he had commissioned an episode of *Sutherland's Law* with the storyline written just for me. He gave me the dates, but when he called back to confirm, his dates had slightly altered and I was already committed. There was nothing to be done about it; I lost the part, and I really wept over that one. I met Frank years later, and he reminded me about that episode and commented on how good I was in it! I should have kept quiet, but I reminded him that I had been unable to do it – I guess that Terry Cavers who got the role must have been alright!

I quickly got over the disappointment as I was straight back into the Perth Summer Season and had no sooner started rehearsals when I had a call from Robin Hardy, director of *The Wicker Man,* suggesting that he visit for a few days to discuss parts for me in not one but four pictures he was to be directing. Naturally, I was very excited, especially as he had mentioned that David Niven was to be starring in one of them, so I booked him into a small hotel and awaited his arrival with a keen sense of anticipation. Mum had agreed to put him up for his first night, so that I could return the hospitality he had shown to me when I was in London – although I have since wondered what he made of the tiny back bedroom and Z-bed therein!

As soon as he arrived, he took me out for a quiet drink in a country pub, and I ordered a Dry Martini, a fairly naff old drink which you used to pour straight from the bottle, but Robin assumed that I was meaning the real gin-based cocktail and I didn't have the nerve to admit to my lack of sophistication. I squirmed with embarrassment as he proceeded to explain the measures to the young barmaid, finally going behind the bar and mixing it himself; I forced the potent drink down in order to hasten our departure. That evening he outlined what he had in mind for me in his first three pictures, but before he would discuss them in detail, he wanted me to read the script for the fourth film in which, he assured me, I could have any part I wanted. Moreover, as he planned to make this particular movie in Scotland, there would probably be parts in it for all my friends as well! I went to bed to peruse the script which, he said, was entirely his own work. I took one look at the title, *A Billion Women to Lay,* and my heart sank.

The following evening he took me out to a favourite restaurant, Timothy's, to discuss it all. I tried to focus his attention on the parts in the other three movies, but it soon became clear that he was much more interested in auditioning me for the part of his next wife! We had lots of champagne, grew rather tipsy and, as the evening wore on, he became rather flirtatious, quoting romantic poetry; but it all seemed light-hearted, and I was flabbergasted to find him on my doorstep the following morning under the impression that I had agreed to an afternoon in bed! It was awkward, and I suggested that we go to the Traverse Theatre instead, which put him in a foul mood for the rest of the day. He hated the play, and walked out of the auditorium, which was mortifying in such a tiny venue, because it was obvious to everyone, but I managed a few words with Mike Ockrent and the cast afterwards, made my excuses and we left. We drove back to Perth in silence, and the following morning I received an apologetic note with a forwarding address, which was 'c/o Bucks Club' (a very smart Gentlemen's establishment founded in 1919), just in case I still wanted to make contact. He had cancelled the rest of his hotel booking and made a very hasty departure. Bang went my life in the movies! I guess this was my closest encounter with the 'Casting Couch', and it came as no surprise that none of the four films were ever made. It would be many years before we met again.

Over the next few weeks everything fell into place, and Terry and I moved into our first little flat together at number 6, Victoria Street. This was a major commitment, and one I had to tell my folks about. I told mum first when they were up seeing a play, and Joan Knight made her even more tearful than she already was by bouncing across the crowded bar, shouting, "Don't worry, it will all be wonderful darlings!" – which kind of insinuated that everyone but mum knew about our plans. Mum passed on the news to dad and, as she had predicted, he was horrified and wrote me a very emotional letter, expressing dismay about his friends and relatives in Perth finding out, and he finished by saying that if I ever walked down the aisle it wouldn't be on his arm! Gradually he softened and mum and dad eventually honoured us with a visit to the flat. It must have been difficult for them because, although estranged, Terry was still married – but we had a lovely summer season with many Sunday meals at the *Isle of Skye Hotel*, where we sometimes even took to the small dance floor. This hotel was a favourite haunt until the carvery closed in 2019.

In the meantime, the season opened with *Move Over Mrs Markham* followed by *Cowardy Custard,* in which I had the pleasure of working alongside the delightful Kevin Whately in many of the romantic numbers and again in *The Day After the Fair* by Frank Harvey – which was Terry's début as a stage director. Kevin played a budding young barrister from London on a tour of the Western

Circuit in the late nineteenth century whose looks, sophistication and charm bewitch an ill-educated servant girl, a part in which I was ideally cast. Kevin was not ideally cast, and it soon became clear that what you saw and heard was what you got, so that when the final curtain fell you were left in no doubt that in this production things had turned out for the best when he ended up having to marry the servant-girl! As everyone knows, Kevin found his metier and went on to have a very successful career in television.

1975, Perth Theatre – The Day After the Fair with Janet Michael, Judi Maynard, Martin James, Hilary Paterson and Kevin Whately.

It was during this time that I had a strange and infuriating correspondence with Dundee Rep. We heard one day that they were planning a production of *The Wizard of Oz*, and although I had never seen the film and Judy Garland was hardly known to me, I was happy that Terry thought I was ideal casting for Dorothy. I spoke to Joan about it all, and she was extremely enthusiastic. She took over, saying, "I'll ring Stephen right now darling – I'm sure he'll be delighted to have you!" She immediately called him and told him that if he wanted to have me in his 'Wizard', she was happy to release me. I didn't hear the other half of the conversation, and it didn't really cross my mind that he might be resistant to taking a casting suggestion from the formidable Miss Knight. Joan informed me that his Associate Director, Robert Robertson, was to be directing the show and I should make personal contact with him. The only problem was that there was someone in their current company who they were considering for the role. I knew that this girl was a good actress, but no singer, so I was not unduly worried. I left Joan's office feeling quite optimistic and grateful to her for helping out. I decided to do a follow-up letter, little realising that it was the beginning of a ridiculous, lengthy and ultimately pointless correspondence.

Terry also wrote to Stephen, with whom he had worked many years previously, assuring him that I was indeed 'The Nation's Dorothy'. Whether all this outside interference conspired against my playing the role, I'll never know, but I think I can surmise because of the outcome. In response to my own letter, I received a letter of acknowledgement from Robert, and this was the first of many. I can't remember what they were all about, but these missives went back and forth until I eventually received one telling me when the auditions would be held. I had already done a number of productions at Dundee, including roles where I had to sing, but Dorothy was the leading role, so maybe having to audition was reasonable enough. When you compare the situation back then with the way things are today when people can have eight or nine recalls (mainly done via self-taping) before a management makes up its mind, it doesn't seem nearly so outrageous as it felt to us at the time.

But I was disappointed, as not only were they not offering it to me, they were opening it up to actresses from all over the country. Here I was, a local girl with all the right attributes (according to Terry Wale!), and they chose to hold open auditions. To make matters worse, Robert came in to see the current show, *Cloud Nine*, and went backstage afterwards to invite another girl in the cast to come to Dundee to audition for the role.

I began to feel uneasy, and my feelings were justified when actress, Thelma Rogers, Robert's wife, managed to seek me out one day, and told me in no uncertain terms that I should not even think of auditioning. She was a highly strung, nervous lady, clearly very uncomfortable with the whole business and she wouldn't give me any details beyond saying that there was no way I was going to be given the part. I might have been the 'Nation's Dorothy', but maybe not Dundee's. So, after discussing it with Terry, I decided not to audition, but said that I was still very interested in playing the role. So sure were we by this point that things were not going to work out, Terry and I booked a holiday for the period in question, and when Robert came into the Perth bar one evening to break the news that the part had gone elsewhere, I was able to say that we had already made other plans. It was just bravado and I felt very vulnerable, made worse when I found out that the girl I was working with in *Cloud Nine* was the one who had been offered the part. I knew then, without doubt, that I had been right not to audition. Why they wasted my time and theirs for so long remained a mystery, but there seemed to be more to it than quite met the eye.

I swallowed my hurt pride and after *Cloud Nine* was over I got on with my most challenging role to date, Isabella in *Measure for Measure*. If I had any doubts about my ability to play the part, they were certainly fuelled by an overheard conversation in the little Circle Bar. Sitting having a quiet drink with Terry in one of the 'boxes' (where we often used to sit after a show), we suddenly heard the booming tones of Martyn James: "Have you heard who is playing Isabella? Can you imagine? Lesley Mackie as a nun – and a virgin?" I was mortified, especially as there were several newly -arrived actors in the bar. Martyn was leaving, and as our paths crossed I said that if he wanted to gossip about me I would appreciate it if he would make sure I was well out of earshot! The following morning I was summoned to Joan's office to discover that Martyn had already been up there to hand in his resignation on the grounds that he found me impossible to work with! He was covering his tracks, but there was no need, as I wouldn't have reported him for a bit of gossiping. Once I gave my version of the 'incident', Joan just laughed heartily and said, "Oh, that's Martyn for you darling!" Martyn kept up a stony silence for the rest of the week, but I finally went up to him and said it was all very silly and we ought to make up and be friends. "Quite right", he said. "No hard feelings!" – as if he also had an axe to grind! Ah well, it was better than not speaking.

1975, Perth Rep – Measure for Measure with Philip Lowrie.

Actors are terrified of missing a single performance or of being a minute late. However, if you were in favour with Miss Knight, she would let you go elsewhere and do other things if it was at all possible. Despite having a leading role in *Measure for Measure,* I was allowed to go to Glasgow to do a radio broadcast, and her characteristic generosity nearly rebounded on us all. On the return trip, the train came to a grinding halt just outside Gleneagles and a guard informed us that we might be there for some time. Panic stricken, I told him through floods of tears that I was playing a leading role at Perth Theatre, and I had to be there by seven o'clock, so he agreed to call the theatre and let them know what had happened. Shortly afterwards he returned and, with a reassuring smile, told me that all my worries were over as the people at the theatre now knew where I was. I was living through every actor's nightmare, and no one understood why I was still so worked up; it was very different from someone in what you might call a 'normal' job failing to turn up at the office. To me it was cataclysmic! And the same applied to being late for any show. No excuse was good enough, short of sudden death! I just had to sit and sweat it out until the train finally got moving at a quarter to eight.

Joan was waiting for me in her little Morris Minor, so I jumped straight into the car and we sped through the streets of Perth. It was now a little after eight and the show had been due to start at 7:30. Joan told me that the audience had been sent away to the bar for a quarter of an hour, and when they returned at 7:45, they were sent away for another 15 minutes with the proviso that at 8pm the show would go on whatever happened. As I crashed through the stage-door, I was met by the sight of Trina Crichton, our lovely deputy stage manager, who was quaking in my nun's habit and clutching the script. I heard the cue for my first entrance fast approaching as she willingly, nay enthusiastically, threw off the costume and, having managed to get almost everything on, one very overwrought novice nun, minus her wimple, lurched onto the stage. Not an experience to repeat but, on the plus side, I heard that the bar did record business that night!

Terry stayed on after 'Measure' to do *Habeas Corpus*. I had also been asked to stay on, but I went off to London to do a television play, which Joan, of course, took very well. This, however, was the time of one of Terry's close shaves with the megalomaniac side of Joan. We had heard stories about actors and critics who had been banned from Perth Theatre because of various misdemeanours, so we were aware that she was a lady you did not cross. He had planned to stay on for *Dodwell's Last Trump* and to play Idle Jack in the Christmas Pantomime, but having read 'Dodwell', he decided that he didn't want to be in it, and as far as the panto was concerned, he felt that the character should be played by a Scot. He politely declined and, having gone to the trouble of writing an explanatory note, went to discuss it in Joan's office. She had obviously decided not to read or just to ignore the note, because she barely let him get a word in edgeways. She accused him of backing out because he wanted to play Dodwell and not one of the subsidiary characters, and he had to understand that Martyn was due a leading role. He was welcome to that one as the play was one of Perth's major disasters.

We were beginning to learn just how little it took to fall out with Miss Knight, and I discovered 20 years later that even one as favoured as myself could be thrown onto the cutting room floor for no apparent reason; but that was the future and, fortunately, Terry's little episode was not to cause any permanent damage. He was offered another job for Christmas in *Toad of Toad Hall* at Birmingham Rep and, although he had always played Ratty in previous productions, this time he gave his one and only Moley, which was a change, if not a particularly welcome one. He did, however, glean one of his favourite 'bad' reviews, being described by one critic as 'dismally charmless'!

I spent a very full fortnight in London doing the telly play and seeing numerous friends, and it was during that visit that I saw Mike Naylor for the last time. We met for a drink, and by the time we left, Mike was paralytic; having failed to hail a taxi we staggered to the Tube. I let him go ahead of me down the escalator and, a short time later, I followed on. As I moved slowly downwards, I caught a glimpse of him coming up the escalator on the other side, slumped over the moving rail, so I braced myself and just kept on walking until I stepped onto my train. It felt heartless, but I called his office the following morning to check that he had arrived and, amazingly, he had. So at least I knew he was alive, even although he had perhaps spent the night in a gutter. It was not a healthy friendship for me to pursue and I never saw him again or heard any more about *A Postal Order from My Granny*. Years later, in 1988, when I was doing *Bells Are Ringing* in Cheltenham, a lady and her daughter stayed behind one evening after the show. It was Mrs Naylor, who told me that Mike had died of throat cancer a few years before. I always felt that he would come to an untimely end, but we'd shared a few laughs and adventures during our brief friendship. I left London and reached Birmingham in time for Terry's opening night of 'Toad'. I left him with his two shows a day and headed back to Perth for the Spring Season.

I had the usual varied batch of roles, from the Chinese 'Mistress' in *On the Spot* by Edgar Wallace, to Antigone in *Antigone*, but my favourite play of the season was *Absurd Person Singular*. I was probably too young to play Jane, the obsessive housewife, but I loved it, and still consider it one of Ayckbourn's most hilarious black comedies. Plays still opened every second Tuesday, with rehearsals for the next play commencing the following morning; and yet, despite this rigorous schedule, my diary is full of walks up Kinnoull

Hill, swimming, saunas, having friends round for meals and many other social activities. When did we learn our lines?

Early in the season, Joan again allowed me to leave the 'Fair City' to audition for the soubrette part in the West End revival of Leonard Bernstein's musical version of *Candide*. I got through the first audition and a few weeks later headed for London again to face a second, this one in the presence of the internationally acclaimed director, Hal Prince. I walked tentatively onto the stage of Her Majesty's Theatre, sang my prepared song, and was then asked to read a short scene, at the end of which I heard an argument going on in the darkened auditorium. I knew that I was being considered for Paquette, a nice character part, but it seemed that Hal Prince now wanted to offer me the Juvenile leading role of Cunégonde, which was already on offer to somebody else; this was the substance of the argument. Fortunately for me, Cunégonde was not your conventionally pretty and romantic leading lady, but quirky, characterful and a little offbeat, so it was right up my street. I was then asked if I could reach a coloratura E Flat, and after I just about managed to squeak one out, I was told that I was now their first choice for Cunégonde. I was to be sent a copy of the aria *Glitter and be Gay,* and after I had learnt it I would return to give them a rendition, and this time they were willing to pay my fare! Things were looking optimistic, as managements only offered expenses if they were sure that they wanted you. I hardly dared to believe that I had landed my first leading role in the West End.

Terry always participated in the telling of this story because, according to him, he heard every word of the dialogue between us whilst he was waiting in the wings for me, although I don't think that he was. As time went by and we told and re-told the story, it had become so vivid to him that he became convinced that he had been there. He was certainly around to support me, and he sent me on my way northwards feeling somewhat over the moon. The following day I was straight into the technical rehearsal of *Oedipus*, which the company and I obviously coped with, although not many theatre directors would have released an actor for an audition on the day before a 'tech'!

For the next few weeks hysteria and jubilation reigned supreme as I practised *Glitter and be Gay* in every spare moment.

But then the dreaded letter arrived. Hal Prince was perfectly happy with his casting, but he could not get the theatre he wanted, and British Equity would not grant a work permit to Joel Gray (the American male star they had cast as Dr Pangloss), so the show was to be indefinitely postponed – which, as it turned out, meant for ever. I was naturally devastated, but I was learning what a lottery our business is and how an entire career can be altered by one piece of good or bad luck. I shed a few tears but had little time to mope.

It was during this spring when I spotted that the Edinburgh Lyceum was planning a production of *The Wizard of Oz* for autumn 1976, and I went across to Edinburgh to sing for the director of that show, a lady called Anna Barry. She seemed keen from the start and virtually offered it to me on the spot. This was compounded by my erstwhile friend Thelma, who was now working at the Lyceum. She sent me a card with congratulations as she had seen a cast list go up backstage in the theatre. I was delighted – after all, the Edinburgh Lyceum was a bigger and more prestigious theatre than Dundee – and although I had not been officially informed I was surely going to get the chance to play Dorothy Gale after all.

But time passed, and I couldn't understand why I hadn't received confirmation, never mind a contract or the train fare that they had promised; theatres sometimes did pay expenses back then. I wrote to Anna asking if I was going to be given the fare, and I received it by return of post. There was no contract, however, only a kind of havering explanation as to why I had not been given the coveted role of Dorothy, and this was despite her verbal offer on the day of my audition, not to mention the cast list on the notice board backstage. I discovered shortly afterwards that the part had gone to Tricia Scott who, although she was a good little actress, didn't sing at all. When I heard that the theatre was paying for her to have singing lessons in London in preparation for the role, it all fell into place. The new director of the Edinburgh Lyceum was none other than Stephen MacDonald, and I knew then that it had been Stephen and not Robert who had been at the root of the Dundee problem. It was just another rebuff from a man who did not appreciate other directors – or actors – giving them unasked for advice. We felt that he had been prejudiced against me by various things, but mainly by the interference of others. Some directors are extremely autocratic and like to acquire their own favourites, and as well as the *Pygmalion* aggravation when Joan released me to do a telly, there may also have been another factor. Being one of Dundee's own, given special attention in the press as a local lass, maybe he just wanted to take me down a peg or two; as if you need to do that to any actor – the business will soon do it for you. I did take it quite personally though, as there was always the feeling of an intentional slight. The 'Dorothy' incident troubled me for a long time, and I always hoped that one day I would meet Stephen again in convivial circumstances and put 'Wizard' behind us. Sadly, our paths never crossed before Stephen threw off this mortal coil, so I never had the chance to renew our acquaintance.

Robert eventually took over the running of Dundee Rep and oversaw its transition from old, converted church to new building in Tay Square. He invited me to be in the opening production, *Tonight We Celebrate,* but having heard on the grapevine that it was to be avoided at all costs, I politely declined, citing another possible job as an excuse, but I don't think that went down too well as far as any future work was concerned. Also, his marriage was soon to break up and, having behaved rather badly, he didn't want friends of Thelma's around to make him feel uncomfortable. He presided in Dundee for over ten years, and he never asked me again. For the record, *Tonight We Celebrate* was an unmitigated disaster.

People have oft times asked why I chose to work so much in Perth, insinuating that I made a choice, and seemed surprised to find out that actors have little control over their own destiny, as it was always a disappointment not to have worked more in my hometown. The preceding saga perhaps goes some way to explain my absence from the Dundee stage from 1974 until 1997.

My relationship with Terry was still alive, albeit with highs and lows. I wrote fondly in my diary of our 'Candide' meeting in London but, only three months later, having gone to see him in *Anastasia* in Birmingham followed by a week's sojourn in Bournemouth when he was on tour with the play, I felt that something was very wrong; he was totally preoccupied and seemed to have little time for me. I moved into Blackheath with him for a couple of weeks, but he shut himself away to devote himself to his play about Jessica Mitford and, even when he did take a break, I had the distinct impression that my presence was somewhat de trop. He had been commissioned by the Scottish Arts Council to write the play for Perth Theatre, so he had a deadline. With the benefit of hindsight and a comprehension of the kind of isolation writing requires, I can now understand the privacy he craved, except it wasn't quite as simple as that. I think it was the stickiness of our relationship which made me jump at the first job which came my way. I was asked to go and do a play at the Young Lyceum in Edinburgh, so I packed and left at once and, although it was a decent part in a play called *If You Died with A Face Like That*, within a fortnight I was offered a lovely job in a Granada sitcom. Although I went to great lengths to see if commuting to Manchester was a possibility, it was not to be. I somehow seemed fated not to work at Granada; when I was at Ochtertyre playing to a handful of people each evening I missed out on *Coronation Street*, and that was just the first of many jobs I had to turn down over the years. I liked to keep my diary full and never left gaps if I could avoid it. I didn't seem to have the right kind of advice back then, but in an overcrowded profession I suppose it's difficult for an agent to advise a client to turn down work. Twenty years later I went to STV to meet John Temple, the producer of *High Road*. He said, "I remember you well, because you were the flavour of the month at Granada in the '70s." And yet I never worked there once.

Neither had things worked out for Terry's play *The Other Day*; Jessica Mitford, the heroine of the piece, had gone along with it until the last minute, when she suddenly decided that she no longer wanted her family to be portrayed onstage. A more likely explanation was that Tony Richardson had bought the rights to her autobiography, *Hons and Rebels*, on which Terry's play was largely based. She was sure to make a lot more money if her book was turned into a film, although how a production at Perth Theatre could have affected a Hollywood movie is bewildering; as it turned out, the film was never made. He was devastated; he had been working on it for over a year and was very nervous about breaking the news to Joan, as things had almost reached the casting stage. True to form, when you were down, Joan would drag you up again, and she responded by asking him to play Jack Tanner, one of the biggest roles ever written, in *Man and Superman* – and also to use the knowledge gained from his research on the Jessica Mitford play to create and direct a project for the Theatre in Education on the Spanish Civil War; so with plenty to divert him from the disappointment, he was heading back to Perth.

I was also returning to Perth for the Ayckbourn trilogy, *The Norman Conquests*, and Terry called to ask if there was any chance of us sharing digs again. I wasn't sure about it, but we did end up sharing a room in Rose Cottage, where there were quite a few actors in residence. We quickly found that the spark had indeed gone out of our relationship, and we were just 'mates' for the rest of that summer season; it was clear that we were going our separate ways. After an enjoyable interlude performing the lovely role of Annie in *The Norman Conquests,* it came as no surprise to me when Terry suggested that I should forget the possibility of any future with him. We would always be friends, but I should look elsewhere for romance and marriage – and, if possible, with a younger man. I agreed and was looking forward to pastures new.

Sometimes good fortune creeps up on you unawares and takes a while to reveal itself. Only a few months earlier I'd been disappointed when I'd not been asked to play Dorothy in *The Wizard of Oz* at either Dundee or Edinburgh. Now I had been invited to play it in one of the biggest repertory theatres in the country down in Birmingham, and I was looking forward to the challenge, unaware that my journey along the Yellow Brick Road in Judy Garland's footsteps was only just beginning.

Off to see the wizard

Third time lucky. Clive Perry, one of the directors fostered and favoured by Joan, but with a definite mind of his own, invited me to Birmingham Rep to play Dorothy in *The Wizard of Oz*. He seemed to think that Dorothy might have to tap dance, so I took a few classes in Perth before I left. My other preparation for the role was a trip to Henlow Grange Health Farm in Biggleswade in order to lose a few pounds. Dorothy is a farm girl, and Judy Garland was certainly no sylph, but I felt that I still had a little too much of my 'belated' puppy fat to be convincing as a 12-year-old. I had high hopes of a sudden and dramatic weight loss, so I happily complied with the suggested liquid diet, but it was a tough regime. After 48 hours of waiting for the next carrot or tomato juice, the deprivation of food had affected my nervous system, I became weak and weepy and was transferred from the 600 calorie-a-day diet to a slightly more substantial one. The situation was not helped by watching all the underweight specimens skipping into the dining room to be fattened up and then hearing descriptions of baked potatoes, steaks and chips washed down with port! As the cost was the same whether you were on an increasing or reducing diet, it was all too much for a canny Scot to thole.

Anyway, I arrived in Birmingham six pounds lighter and ready to take on the role I had dreamt of for some time, which would turn out to be one of my all-time favourite parts. I found digs with a lovely old lady called Mrs Cooper and her daughter Paddy. It was a large old house full of large, old furniture. It probably had great potential, but to my eyes it was just very old fashioned. I had a little sitting room downstairs to entertain friends, which was a great bonus. Mrs Cooper is, of course, long gone, and I kept in touch with Paddy until she too passed on.

At the first read-through, I detected an air of discontent emanating from the actress who was playing Glinda, the Good Witch. She had only been sent Act 1 and was now discovering that she had little or nothing to do in Act 2. She invited me to join her for a drink at the *Grosvenor House Hotel*, a 'gay' establishment situated on the Hagley Road, one that I would frequent a lot as time went by. Her name was Amanda Barrie, and I took to her immediately, but ours was destined to be a brief friendship, because she told me that she was planning to leave a letter of resignation for Clive. The following morning, *The Good Witch of the North* had handed in her notice, flown the coop, and we were urgently looking for a replacement.

Clive found one in the shape of Lesley Joseph, who went on to find fame in the telly sitcom *Birds of a Feather. The Wicked Witch of the West* was Ursula Smith, who I knew from my Dundee Rep days, and she and I shared a dressing room. We only had one 'star' in the company, and that was Norman Vaughan. He was a sweet man and we all liked him, which was just as well, as he was being paid about six times more than anyone else and used about a sixth of the energy! Generally speaking, and with minor variations, an equal pay policy existed in most repertory theatres, but Norman was a television personality whose name, at least in theory, would put 'bums on seats', so I guess the rules didn't apply. Of course, as the years went by, commercial pantomimes would be cast from 'soap' stars, sports personalities and mini celebrities from reality television shows, all on astronomical salaries, with talented actors getting the small parts and even smaller pay packets!

Clive just let him suit himself, but while he was uncharacteristically tolerant with Norman, he was very strict with me throughout rehearsals and, after a week, was asking why I was still 'on the book'. Almost everyone was still on the book at that stage, but I realised that he was serious when he caught me one evening as I left rehearsals and asked where I was heading. When I said that I was going to the cinema with the Tin Man (David McAlister) and the Lion (David Foxxe), he told me quite categorically that I was not, and drove me back to my digs. I asked him why he was being so hard on me, and he glibly told me that I had to curtail my social activities until I had my own lines under my belt, so that I could start learning the part of the Scarecrow in case Norman needed a prompt! Being a comedian and used to ad-libbing, Norman was not expected to be line perfect and there were many times when he desperately hissed, "Is it the poppy field next?" I think he appreciated the back-up, and it meant that I knew the show inside out.

Vast sums had been spent on costumes and scenery, with a wonderful designer (Finlay James), and choreographer (Irving Davies), 20 Munchkins (all professionals), a glitzy set with a complicated revolve, and a 16-piece orchestra, which was almost unheard of outside the West End of London. We even had a large farm horse which only appeared in the opening scene and was the second highest paid performer in the show. It was worth its salary, as it succeeded in excavating its bowels as soon as the orchestra struck its first chord, and as this became a nightly feature, it was built in that the farmhands would come onstage with buckets and spades to clean up afterwards.

It was clear that some economy was required, and a week before we opened, I was sent to the local dog pound to look for a dog to play the key part of Toto. I returned with a little white terrier, which looked the part but, at only a year old, was not quite ready for such a demanding role so, with only a few days to go, he was sent off for a crash course in stagecraft. Unfortunately, you can't train a dog in a week, and the technical rehearsal will be ingrained in my memory for all time.

As it was a highly technical show there was a lot of pressure on everyone, and from the very beginning it was clear we were in for trouble. The surface of the stage was very slippery, and the dancers were having a terrible time staying on their feet – a problem they shared with Toto, who was straining at his leash to escape and doing his own version of the splits as he skidded along behind me. I was told to keep a packet of treats in my pocket and pat them to make a rustling sound whenever I wanted him to come to me. As he was supposed to stay by my side throughout the show, this was not going to be practical. The best we could manage was to have the trainer stand in the wings and pat her pocket and, of course, Toto ran straight past me to get to her. Clive was driven at one stage to mutter to me, "Get it behind the set and give it a good kick – you'll never get it to obey you otherwise!"

I tied it by its lead onto the high farm cart and as the orchestra launched into the opening bars of *Over the Rainbow*, the creature panicked, leapt off, and was left dangling by his neck until a member of the stage management team rushed onstage to rescue him from a premature demise! I was quite shaken and close to tears, but a voice from the auditorium commanded, "Tie it up again – it won't do the same thing twice!" This was a far cry from the caring theatre that had supposedly 'saved' this little stray puppy from an uncertain future in a miserable dog pound; its future was well marked.

We settled on using the dog as little as possible and found a way of tying him to an invisible pole in the wings at the beginning of each scene and collecting him each time we continued our journey to Oz. Both the dog and I were wrecks by the time we reached there, and at one point I somehow managed to get in front of the gauze which I was supposed to be behind. Clive was also at the end of his tether; after berating me in no uncertain terms, I got into the right position behind the gauze, and attempted through a vale of tears to sing *Follow the Yellow Brick Road*. Clive started to clap along, shouting, "Sing, Sing, Sing!" in time with the music, and eventually I was so emotionally drained that Irving Davies, the esteemed choreographer, came onstage and said to me in a placatory tone, "Don't worry darling. You know what his problem is, don't you? He wants to play Dorothy – with his hair in a bunch!" Everyone was on my side and, although I didn't appreciate it then, I suppose Clive was too – in his own peculiar way.

1976, Birmingham Rep – The Wizard of Oz with David McAlister, David Foxxe and Norman Vaughan.

But we had a wonderful time, and the show was rapturously received. It was Clive's first production in his new role as Director of Productions at Birmingham, and although it did go over budget to the tune of about £45,000, in the face of such acclaim, that was a mere detail. On the opening night, I made my first entrance shouting, "Aunt Em, Aunt Em", Toto slid in behind me, legs splayed, the audience erupted, and it all went splendidly.

At the finale, as I walked down the Yellow Brick Road to the strains of *Over the Rainbow*, surrounded by so much glitz and glamour, I felt as if I had stepped into a Hollywood movie. And what a thrill it was to discover that the two tickets I had left at the Box Office for friends of my father were, in fact, for dad himself and my brother, Grant, who had travelled all the way down from Dundee to surprise me. They only stayed for a few brief minutes before they drove straight back, but it was lovely to know that they had been there on such a special evening. During the run, many friends and family travelled to see it: Mum (of course), Aunt Mina, Uncle Bill and Uncle Archie to name but a few.

1976, Birmingham Rep – The Wizard of Oz with David Foxxe.

Once we settled into a routine, and despite the two shows a day regime, I was again able to enjoy an active social life. It was a role with its own special appeal, and I still have a lovely ring given to me by Malcolm, who was a member of the crew and a jewellery student at a local college. Sometimes a few of us would venture along to the *Grosvenor*, where the resident pianist would play a snippet of *Over the Rainbow* as I entered, and it was in that hotel that I met a young man called Christopher Scoular who was playing at the Alexandra Theatre in some touring comedy. Over the next few weeks, I came to believe that he might be the young man Terry had suggested I try to find. He came up to see me a few times during the run, and Mrs Cooper let him put his sleeping bag in my little sitting room. I was still having regular telephone conversations with Terry, and I was now able to tell him that I had taken his advice and found a younger man.

Once we'd opened, Clive went on directing me off-stage. He made it plain that he was disappointed by the casual clothes I chose to wear in the bar after the show, and told me in no uncertain terms that he expected his leading lady to wear dresses and skirts in front of the public; neither was I to smoke. He commented on my kaftan which he thought might be hiding a multitude of sins – and I had indeed put my six pounds back on. He was always just around the corner, and I jumped every time I heard him approach. He became well known for having a 'whipping boy' and, on this occasion, I think I was it. In retrospect, I'm grateful for his strictness because it probably did me good, although I don't think it did much to curtail my activities.

As the run progressed, Toto seemed quite poorly, and his symptoms were getting worse. The whole experience was just too overwhelming for a puppy, and he finally cracked under the stress. He was frightened of the music, of the Cowardly Lion and of the audience. One evening as I closed my eyes and wished myself back to Kansas, I was aware of the audience giggling. I glanced down and saw that my ruby slippers were all but submerged in a pool of wee-wee. I picked Toto up from the puddle and, as I cuddled him to me, he suddenly snapped at my face and snarled. There was a ring of foam around his mouth, and it was obvious that he was not well. He was taken away after the show, distemper was diagnosed, and I never saw him again. I was told that he would be looked after, which probably meant that he was put to sleep – maybe by Clive himself! The next day, just before the matinée performance, I was presented with another dog – a baby alsatian, which belonged to the theatre's wardrobe lady, and had never been on a stage before! Ursula and I laughed until we ached at the craziness of the situation but, in truth, the 'Toto' factor made my life very difficult.

1976, with the original Toto.

Because of the problem with the stage, which was either too slippy or too sticky (from a Coca-Cola mixture put on in order to combat the slippiness!), it was decided early in the run that I would <u>carry</u> Toto onstage on my first entrance, so that they looked at <u>me</u> and not the antics of the dog. However, the little alsatian seemed to grow from day to day and carrying him became such an effort that we were getting the wrong kind of mirth, so we went back to the old routine of the dog skidding on behind me. He was no better than the dear departed puppy, just bigger and uglier, and he managed more than a wee-wee on one occasion, which necessitated Norman and I doing a dance routine around a pile of poo. I never understood why they hadn't opted for a professionally trained dog; after all, he wouldn't have cost much more than I did.

The only other fly in the ointment was dear old Norman, who got lazier and lazier as the run progressed, although he might have saved a bit of energy if he'd not had a regular visit from one of the young dancers between shows! It was a bit of a worry as he was playing the energetic role of the Scarecrow and, although he had been a bit of a song and dance man in his day, he certainly didn't have the stamina for two shows a day. He would often sit down in the middle of a scene and just leave me to get on with it while he got his breath back. I remember on one occasion during a matinée, I spotted him lying flat out on a rock. When I asked him later what was wrong, he said quite matter-of-factly that he was saving himself for the evening performance! And this was despite the advantage of being the only member of the cast with a personal radio mike.

Throughout the run I built up a small following in Birmingham and, in particular, I had sterling support from Barbara and Brian Weatherhogg, two local schoolteachers. After seeing the show, they sent me a charming little note saying how delighted they would be if I would join them for a Sunday meal. It was my only day off, but being me, and probably afraid of missing out on something, I got in touch and they collected me the following Sunday. They were Christian Scientists, so it was an abstemious evening. They were obsessed with 'Wizard', and even more obsessed with Dorothy Gale. They talked about the show all evening, and I was treated to a slide show of photos taken by Brian during the performance, which he punctuated with short bursts of song. He even had the score sitting on his piano and wanted me to sing along as he played – but I did draw the line at that.

They often turned up at the stage door after performances to say 'Hello', usually clutching or wearing their crash helmets if they were on their motor bikes. I knew before they came round that they had been in because they always sat in the centre of row B, and at the curtain call they raised their arms aloft, clapping their hands above their heads; you couldn't miss them. I saw them many years later when, quite by chance, I bumped into them in the foyer at

Pitlochry Festival Theatre. We had a friendly chat, but I think they had moved on and their ardour for Dorothy had waned a bit.

I will never forget the feeling of coming down the Yellow Brick Road to *Over the Rainbow* on the last night to take my curtain call. I felt like a star. At the end of the run, there were plans for the production to go to the *London Palladium*, and Clive hoped to surround me with star names while I would be the 'unknown' at the heart of the piece. For a moment, I thought that this might be the chance I had been waiting for, and it was a great disappointment when it fell through. It would have been a wonderful way to continue my 'Judy' journey – to play Dorothy in a theatre where Judy Garland herself had appeared – although at this time I had little knowledge of her or the part she would play in my life; that was all to come. I do get the odd pang when I think about how incredible it would have been to play the 'Palladium'; who knows how it might have changed my life path, not to mention how good it would have looked on the CV?

I got on very well with Ursula, and I now made plans to move into her little bedsit in Golders Green for a few weeks or until I decided where I wanted to be. Ursula was heading off to work elsewhere and was happy to have her room occupied. Chris Scoular and I were about to audition for *The Duenna* which was to open in Guildford before touring, and we were quite excited about that possibility; things seemed to be falling into place for us.

Terry had been in to see 'Wizard' at Christmas with his friend Bernard Lloyd, and on the very last night he turned up again, but this time with Roger Kemp, and insisted that he drive me back to London, which was extremely convenient. He was soon back in touch to arrange a meeting. When we met he handed me a letter which was a proposal of marriage, the last thing I expected. It was not easy to turn my back on this after all we had been through, so I told Chris of this new development and he wrote to Terry asking if he would leave us alone for a while and give our relationship a chance, which was the last thing that Terry intended doing. He was quite persistent, and I suppose that it was his persistence which eventually won out. I had no particular reason to trust him or believe that he finally knew what he wanted, but on the other hand I could not ignore his declarations of undying love. He said that he had never been able to accept that the first lady he met after the breakup of his marriage could possibly be his next wife – until I met someone else.

Things were further complicated by the fact that Chris and I had both been offered parts in *The Duenna* and Chris had already started to book our digs for the tour. It was all so unfair on him, and I decided to go to Dundee to discuss this bizarre turn of events with mum and dad to see if things looked any clearer from a distance. Mum was torn as, although she liked Terry, she had an old-fashioned resistance to my marrying a divorcee, but at the same time she quite liked the idea of my marrying someone! I returned to Golders Green to ponder my future and spent the next few weeks meeting Chris and Terry, and not knowing which way I would eventually turn. Terry did win a few extra points for having a car (even if it was Bernard's!), and whenever I needed taken or collected from anywhere, he was available and willing. It certainly was a star player in the matrimonial dilemma.

On March 8th I was invited to the flat of an old friend from my college days, Celia Preston, and her husband Stewart. After supper, Terry arrived to collect me and drive me back to my digs. He only left the car parked for the length of time it takes to say 'Hello' and 'Cheerio', but by the time we both got downstairs, some overzealous little Hitler had covered the car with stickers saying, 'Don't park here' and suchlike. We trailed up to the flat to get a bucket of water, went back to the car, scrubbed for as long as it took to remove all traces of the glue, and returned the bucket to the Prestons. He must have been waiting to pounce because, hard though it is to believe, the little shit did it again! I could have wept, but Terry stoically faced another sloshing off session and, in a moment of impulsiveness or even madness, I blurted out, "Yes, I will marry you!" Later that night I wondered if I would feel differently in the morning, but when I woke up I knew that I'd made my decision and must now face the consequences.

Although it was awkward, as I started rehearsals down in Guildford, Terry and I began to quietly make plans for our wedding and I'm happy to say that Chris and I managed to remain friends. A few days after opening, I had my first encounter with Norman Punt, throat specialist to the stars! I had contracted a viral infection and was left with virtually no voice at all. Mr Punt painted my vocal cords with some protective substance – a real eye-stinging experience, but he somehow gave me enough voice to get through the evening performance. He'd warned me that I would have even less voice the following morning, but the extra day gave the company time to give Fiona Clare, my understudy, a bit of rehearsal, and though it grieved me she went on as Donna Luisa for the next couple of performances. Many years later I discovered that during the rehearsals she had the personal attention of Julian Slade, composer of *The Duenna* and many other similarly quaint musicals, his most famous being *Salad Days*. Even in retrospect I still feel a little envious about that.

1977, Yvonne Arnaud Theatre, Guildford – The Duenna on Tour –
with Elizabeth Hudson-Evans (née Brown).

Unfortunately, the tour was a bit shambolic, because once we left the *Yvonne Arnaud Theatre*, the set didn't seem to fit anywhere else; in Wolverhampton, I flung open my bedroom windows to warble my opening notes, but due to a backwards leaning piece of scenery they closed straight back in my face. The set swayed constantly and always looked as if it was about to keel over; on one occasion it was supported by a couple of actors who struggled against all the odds to keep it upright.

My most embarrassing moment came towards the end of the show one evening, when I made my entrance from upstage right and ran to the centre of the stage to meet my lover to sing our final duet. As I skipped on, my wig brushed against the scenery and managed to attach itself to a protruding nail. It flew from my head and was left dangling at the back of the stage in full view of the audience. I was left bald as a coot, my hair all tucked inside a flesh-coloured skull cap, which was not a pretty sight, and both of us struggled through the song despite mounting hysteria. I was never so glad to get to the end of a show.

The musical had quite a silly story, and at one point Chris had to stand before the two leading ladies unable to tell us apart because we had our faces covered; the fact that the other actress was a good six inches taller made it one of the more ludicrous moments in the show. That notwithstanding, part of the problem was the absence of any real guiding hand as Lionel Harris, our director, had a heart attack early in rehearsals and was replaced by David Thompson. Once Lionel recovered from the initial shock, he began to summon us to his hospital bed for notes and lessons on how to use a fan. He adored the show, but he was impossible, and Lizzie and I felt that we should mention our hospital sessions to David who was, predictably, less than impressed. But we were young and desperate to please everyone, so we went on taking notes from both directors, and when we reached Eastbourne, Lionel finally returned and proceeded to re-direct the whole thing. David quietly disappeared as Lionel launched into his task.

He told me my hat was badly made; to make sure it was altered he pulled it apart before me. He did the same to my dress, hauling out the padding on one side so that it hung lopsided. His reasoning was that, if he made a total mess of it all, the wardrobe department would have to sort things out, but we only had one girl on tour with us helping with maintenance, so there was little chance of any major repairs. To make matters worse, he came into my dressing-room shortly before curtain-up to tell me about the changes he had made to my main scene with the Duenna, played by Joyce Grant. He gave me the impression that he had already gone through it all with her and there was no need for a stage rehearsal; in fact, Joyce had refused to rehearse with Lionel and knew nothing of the changes. Normally, I wouldn't dream of doing anything which was unrehearsed – and I can't recall what possessed me to do it without reference to Joyce – but somehow Lionel conned me and, as I started the scene in a different position, I saw the look of panic in her eyes, and we both went through agony until it was over; the fact that I looked like something the cat had brought home was the least of the problems. Having caused havoc, Lionel went home to convalesce, and we finished the tour without a director.

I said goodbye to Chris and the company, and Terry and I headed north to assist with the wedding plans. We had an interview with the *Dundee Courier* about our engagement and forthcoming nuptials, then met with Rev Duncan Darroch who used to be my School Chaplain and was briefly coming out of retirement to perform our wedding ceremony. In some denominations, it would have been difficult, nay impossible, for an atheist divorcee to marry in a church, but Mr Darroch was a gentle, understanding man and we both took to him. We chatted at length, and once he had established the sincerity of our intentions, all was set to go ahead. We even managed to arrange the wedding for a Sunday – which was a 'first' for Mr Darroch – so that friends in the theatre would be free to come; it also meant than neither Terry nor I would have to call it off if a job cropped up. However, soon afterwards I did have to turn down a tour of *Oliver* playing Nancy, as it would have been impossible to get to my wedding if the show was playing in some distant southern venue on Saturday October 8th, so a Sunday wedding didn't cover all eventualities.

Before we left Scotland, we had a meal with Joan Knight and Andrew McKinnon. Many months previously when marriage wasn't even on the cards, I had been at a theatre party and walked into the ladies' loo to find one of the doors wide open, revealing Miss Joan Knight sitting on the loo! She was a bit tipsy and shouted to me as I passed: "Darling you won't ever marry Terry Wale, will you? He is not the man for you. Promise me that you won't!" I told her that nothing was farther from my mind and forgot all about it until marriage became a possibility. So, on that evening with Joan and Andrew, I apologised, tongue in cheek, for breaking my promise. She laughed heartily and declared that she was delighted, and at that moment she may well have been, but as time passed, Joan's feelings would change.

We headed back down to London having done as much as was possible in the time we had. Terry and I had managed to see quite a lot of each other over the previous two years, so it was ironic that we were soon to spend three months apart before the wedding because Terry had been offered a season at the Chichester Festival Theatre, down on the Sussex coast, and Joan Knight had invited me back to Perth. Terry left almost at once for his read-through of *Julius Caesar,* directed by Peter Dews. He was to be playing Calpurnia in an all-male production, and although he had often played female roles in his youth, it was the first time he had been cast as a middle-aged woman!

Bernie was still in the flat in Blackheath, but was about to depart on a two-week tour of the capitals of Europe with the Birmingham Repertory Company, doing two plays, *Measure for Measure* and *The Devil is an Ass.* On the morning of his departure, I was in the flat planning my trip to the 'dole' when the phone rang. It was Clive Perry calling from Birmingham. One of the actresses in the plays had taken ill with suspected appendicitis and was I free to take her place on the European tour? After the initial shock, I began to feel quite excited, and quickly sorted out my things. My suitcase was still packed, and for some unknown reason I had my passport with me. After leaving a message in Chichester for Terry, I climbed into a taxi with Bernard, and we headed for the airport. On the journey, Bernie told me what my parts in the plays would involve. It all sounded straightforward, which was just as well as I would have to learn the lines on the flight to Zurich and, once there, there was only one day's rehearsal. We checked in at Heathrow's departure desk, after which I was introduced to the other members of the company. As we stood around chatting, a call came over the tannoy system for the Company Manager.

At that moment, I was blissfully unaware that my little dream was about to be shattered, as it turned out that the call was about the missing actress, Janet Maw. Apparently, she was only suffering from the severe effects of a tummy bug and would be well enough to take a later flight and join the company in time for their first performance. This gave the Company Manager a difficult choice, but I knew in my heart that there was only one decision he could make. Janet had already served her time on a lengthy British tour, which included exotic venues like Bradford and Wolverhampton, so she deserved the foreign trip. It also meant no extra rehearsals for the rest of the cast, so that was that.

My luggage was recovered but I was unable to retrieve Terry's flat keys, which I had just sent to him by registered post. I managed to catch Bernard before he left for the departure lounge, and he gave me his keys with the proviso that I would be at the flat for his return. Having wished the company good luck I waved them off, fighting back tears as they all disappeared from view. It was only then that I allowed myself to cry as disappointment flooded over me. I felt cheated, but I knew that I would have risen from my sickbed to tour the capitals of Europe! I've always wanted to work abroad but something has always managed to get in the way. As the tears flowed, I poured out my tale of woe to the taxi driver as we returned to the flat, although he had to make a detour to take me to Chadwick Street so that I could sign on as unemployed. He waited for me before driving south to Blackheath, even coming in to re-connect the electricity supply and have a cup of tea. The taxi cost £20 which was quite a lot back in 1977, but I knew that Clive would see to it that I wasn't out of pocket; in fact, he also sent me a book token and a bunch of flowers, but it was cold comfort when I thought of what I was missing, and even more depressing when I received Bernie's postcard telling me of the delights of Europe and the success of the tour.

I put it behind me and spent most of June down in Chichester with Terry. I saw his opening night, and it was so convincing watching him play a woman that it almost made me think about cancelling the wedding! After a quick trip to Bristol to have a fitting for my wedding dress which was, surprisingly enough, to be made by Dawn Pavitt, Terry's ex-wife, I headed north to start rehearsals for two plays, *The Matchmaker* and *The Hypochondriac*. My rehearsals coincided with another momentous event, which was the wedding of my old pal, Doreen. We had made a schoolgirl promise that we would be each other's bridesmaid, but Doreen had a younger sister; as they couldn't afford to dress two bridesmaids, I had to settle for being a guest! Her wedding was quite chaotic, but great fun. I sang *Evergreen* at the reception, but my abiding memory is of Doreen's mum, Irene, taking off her wedding hat and using it to collect money for the bus driver on the way to the reception. Doreen married her wood sculptor and became Mrs John Spielman.

After rehearsals one evening, I stayed behind with the company for a couple of drinks at a favourite pub, *The White Horse*. I tried a drink that was new to me, a Carlsberg Special (echoes of Southern Comfort!), and after a couple, realised that I had missed my train. So I decided to have another to pass the time until the next one, and by the time I left the pub I was not only feeling rather drunk, but also quite ill. I remember whoever it was who dropped me off at the station, asking me if I was really fit to travel. I assured him that I was, and staggered onto the platform. I boarded the train and with enormous relief settled down to have a short nap. I was wearing a spotted blue and white sun dress with a little shoulder bag, an outfit that had seemed quite appropriate as I left for rehearsals in the morning sunshine but was now a little incongruous in the cool of the evening. Predictably, I fell asleep but awoke with a start when the train suddenly arrived at the station.

I became aware that my head was resting on something soft, which turned out to be the shoulder of the man sitting next to me. "Is this Dundee?" I asked, and was horrified to discover that we were pulling out of Stonehaven. The next stop was Aberdeen, and John, the man beside me, offered to help me when we got there. We found a guard who informed me that there would be no train back to Dundee until 6am the following morning; he also said that I would be lucky to find any accommodation because the Brass Band Festival was on and the town was choc-a-bloc, but I was welcome to sit in his office until the early train. The thought of sitting on a hard chair under lurid strip lighting was a mind-numbing way of spending the next ten hours, especially with a hangover, so I was grateful and relieved when John suggested that I go back with him to his mother's house on the outskirts of the town. He explained that he worked on the oil rigs – two weeks on and two weeks off – and when he was working, he came up from his family home in Dunoon and stayed with his mum before heading out to the rigs. This offer felt like manna from Heaven, so I found a call box and phoned mum to let her know what was happening, explaining that I had fallen asleep on the train. She wasn't daft, sussed that I had been drinking, and was horrified that I was about to put my trust in a total stranger, but I tried to reassure her that he was middle-aged, couthy and seemed very nice, and in any case I was to be staying in his mother's house. Mum was not at all happy, but I felt I had no choice.

I did suggest to him that he call his mother to see if she minded my coming, but he insisted that there was no problem, hailed a taxi, and we headed for his home, where there was no sign of a mother; I began to feel very uneasy. His story now changed, and he explained that his mother had departed for a lengthy world cruise to celebrate what would have been her Diamond Wedding, had her husband still been alive. Warning bells were ringing and when he offered me a drink, I declined and asked him if he could show me to a room as I was ready to collapse. He then started to prevaricate about the sleeping arrangements, and the problem seemed to be that he didn't want me to sleep in his mother's room, as she was bound to notice and give him a hard time when she sailed back into Aberdeen. This seemed a ludicrous excuse, considering that he was a mature man, and I began to wonder if his mother was alive. I offered to sleep on a chair, but after a lot of debate, he said that I could have his bed and he would sleep on the sofa. He phoned to book a cab for the following morning, offering to drop me off at the station before heading out to the rigs. It seemed that chivalry was not quite dead – or so I thought.

After removing my little sundress, I climbed into bed and oblivion. I was rudely awakened by the arrival of a small, tubby, middle-aged naked man, who clambered into bed beside me. I virtually threw myself from the other side and the next few minutes, had I not been so scared, were almost farcical. He chased me round the landing of his house until he eventually managed to pinion me against the wall. As he stood there stark naked, I sobbed, begged and pleaded with him, but he was equally desperate. He said that he had been married for 20 years, had a son of 16 and had never been unfaithful to his wife. He had a male fantasy about the kind of accidental encounter we'd had, and I was obviously not living up to expectations. He finally relented and slumped onto the trunk at the top of the stairs, allowing me to escape back to bed, although I felt decidedly uneasy lying there.

Suddenly, at around four o'clock in the morning, the light snapped on, and he burst in again, fully clad this time. He said that he could not sleep, knowing there was a young woman in his bed, and he asked me to get dressed and leave. This, I feel, was the worst of all his deeds – to put me out in a strange, cold city in the middle of the night – but I was lucky enough to pick up a cab, where with a touch of déjà vu about my taxi journey from the airport only a few weeks previously, I related my tale of woe to the driver, who took me back to the station.

I found the guard who I had spoken to only a few hours earlier. He was sitting in his little office with a couple of policemen, and I regaled them with my sorry tale, but even if I had wanted to report the man, I had no idea where I had been. I sat there until it was time for the train, exhausted, my face smeared with mascara, and quite inappropriately dressed for the chilly crack of dawn. I arrived back home, passing mum on the path as she headed out to school. She asked if everything had been alright, and I responded in the affirmative; I never did tell her the whole story, although she probably sensed that I'd landed myself in a bit of a scrape.

I cleaned up and rushed off to Perth, and only a little behind schedule, got to rehearsals, where I attempted to explain. There have been some excuses for being late, but I think that my Aberdeen story takes some beating. I don't think that anyone quite believed it, but every word of it was the truth – another story which I would tell for the rest of time. Terry and I were apart for about ten weeks and it was clear that I needed a minder to help me curtail my adventures and take things a bit more seriously. Maybe I would suddenly acquire maturity with the approach of my marriage.

- 8 -

The bells are ringing (Stay six days and see six plays)

It had never been part of my life's plan to marry an actor. In a profession that boasts over 85% out of work at any given time, it would have been more prudent to seek out a nice doctor – a plumber would have been too much to hope for! So when Terry proposed I was faced with a dilemma, for not only was he an actor, but he was also considerably older than me; as if that wasn't enough to contend with, he had been married before. Nevertheless, it was now all arranged, and mum was dealing with most of it on her own, dad not being of much help in practical matters. I sought Terry's opinion from time to time, but he was happy to let us get on with it; he had other things to occupy his mind, and one was his impending divorce. For some reason there had been a backlog of divorces, and the wheels were moving very slowly. His solicitor, Jim McGoldrick, had guaranteed that Terry's would not be a problem, but it had not yet come through. Terry didn't want to alarm us, but realised that if he didn't tell us we might be faced with the nightmare of a last-minute cancellation – or even a bigamous marriage! He went through hell until it was finalised, just in time for the calling of the wedding banns. I can't recall if I ever shared the details with my folks, but I'm glad that even I wasn't aware of just how close a call it was.

Although we had our own concerns, there was one truly tragic event a few weeks before the wedding, and that was the untimely death of Lesley Sinclair. She had a massive brain haemorrhage and was gone at only 23 years old. Her mother, Bunty, was an old friend of mum's, and I had known the family since my childhood as they lived round the corner from our flat in Tait's Lane. I have always thought it incredible that, despite the loss of their daughter, John and Bunty Sinclair still came to our wedding, sitting quietly on the sidelines during the reception; it must have been agonising for them.

Having performed our two plays in Perth we then took them to *His Majesty's Theatre* in Aberdeen, and it was here that Terry and I were eventually reunited. We had spent hours on the telephone during the long separation, but it was strange being together again. I think we both found it hard to believe that within two weeks we

101

would become a married couple. We returned to Perth where I was doing the two plays in repertoire until the end of October.

1977, The Matchmaker on Tour – with Billy Hartman, Tony Roper and Anne Kidd.

We squeezed our wedding in between a Saturday night 'Matchmaker' and a Monday evening 'Hypochondriac'. It was a wonderful day, despite a gentle drizzle. Terry's mum and dad came up from London but, unfortunately, his brother Peter and his wife could not make the journey as Annette was pregnant with her first child and suffering from morning sickness. Peter was going to be one of the ushers, but we replaced him at the last minute with Ralph Riach, who we had met in Perth as a theatregoer, and who had become a friend. He was an architect and an enthusiastic amateur at this time, providing digs for visiting actors, but after a few years and against all advice, Ralph gave up the day job, went to the RSAMD to train as an actor – and had a good career in the business. Brother Grant was Chief Usher, our Best Man was Andrew McKinnon, Associate Director to Miss Knight and a good friend of us both, and of course, my Matron of Honour was Mrs Doreen Spielman.

When I think of the expense of a wedding nowadays, I'm sure that we kept to a very tight budget, although it was quite a large affair with 80 guests, which my parents paid for. Doreen wore a Laura Ashley dress of mine, with an additional three inches of lace added at the bottom to make it the right length, and she handed it back afterwards. Terry's folks were older and couldn't contribute at that time and, in any case, it was still traditional for the bride's parents to cover most of the costs. We certainly didn't have much money, and Terry was still in debt to me to the tune of about £70. Just prior to the 'Duenna' tour, we went to buy an engagement ring, and chose a dainty one with a small sapphire set in diamonds. It was a modest £45 and when Terry handed over his Access card to pay for it, the assistant decided to do a check. Terry quietly asked me to leave, and when he emerged a few minutes later minus the ring, he said that his account was overdrawn and he had left a £5 deposit. I probably lent him the rest. For the record, over the years, Terry became extremely thrifty, taking control of our finances, doing the tax returns and happy that we usually managed to have some money in the bank. He was so thrilled to be in this position, that by the time we were more financially secure he preferred saving to spending.

I paid for my own dress, but the details remained a secret from the guests. Terry's ex-wife, Dawn, was a dress designer, and although it had seemed a good decision on our part to ask her to make my dress, we knew it might seem a little bizarre to certain relatives and friends, so we just told people that it had been made by a designer friend. I had been down to Bristol on a couple of occasions and Terry brought the finished article up with him at the end of September; luckily it fitted.

Everything went smoothly thanks to mum's organisation. It was all very simple – no hairdresser, manicure or pedicure. The only problem I had was in finding an invisible way to secure the little pearl skull cap on my head, but by the time the cars arrived we were all ready to go. I savoured the drive through the town alongside dad and, despite the rain, it was uplifting to see a small crowd gathered outside St Peter's Church. I remember the last moment before we walked down the aisle, when dad turned to me and said that I looked 'nice', then we heard the strains of *St Anthony's Chorale* and made our entrance. We were lucky to have John Scrimger as organist, Musical Director at Perth Theatre and one of the best.

I risked one sideways glance at mum, but I felt quite emotional and didn't linger; dad handed me over, having made a loud noise as he accidentally kicked the front pew (a moment caught forever on the old reel-to-reel tape recorder which I had planted at the front of the church), and then he joined mum. Terry looked dapper in his cream suit, which contrasted nicely with his brown hair, recently dyed for the occasion. It had been some time since Mr Darroch had conducted a wedding, so he was probably as nervous as we were, but he had a natural warmth and sincerity. It was a lovely, personal service and we couldn't have wished for a better minister. As it turned out, it was the last one he ever did because he died only a few weeks later from an existing heart condition.

Terry's hand trembled as he placed the ring on my finger, but that was maybe because he was fearful that the Access men might appear at any moment to reclaim it! As we signed the register, Neil Young, son of our next-door neighbours, sang *Oh Perfect Love,* and we eventually marched out to the strains of the *Trumpet Voluntary* by Jeremiah Clarke (often attributed to Henry Purcell), and were greeted outside the church by a number of people including the local press. Although I was a bit of a local celebrity, I had competition on this occasion from Brendan Price, an actor friend of Terry's, one-time Chief Weasel in *Toad of Toad Hall* and now appearing in a popular television series. After a few more photographs in the university grounds we headed to our Reception at the *Queens Hotel.*

Terry wished that he had learnt his speech instead of just leaving it to chance, and only just remembered after a prompt from me to thank my folks. As a writer he excelled, so he should have prepared, and it paled somewhat by comparison to Andrew's, which was well polished and ended by wishing us 'the patience of Job, the wisdom of Solomon and the children of Israel' – an awe-inspiring toast! It was great to see a few of the older family members, including my Gran Mackie, who had threatened not to come when she heard it was on a Sunday – never mind the fact that I wasn't wearing a veil!

My only disappointment of the day concerned the gift from Brendan. As he handed it to me, he launched into instructions as to how I should treat it, not to put it onto direct heat, only in the oven and so forth, and Terry promptly took it from him and went upstairs to the room where we were storing any newly-arrived gifts. Foolishly, he was holding it by the string which was tied round the parcel; just as we reached the room it snapped, and the parcel fell to the floor shattering the gift into many pieces, leaving nothing intact but the lid of a rather expensive Elizabeth David casserole dish. We returned to the reception and thanked Brendan, and we never did tell him what had happened. I can't recall if Terry danced at all, although I had given him lessons in a few of the Scottish ones prior to the event, but I danced a bit, and even sang *Bobby's* (Terry's) *Girl* at the request of Chrissie Rhynd, the well-known Dundee violinist.

Leaving all the merriment behind, we eventually left for Ballathie House Hotel, where we knocked back a bottle of champagne and collapsed in a heap. It was straight back to work the following day, and so our real honeymoon would have to wait. With or without the trimmings, I was now Mrs Terry Wale.

Looking back after all these years, and despite my earlier reservations, I have no doubt that marrying Terry was the best decision I ever made. Many show-business marriages suffer from long and frequent separations that are part and parcel of an actor's life, but in the early days we were seldom out of each other's sight. We always considered it a privilege to work together, and over the years we were fortunate in this respect, working together as actors, as director and actress, and eventually creating our own shows and cabarets, even trying our luck as co-producers.

We were now into rehearsals for *Blithe Spirit,* in which we were playing supporting roles to Rikki Fulton as Charles Condomine. This was an unusual bit of casting, and it sometimes seemed as if the character had strayed in from another production altogether. "Mmm, Golden Shred, delicious!" he extemporised as he kissed his wife at breakfast. Character and dialogue were freely adapted to suit Rikki's persona and undoubted talents. The curtain rose to his rendition of Irving Berlin's *Always* at the piano. The fact that Charles Condomine hated the song and couldn't bear to hear it, let alone play it himself, didn't seem to matter. Rikki was determined to start the evening off with a bit of a solo and collect the round of applause that sometimes capped his virtuoso performance. Anne Kidd and I had the unenviable task of playing the opening scene while all this was going on, and I think a good deal of the plot went unheard. Still, the audiences seemed to like it, and Sir Noel was no longer available for comment. Rikki ran rings around the young and relatively inexperienced Andrew McKinnon, who even allowed Rikki's two small yapping dogs to attend rehearsals, and they not only stunk (due to some bowel disorder!), but howled whenever Rikki played the piano.

We were staying in a flat next door to Rikki and his wife Kate Matheson, who was playing the part of his second wife, Elvira, and on one occasion they asked us to join them for a meal. We didn't relish the idea of an evening with Rikki's two little farting dogs, but we went along and, true to form, Terry took the opportunity to casually comment on 'Andrew's silly idea' of having Rikki play *Always*. Rikki quickly stated that it had been his idea, which of course we knew, but we looked suitably surprised. Terry had made the point, although it didn't change anything. Despite Rikki and his antics, we would have just enjoyed being and working together, had it not been for a very dramatic occurrence, which sent shock waves through us and had repercussions for some considerable time.

About two weeks into rehearsals, Terry received a telegram from Dawn, asking him to call. Her partner, Charles, had taken his life by jumping from the Clifton Suspension Bridge and Dawn was in a desperate state. She had heard the news on television and knew from the description that it was Charles. Although he suffered from manic depression (now called bipolar disorder), the suicide was unexpected and devastating. This event marked the start of a difficult year for Terry and I, as he was torn between her obvious need for his support (involving almost nightly phone calls), and the strain it was putting on us as newly-weds. The phone calls went on for a year, and Terry also made a few trips to Bristol to offer support. Looking back, perhaps his behaviour was admirable as there are not many divorcees who would take on the burden of an ex-wife's grief for the man she had left him for, even to the extent of accompanying her to scatter Charles's ashes.

A week after the play closed, I was on my way to Birmingham to play Belinda Cratchit and Little Fan in *A Christmas Carol*. Clive had nothing more exciting to offer Terry than George the Bystander, but he thought we might like to spend our first Christmas together. We appreciated this gesture, and he even let Terry start a week late in order to stay in Perth beyond the opening night of *Waiting for Godot*, which Terry had directed. So I settled into Mrs Walsh's digs, the same landlady I had stayed with during *The Duenna*, and this time we shared the flat at the top of the house with Ursula Smith, who was also returning to Birmingham for the Christmas show. By the time Terry joined us, rehearsals were not exactly going well.

1977, Birmingham Rep – A Christmas Carol with Bob Grant.

For some reason the choreography took up most of the rehearsal period, and Clive seemed happy about that. In contrast to the previous Christmas, he sat in the auditorium for much of the time, blowing his whistle if he wanted to comment, and did little or nothing on 'the book' until the last few days. We were all worried, and I can't imagine how the actor playing Scrooge (Bob Grant) must have felt. Having been very dictatorial during 'Wizard', Clive was now so laid back that he was hardly there at all. Apparently, this was all to do with 'est', a course in self-knowledge and striving for tranquillity, which must have led him to believe that the show could direct itself.

Terry had been looking forward to a relatively easy time; as dancing was not his strong point, that aspect was irksome, and he certainly hadn't reckoned with Lesley Joseph, who was also back in Birmingham, lured, no doubt, by the promise that the part of Caroline, George's wife, was more substantial than it was. Not being backward about coming forward, Lesley J. persuaded Clive to build her part up and scenes were added daily, until the minor characters of George the Bystander and his wife, Caroline, threatened to take over the show. But it all came together – after a fashion – and we enjoyed our first Christmas together in snow-bound Edgbaston. Ursula had very sweetly booked herself into a hotel for a couple of days to give us the flat to ourselves and we had an idyllic day – a huge meal, then a long walk on a frosty afternoon, totally alone together.

The show over, we drove back to 137, Purves Road. There had been a lot of debate about our moving in. Terry's dad, Sid, was very keen to have us there, but Lily was very equivocal and unable to come to a decision. What we didn't realise then was that her mood changes and indecision heralded the arrival of early-onset dementia and a twelve-year period of disintegration. Although we were to have the upstairs flat, Terry had his own reservations about moving back to his childhood home and such proximity to his parents. We stayed at the Blackheath flat until everyone appeared to be happy with the move.

Lily said, "Yes", and before she had time to change her mind, we packed up all our goods and chattels from Vanburgh Park, hired a van, and moved into Kensal Rise. The upstairs flat had previously been occupied by the Smith family, and both the Smiths and Wales had paid rent to a landlord. However, at some point, the opportunity arose to purchase the property, and Sid managed to secure the amount required, which he had managed to knock down from £2,000 to £1,850, and thus the Wale tenants became the landlords. The Smiths moved out, leaving most of their stuff behind, and the flat had lain empty until our arrival. It was a two-bedroomed flat with a spacious lounge, tiny bathroom and a miniscule kitchen/scullery. It was all very old-fashioned, but it didn't take us long to appreciate that moving into the family home was one of the wisest choices we ever made, as it saved us a small fortune in rent over the next ten years.

Despite the lack of a dining table, we managed to do quite a bit of entertaining in the early days of our life there. I recall one occasion, when we had invited Sue Yelland (designer from the 'Welly Show' and 'Wicker Man') and her partner Graham Attwood round for supper, as that was not one of our more successful evenings. They arrived with a set of mixing bowls as a wedding gift and a bottle of Bollinger, and although I had no idea that it was one of the best champagnes, I was aware that it was not a particularly suitable accompaniment for the chilli con carné I had concocted, which was swimming in sauce, as was the cucumber raita, and it was virtually impossible to eat it on our laps without the juices slopping over the edge of the plates and onto the floor. The garlic bread was soggy as I had forgotten to remove the foil at the end of the cooking, but it was at least edible.

Sue had introduced me to the joys of garlic bread a few years previously at her home in Barnes; indeed, she introduced me to garlic. So taken was I with the bread, that I asked for the recipe and decided to try it out back home for the folks and a couple of friends. It went disastrously wrong on that occasion, with the result that it was inedible and stunk the house out for days. It was very simple: 4ozs butter, 2 crushed cloves of garlic and of course, a loaf of bread. I had mistakenly thought that two cloves meant two bulbs and had added over 20 cloves to the mix. So this was my second attempt and although they seemed to forgive its imperfections, Sue was an excellent cook, and I often wondered if it was one of the reasons that we never heard from them again! Anyway, having settled into our London flat, we seemed to have no sooner caught our breath before we were heading north again for a season at the Pitlochry Festival Theatre.

With an eight-month stint ahead of us, we loaded everything into our old Rover 100, and set off for the 'Theatre in the Hills'. On the way north, we celebrated Terry's 40th birthday at *The Angel Inn* in Corbridge, where we had a lovely meal and stayed overnight. 'Stay Six Days and See Six Plays' was the slogan with which Pitlochry enticed its audiences. What it meant, and still does as far as the actors are concerned, is that once all six plays have opened, there are gaps of anything up to a week between performances of the same play, and consequently almost every night is just as nerve-racking as the opening night! We were in five out of the six plays, so it was just as well that we managed to rent a lovely cottage just a stone's throw from the old tent theatre. It provided a haven, not only for us, but for many other members of the company who were far from home and without their partners. It also had a spare bedroom, which was to prove very useful for family and friends throughout the season.

We were certainly kept busy with major roles in several of the plays. Rehearsals were intensive at the start, as the first few plays opened in quick succession. The company were, in the main, very jolly, although after a time some relationships became rather strained. As there was also a tour at the end of the season, it was a lengthy engagement. We became very friendly with an actor/ musician called Malcolm McKee, a keen socialite always at the centre of things. Once all the plays were up and running and our days were free, we filled them up with extra-curricular activities, and collaborated with him on a light musical evening which we titled, *Are We Keeping You Up?* Putting that together and trying it out in front of friends and family in Ralph Riach's drawing room kept us fully occupied in the pleasant summer days. We then performed it as a late-night theatre bar show and also on the tour, so it had a life, albeit a short one, although Malcolm went on to do it with other performers. Unlike some of the actors who were spending many months alone in digs, we were lucky to have each other. We certainly made the most of our time with a lot of socialising, but after a while we began to feel the need of a little more privacy from the endless stream of visitors to the cottage.

We had been invited to Pitlochry by our old friend and Best Man, Andrew McKinnon, who had taken over as Director of Productions. It seemed to us that Andrew wasn't so much a man of the theatre as an academic – and a clever one at that! Everyone had their minor gripes, but Terry had the worst of it in *The Tempest,* which had a set designed to make anyone sound like a baby elephant – and when you are playing Ariel, this was not ideal. We both enjoyed *The Caucasian Chalk Circle,* myself as Grusha and Terry as Narrator – both major roles.

We managed to get a lot of fun out of an old Ben Travers farce called *A Cup of Kindness,* which was so corny we had to resort to all sorts of tricks in order to raise a few laughs. When the elderly author of the piece came to see the show, he wrote in the visitor's book: 'Not one of my best'. There was also *Know Your Own Mind,* a comedy in five acts by Arthur Murphy, written in 1777, and not a well-known piece for reasons obvious to us all and soon re-titled *Blow Your Own Nose* – very witty I'm sure! It was the one play in which Terry had a 'dry', as coming back to that convoluted language after a week away from it, eventually got to him. However well you'd learned your lines – and Perth had been a wonderful training ground - a repertoire season has specific requirements. If you have long gaps between performances of each play, other techniques are essential, and once you're in four or five plays, going through the lines on a daily basis becomes part of the routine; and that applies to everyone, as cues from other actors must be accurate.

1977, Pitlochry Festival Theatre – The Caucasian Chalk Circle with Terry Wale.

But our favourite play of the season was Terence Rattigan's *While the Sun Shines,* in which we both had delightful cameo parts. But thereby hangs a tale: the company had been divided into two, one group to be in the Rattigan, and the other group in *The Shooting Range,* a new play which touched on the subjects of incest and cancer, not the usual Pitlochry fare. We were in the fortunate group, and some of the other cast expressed disappointment when they first got their scripts. As time moved on, they not only found the commitment necessary to go onstage and play their roles with conviction, but began to talk of the piece with genuine enthusiasm and something approaching glowing terms. They all liked the writer, as did I, and that was an important factor. I think I am being honest when I say that I have always tried to remain objective however an audience reacts, and this was particularly true of *A Cup of Kindness*. We knew it wasn't that good, although that never stopped us endeavouring to get laughs – but even when we got them, it didn't change our opinion about the quality of the piece.

1977, Pitlochry Festival Theatre – While the Sun Shines, with Graham Poutney.

During the rehearsal period we made a few trips over to Perth, on one occasion to see *Jacques Brel is Alive and Well and Living in Paris*. We were with Ursula Smith on this occasion, and after the show she said something to me in the loo which, in retrospect, was extremely prophetic. She had not enjoyed the show very much, and as we were about to make our entrance into the throng, she said, "Come along darling, we are going out there to lie through our teeth!" And she did, telling everyone how good the piece was and how wonderful they had all been. I should have taken note because only a fortnight later Bernie Lloyd came up for a few days, and it was just unlucky that the first play we had lined up was the opening night of *The Shooting Range*. I had to call off at the last minute due to a throat infection, so the boys went along together. As expected, there was little to redeem it, and as Bernie emerged from the auditorium he proclaimed with his usual projection, "Unmitigated rubbish, shouldn't have been allowed on the stage!" Conscious of the fact that we were part of the season and had to go on working with the company, Terry hastily nudged Bernie and whispered that Kenneth Ireland, the overall Director of the theatre, was just behind him. "Kenneth who?", Bernie boomed, at which point Terry decided that the best plan of campaign was to hustle Bernie out of the building and avoid any more tactless (rude?) comments in front of the company. They rushed back to the cottage to give me a blow-by-blow account.

It had not occurred to them that anyone would even notice their absence, but at rehearsals the following morning, Terry was greeted by a stony silence from a few actors, but from Ms Smith in particular. She kept it up for about a week until she could no longer contain herself, and eventually she took me aside and asked if I knew why she was so upset. I admitted that I had a fair idea, but as I hadn't been there on the evening concerned it had little to do with me. She blurted out that she expected no better from Bernard, "because he's rude to everyone", but she expected better from Terry, who she considered a friend. I tried to explain why they had made themselves scarce, but she came back at me with her line, "Why can't he learn to lie through his teeth?"

Looking back, it might have been better to brave the bar after the performance and choke out a, "Well done everyone", but Terry would have been on heckle pins with Bernie, who could never be trusted to say the right thing. Whereas we would never give an unasked-for opinion on an opening night, there is always the risk that someone in the cast will ask what you thought; in that situation, an actor lays himself wide open. It's certainly one of the tricky aspects of our business, but if we went along with the 'praise at all costs' theory, people would never know when you truly enjoyed a performance and genuine congratulations would become totally meaningless. Ursula took none of this on board and, at the end of our conversation, said that she couldn't possibly forgive Terry unless he apologised and said something complimentary about the production. I conveyed this to Terry, who was very irritated by it all, but ended up back on speaking terms with her. I went to see the play a few days later, rushed backstage and said, "Well done", and everyone seemed to be happy.

Having opened all six plays, we were asked to take part in 'Plays in Progress'. These were one-act plays which a small cast rehearsed for a week and then performed before the public on a Saturday morning. I was in *Kind Milly* by Ena Lamont Stewart, a rather quaint little piece, and we had some private hilarity about it, but it was actually very well received, and I had one of my best reviews of the season: *Lesley Mackie either had all the best lines or made it seem as though she had. Miss Mackie can do that whatever the play is!* I must admit that it was quite terrifying, as trying to cram in the lines over a few days for only two performances was not easy, and I had my only 'dry' of the season in this little piece.

We made new friends in the town, including the minister Frank Martin and his wife Ann, who involved us in a church service where I recall singing, *We Plough the Fields and Scatter (Godspell version)*, and we kept in touch for many years. With the five main plays, the Saturday morning plays, *Are We Keeping You Up?* and other social activities, it was a packed season. We had virtually every member of the company round for a meal and many visitors to see the plays, no doubt tempted by the fact that we could offer them a bed afterwards. We had my cousin Dianne over from Canada, Terry's agent Norman Boyack and his daughter, family friend Jim Swan, cantankerous Bernie and, of course, the folks. Grant came to convalesce after breaking his leg in a football match – apparently, the crack echoed round the pitch!

I had a little accident myself, although nothing as serious as a leg break! To combat my hay fever and blocked tubes, I had bought a little Pifco facial sauna, and during a session there was a bang, the mask flew off the appliance, hitting me and splashing my face with boiling water. For a second I thought I had been blinded, but after I calmed down we examined the damage; although I found that I'd lost some skin from my face and the outside and inside of my nose, it wasn't serious, but the burns and redness on the surrounding area meant that I was unable to use make up for a couple of weeks. We took advice and tried to pursue Pifco for damages, but after a meeting with a Glasgow solicitor, we backed down. We had no financial resources and we realised that it would be silly to take on the might of a company like Pifco as we might lose more than a few bits of skin! We ended up with a letter from them admitting no liability but enclosing a cheque for £11 to replace the sauna. Despite the nasty episode, I bought another one, and when it packed up after a few months, being a glutton for punishment, I even bought a third!

There is one person I have only made brief reference to, and that is Kenneth Ireland. Kenneth was in a very privileged position at the theatre, being one of the founders of the Festival Theatre, and responsible for much of the running of the building and for most of its artistic policy. He was married to Moira Lamb, a lovely lady who had been employed there for the previous 13 seasons, playing some wonderful roles, although she had limitations as an actress. Kenneth was an amiable man, and more of a businessman than a man of the theatre. He was strangely naïve; in fact a book could have been written about his many faux-pas and sayings.

He lived with his family in Knockendarroch House, which was a beautiful historic building full of works of art. The story went that, when he first arrived in Pitlochry, it was suggested that Knockendarroch be designated as a building to house actors, to which he replied, "Oh it's far too good for actors", and promptly moved in himself. He did say, in my hearing, that 'actors only live on beans on toast', so the tale may well be true. My most vivid recollection of a 'Kenneth' story was that on one occasion, our Company Manager, Terry Bird, spotted a questionnaire on Kenneth's desk. It was a survey to ascertain the management's treatment of employees. To one of the questions, 'Do you employ coloured people?', Kenneth had responded, 'Yes, we have one in the workshop, and we are thinking of employing another, so that he will have someone to talk to!' We all gasped and then laughed, because it was such an outrageous response, even back then – but, by his lights, he had answered the question honestly, if naively, and we instinctively knew that no malice was intended; 44 years later, people must find it hard to believe that a kind, well-meaning person appeared to have no concept that this could be construed as offensive.

He invited the company once a year for a soirée, when we all had the opportunity to enjoy a light buffet and have a look around

Of course, he clearly didn't consider Moira a lowly actor, and probably saw her as a different breed who didn't really need to work at all but graced the Pitlochry stage with her presence as one of the Grande Dames of the British Theatre. When we returned a couple of years later to see *The Importance of Being Earnest*, he welcomed us warmly, fussing around us like an old hen and squeezed us in on stools at the back of a packed auditorium.

1978, Pitlochry Festival Theatre – A Cup of Kindness with Graham Poutney.

He apologised in advance for Moira's voice which was under par due to a throat infection. He was obviously concerned that nothing would get in the way of her definitive performance as Lady Bracknell. As the lights dimmed, he shoved his head through the curtain at the back and whispered, "I'm sure you'll still find that her 'A Handbag?' has its own special nuance." That moment passed by virtually unnoticed, but she was not helped by the colour of her dress, which matched the chaise longue so, when sitting on it, she was all but invisible.

A few years later Kenneth was squeezed out of Pitlochry, and whatever people felt about him there was no doubt that he adored that theatre, gave much of his life to it, and did not deserve to be treated so badly. He eventually moved with Moira to Edinburgh, and died in 1999 after major heart surgery at the age of 79; she always felt bitter about the way her husband was treated, and never returned to the 'Theatre in the Hills'. We kept in touch, and she said in one of her Christmas cards that Terry's 'Round Robin' each year was one of the major highlights of her life and one of the few things that made her laugh out loud.

When the season ended on September 30th, there were some who were not in either the Rattigan or the Shakespeare, so they just collected their holiday pay and scarpered. Those of us in *While the Sun Shines*, which went on the longest, had to face the prospect of a dreary tour, made more daunting by a compulsory fortnight's break in the middle. Terry and I decided to use some of the time to have a belated honeymoon, but most of the company were twiddling their thumbs, paying for digs, and unwilling to spend money on going home when they were due to finish in a matter of weeks. The management gave us the paid, two-week, cold and wet winter break instead of holiday pay, which was definitely not the same as money in the hand at the end of the job!

As we all stood on the stage after our final performance on September 30th, Kenneth gave his usual address to the audience, "It has been a wonderful season", he said, "and a wonderful company. Next year", he went on, "we hope to have an even better one!" And so say all of us! We completed the first leg of the tour, and headed off to the Greek Island of Kos, blotting out the knowledge that our short break would be quickly followed by a return to the frozen North.

- 9 -

Beware of Greeks bearing gifts

Why book a holiday on the moon when you can go to the Greek island of Kos? First impressions were none too favourable. Its lunar landscape was the first thing that struck us about the place as our coach bumped along the road from the airport. On our arrival at the hotel, we found that the rooms were not ready and, after a whole night without slumber, lying around in the foyer was not the most promising start to our 'honeymoon'. After a few hours of sleep, and optimism restored, we headed out to make the most of our seven-day holiday.

Kos is the nearest island to the Turkish coast and the recent conflict between Greece and Turkey meant that, where it didn't resemble the moon, it was very much like a fortified garrison. The military presence was everywhere. Our first attempt at sunbathing was rudely interrupted by shouts of "Mines! Mines!" We had obviously chosen the wrong beach and so we picked our way gingerly back towards the relative safety of the hotel pool. There was, however, a different fate awaiting the unwary female tourist in the shape of 7,000 frustrated soldiers, many of whom were out of control. It made no difference if you were escorted or not, you still had to ignore the comments and dodge the hands. It was amusing for a day or two but became a real irritant.

We made a few friends on this holiday, in particular a couple from Manchester called Alf and Lynda Jacob. Lynda was a big-breasted woman, so drew quite a lot of attention from 'the military'. On our first night out we were joined very quickly by a group of soldiers who imbibed freely from our carafes and wouldn't leave us alone. One of them asked me up to dance, and as we moved around in the Greek fashion, our arms encircling one another, most of my energy was required to keep my partner's hands on my waist. I was pestered by a rather surly soldier who would not take 'No' for an answer. Terry did his best with comments like "She is my wife" and "Hands off", but to no avail. In a final steely-eyed confrontation, the soldier exerted too much pressure on the wine glass he was holding. It was meant to be a macho gesture of defiance and he probably thought he was squeezing a beer can; either that or he was completely round the twist. The glass shattered in his hand, blood spurted everywhere, and he was taken off to a local hospital for stitches. With his departure I then had the attention of the captain, who asked if I would meet him the following evening. I reminded him of my marital status, but he seemed happy to invite Terry along as well! We didn't keep that assignation.

After a couple of days of sun, sea and sand, we opted for a quiet evening in the hotel with another couple from London, Shirley and Harry Wheeler. We were hardly settled at our table when a one-legged man hopped up and asked me to dance. He had no wooden leg, no crutches or aid of any kind, just one strong-looking, trousered leg, so to the strains of a John Travolta track, and with only one other couple on the floor, I danced rather self-consciously while he hopped around manically beside me, doing leaps, twirls and generally showing off. When I sat down, he then asked Shirley up for the next dance, which was a Viennese Waltz. He was very adept and managed to execute the steps without either losing his balance or landing on her feet. We discovered that he was an Austrian paraplegic champion in various sports: swimming, diving and skiing – and certainly a Champion Pest! He would not leave us alone and his disability made it very difficult for us to be blunt. He went on to display his other gifts, making instrumental noises while pulling Terry's nose, ears and whatever else he could grab hold of, and his trumpet was exceptional! Our patience finally ran out when he revealed his pièce de resistance. He picked up a flashcube for my camera, put it in his mouth, crunched it between his teeth – and it flashed! This was the final straw, and after a rant from Terry about meddling with other people's property, we all rose and moved to another table.

The following night we headed for a Greek night out, which was an organised outing a few miles out of town where we partook of the usual Greek fare before the obligatory Greek dancing. Terry has always preferred to sit on the sidelines, so he was quite happy when a big, sturdy-looking Greek took me up onto the dance floor. After a while he asked if I would go outside with him so that he could teach me the proper Greek steps, and went over to ask for Terry's permission, inviting him to watch if he wished. Knowing that Terry had us in his sight lines, I went off for my lesson. It was fun, and after a time Grigoris asked if I would like to go with him to pick mandarins. Thinking this must be a local gesture of friendship, I checked it out with Terry who seemed to think it a harmless enough pursuit, and he waited patiently while we headed through various gardens with Grigoris picking mandarins as we went. We were probably trespassing on private property, but he seemed relaxed about it all, so I presumed he knew what he was doing. We returned to the taverna with our pockets bulging, and we settled down to have a chat and get to know a bit about him. In fractured English, he told us that he was quite a political animal. Terry spoke with him about the Greek Colonels and the recent war with Turkey and found him *simpatico*. He was of peasant stock (our opinion!), and his conversation was peppered with declarations like, "One day I go Montréal", "I run for Greece", "I bring medal back for my country", "I big strong boy". It was entertaining but highly improbable as he was already 31 years of age with an 11-year-old daughter. Throughout the evening we had been rather taken with Andréas, our Greek Cypriot bus driver who had provided some of the entertainment, and I was not the only one to gasp as he picked up tables in his teeth. As well as this unusual gift, he was dark, stocky and very dishy. During one of the dances I ended up dancing opposite him, he picked me up, put me on his shoulders and I was the envy of many.

We seemed to have chosen an island which was bubbling over with sexual frustration, but it was reminiscent of many other Greek islands, where the lifestyle was still strict, and unmarried Greek girls were not readily available. On Kos, the problem was more extreme as there were far too many men requiring the attention of the foreign tourists, who were probably resented by the local girls whose marriage prospects dwindled as the men sought easier gratification elsewhere; there was definitely one law for the goose.

The following night was our last and we had arranged to meet Grigoris at a nightclub to have a drink and say 'Bye'. He was very protective of me throughout the evening, and as we departed he asked me if I would go with him for the last time to pick mandarins; as Terry raised his eyes to the heavens I trotted off with him. We returned with the oranges, Grigoris collected his little Lambretta and offered us a lift back to the hotel. There was no way he could squeeze us both on, never mind the fact that the bike wouldn't start, but he persevered as he bumped it along the road. As he muttered "I will conquer this beast", it eventually came to life, and although there was only about half a kilometre left to go, he was so insistent about the lift that Terry suggested that I mount 'the beast', and he would follow on.

Grigoris and I reached the foot of the hotel driveway in a matter of seconds, and as I got off the bike my only thought was that I would now have to spend another five minutes of 'I swim for Greece' until Terry caught up with us. Grigoris suddenly went very quiet, and without any preamble said, "I go crazy for you now", took hold of me and pushed me down onto some raised brickwork only a couple of feet from the ground. I was now in no doubt of his intentions, and knowing how near Terry must be, I tried to distract him but to no avail. There was no point in trying to fight him as he held me down, accomplished what he had set out to do, and muttered, "I go now" before heading back to his bike, which again failed to start.

Terry was now in sight, and I saw him stop to shake hands with Grigoris. Apparently, he thanked him for bringing me back, and wished him well before Grigoris continued to jerk his bike down the road. As Terry approached, he saw that I was in tears, and after a garbled explanation, he raced back to confront Grigoris before he disappeared into the night and out of our lives. Terry blurted out, "Did you rape my wife? Lesley tells me you raped her, is that right?" From this point, Grigoris failed to understand a word of English. Looking bewildered, he said "Rape, what is rape?" Terry did not know what his next move should be, but he followed his instinct, raised his arm and with all his weight behind the blow, he caught the big Greek fair and square on the chin. His aim could not have been surer but, to our amazement, Grigoris' head moved all of two inches. For a moment I thought he might retaliate, but he just looked wounded as he said something I will never forget, "Why you hit me? I your friend."

As he wandered off, we were left to come to terms with this awful event on the last night of our 'honeymoon'. We sat up all night weeping and castigating ourselves for our stupidity. Things often happened to me, but this was much more extreme than anything that had occurred in the past. By the time we had gone over and over it, it was time to catch our early morning flight. We were highly charged emotionally and somewhat stunned.

We wanted to get on with our work as if nothing untoward had occurred, to try and lock it away until we were back home in London. The fact that it happened in a foreign country may have made it easier to deal with, and as time passed it became strangely unreal, like a bad dream which had happened to someone else. There was also the friendship factor; we had spent some time with Grigoris, and considered him a holiday acquaintance, so I don't think I ever felt afraid that he would hurt me, whereas if a stranger jumped out of a dark lane, the fear and repercussions would have been traumatic, and might have haunted me for many years.

In the early days after our return, it certainly would not have been an easy subject to discuss over dinner, but as the months went by, we did exactly that. I was aware that women might not comprehend how I had come through it so easily, so I was careful not to make light of it.

We returned to Scotland to continue the tour and, after the pleasant weather in Kos, the climate was rendered even more dreary. The final week was epic in its awfulness – Peterhead, Troon, two nights in Dumbarton, two nights in Livingstone and our final night in Musselburgh! It rained for the entire week, and we were permanently damp and frozen. After such a long season, it was with a mixture of sadness and relief that we packed up and headed back to London with a brief stopover at *The Angel Inn* in Corbridge, just 'for old times' sake'. We were heading to our first real home and the start of a new life in Purves Road.

Just before the tour came to an end I'd made a hasty trip down to London to meet Alan Dosser, who was to be directing a new musical for the English branch of the 7:84 Company. It was *Bitter Apples*, written by political playwright, John McGrath, set in 1968 when much of the world was in a state of revolt. I enjoyed the interview, but on my journey home was somewhat disappointed as I perused the script. My character was Bessie, one of the leaders of 'The Liverpool Liberation Army'. I think that they had thought of me for the part because of my portrayal of Alison in *Just Your Luck* a few years previously, but I had changed quite a bit since then and wasn't convinced that I could easily convey the image of Scottish toughness that was required. After a lot of pressure, I agreed to do it, albeit with grave misgivings, but once I was back in London it was cancelled and all the actors involved received two weeks' pay as compensation – which was rather nice, although it was going to put me in a very difficult position in a few months' time.

I had no other work lined up and, for the first time, began to experience the real chill of unemployment. Based in Scotland, I had always felt relatively secure, rarely out of work for longer than a few weeks at a time, and even then there was usually a job in the offing – and the comfort of knowing I was amongst 'my ain folk'. London was a different proposition altogether. We had been in Pitlochry for over seven months and, although 500 miles from the Big City, we felt we were at the throbbing heart of the theatrical world, although we might as well have been on a different planet. Only our friends knew where we had been, and even some of them had no idea where Pitlochry was and wondered why we had chosen to hide ourselves away for such a long time. Many actors enjoy a love-hate relationship with London, and at this time (and probably even now) some chose to turn things down from time to time, rather than risk missing out on 'the big chance' by accepting work in the provinces.

So life in London was not without its frustrations, but Terry was working at the Old Vic, giving his 'Ratty' twice a day in *Toad of Toad Hall,* and we had a flat to decorate and furnish, so it wasn't as bleak as it might have been – and I did have another West End chance towards the end of 1978. Mike Ockrent was to be directing *Once a Catholic* at Wyndham's Theatre and, remembering his encouraging words to me as I left the Traverse Theatre, I was delighted when he made contact about the lovely part of Mary Mooney. The play was set in a convent in Willesden, but my London accent was pretty good, so I felt reasonably confident when I went along to read for Mike.

The audition went well, and he gave me the impression that it was 'in the bag'. I then received a call asking me to come along to meet Mary O'Malley, the writer of the play, who had casting approval. What I didn't know was that she only wanted actresses who came from the Willesden area, or thereabouts – and preferably with a convent background! During our meeting, I chatted in my own accent and bombed myself out completely. I wish I had been asked to read from the script, giving me a chance to show how right I was for the part. Mike was most apologetic and, to give him his due, he made contact again nine months later when they were recasting one of the other 'Marys'.

This time he suggested that I take over the part of Mary Gallacher, which was not quite so much fun as Mary Mooney, but a nice part all the same. He again made it plain that he wanted me to do it, but there was one other actress who the producers wanted to see, and she was Janette Foggo. We were like chalk and cheese, she being tall and gawky so, after the interview, we both waited in agony wondering whether they wanted the chalk or the cheese. As usual, it was about matching up with a boyfriend, and it was obvious that the producers could not agree. Janette and I kept in touch to see if either of us had any news. The result was that she was offered the nine months work and I had another disappointment to add to my growing list of 'close shaves'.

But even in the late '70s, things were changing in the theatre. It was around this time that I auditioned for the part of Yul Brynner's head wife, Lady Thiang, in a revival of *The King and I*. I thought I had the essentials for the role; I was petite with very black hair, the songs suited my voice, and with a bit of judiciously applied make up I knew I could pass for Siamese, at least onstage. I survived all the auditions until there were three of us left, so I knew that I stood a good chance. The other girls, however, were the real deal. I don't know if they were born in Bangkok, but they were oriental, and they could sing too, so that was that. Fair enough – and it would reach the stage where, short of being a 'star' (when you could get away with anything!), all casting in theatre had to be authentic.

There was no point in dwelling on lost opportunities, but I think that it meant a lot to mum and dad who found it hard to come to terms with me being out of work at all.

We had our first Christmas at Purves Road with Sid, Lily, Pete, Annette and our eight-month-old nephew, Steven. Sid seemed delighted to have us in the upstairs flat, as nothing pleased him more than having his family around him. As 1979 dawned, and over a year since Charles' death, Dawn was beginning to adjust to life again, and was becoming less dependent on Terry's phone calls, which was just as well, as our finances couldn't have taken the strain for much longer – no such thing as unlimited minutes back then! We had few resources, which resulted in the loss of our dearly loved car 'Estelle'. She was just too high maintenance, and when the clutch finally went, her death knell was sounded as we couldn't afford a new one and we had to accept the meagre £50 that the local garage offered to tow her away. The tyres were worth more than that, but we were in no position to argue. Within a few weeks, we spotted her in the area, all spruced up and looking like a million dollars, so it wasn't the write-off we were led to believe. Our only little piece of luck was in selling the number plate, 100 DBM, just before the breakdown and we got £110 for that – more than we got for the car!

1979, STV – Charles Endell Esquire with Patrick Doyle.

I was soon heading north again for a summer season at the *Adam Smith Theatre* in Kirkcaldy, not the most exciting of places, and most famous for the linoleum industry and the odour emanating from the linseed oil used in its production, immortalised in a poem by M.C. Smith, *The Boy in the Train*, about an excited child on his way to Kirkcaldy: 'For I ken mysel' by the queer-like smell, that the next stop's Kirkcaldy'!

The year had been pretty bitty until then with my most enjoyable venture being an episode of *Charles Endell Esquire* for STV, playing a punk rocker in a band called *Blunt Instrument*! 1979 will not go down in the annals as particularly exciting for either Terry or myself although, as far as Terry was concerned, it did lay the ground for a better 1980. He went down to Salisbury to take part in a musical called *Miss Leading Lady,* and the pay-off came in the summer when we were both up in Scotland; he had a call, offering him a lovely part in a two-hander show – again down in Salisbury – called *Make the Little Beggars Hop.* It had been written by Ned Sherrin and Caryl Brahms, was to be directed by Patrick Garland, and there was a distinct possibility that with Timothy West playing Sir Thomas Beecham, it might well transfer to the West End; something to look forward to.

1979, Adam Smith Theatre – When We Are Married with Martyn James and Janet Michael.

The season in Kirkcaldy was under the banner of Perth Theatre. I had lovely roles in *Boeing Boeing, When We Are Married* and one of my all-time favourites, the part of Jackie Coryton in Coward's *Hay Fever*. Clive Perry was, yet again, on great form with this play and much of his comedy business was hilarious.

On a sadder note, I also remember that summer as the one in which Miss Cita Angus died. She had been such an influence on my early life, and I was very disappointed when rehearsals prevented me from attending her funeral. She had dreamt of being an actress, but her father had forbidden her from entering such a debauched profession. I believe that, with her help, I became the actress that she had always wanted to be and, up to a point, she lived her life through mine. She was madly eccentric, but over the years her eccentricity became dottiness; she spent her last few years in a dementia unit in Fife, where she had a severe stroke, rendering her virtually immobile and totally confused.

Towards the end, mum and I went to visit her, and it was a pitiful sight as she was carried in to see us, with a nurse supporting her on either side and her legs trailing along behind her. We had a conversation of sorts and, although it was impossible not to feel pity for her plight, it was not without humour. Having sat with us for a while, Cita suddenly turned to mum and said, "Do you ever see Lesley Mackie? She was my star pupil. I hear she's doing rather well. Could you ask her to send me a pound?" Even although she seemed not to realise who I was, something must have connected in her poor brain for her to mention me I suppose – unless she said the same thing to everyone! Having just watched another lady eat a pound note which had been handed to her, we said our goodbyes to Miss Angus and left. We never saw her again.

I also remember Kirkcaldy because it was during that season that *Bitter Apples* raised its head for the second time. I knew that I was somewhat compromised by having previously accepted the job a few months earlier, gaining two weeks salary when it was cancelled. Suddenly, it was all on again, but the last fortnight of my summer season clashed with the first fortnight of their rehearsals and, although they seemed prepared for me to miss them, it was a new play with all the complications which that entailed. I decided that there was no way I could cope with heading straight down south when we finished, arriving halfway through the 7:84 rehearsals. So, reluctantly, they said that they would re-cast the part. I was suitably disappointed but, privately, heaved a sigh of relief and put it out of my mind.

But that was not the end of the story. After Kirkcaldy, we returned to Perth Theatre to finish our season, and just before it ended the 7:84 came back to me again, begging me to come straight down. Apparently, the actress who had been cast as Bessie was not coping with the job as well as caring for her young child, and had left the company somewhat in the lurch. So they persuaded me, despite the short rehearsal period remaining, to come and save the day! This time I felt I had no option. As soon as I finished on the Saturday night, I caught the 'sleeper' down to London, and prepared to go to rehearsals on the Monday.

1979, 7:84 Company – Bitter Apples with Chris Darwin, Matthew Kelly and George Costigan.

John McGrath's reputation, not only as a playwright, but also as founder of the Scottish 7:84 Company, should perhaps have ensured some enthusiasm, and my scepticism had nothing to do with the company's politics and its left-wing bias. I hadn't been too keen on the script or the part from the beginning and I thought I had done everything I could to avoid committing myself, except to say "No" back at the start. Fear of unemployment or of offending influential people leads actors into all sorts of jobs they wish they hadn't accepted, especially when something much more suitable comes along as soon as you've signed the contract, which is what happened when Clive Perry invited me back to Birmingham to play a lovely part in Ayckbourn's *Bedroom Farce*. But the offer came too late, and having already lost one actress and two weeks' rehearsal time, the director of *Bitter Apples* was not about to wave goodbye to me too. One lesson I was to learn from the experience was that, in future, I would put more faith in my instinct.

The plot spanned a period of ten years, from the heady left-wing idealism of 1968 to the disillusionment of 1978. It encompassed too many political events, and even quite a large cast found themselves playing as many as four or five characters each, as the story sprawled from Vietnam to Paris and from Chile to Wenceslas Square. At the centre was a motley crew of young people calling themselves 'The Liverpool Liberation Army', at whose head was a character called Bessie. Yes, that's right — Me!

Bitter Apples in rehearsal with Matthew Kelly, Mike O'Neill, Alan Tall and George Costigan.

It didn't take me long to realise that a lot had happened during the fortnight I had missed. The part of Bessie, which had not impressed me much when I first read it, had now been cut to the bare bones, and there was very little left to 'get my teeth into'. The prospect of heading out on tour in a part like this didn't fill me with enthusiasm. The only glimmer on the horizon was that the show was running at an epic five and a half hours so it had to be cut; with a bit of luck Bessie might disappear altogether.

By the time we opened in Liverpool, it was still coming in at three and a half hours, and we spent the next fortnight rehearsing in a desperate attempt to reduce the show by another hour. I was just hoping that they would leave the songs untouched as it was the part of the show that I really enjoyed. I still had the feeling that I was not ideally cast as Bessie, the tough down-to-earth leader of the Liverpool Liberation Army, but after a hasty consultation with my husband I pulled on a woolly hat and it seemed to make all the difference.

While all this was going on, Terry was having his own problems. He was at the Belgrade Theatre in Coventry, rehearsing a two-character show, Anthony Shaffer's *Sleuth*. His fellow-actor, Ronald Lewis, who had been something of a matinée idol back in the '50s, had been struggling with his lines from the start of rehearsals, and Terry had a sense of foreboding about the production. On the opening night just before curtain-up, Terry heard a loud noise, and found Ronnie collapsed and unconscious in his dressing room. Epilepsy was eventually diagnosed, but the performance was cancelled, and the search was on for someone to take his place. They procured the services of Ronald Leigh-Hunt, who had played the part on two previous occasions, and Terry and he met for the first time on Monday morning, three days after the cancelled opening. They rehearsed all day, and the curtain went up on Monday night. Unfortunately, he had a prior commitment and had to fly off to Sweden the following week, so the director, a former actor, took his place for the rest of the run. The result was that Terry was rehearsing the play every day, as well as performing it every night for the entire run.

In spite of this, on a couple of occasions he actually drove the 116 miles from Coventry to Liverpool after his show to give me a bit of moral support. *Bitter Apples* was still so long that he was well on his way by the time our curtain came down, and when he arrived in our recently acquired and battered old Fiat, the company were still in the bar having a drink or two, and I invariably had a few stories to make his journey worthwhile. He was keen to have a chat with Alan Dosser our director, because we were desperate to persuade him to release me to do the Birmingham job, but Alan's own life was a bit of a mess back then, and he was invariably on the road to oblivion by the time Terry managed to corner him. I did have an understudy, and still felt as if I had been bulldozed into the production, but with the benefit of hindsight I don't think it was reasonable to expect him to recast at this stage. We were too used to Joan Knight, who was often willing to let someone go if they had a better offer elsewhere.

And then there was the company; an interesting and friendly group, not one of whom I had ever come across or worked with before. Being the 7:84, there were inevitably quite a few extreme 'Lefties' around; although I had grown to be somewhat to the left of centre myself, I was aware of the darker side of politics on the day when Lord Mountbatten was blown up on his boat off the Irish coast by the IRA. Most of the nation was stunned, but I recall a couple of individuals expressing surprise that people should get so het up about the death of someone, just because they were an establishment figure. I knew what they meant, but where was the compassion? Politics without feelings.

My boyfriend in the show was played by Matthew Kelly, who eventually became a big television star. He was six foot four inches tall, so with my being five feet it was an amusing pairing. Onstage one night, he allowed his dressing gown to fall open for a brief second, revealing himself in all his glory, then he giggled and covered himself up. It was a completely gratuitous moment, which is, of course, why he did it. Just a little piece of 'Matthew Madness' and I honestly don't think he meant to do it again. Alan Dosser, however, thought that it added a certain *je ne sais quoi*, and so it was kept in. It certainly raised a few laughs in Liverpool, but Nottingham was a different matter altogether. There was a big reception on our opening night there, and the guests of honour were the Lord Mayor and his entourage. Matt skipped onto the stage, his dressing gown fell open as usual, and the entire block of Town Councillors stood up and left. Headlines in the local paper the following day read 'Actor's little slip shocks the sheriff!' – it even got a mention on Ned Sherrin's late-night radio show, so at least we got some publicity out of it.

George Costigan was another free spirit who enjoyed being as unpredictable as possible. I remember on one occasion when a couple of latecomers arrived during his opening speech, he used their late arrival to his advantage and managed to get a few legitimate laughs. When Terry later commented on how well it had worked and suggested that it might be a good idea to plant a couple of latecomers, he just said, "Oh, I couldn't do the same thing twice." To ring the changes, he would come onstage backwards, or throw himself on the floor and play an entire scene in that position, and on one occasion he didn't come on at all – just to keep us on our toes. One night, he entered clutching a toilet seat and placed it over my head just as I was about to sing. He then pulled my hat down over my eyes which added nothing to the scene and made singing almost impossible.

I almost felt a sense of relief when I contracted a nasty chest infection during a week in particularly damp digs, as it afforded me a couple of nights away from the trials and tribulations of the Liverpool Liberation Army, not to mention the incongruous moment when I had to appear as a GI in full battle gear. I mean, at my height, I was the perfect candidate for a Viet Cong insurgent! Nevertheless it had its moments, I liked the company, shared a few laughs, and forged a lasting friendship with Diana Davis. A sad postscript to Terry's Coventry engagement was that only a couple of years later, Ronnie Lewis took his life at the age of 53, a tormented soul indeed.

The 1980s lay ahead, full of the usual ups and downs, but destined to be, in many ways, the most significant and fulfilling decade of my life, both personally and professionally. Not to mention the most thrilling…

- 10 -

Forth, pilgrim forth! (Touring days)

1980 started well when Terry's play from Salisbury, originally called *Make the Little Beggars Hop* and now re-titled *Beecham*, transferred to the West End. For a while, at any rate, we had financial security. Terry got on well with Timothy West, who was playing Sir Thomas, and although he was there as a kind of 'feed' for Beecham's wit, he was the only other person in the show and shone in his own right, as well as providing wonderful support for Tim. They both enjoyed it immensely, despite the minor irritation of Tim's understudy, Richard Huggett, who sat in the Circle Box each evening, studying Tim's performance whilst sipping champagne. He was desperate to go on, and even had the brass neck to ask Tim and Terry if they would mind missing a performance so that he could organise a special matinée to give the two understudies a chance. He planned to invite various agents, producers and casting people, but that never did happen. He was a character, and in his own way was a great supporter of *Beecham*. He lived in a little flat in Soho directly above a prostitute, and he gave her a poster of the show which she apparently placed in a position that gave her clients a clear view of it when they were in action. Sadly, and despite Richard's efforts, the play only ran for three months, but they took it elsewhere after the run, including a six-week tour of New Zealand in 1983. It was finally televised, and in its transition to the screen became an epic with the introduction of the entire Hallé Orchestra.

In writing this lengthy tome, I have used my diaries as a guide throughout, and 1980 is one of the very few that are missing, although my memories of that year are still quite vivid. The reason for the lost diary is because of a holiday in Rhodes. One evening whilst enjoying a meal in the Old Town, the table rocked from side to side whenever we moved, so I propped up the offending leg with my diary and chequebook, and there they remained. We never had the opportunity to return and retrieve them, so the recollections for this year are entirely down to my memory.

Our three weeks in Rhodes was the longest holiday we ever had. When we arrived at the airport, we joined up with another couple who were headed for Lindos, a pretty little village, which became a very popular and expensive tourist resort; at that time it was still virtually untouched by tourism. As it was May, just before the High Season, we had no trouble finding accommodation. As our taxi arrived in the village square, we were surrounded by locals who all seemed to have rooms to let. We went along the main drag and were offered a villa for the princely sum of £5 per night. It even had its own lemon tree, which I would climb in the early evening to pull a lemon so that Terry could mix my pre-dinner Bloody Mary. What bliss!

After a week in this idyllic, white-painted village, we decided to take a boat to Kos to eradicate the bad memories of our holiday less than two years previously. The soldiers had now departed, and the island had become much more tourist-orientated, so we were curious to see how things had changed. It looked a lot prettier, as May is a better time to visit than October when all the flowers and foliage have been scorched by the summer sun. We booked into a hotel, and as we were travelling under our own steam we decided to look at the notice board to find out what outings were on offer. The only tourist information seemed to be in Swedish, but we worked out that one of the trips, illustrated with drawings of dancing and eating, might be the one for us, so we sought out the Swedish representative to find out if we could tag along. He spoke little English but told us that we would be very welcome. So, on the appointed night, we put on our glad rags, and went to board the coach. As we settled into our seats, he spoke into his microphone, "To our two English guests – Welcome." The passengers applauded, and those were virtually the only words of English that were spoken throughout the evening.

As the coach pulled in to the taverna, a vague sense of recognition stirred in me, and the feeling was confirmed when I spotted a lone figure sitting outside at a table, drinking a glass of wine. As we moved closer, I saw that the figure was indeed our one-time friend and assailant, Grigoris Houlis. We went inside, trying to ignore this unexpected encounter with the past. I was invited to dance by one of the Swedes, and as we moved around the floor I found myself opposite Grigoris, so was forced to dance with him for a few seconds until the circle moved on. He gave me such a look of hauteur and defiance that it was a relief when I left him behind. Later on, I glanced outside and spotted him teaching a girl to dance, just as he had done with me in exactly the same place less than two years before. I felt that I should warn her before he took her off to pick mandarins, but none of the Swedes spoke much English, and it would have been too difficult to explain, so I did nothing. Fortunately, he didn't have time to take her for mandarins before the coach departed.

We stayed in Kos for a few days, and we spotted Grigoris on two other occasions, but it was a small island. In a bar when we'd stopped to have a drink, I mentioned his name to the barman who laughed and said, "He is crazy for the women!" Hmm. We spent our final week in Lindos, and many years later we returned, but we never went back to Kos.

With some trepidation I now faced the prospect of another long tour. The recently formed New Vic Company was about to start rehearsing Phil Woods' updated version of Chaucer's *The Canterbury Tales*. They had already premièred the show in Leicester and were extremely confident about its future. The cast consisted of five men and two women who were all, excepting one of the actresses, available for the tour; this is where I came in. I had already met Micky O'Donoghue, one of the founder members of the company, the previous year when I worked with him on *The Anatomist* (starring Patrick Stewart) at the BBC; he said then that he would be back in touch. He was a one-eyed, larger-than-life character by any reckoning, a bizarre man who found it difficult to separate fact from fiction, and I never really expected to hear from him again; but he did get back to me, and on this occasion he managed to sell me the virtues of the show with such enthusiasm that I could hardly say no. Obviously I was about to embark on an earth-shattering theatrical experience, and I was going to have the time of my life.

This promise was made good right from the start with a day trip to Boulogne, organised by Micky, so that the entire company could have a day out together before getting down to work. We had a jolly meal and a few laughs, but I quickly realised that male chauvinism played a big part in their humour. They had managed to secure the services of Michael Bogdanov, director of the original production, and his name on the poster was something of a coup as he had become an Associate Director at the National Theatre. During our run he found a level of infamy when Howard Brenton's, *The Romans In Britain*, resulted in a private prosecution in which Bogdanov was accused by the Christian morality campaigner, Mary Whitehouse, of 'procuring an act of gross indecency' in one scene where two male actors simulated anal rape. The scene of homosexual rape would, she said, be an incitement to some men. The case was eventually dismissed. I was looking forward to working with him, although his contribution turned out to be minimal. He didn't really direct the show at all; he just presided over the rehearsal process, and I was pretty much left to my own devices. He was definitely 'one of the boys', and the New Vic Company was very much a boy's world. He was only available for one week, so we only had a week's rehearsal. This was fine for the rest of the company who had done it before and knew exactly what they were doing, but quite a challenge for me. As it turned out we had a lot of fun, although the next few months were not entirely a bed of roses.

1980, The Alternative Olympics – publicity event for The Canterbury Tales.

It was July, the weather was perfect, and we opened in Poole for a three-week run. For me, this was the highlight of the tour, somewhat marred, however, by the introduction of 'Street Theatre', in which we were all expected to participate. It was obviously regarded as an inexpensive way to publicise the show; well, we didn't get paid for it, so they had a point. We called it 'The Alternative Olympics' but I found it exceedingly embarrassing, possibly because I had no special skills in this area. Micky tore up telephone directories with his bare hands, Big John Labanowski lay on a bed of nails and stubbed cigarettes out on his tongue, Bev Willis did some roller-skating and Kate Versey swallowed 'wagon wheels' whole – a nauseating spectacle. They finally came up with a stunt for me, a lame trick which was neither spectacular nor funny, which was to catch a flat iron in my teeth. I was introduced as 'The Mighty Microdot', at which point I flexed my muscles. As they informed the crowd of the feat which I was about to perform, I bared my teeth to the assembled throng. It involved an iron attached to a long piece of elastic, which I held between my teeth as one of the lads walked into the distance holding the iron until the elastic was taut. After a big build-up he shouted, "Are you ready?", at which point I opened my mouth to speak, the elastic popped out, and the boy fell backwards as the flat iron whacked him in the goolies! Hilarious!

I began to dread Monday mornings in each new town and especially when we got a bit closer to London, where the public, not quite as imbued with the holiday spirit, gave us a wide berth and were less inclined to stop and watch, having more important things to do. I eventually dropped the stunt in favour of handing out leaflets, although I always believed that we must have put off as many of our prospective audience as we enticed in to see the show.

There was also the pre-show to contend with. Four of the company had a tale to tell in which the rest of the company participated, and as the show was structured as a competition between these tales, we were expected to accost the audience in the bar beforehand to persuade them to vote for us at the end of the evening. It was a perfectly valid way to start the show and set the tone for the rest of the night, but I hated going up to people enjoying a drink to assail them in this way, especially as we were supposed to be selling badges and other memorabilia at the same time. To make things more awkward I was the Cook, and as *The Cook's Tale* was just a folk song with the company joining in for the choruses, I didn't have a hilarious character to hide behind. On our opening night, Bogdanov (aka Bodger) tailed me, egging me on and making me feel even more uncomfortable.

Despite my misgivings, everyone's confidence in the show was borne out by audience reactions up and down the country. Geoffrey Chaucer might have been turning in his grave, but it was great fun and the public loved it. The main source of hilarity was Micky as the Miller, whose function was to disrupt the tranquillity of the vicar's garden-party, which was the setting for the play, with lewd remarks, bawdy jokes and general grossness. During the pre-show he was virtually leaping on women in the bar, commenting loudly on their 'booby roubles', and looking as if he was about to grab them in his podgy hands. He was of course, for obvious reasons, excluded from the story-telling competition. Having created havoc throughout the show, and winning himself many friends in the audience, he finally comes onstage and, with their support, is reluctantly allowed to tell his tale. It is, of course, just as rude as everyone hopes, and the volume of the applause declares him the winner. That was how the show was structured, and even though the Miller's Tale was far from being the best, and one or two of the other actors became competitive, trying hard to win the 'prize', it always worked out – well, almost always.

My tale, which consisted of a rather attractive folk song and no jokes at all, was never in contention. At least, it wasn't until one night in Edinburgh when 23 members of my family and friends made such a formidable noise that, for the first and only time, I won the competition. It was in Edinburgh, too, that we experienced the only complaint about the refreshments we served up between tales. Most audiences seemed to enjoy the novelty of coming onto the stage for mulled wine and mince pies, even if the quality of the wine deteriorated during the tour, and usually ended up as a hastily mixed concoction of wine and lemonade, often bunged together five minutes before the show started. The trouble arose, not because of the wine, but because 'mince pies' in Scotland are sometimes filled with minced beef instead of dried fruit and are not ideally eaten cold! We discovered the mistake just before the show when we found the pre-ordered trays of greasy cold meat pies lying in wait for us. I was all for sending them back, but the company, opportunists to a man, tried – unsuccessfully it must be said – to foist them on an unsuspecting public. Even the most accommodating of audiences could not have stomached one of those, washed down with a cup of diluted red wine!

It was a long tour, and some dates were more memorable than others. Bath and Oxford were delightful, apart from the church bells which rang every quarter of an hour – even during the night – and drove me crazy. Bradford, however, was seared into my memory for very different reasons. After packing them in all over the country, we played the Alhambra Theatre to near empty houses. The serial killer known as the 'Yorkshire Ripper' was still at large, the city was living in fear and few women dared to venture out alone in the evening. Terry had a word with the lads, asking them to keep a look out for the girls in the company during the Bradford week. "What do you take us for?", they chorused. Obviously he took them for a bunch of male chauvinists, or he wouldn't have had to mention it in the first place. Wild horses couldn't have dragged them away from their pints and their late-night curries. I was sharing digs with the girl from the wardrobe department, so I had company, but we still found the walk back quite unnerving.

On the very last night, Jackie had arranged a lift back to London, and I suddenly found myself standing alone outside the theatre, sinking under the weight of half a dozen plastic bags filled with all my bits and pieces from the dressing-room. It was bitterly cold and there wasn't a soul in sight. I had no choice but to head back to the digs, and I panicked, couldn't remember the way, and finally had to go into a taxi rank to ask for directions. It turned out I was just a block away, and only had to cut through one alleyway to reach my street, but I stupidly started to hurry down the lane, seeing the shape of the 'Ripper' in every lurking shadow. Panic-stricken, I managed to convince myself that I had finally run out of luck and very nearly stopped at a phone box to say goodbye to Terry – but decided to keep running instead. I finally made it, and with my heart thumping I slammed the door behind me. I can't imagine what state I would have been in had I known that the most recent murder had occurred within a few hundred yards of my digs, and that, days later, another killing would take place – also in the same area. For the record, Peter Sutcliffe was finally caught on January 5th, 1981, and the nation breathed a sigh of relief.

After the tour, we had a six-week season at the Roundhouse. It was good to be back in London, and loads of pals came along to see the show. It didn't appeal to everyone though, and one of Terry's director friends, Patrick Garland, hated it, but wrote to me afterwards, referring to me as a 'good deed in a naughty world'. On the last night at the Roundhouse, Terry got a special mention at the curtain call because he had seen the show 16 times, so it must have had *something!*

They decided to extend the tour by another few weeks, but I'd had enough, so they auditioned for a new Cook, and another lucky lady joined the ranks. In truth, I enjoyed a lot of it, and have happy memories of company meals in Italian restaurants when Micky would serenade us and other diners with his Italian arias. The most wearing aspect was the schoolboy humour which rarely transcended beyond the level of John Labanowski, whose speciality (as well as lying on a bed of nails and stubbing out cigarettes on his tongue!) was emitting huge farting noises, blaming the nearest female and then making great sport of pretending that her tights were filling up with air and about to explode. Time to move on and I had another tour lined up...

There was only a three-week gap before the onset of rehearsals for *Much Ado About Nothing* with the New Shakespeare Company. Terry had one of the major roles, but I was happy to play the small part of Margaret. Before it all began, I made one of my usual trips north to see the folks and as many relatives as possible. I probably saw more of them all then than I did after we eventually moved up to Perth. I also made a point of visiting a tiny man called Tom Connelly and his large wife, Flo.

I seemed to attract some rather unusual 'fans', but Wee Tommy was the most bizarre. I first met him in 1973 when I was working at Dundee Rep. A few of the company used to go down to the Tay Textiles canteen for lunch, and I spotted a little man coming in on a daily basis for a bowl of soup and a pudding. I approached him one day and asked if I could join him. That was the beginning of a quaint friendship, and Tommy started to come to the theatre. He had no critical faculties, but he liked to watch me on the stage, and always brought me a bag of sweets. When I moved on to Perth Rep, he started to come up on the bus, and at the end of the matinée I would meet him and occasionally accompany him to the bus station. It was a source of hilarity to some of the company as they watched me link in and walk off with this tiny man, who was not only smaller than me, but moved like a little clockwork toy. When I wrote to him in 1977 to tell him of my impending wedding, I was surprised to receive a note of congratulations but also expressing disappointment that it had not been him! I had no idea that he had romantic notions; in fact, nothing could have been further from my mind.

Only one year later, he bumped into an old flame at Leuchers Aerodrome, they fell for each other again and married soon after. Tom must have been around the 70 mark and Big Flo only a few years younger, but it was a first wedding for both, and I persuaded Terry to come along with me when I went to visit the newly-weds for the first time. We had no idea what to expect, and when we arrived, Tommy told us that Flo was hiding in the kitchen so that she could give us a surprise. This large woman suddenly jumped out wearing an ape mask and making monkey noises – the perfect introduction to Big Flo. She was a cleaning lady and, although somewhat 'off the wall', she seemed affectionate towards Tommy, who she called her 'Wee Cuddles'. As we left, and still wearing her mask, she threw herself in front of our car and Terry only just managed to brake in time. They were simple folk, but they were company for each other, and over the years we had a few laughs.

As mum and dad lived quite close to them, mum somehow got involved and invited them round to join the family at the traditional New Year's Day party at 21, Nairn Street. This was the start of what became an annual visit from Tom and Flo, who looked forward to the social occasion, always keen to 'do a turn'. His was *The Laughing Policeman*, accompanied by mum on the piano or by himself on the accordion, which he somehow managed to trundle along, although I have a feeling that Grant used to go down to pick them up! Flo threw herself into it – in an improvisational way, either doing the Can-Can or whatever she felt like at the time. She seemed to get crazier every year, and on one occasion she arrived in a pair of shorts, lay down on the floor and proceeded to do leg exercises.

When mum and I visited their little flat, we were usually forced into a sing-along, which always reduced us to hysterics. Tommy had accumulated every instrument under the sun: an organ, an accordion, a trumpet, a guitar, various keyboards, and he couldn't really play any of them. The organ was his favourite, and on one visit we tried in vain to recognise his song selection, humming along as best we could; during one particularly obscure tune, he stopped and said, "Do you not know this one?" We almost roared when he said it was *On Mother Kelly's Doorstep* and gamely joined in the next chorus. We always ended up with tears streaming down our faces, which I tried to put down to my hay fever if it was a summer visit. We eventually took our little daughter to visit, and Flo couldn't wait to thrust gifts at us. She ripped magnets from her fridge (They were glued on!), and filled a black plastic bag with everything she could lay her hands on, including her little pouffe. We returned most of it, but she was not an easy woman to put off. Sadly, as time went by, she spent a bit of time in Liff Hospital which dealt with mental health problems, and I think that Wee Tommy suffered the odd beating up, but back at the start of the '80s they were still enjoying life.

After all the socialising, we returned south to get on with 'Much Ado', and we took the opportunity to do a bit of house-hunting in some of our touring venues: Bury St Edmunds, Kings Lynn and Lincoln, as we had our sights set on a little country cottage. We saw some very attractive places, but nothing quite won us over. It was my first experience of looking at properties and I found it difficult to resist putting in an offer on every house – just to please the vendors!

At the end of the tour we had a party, and Terry and Graeme, another cast member, decided to hand out 'Awards'. The play had been set in 1914, so they geared the 'gongs' to World War 1, with an 'Over the Top Award' (for overacting!), a 'Mustard Gas Award' (which went to a young lady who farted with nerves before each entrance), and a 'Wilfred Owen Poetry Speaking Award' – which went to the actor who had given the worst reading of any line in the play. Most of the company took it in good part, but a couple of actors took it personally and walked out in disgust. The rest of us found it hilarious, but maybe the boys went a bit far!

We had a few weeks back in London before heading off to Paris to celebrate my 30th birthday. It was our first time together in that romantic city and we walked for miles. On our return, Terry joined the cast of *Amadeus* when it transferred from the National Theatre to Her Majesty's, where it ran for almost 14 months, and provided us with a good deal of security. It is ironical, however, that while most actors dream of a long, successful West End run, few know how to cope with it. Sooner or later the mind rebels against the endless repetition and you're haunted by the fear that it will suddenly go blank. You try to distract yourself and get on with your life, but if you allow yourself to become too distracted, you know you won't be mentally prepared for the show, an obligation you can begin to resent. Then, of course, you feel guilty for resenting it when thousands of actors would give anything to be in your place. The result is a lot of stress which, for Terry, came to a head around Christmas when I was playing in *Jack and the Beanstalk* down in Leatherhead.

The relentless months were broken up for him from time to time by the occasional Sunday performance of *Beecham*, which afforded a little alternative stimulation, but the gaps between these engagements were so wide that he and Timothy had to meet up and re-rehearse for each one. One weekend in July when they were about to head to Bury St Edmunds, Tim discovered that he didn't have a 'dresser' and, not being particularly busy at the time, I gaily offered my services. Before the show, he gave me a full list of his changes but no specific advice on how to go about it. I had never performed this task before and never did again; it was a nightmare.

Tim was seldom off-stage for more than two or three minutes at a time and so we were working against the clock. I laid out all the bits and pieces and awaited his first exit. As I held out his trousers, the braces fell inside, and his legs got completely entangled in them. We somehow unravelled the chaos, but there were collars to be studded and shoes to be changed. I had laid them out, but was unaware that a good dresser would have knelt and helped him into them with the aid of a shoehorn. He made his next entrance in a state of total disarray, his braces hanging down, his white scarf hanging loose and his dressing gown hanging open revealing his under-dressing for the following scene. I spent the rest of the evening on the verge of a panic attack, but Tim never panicked or seemed flustered and was, in fact, extremely good-natured about the whole affair. In my defence, he should have realised that he needed a trained dresser, but I should never have volunteered. Unsurprisingly, he never called on my services again, but from that day forward I looked on 'dressers' with renewed respect, and would never underestimate the skill of a good one.

By the time I finished *Much Ado About Nothing*, I was becoming a little bored with my work situation. I had done three tours within two years, and none of them particularly satisfying. Things seemed stagnant, and it hit me hard because I had worked constantly in Scotland and was beginning to wonder – as my mother did – if I had been wise to move away. When I look at young actors today, I am so aware that those were indeed the 'Good Old Days'; nowadays they put out the flags if they get a recall – or even an interview! There was the added frustration of not getting pregnant, and this was the start of five years of all sorts of tests and examinations and much prodding and probing.

Terry had his own tests to contend with, although they were a lot simpler, usually involving the donation of sperm. We established quite early on that Terry had a low sperm count, but they had to make sure that there wasn't a dual problem. One of the worst I can recall was the fallopian tube X-ray. It sounded like a simple proposition to inject dye into the tubes, but it took longer than I expected, and I began to experience a lot of discomfort. I must have started to panic because I had the tell-tale spasms in my hands and feet, and I told the nurse that I had started to hyperventilate. She said that if I could just hang on for a couple of minutes, it would all be over. My breathing was already out of control, and lying there with a needle inserted somewhere in my innermost being, my stomach muscles seized up and I finally lost my powers of speech. I tried to let them know what was happening, but no one recognised the symptoms. Instead of putting a paper bag over my mouth in order to allow me to breathe back some carbon dioxide, they slammed an oxygen mask over my face, which was the opposite of what was required to bring me back to normal. I was totally disorientated and on the verge of oblivion, but eventually someone realised they were on the wrong track and reversed the process.

Once the worst was over, a nurse helped me to get down from the bed, but my legs buckled under me, and I could barely stand. As I shakily attempted to dress, the doctor came over and said, "You're a bit of a coward, aren't you Mrs Wale?" If I hadn't been so shaken I would have given him a piece of my mind. His face remained imprinted in my memory for some time. I was not a pretty sight when I emerged from my X-ray as white as a sheet, hair standing on end, looking and feeling as if I had just been through a major operation. Later that day, we had a visit from a friend who just happened to be a nurse, and she told me that I should have had a sedative before that procedure was carried out, so perhaps I wasn't such a coward after all.

We turned to a private doctor in Harley Street, but as time wore on we tried to put it out of our minds and let things take their course. We had seen the lives of others taken over by the desperation to have a family and, much as we wanted a baby, we felt that life was just too short to let our fertility dominate ours.

- 11 -

Light at the end of the tunnel

In the summer of 1981 I was feeling the cold wind blowing, so I accepted the first job that came along, and at least it wasn't another tour. I decided to go to the Belgrade Theatre in Coventry and participate in the Mystery Plays; not my 'Dream Job', but the setting was to be the Coventry Cathedral which should have been an intriguing experience. I hadn't seen a script, but the director, Michael Boyd, made it sound reasonably tempting, although I should have known better than to accept a job based on a director's promises. I knew that I had three parts: a 'meaty' Messenger, Celedonius' sister, and the mother of a murdered baby, who had two songs to sing, one of them a duet. Despite endless calls, the script did not arrive until two days before I left for Coventry, and I discovered that the Messenger had all of five lines, Celedonius' Sister was a deaf mute with little function in the play beyond being in the throng, and the singing role had one duet and no lines at all. I was in an awful position because I had signed the contract; this was the weekend, and I was due to start rehearsals on Monday morning. I decided to go, and sort things out with the director after the read-through.

Apart from the five lines, I was silent throughout, and Michael agreed to come along to my flat to talk things through. He was fairly honest about his motives for the minor deceit he had perpetrated and, after apologising, said that he really wanted me there to supervise and lead the children's choir, but he would do his best to build my parts up a bit, make the Messenger more 'meaty' and help me make something of the deaf mute. I mean, I knew it wasn't going to be Kattrin in *Mother Courage* but maybe something could be done. I had already settled into my little theatre flat so, despite Terry's advice to pack my bags and head home, I decided to try and make the best of things and throw myself into it with a show of enthusiasm. The parts did not live up to his promises, but as the production took shape I realised I was more than happy to remain on the sidelines.

We spent the first few days getting to know one another, playing such challenging games as *Grandmother's Footsteps,* which was tedious and without any useful purpose that I could see. I only knew one other cast member, and that was Elizabeth Sinclair, an old acquaintance from the RSAMD, who was playing The Virgin Mary. Being a timeless and universal story, the director had decided to ignore time and place, but when the Angel Gabriel appeared in a flying suit as a World War 1 pilot, and Herod played *Some Enchanted Evening* on the violin, credibility was stretched to breaking point. It all seemed strangely at odds with the atmospheric setting of the old cathedral. In a pre-show pageant, I played Daniel in the Lion's Den, wearing a three-piece trouser suit, huge spectacles and looking for all the world like Ronnie Corbett. There were three other pageants, and all four happened simultaneously. Adam and Eve, however, wore nothing but body stockings and it was no surprise that they were the ones who drew the audience!

It was a shame to see such a beautiful and poignant setting as the ruined Cathedral so sadly misused, and Coventry decided not to do the Mystery Plays the following year which, I think, was a fitting postscript. I had no regrets about doing the job because I made two very dear friends in Diana Kyle (who shared my duet) and Cathy Jayes, a Musical Director with whom I worked on many subsequent occasions. Nothing shocks or surprises in this business, not even the fact that Michael Boyd ended up as Director of the Royal Shakespeare Company and stayed for a ten-year tenure, clearly making quite a mark.

Terry always had a hankering to live by the sea, and we'd started to look on the South Coast, but the prices were somewhat out of our reach, so Brighton would have to wait. Nevertheless, on one of his many trips to Coventry, Terry and his friend, Gordon Griffin, stopped off to view a tiny cottage in the village of Milton, near Banbury, and from the moment he set eyes on it, he knew it was the one for us. It was so dinky, with only a tiny front patio to tend, but the search and sale took a few months to go through, so we just got on with our lives in Kensal Rise. It wasn't until the spring of 1982 when we finally moved in.

Due to a couple of coincidences, I was suddenly offered a part in *A Criminal Suggestion* at the Thorndike Theatre in Leatherhead. It was written by Philip Guard, with whom I'd worked at Ochtertyre, and it was to be directed by John Doyle, who was a contemporary of mine from the RSAMD. I loved my part in the play, a simple Suffolk lass, and before the onset of rehearsals I met up with Philip who had lived in Suffolk for some time and was able to give me a bit of help with the accent. I remembered him as a clever and erudite man, and although I had observed a little of his intolerance, I was seeing a very different man now.

1981, Thorndike Theatre, Leatherhead – A Criminal Suggestion with Philip Guard.

Even before the onset of rehearsals, things were not going well between Philip and the Thorndike management. Phil had suggested Iain Cuthbertson for the leading role, excellent casting as the affable doctor who was, in fact, secretly conducting experiments in his laboratory on his murder victims. Philip was livid when he discovered that Iain had been offered the usual rep salary, as there was no way that £80 per week was going to tempt him to Leatherhead. Philip took this as a personal affront, believing that the attitude of the management reflected a contempt for his play.

After much discussion and acrimony, it was decided that Philip himself would play the role. Fine actor though he was, this was not a good idea. He had a rather foxy face, and from his first entrance there was a danger that the audience might suspect that he was the villain of the piece, so we went into rehearsals with a slight handicap. There were numerous problems, made worse by Philip being on the spot to witness them. As the days passed, his paranoia grew, and although there was no doubt that there did seem to be a somewhat cavalier attitude to the finer points of the production, he began to imagine that the whole world was against him. He just about had an apoplexy over the false economy of using brown envelopes rather than white ones for onstage use, and even the sound of a member of stage management whistling (considered to be bad luck in the theatre) in the corridor was taken as an act of impertinence – and he was not at all impressed by John Doyle, who he also felt was not on his side. John was a very talented director who had recently taken up a post at the Swan Theatre in Worcester, but as a guest director he departed once we opened and was not able to give much aftercare to the production. There was always something missing onstage, and even splashes of blood and gore not washed away from the night before. Bookings were not wonderful, and Philip's frustration was exacerbated by the Box Office staff who seemed reluctant to give him details of audience figures when he made enquiries on his arrival each evening.

At the helm of the theatre was an amiable director called Roger Clissold, but in the face of his apparent lack of effort to invite any London producers along to view the piece, he became the target for all the fury bubbling up inside Philip. On one of our many train journeys back to London, when raging about Roger, he told me that he had succeeded in exterminating three people by sending death wishes to them – although he'd had little success with our theatrical agent, Felix de Wolfe, who went on to live to a ripe old age. I had my own minor gripe about Felix; when I first met him, he asked me what I was going to do about the 'dreadful noise' that came out of my mouth (my Scottish accent!) – although he did take me on. I usually welcomed a chance to use different dialects, but I never thought it right to lose my accent in an interview situation, unless I was reading from a script. I believed I'd lose my personality if I did that – but I bore him no grudge. Everything for Philip was blown quite out of proportion, and after a particularly frustrating show one evening when everyone had let him down, including the cleaning ladies who were reluctant to let us out of the main door as they locked up, he grumbled loudly as he exited, and shouted up at the building, "I wish you cancer by Christmas!" This venomous outburst was directed at Roger, and although, sad to say, he did die at a fairly young age, it was 17 years after Philip's curse.

On the last night of the run, we were leaving the bar when Roger rushed across to thank us and say goodbye, and as the lift doors closed Phil responded, "I don't want to thank you for anything Roger." Despite his provocative behaviour, I had a sneaking fondness for Philip as he could be such wickedly entertaining company. He eventually became so disillusioned with the business that he went to live in Italy and continued to write novels and plays for the entertainment of his devoted partner, Denise Hurst, and the many stray dogs he had acquired. I eventually lost touch with him, but after many years made contact through one of his sons, actor Christopher Guard. Philip and I corresponded for a while, but after sending us many entertaining letters and plays, I presumed he just lost interest and stopped writing.

I stayed on at the Thorndike to do the Christmas pantomime, but it was a tortuous winter; the weather was appalling, and British Rail was in a state of chaos, so that commuting became a major problem. It didn't seem to matter whether the train said Waterloo or Victoria, it was always re-routed to the other one. Terry used to meet me after *Amadeus* each evening, so he was usually waiting at the wrong station, and had to drive to the alternative when the train failed to show.

The weather deteriorated and getting to and from Leatherhead became a major challenge. I had various lifts on offer, and although we always made it through the blizzards, it was a constant battle. It was a difficult Christmas with both of us working, but for some bizarre reason we invited Terry's cousin Mike, his wife Aileen, and their family over for lunch on Christmas Eve. These 'Wales' had only recently come back into Terry's life when they turned up at the Apollo to see him in *Beecham* and, from that time onwards, they remained amongst his closest family members. Having managed to fit in all the shopping, we were up late on two nights, chopping and preparing for the onslaught, but we'd agreed that we would leave it at that as far as the cooking was concerned; we'd have Christmas dinner at Pete and Annette's, and be back to work on Boxing Day with two shows each.

On Christmas Eve, Terry marched in with a vast turkey. I asked why he had bought such a huge beast when we'd made our eating plans, as I certainly had no intention of cooking on Christmas Day. He seemed to think we had discussed the matter and I'd agreed that it would be a good idea to cook the beast and have pounds of turkey to keep us going in sandwiches for the rest of the run. In the face of my intransigence, he flew off the handle and flung the bird at the door of the back bedroom, where it fell in a bruised heap onto the floor. I realised then that Terry was not in a healthy frame of mind, but we managed to pull ourselves together, and although I was still hoovering when the family arrived, the Christmas buffet went smoothly enough.

To save ourselves any further hassle, we went out that evening for a Caribbean meal, but made the unfortunate choice of curried goat. It was a change, albeit tough and inedible, but we didn't have the energy to complain and reflected that we would have been better off with the big, bruised turkey. Terry oversaw the shopping over the festive period, and that burden contributed to his blues. I still recall telephone calls when he would ramble on about the agonies of shopping in Sainsbury's, with garrulous women blocking his way while they chatted in the aisles, followed by the scream-inducing wait in the checkout queue. I would come off the phone and share a laugh with Moir Leslie, who was playing the Good Fairy, as she was having similar problems with her husband Phil, but the worst was yet to come.

Our musical director had shown more than a passing interest in me, and although Terry found it amusing at the outset, the situation began to rankle with him as his own state of mind deteriorated. He started to talk of coming down to confront our MD, and he might well have done that at the opening night party, had a wheel not flown off his car just outside Buckingham Palace. He was stuck in the freezing cold waiting for the AA while we partied, and he never did reach Leatherhead.

When he finally made it down to the Thorndike for the Christmas party, I had warned the MD about Terry's current state of mind and specifically requested that he refrain from asking me to dance. I was nervous because, although he was aware that Terry was going through a tricky time, he was thick-skinned, and regularly asked me if I would like to jet off to Florida for a holiday at the end of the run! We had no sooner sat down, when he bounced over and asked me to dance. I eye-balled him and declined in a desperate effort to keep Terry calm but, undaunted, he then went up to present a few silly awards. Whilst sitting in the pit, he amused himself during some of the dance routines, by trying to spot the colour of the ladies' knickers so, with great aplomb, he announced the winner of 'The Naughty Knicker Award'. Terry bridled as I collected my award (a pair of tartan knickers!) with as much dignity as I could muster, and the rest of the evening passed without too much aggravation.

We were on the point of leaving when our incorrigible friend came over and suggested to Terry that they might meet up in town for a drink one evening after *Amadeus*. Terry rudely declined and hustled me hastily towards the exit. I was livid that he seemed to have got things so out of proportion and had lost his sense of humour over the whole affair, not to mention the fact that we would now be the subject of company gossip. We had a blazing row on the way home.

The next morning, Terry awoke, surprisingly full of the joys, and apologised profusely for his churlish behaviour of the previous evening, and despite appalling weather, volunteered to drive me to Leatherhead for my matinée performance. Snow was still cloaking the countryside, the roads were dreadful, and it began to look as if we might be late. We were heading slowly along the A3 when Terry suddenly went rigid and yelled: "I've got a matinée too!" Neither of us had remembered his matinée, which was due to begin 30 minutes later than mine. Suddenly all hell broke loose. "I'm driving the wrong way", he shouted. "Look for a taxi!" "A taxi?", I screamed back. "On the A3? You must be joking!" He was in a terrible state, and we were skidding all over the road. I tried to calm him with time-honoured phrases like, "It's only a show" and "You've got an understudy!", but they were having no effect and I finally shrieked, "I don't want to die today! *Amadeus*? *Jack and the Beanstalk*? What does it all mean?" He dropped me at the stage door just 20 minutes before curtain-up and having left him slumped over the steering wheel, I called Her Majesty's Theatre and told them that he wouldn't be there for the matinée.

I had not reckoned, however, with the actor's determination. Having pulled himself together, he headed back for London. The snow had eased off and he calculated that, if he put his foot down, he might just about make it in time for his first entrance. Missing a show was unthinkable. With two minutes to spare, he dashed through the stage door, all but tore the costume from his understudy's back and staggered onto the stage. It was crazy behaviour, and the stage manager really shouldn't have allowed him to go on in that state. He did feel guilty afterwards and went to the management to ask if his understudy could do a matinée the following week, but that wasn't permissible without a genuine crisis so, although *Amadeus* was to run for another six months, poor James Bryce never did get on.

After that little episode, things did improve, but it shook him up and he went to the doctor, who diagnosed his condition as Housewife's Syndrome, and prescribed tranquillisers. I don't know what housewives would know about playing in a long run, but they do know about boredom and repetition, which were at the root of the problem. Terry never did take any of the pills, but managed to get back on course and completed the run without any further dramas.

The best thing about the spring of 1982 was that the cottage became ours on March 14th, so for the next few months we went to Milton whenever we could, to get it fit for purpose, which helped to take my mind off the dearth of work and Terry's mind away from *Amadeus* – well, at least on Sundays! Our many visits to B&Q, Texas and MFI for paint, fixtures and fittings for our little cottage were interspersed with doing the painting and getting the fixtures fitted. The background to our own domesticity was the Falklands War. We were confronted daily with a barrage of appalling headlines from the Sun newspaper like 'GOTCHA', which was how they summed up the unnecessary sinking of the Belgrano and the loss of hundreds of Argentinian lives. Mrs Margaret Thatcher, our Prime

Minister, made speeches about our wonderful forces and impending victory, which roused the usually apathetic Brits into a frenzy of patriotic fervour. I'm slightly ashamed to admit that I shed a tear or two as our fleet sailed off amidst much flag-waving and with the stirring sound of brass bands echoing in their ears. We won that war, for what it was worth and, sad to say, Mrs Thatcher reigned supreme for many years.

Most actors are forced to subsidise their careers by taking on other employment, so I suppose I've been very lucky not to have been put in that position. This was not to do with an overabundance of work, but more a reflection of rather good management with limited resources, and our needs were so much less back then; with no computers, iPads, mobile phones or rent, we were pretty low maintenance. Even so, I was becoming restless, and I made a feeble attempt to find alternative employment when I went to a brief training session on the techniques of selling Teflon ironing pads, and was immediately booked to start work the following morning in an Army and Navy department store somewhere on the outskirts of London. The doubts set in even before I arrived back at the flat, and I cancelled that same evening.

The cottage was a little haven. I only had a tiny border to tend, but it was very therapeutic and there was rarely a weed to be seen. Over the three years we lived there, I tended it with loving care. As our address was 4, The Bank, we named our cottage *Wild Thyme,* as in 'I know a bank whereon the wild thyme blows' which we felt gave our home an air of bijou grandeur, and to complete the illusion, I planted a little of the same at the end of my border. We even managed to get on our bikes. Bloxham, our nearest village, was one and a half miles away, and I made many a trip for the odd pint of milk or loaf of bread. As time passed, we realised that Milton was a little too quiet for us, and although it was an ideal weekend cottage we could never have adjusted to living there on a full-time basis.

And there were other drawbacks; if Terry was away and I was left alone in the evenings, I would sit watching the telly with the hoover by my side, ready to suck up the giant spiders that suddenly scuttled across the floor. Wood lice too were always in evidence, and although it was lovely to have a big roaring fire it was no joke getting up early in the morning to light it – but for the moment, it was summer, we had our own place, and it was a wonderful escape from London. Having decorated and furnished it to our satisfaction, we had our very first visitors, mum and dad. Even though dad's only comment was that it reminded him of a 'coo-shed', the pleasure we took in our new home was undiluted. They brought us a house-warming present in the form of a wooden plaque to go over the door with the inscription, *Wild Thyme*.

I was not in a good state of mind however, as despite a few interviews, nothing was happening. I needed to work, and there was still no sign of a baby to distract me. As I hadn't driven for many years and Banbury seemed the ideal place to get back on the road, I took a few refresher lessons, but as *Amadeus* was still running we were living in London for most of the week, so I had to take them down there. I drove around the busy Kilburn area with Dalton, my West Indian instructor, and after six sessions I was ready to go: fat chance. I should have waited until Terry's run was over and taken the lessons in the Cotswolds, which might have given me the confidence I needed to get going again and ultimately gain more independence. I had always accepted that Terry did the driving – as did he – and it was going to be another 14 years before I eventually got back behind a wheel.

Amadeus closed on July 17th and Terry was free at last, happy to have a bit of respite from the nightly routine. Towards the end of the run, he had been doing a bit of office work for his friend and agent, Norman Boyack. They had worked together many moons before in a large theatrical agency, and when Norman broke away from Richard Hatton's, Terry also left and returned to acting under Norman's representation, remaining with him until Norman gave up the business. They were great mates, which was not perhaps the ideal relationship for actor and agent. Norman had no qualms about getting Terry in to look after the office, but it had become a little disconcerting to be constantly negotiating on behalf of other actors when there seemed to be nothing on the cards for him.

One day, he decided to ask Norman if there was a reason why he wasn't getting any interviews. He was ready to hear that no one was interested, even that he was difficult to cast, so when Norman said: "Do you really want to know?", he braced himself for the truth. "It's because I never put you up for anything", said Norman with barefaced frankness; and then he fell about. It says something for their relationship that, even after that admission, Terry remained with him, but as Norman said at that time, changing agents was 'like changing deckchairs on the Titanic' – and that just about summed things up for everyone.

The seeds of my long connection with the play *Piaf* were sown that summer. Terry and I had seen Jane Lapotaire play the role at the Piccadilly Theatre in London back in 1980. She gave a fine acting performance, but her singing was not strong and to avoid comparisons with Edith Piaf, she hardly sang any of the well-known songs, which lessened the dramatic impact. It's not a great play but the central role of Edith Piaf is a wonderful vehicle for the right actress; a strong cast is essential, but it succeeds or fails on the strength of the central performance. After the London production closed, it was inevitable that other theatres would start to do it and I was disappointed not to land the part in a production at Farnham, but as they say in Scotland (although I don't believe it!), 'What's for ye will no' go by ye!'

1982, Swan Theatre – Cabaret with Christine McKenna, LM, Tina Gray, Hilary Cromie and Jacquie Crago.

As I was soon to find out. John Doyle, who I had only recently worked with, invited Terry to play the Emcee in *Cabaret* at the Swan Theatre in Worcester. He had a couple of big parts lined up for me later in the season, but asked if I would like to come along for the ride and play one of the Kit Kat girls, the tacky chorus line in the Berlin night-club which is at the centre of the show. As it turned out, I had a variety of roles, including that of an undersized gorilla, and I don't think I have ever had such unadulterated fun in the theatre before or since.

1982 - Swan Theatre. Cabaret with Terry Wale

The offer came at just the right time, particularly for me. We could not have known, however, that this job was to become a highlight for both of us and the benchmark for all future jobs. It is notoriously difficult to make lasting friendships in such a nomadic profession, but such was the camaraderie at the 'Swan' that, over a period of five weeks, friendships would be forged that would last a lifetime. Terry and I were about to embark on a long and happy relationship with that tiny theatre; in fact, it became one of our all-time favourites.

- 12 -

Cri de coeur

Cabaret was a joy, and Terry was a wonderful Emcee. We had some interaction, especially in his number with the gorilla in which I had comedy business with a banana. It was usually snaffled by a hungry actor or member of stage management as soon as the number was over, but as the run progressed I suggested that the banana became something of a prize, a reward for a 'cock-up' in fact. Those of us who had the time and inclination observed the show throughout the evening, nominations were put forward, and whoever made the most amusing and noticeable *faux pas* was awarded the banana at the end of the night. The Banana Awards were born.

So obsessive did it become, that even John Doyle used to give his notes in the form of Banana nominations. All this nonsense did not impair the quality of the show, nor (I hope) did the nightly visits to *The Cellars*, a local bar. Many an hour we whiled away with members of the company, including Cathy Jayes, who I had so recently worked with in Coventry. Sometimes we staggered home at 5am, and I don't know how we did it – halcyon days.

At the end of the run, we had a little party; we knew that John was going to present 'bananas' in various categories, and one specially made Golden Banana for the person he felt had made the biggest contribution to the show. We all had hopes and I recall Tina Gray, one of our Kit Kat Girls, preparing an acceptance speech – just in case. I won the Golden Banana, mainly, I think, for instigating the whole idea, and as I went forward to collect my prize, I felt as though I had won an Oscar. So choked was I, I could barely splutter out, "Thank you", never mind a speech, and I knew that if I ever did win one of the prestigious awards, it couldn't mean much more than this. Tina read out a poem that she'd written, extolling the virtues of the company, and a great night was had by all. It had only lasted a few short weeks, but there was an extraordinary feeling of camaraderie, a spirit that would continue in future productions. I still have my Golden Banana in pride of place in the study.

Apart from banana fun it was a good production and a number of friends and family came to see it. I was so delighted to be working again; the spell seemed to have been broken, and after *Cabaret* I had the Christmas show to look forward to. It was to be *The Wizard of Oz*, a small-scale production compared to the Birmingham one of six years before, but it turned out to be just as enjoyable and it confirmed the role of Dorothy as one of my all-time favourites.

So, for the second time in my life, I started rehearsals for 'Wizard', and Terry was cast as the Wizard and Mayor of Munchkinland. For someone who had succeeded in avoiding pantomime throughout his career, he came pretty close to it with his mayor! It was a relief to have no dog this time, and only one child asked where Toto was, which goes to show that if you believe in something enough you can make children believe in it as well. It was a lovely company, and we kept each other going, despite the occasional day when we had three shows. At the grand old age of 31, I was thrilled to be taken for half my age, at least by one elderly man who helped Front of House and opened the curtain every performance to allow me to make an entrance. He ventured one day to ask me how old I was, and was amazed to discover that I was over 16! My most galling moment came after a matinée when a little girl stayed behind to meet Dorothy, and to invite her to her home for tea. I changed quickly, headed to the foyer, and as I approached she burst into tears. "But mummy, she's a lady", she wailed. I should have stayed in costume and invited her to meet me backstage; I hate to think I took away any of the magic.

By way of an extreme contrast with the 12-year-old farm girl, I was to follow it with a part that, although I didn't know it at the time, was to become a milestone in my professional life, not to mention the greatest challenge I had ever faced. It had not occurred to me when I first saw the production in the West End, that the character of Edith Piaf would become so much a part of my life that I would end up feeling that the play *Piaf* by Pam Gems had been written especially for me; would that it had been.

The central character is strong, combining all the ingredients an actress could wish for: laughter, tears, and a timespan of 30 years, covering Piaf's stormy life from the age of 17 to her untimely death at 47, racked with pain and terminally addicted to morphine; not only that, but there were 12 songs, all to be sung in French. In coming to terms with the character of Piaf, I was concerned about the excessive use of strong language throughout the play. It was essential that the audience should feel sympathetic towards the 'Little Sparrow,' and I was worried that all the four-letter words might alienate them. Warmth would be essential. Our set was stark and simple, musical accompaniment was confined to a piano and an accordion, and the entire budget for the production – for set and costumes – was in the region of £600, which was a wonderful example of what can be achieved with limited resources. As I waited nervously in the wings on opening night, I knew that if I were to do justice to the original, I had to make them care about her. That was my over-riding ambition at that moment; certainly I could not have imagined, along with the company, just how great an impact we would make.

1983, Swan Theatre – Piaf.

I remember vividly our first standing ovation. It was the first Tuesday after we opened, and as the audience rose to their feet I felt an unprecedented rush of excitement. I glanced around at the rest of the company, whose faces were wreathed in smiles. After so many uncertainties, we knew we had made it, and I think there was a standing ovation every night for the rest of the run. I was earning a pittance in a small repertory theatre in the heart of England, miles away from the bright lights of London, and yet I was getting a taste of something that many accomplished and successful actors never experience throughout their entire careers.

1983, Swan Theatre – Piaf with Karen Mann.

The newspaper reviews were ecstatic. According to the various critics I was 'electrifying', with a voice that 'holds and haunts and challenges, defying its audience to escape from its spell', and a performance of 'stunning memorability'. In the face of such unstinting praise, it was as well to remember that I had never been blessed with a part like this before. Now and then one comes along and you know, instinctively, that it belongs to you. Edith Piaf was one of those parts. It was my coming of age as an actress, and I felt quite bereft when, three short weeks later, it came to an end. Little did I know that another part, equally rewarding and, if anything, even more demanding than Piaf, was about to be created, and created especially for me.

Terry was in the company and, sitting onstage one night, had suddenly been struck by something I did, a look or a gesture, that reminded him for a moment of Judy Garland. That impression, brief as it was, stayed with him, and over the next few days began to develop. When he finally took his idea for a play about Judy Garland to John Doyle, he was offered the sum of £1,000 to write it for the Swan Theatre. It would be another 18 months before *Judy* saw the light of day, and had Terry known what lay in store for him he might not have been quite so keen to take it on.

1983, Piaf, with John Doyle (front right).

The only problem I had during the *Piaf* run was an excessive thirst and endless visits to the loo. Things were not helped by the numerous drinks I had to consume during the show. We found it hilarious when I had to have a makeshift loo installed in the wings, a chamber pot with a piece of wood on top, as I just couldn't make it through the second act and there was no time to leave the stage area. I had about a minute to spare at one point, and I used this little oasis on a nightly basis while Ginni Barlow stood guard in her nurse's costume. I had no idea that my 'symptoms' were the manifestation of a very rare 'condition' which would soon play a prominent role in my life. I left Worcester feeling very elated, if a trifle hoarse.

I was now on my way to play Maggie in *What Every Woman Knows* at the Thorndike Theatre in Leatherhead. Roger Clissold, who was still at the helm, thought I was born to play the part. That may have been true, but perhaps not in this production. I had turned down a Noel Coward play at the 'Swan' to do the James Barrie play and I soon began to wish I'd stayed in Worcester. I was back in Kensal Rise with daily to-ing and fro-ing down to Leatherhead. I still had a very dry throat but thought that was partly attributable to the rigours of playing Piaf.

1983, Thorndike Theatre Leatherhead – What Every Woman Knows with Benny Young.

Roger professed to love the play, maintaining it to be a favourite of his, but he was not over-inspired. With some frustration along the way, but with a lot of input from the company – particularly from John Grieve playing dad – we got there in the end. I think that my 'Maggie' was fine, but it was hard to remain enthusiastic in a rather lacklustre production. I did, at least, have some time off during the show, so there was no need to install a potty, although I was consuming copious amounts of tea saturated with honey to deal with the thirst. Because of the dryness I also started to have coughing fits onstage which I managed to conceal until the final performance. As the curtain came down on Maggie laughing with joy, she was choking fit to burst.

Next on the agenda was a holiday in Yugoslavia, a country Terry was already in love with, and very exciting for me as we drove through many countries to get there. The atmosphere felt good, and the spirit of Tito was still around. There was certainly no hint of the dreadful turmoil the country would be thrown into in the '90s when all the different ethnic groups would be literally at each other's throats. We met a few of Terry's old friends, we bought a few souvenirs, but the one special item that we acquired during this trip was a lovely painting of a winter scene on glass, which still has pride of place in our bathroom and remained one of Terry's favourite works of art. As we left for our long drive back, I don't suppose that either of us thought we would ever see any of those people again.

The next big production was my brother Grant's wedding to Maggie. Terry wasn't free to come, so I headed north on my own to be at the event and to make my own small contribution by singing *The Eriskay Love Lilt* during the wedding ceremony in the local kirk. The following day a few of the wedding guests came back to Dundee for tea and a chat. The conversation turned political, was focusing on the 'Unemployed', and they were coming out with the kind of jargon you would expect to see in *The Sun* newspaper. Aunt Bessie took the biscuit when she came out with: "Well, I haven't come across any of those homeless and unemployed people that you keep talking about!" To my eternal regret, I heard myself saying snippily, "Well, you wouldn't, would you? Not in Chislehurst!" before I left the room. But I was fond of my aunt, and I hated upsetting mum, who came to my bedroom and said that I ought to see a doctor; when I woke up the following morning she had already made an appointment for me. I was on the point of saying that having left-wing sympathies was not usually considered to be a medical issue, but I decided that it might be worth going to check up on my thirst and my nocturnal visits to the loo so, singing *The Red Flag*, I went along to see the family GP, Dr John Foster. Our political differences were about to change my life.

Diabetes was suspected, but the test was negative, and I left a blood sample to be sent to Ninewells Hospital for analysis. I was on the point of returning to London when the results came through and I was advised to head straight to St Mary's Hospital in Paddington, where a bed had been reserved for me in the Metabolic Unit. All I knew was that I had a severe potassium deficiency but had no idea what that meant or how serious it was. I arrived at St Mary's for the first of many visits and was allocated a place in a ward with three other ladies, and as they all had weight-related problems I spent a sleepless week, serenaded nightly by the sounds of snoring. Many of the patients were there to lose weight, either because of ill-health or in preparation for a major operation, and the unit could only justify its NHS funding by treating obese patients if they had a related medical problem; any person who was there simply to get some assistance with dieting had to pay for the treatment. One of the inmates was so massive that he couldn't sit on any of the chairs. He was sleeping in the private Lindo Wing and was over from Saudi Arabia in order to lose half his body weight. By the time I arrived, he had been in residence for over six months and was planning to stay as long as was necessary. If he ever reached his target weight, he faced major surgery to remove the mounds of flesh which would be left hanging from his body.

As for myself: Bartter syndrome, a very rare condition, was mentioned, but at this stage they could not give a conclusive diagnosis. (It wasn't until I had a genetic test in 2013 that it was discovered that I actually had Gitelman's syndrome). They conveyed to me that I had something extremely dangerous, and whether I had been born with it or developed it over the years, was all for further investigation – but I was left in no doubt that unless I could get my potassium level up to something approaching normal, my body's organs, particularly the heart, could malfunction. So emphatic were they, that I was convinced that a heart attack must be imminent, and I might not be long for this world. As time passed, I came to accept that I had a rare condition that my body had perhaps attuned to over the years, hence my seeming ability to cope with it. Nevertheless, I was grateful to have their interest in my case as I had no way of knowing whether things might have become untenable as the years went by – and I couldn't forget that I had been really suffering with the excessive thirst and urination, so my hope was that at least these problems could be resolved.

I stayed in the hospital for a week, but time was short as I was soon to start rehearsals in Chester. Although the Professor was keen to do a biopsy to get a look at one of my kidneys, he would have to keep a rein on his renal obsession for a little bit longer. He tried to convince me that I was not fit to work, but I was not going to give up a job when I had clearly been living with this condition for some time – and no one knew what to make of it in any case. As I left, Professor Wynn said to me, "You must understand that you are a very sick woman Mrs Wale", which was not very encouraging. I left St Mary's with a ton of potassium, a drug called indomethacin, and a modicum of anxiety. If I had known what I was about to embark upon in Chester I think I would have chosen to stay in the Metabolic Unit!

Still flushed with my Swan Theatre *Piaf* success, I was eager to play the part again and had leapt at an offer to do so at the Gateway Theatre in Chester. Malcolm McKee, an old friend from Pitlochry, had put me in touch with Sue Wilson, the Artistic Director, and at a preliminary meeting at the *Spotlight* offices we had a brief chat, I gave a quick burst of song, and she offered me the job.

It's never easy when you've played a part before, especially a whacking great lead like Piaf, because you must resist the temptation to say, "When I did it last time". I had high hopes of avoiding this, as she made it clear that I was being asked because I had so recently played the part in a successful production. She wanted to add a couple of songs, and have Marlene Dietrich instead of Josephine Baker as Piaf's friend, which was fair enough, as at that time Marlene was probably easier to cast than Ms Baker. Apart from these changes, she agreed that, with various versions of the script to choose from, she would use the same one we had worked with at the Swan Theatre. I offered my script so that she could make copies, but she said she'd be in touch if she couldn't get hold of it from Worcester.

We spent some time at the cottage before I left for Chester but, to my dismay, I had a call from Sue to say that she hadn't managed to get hold of my version of the script, so had ordered copies of the published version. I failed to understand why she hadn't come back to me sooner, but time was running out, so I arranged to go over to Chester to see what could be done. We spent an entire afternoon juggling the two scripts until we felt we could work with it, but I was beginning to feel distinctly uneasy. Deeply depressed, I returned to the cottage and, with a heavy heart, headed for rehearsals a few days later.

1983, Chester Gateway Theatre with Jackie Lye.

We got off to a bad start when she failed to introduce me to the company, all actors who she had worked with before, and who were currently in *The Elephant Man*. Apart from Malcolm, who I was to be staying with for the duration, I knew no one. We were handed sheets of re-writes, based on our script conference of the previous week, and we then had a read-through followed by a look at the set and costume designs. I was expecting a slight variation on the little black dress I had worn in Worcester, but was astounded by the array of coats, hats, furs and feather boas. I knew there was virtually no time to change, so when I was meant to get into all this finery quite bewildered me. It was suggested that I might manage a change or two during Marlene's numbers, as she was to be singing a couple of songs and could easily sing another. I was aware that too much focus on another singer might upset the rather fragile structure of the play and diminish the impact of the evening, but I was in a very difficult position, because if I didn't go along with this, it was bound to be interpreted as selfish. I felt powerless, and it wasn't long before every suggestion I made was treated as an intrusion. Actors work with all sorts of directors, some of whom would prefer you to do as you're told and keep your opinions to yourself. There are, however, a handful who welcome an actor's input and who believe that putting on a play is a joint responsibility; these few we treasure.

The coterie of actors who made up the permanent company were obviously unaware of all that had passed between us at that early meeting, nor were they about to bite the hand that was feeding them. From their point of view, I was an incomer who wouldn't let the director get on with doing her job. I imagine that some of them thought I was temperamental and a bit of a diva, which couldn't have been further from the truth. I was just desperate for the production to work and for the play to have a similar effect to the one we had experienced in Worcester.

Terry was with me for the first few days before his departure for the New Zealand tour of *Beecham* with Timothy West, and I only survived that first week because he was around to hold my hand. He felt that he had seen and heard enough to advise me to consider backing out, but I never saw that as an option. Before he left, he was able to attend an open rehearsal of *Piaf,* because it was Chester policy during each production to allow members of the public to come in on one day to observe the actors at work. They paid 50p to witness a 'normal' rehearsal with no concessions made, but not only was I asked to avoid any dissent, but Sue also requested that I sing a few numbers to provide some entertainment. I did as I was told to avoid conflict, and Terry sat quietly seething. He left that day, and I had to survive for the next month with only phone calls and letters to ease the pain and isolation.

The play was most effective on a simple level, but it was Ms Wilson's 'swansong' as she was soon to depart the theatre, and she obviously wanted to go out with a bang. We didn't need a complicated set, numerous costumes, flashing lights and fussy staging; we were in the back streets of Paris, not on Sunset Boulevard, and everything was ill-conceived from the opening scene which was full of jugglers and people doing acrobatics, when it should have been a tiny figure in black singing in the street. As she sings, Piaf is approached by a smartly dressed gentleman, and as he lays a hand on her shoulder she starts and says, "Get yer fuckin' hands off me, I ain't done nothin'." The actor playing Leplée felt that it would work better if he didn't touch me, and when I queried the logic of this, Sue said I should do as he suggested to see if it worked. How could it work? That was the opening line, and from that point onwards things just got worse.

I argued and challenged, and the company grew weary of the daily conflict. In the early stages, a few members of the company seemed sympathetic to my plight, and I recall Jackie Lye, the girl playing Toine, saying, "You'll have to watch – the way things are going, the play should be called Piaf's Mates!" This was a reference to the fact that Piaf appeared to be a secondary character, usually facing upstage, so that the other actors in the scene were in the dominant position. A strong company is essential, but too much focus on the other characters throws the balance of the play and exposes its flaws, but I was told that I had to let the others 'have their moments'. I knew that I had to choose between toeing the line and retaining an element of popularity or sticking to my guns and getting up a few noses, so I took the only path I knew, which was to be true to the play, and rehearsals deteriorated into what I can only describe as open warfare. One day, things reached such a head that Sue stopped the rehearsal and asked me to come to her office. She said, "Why won't you trust me?" – not a line to inspire confidence.

Towards the end of rehearsals, we had a row about the end of the play. Having agreed to use the device of combining *No Regrets* and *Les Trois Cloches*, finishing with a section of *No Regrets*, she decided that she wanted the last segment as an encore after the curtain call. This was a play, not a musical and I felt it would be wrong to sing an encore – and this suggestion came from a woman who, I discovered, didn't believe in curtain calls.

There were a few who seemed to understand what I was going through, and I remember John McCardle, Gareth Tudor Price, Michelle Butt and Jackie Lye with fondness. As far as certain others were concerned, everything I did seemed to have repercussions. Early on I had some enjoyable chats with the lady accordionist and, believing her to be 'outside' the situation, I poured my heart out to her one night over a drink. How could I have guessed that she and Sue were already very close?

I was also suffering from nausea and an inability to eat, which as well as being stress-related, I suspected might be partly due to a potassium-saving drug I had been given to take. I wrote to St Mary's and was advised immediately to stop taking the Indomethacin, which might be causing the problems. And through all the trials and tribulations, I had no one to lean on. Malcolm, my old friend and current landlord, as well as being an actor, was also assistant director and part of Sue's inner circle. While I understood that he didn't want to take sides, I couldn't understand why he didn't offer a listening ear – even when he saw me weeping at his home in a state of abject misery. Terry was more dismissive of him than I was, maintaining him to be 'on the cutting room floor of our lives'. In fact, that's where he stayed until over 30 years later when we renewed contact through Facebook and moved on with no mention of past times!

The day of the technical rehearsal dawned, and I surveyed the wondrous set. There were a series of rostra to be trundled on and off between scenes, but the scenes were all so short that it was bound to be disruptive. They were also placed so far upstage that the audience were going to feel uninvolved in the action. Although they were eventually moved downstage a little, I still felt it was going to be Set 1 Actors 0. Each time I sang, a glittering array of lights above my head flashed the word 'Piaf' on and off, and some of the quieter scenes had an intrusive musical backing which destroyed the atmosphere. As there was no food available in the theatre, I found myself heading out in a meal break, complete with my Piaf wig under a headscarf, trailing round Chester looking for a bite to eat.

The technical finished at 3am, and totally exhausted I made my weary way back to the digs.

On the opening night there were still many problems to face, the most absurd being the scene with Marcel Cerdan, the boxer. Being a post-coital scene it should have taken place on a bed or something very like one, but despite many trucks bringing on various items of furniture, it seemed that a bed was out of the question and we had to make do with a sofa. Marcel was in shorts and boxing boots and the scene opened with a slow waltz before we drifted back onto the sofa to commence the dialogue. The very notion that, having had sex with his boots on, he would jump up to have a wee dance was going to get titters, if not guffaws, from the audience, but we did it. The reaction was muted at first, then they just fell about. John whispered in my ear, "I'll kill her", but it was too late to have regrets, although we did not dance again. At the end of the show, against all the odds, the audience applauded enthusiastically, we took our curtain call and left the stage. The applause continued, so I decided to go back on for a second call, bringing the rest of the company on to take another bow, which did not feel excessive.

1983, Chester Gateway Theatre – with Gareth Tudor Price.

On an opening night most directors come backstage afterwards and say something encouraging about the performance, but Sue said, "Why did you come back for a second call? We don't really like curtain calls in this theatre". In my experience, most actors and audiences do like curtain calls, and I have always felt that it's mildly insulting to an audience not to accept applause with grace, but there had been no card, no compliments, and she even appeared to grudge the applause. Her partner, Sunny, came to the dressing room, and after saying that she had enjoyed it, she asked why I hadn't sung an encore. I explained about it not being a musical, and got the retort, "You're paid to do what the director wants you to do." "Not enough", I retorted, which was not what I ought to have said, as money had nothing to do with it, but I was at the end of my tether. Never before or since, on an opening night, have I entered the bar and had to search for a friendly face, but that was Chester, and not only on the opening night!

By this time the Farnham production of *Piaf* starring Adrienne Posta had reached Manchester, and that production drew letters of complaint which appeared in the local newspapers. There is little doubt that our audiences were affected by its proximity, although we did receive good reviews and played to reasonable houses. Yes, it seemed that Sue had 'got away with it' like many a director before her, and I believe that I played no small part in making her 'swansong' sweet, but at some cost to myself. I spent most of my days alone and often went to sit on a swing in a local park, where I quietly practised my Garland songs, which was soothing and escapist. Although I would rather have saved my voice, I sometimes went for a drink with the company after the show, but that became increasingly tricky as things were not always going smoothly onstage and it wasn't easy to avoid areas of contention.

There were numerous examples of what I considered totally unreasonable behaviour from both the director and some of her cast. During the scene in the nightclub where Piaf talks to Papa Leplée about her dead baby, there were a few people sitting at tables to provide an ambience. They were encouraged to develop personas, and on one evening, not only did we play the scene against the usual piano accompaniment, but we also had the very audible sound of chatting and giggling at one of the tables, which culminated in a crash, finishing off any chance of creating an atmosphere downstage. I was told that although the crash had been accidental, they had been asked to try things out, and they were 'being lesbians', whatever that meant! When I took the matter to Sue, she told me to relax and trust the company who she knew and loved; in directing it as an ensemble piece, she created a situation where some of the company saw Piaf as just another character who appeared in their scenes and threatened to take away their 'moments'. She also gave Kattrin, the DSM who was 'on the book', *carte blanche* to decide whether we should take a second curtain call, and for reasons best known to herself, she usually decided not.

Many friends questioned the lack of a proper call, but occasionally it did feel as if the applause was dying a little and I lost the will to argue. It took actor friend, Bernard Lloyd, to inform me that the reason the applause was dying was because she was bringing up the house lights after my first exit, which is one sure way to kill applause. On one occasion when I said to Kattrin that I thought we should go back on, she said "No", and I shouted in despair: "So much for the bloody actors", and I was reported for rudeness. The memory still rankles, and I sincerely hope that if she continued in the business, she learnt not only to respect actors, but that curtain calls should be looked on as a measure of success and not as something to be sneered at.

Quite a few friends made the trip to Chester: Alf and Lynda (who we had met on our Kos holiday) came from Manchester, Di Davis from *Bitter Apples* days, dear Bernie who came to give me a shoulder to cry on, Joan Knight and John Scrimger, who were there to view the piece before we did the show in Perth, and lots of chums from Worcester. It was lovely to see them all, and they helped get me through.

During the final week of the run, I was commuting to Worcester for *Pinocchio* rehearsals, which was no easy journey. With the help of the 'Swan' friends, we just about managed it. One evening, it was John Doyle who took me to Chester for the evening performance and drove me back to Worcester. On the last Thursday, Cathy and her partner, Steve, were in to see the show, and on that night all had gone well, and I came offstage feeling quite exhilarated. I was chatting away to the girls in the dressing room, when I suddenly realised that I was talking to myself; they had all gone. Sue suddenly appeared out of the blue and, in my innocence, it crossed my mind that she was finally going to offer a few words of encouragement. Her opening gambit was, "What are you going to do about your performance?" I started to shake visibly as I listened to her telling me that two actors had gone to her with complaints. An actress was upset because I had cut a couple of her lines, and the actor playing Angelo thought that I had cut his 'round' at the end of *Deep in the Heart of Texas*.

1983, The Gateway Theatre, Chester – Piaf with Jackie Lye and Malcolm McKee.

The scene was quite simple; Angelo, with Piaf's support, is auditioning for the manager of a nightclub. Throughout rehearsals the song was becoming sillier and sillier, until he was even performing bunny hops as he sang a line about rabbits. Such an interpretation could only make Piaf look foolish, because Angelo was her protégé and he was supposed to be Yves Montand after all!

Things did settle down and the scene usually went very well. At the end of the song, I applauded with shouts of, "Wonderful, marvellous", which usually encouraged the audience to join in – but the round was simply a bonus, as he was, in effect, singing for the three characters onstage. Well, on this Black Thursday, everything was the same, except that he did not get his round. I was astounded that he saw fit to complain but (if he did!) here was Sue giving it credence and she hadn't even seen the show. For the umpteenth time I tried to reason with her, but to no avail. She said that I wasn't giving enough to the rest of the cast, and I told her I was giving my all. "Who to?" she responded. "To them, or to the audience?" There was no answer to that, and I headed for the bar where Cathy and Steve were already feeling uncomfortable. Anny Tobin (Marlene) had introduced Cathy as the MD from the Swan production, and the atmosphere was rather icy. I spent a few minutes with Di Davis and a casting director from Granada, but Cathy and Steve were so taken aback by the bad feeling surrounding me that they were keen to head back to Worcester as soon as possible. During that journey I was closer to a breakdown than at any time during the run, but I was with friends and the tears flowed uncontrollably. I'm just glad that it happened with them.

I rehearsed *Pinocchio* on the Friday and headed back to Chester for my penultimate show where a lovely bouquet was waiting on my dressing table. The card said, 'From an Admirer', and the flowers were a great morale booster. I was later to discover that they had come from Cathy and Steve; it was a lovely gesture and one that I will never forget. Act 1 passed without incident, but just before the opening of Act 2, I was standing in the wings with Anny (Marlene) when she asked me how I was feeling. I assumed that the enquiry was related to the previous evening, and I quickly gave her my tale of woe about the horrendous car journey, but said that it had been cathartic, and I was feeling a bit better. I heard the intro to *Mon Dieu* and went on for my opening number. At the end of the performance Anny rushed over to me and, to my utter amazement said, "Don't ever tell me about your feelings just before I have to go onstage!" Actually I was the one who had to go onstage at that point

– her entrance was much later – and she was the one who had asked me how I was. It seemed that I could never do the right thing.

One show to go and I laid out a few bottles of wine for the company; I wanted to end on a civilised note. I spoke to a charming actor who had been in to see the show, and while we were chatting, Sue and Sunny came across to say 'Goodbye' to him. They ignored me in a very deliberate way, and after they left he asked me what was going on. I told him a little about my Chester experience, and he said that he had been talking to Sue at the interval, when he had commented that Piaf was a killer of a role with the success of the evening resting firmly on her shoulders. She responded that she did not agree with him, which said it all. I went back to Malcolm's house, clutching a single red rose which had been handed in by some people from Worcester. As I walked into the lounge, I was greeted by the sight of Sunny and Sue who had come back for coffee. I braved it out for a few minutes but as soon as the Perth *Piaf* was mentioned, Sunny quipped, "Well, you'll have to do what Joan Knight wants". I quietly responded by saying that I was sure we would be in agreement about the approach to the production, and went to bed.

As I tried to sleep, I hoped that the healing process could now begin. It was over, but it would be a long time before I was over it; I don't think that I will ever shake off the memories. When you are playing a mammoth role like Piaf and the success or failure of the show rests largely on your shoulders, you have a right to expect, at the very least, the support of your director. In this case, my confidence was undermined every day, and very deliberately too. With Terry in New Zealand, I didn't even have a shoulder to cry on. The experience toughened me up, no doubt, but it was still painful and, to this day, remains something of a mystery. At least I knew that Terry would soon be on his way back to join me in Worcester, where we would go through our mutual experiences for days. Returning to the 'Swan' was a balm to my wounded spirits, and the Chester era was at an end. You will guess from the length of this tale, that it was probably the worst and unhappiest experience of my entire career.

Year of little legends

Playing the part of Pinocchio was not the ideal way to recuperate, but at least I had a few chums around. Terry had missed the first week of rehearsals, so he'd a bit of catching up to do. It was a tremendous relief to have him back and to share our experiences. Although he had got on splendidly with Tim West, he hadn't really taken to New Zealand as a country and felt very helpless knowing what I was going through on the other side of the world. Despite our many phone calls, there were still endless stories to tell.

1983, Swan Theatre – Pinocchio with Charles Bell.

We threw ourselves into rehearsals which involved a few tricky dance routines. Alan Radcliffe and Marcia Gresham were actor-dancers who were making their debut as choreographers, and they were keen to pull out all the stops. They were also playing the Fox and the Blue Fairy. The lovely Cathy Jayes had composed the music, and in my opening number there were so many moves and steps to execute, that there wasn't much hope of singing at the same time. Cathy, true to form, was very stoical, but they eventually simplified the routine enough to give the song a chance. As soon as Terry arrived, he was presented with a rather complicated Mr Cricket song and dance, which was also reduced to something a little less frenzied. Just for the record, the dancing Blue Fairy and the Fox eventually married and became the parents of Harry Potter (Daniel Radcliffe) – yes really – and they lived happily ever after.

Towards the end of the run we were feeling a bit miffed because there had been no review in *The Stage*, our trade paper. Every other Christmas show in the country seemed to have been covered, so Cathy, Terry and I went to the theatre office and asked them if they would chase it up, and whether or not it was due to prompting, the review soon appeared. We thought that we were rather good, so it was a blow to our pride to see my woodenness described as only 'skin deep', Cathy's music as 'derivative', and Terry's Mr Cricket as 'a tired old conscience whose jumping days are long gone!' Funnily enough, that was so negative it made us laugh and it remained one of Terry's favourite reviews. I thought Cathy's music was charming and Terry was very energetic – in fact, his brother Pete thought that he had a trampoline in the wings to assist his bounce onto the stage, and John Slim of the Birmingham Post found my puppet a 'revelation', whatever that meant! Critics are all very well if you agree with them, I suppose. Minor niggles aside, we had a happy time in the show, which helped distance the Chester *Piaf,* but I still felt a little apprehensive about facing my next job, which was to be *Piaf* in Perth.

Sue Wilson had just taken over as Director of Productions at Pitlochry Festival Theatre, a mere 25 miles north of Perth, so I was determined that she should hear glowing reports. I needn't have worried. I found myself surrounded by a supportive company, I had a sympathetic director in Joan Knight, Terry was my Papa Leplée again, and we were working with my original script. A few days into rehearsal Joan took Terry aside and asked him why I was constantly 'upstaging' myself; I was so afraid of causing any waves with the other actors that, without realising it, I was tending to take a back seat, but I soon settled into the production which, strangely enough, featured Edith Piaf as the central character.

At one point during rehearsals, the actor playing Angelo asked why I was clapping so enthusiastically at the end of his 'audition'. "You're not trying to start a 'round' are you?" he asked. I said that might be the outcome, and he begged me not to, as it was not an intrinsic part of the scene – and he was also a little nervous about the quality of his singing! I was grateful, and in that moment I knew that Chester had been an aberration, and felt quite vindicated. I was once again with a company who seemed to understand what the play was about and what their function was. I can't underestimate Joan's part in making that possible, as she made it clear from the outset where the focus should be.

1984, Perth Theatre – Piaf with Iain Stuart Robertson, Paul Morrow and Anne Smith.

Yes, I was back in Perth, and it was like a homecoming. The atmosphere throughout the theatre was especially welcoming in those days, and on this occasion it was electric. Joan was taking a big gamble as nobody knew how Perth audiences would respond to the play, and in several theatres up and down the country, word was that they had walked out in their droves. Fortunately, the people of Perth were made of sterner stuff and the 'House Full' sign became a fixture on the pavement outside the theatre. It was, for me, a wonderful and fulfilling episode, similar to the Worcester experience, and made all the sweeter because I was on my home ground. The reviews were wonderful, with Graham Fulton surpassing himself, saying that it was a 'performance that was nothing short of remarkable'.

1984, Perth Theatre – Piaf with Terry Wale.

On the last night, some of the usherettes clubbed together and threw flowers down onto the stage from the Dress Circle – a magical moment, made all the merrier when fellow-actor, Martyn James muttered, "It's like working with Torvill and Dean!" I had played many parts on that stage, but nothing quite like this. Uncle Archie was at the final performance, and as the three of us drove back to Dundee, we were stopped at a police road check. The policewoman looked into the back of the car, where I was surrounded by flowers, and asked for my autograph. It seemed that *Piaf* had altered my status – well, at least in Perth and Dundee!

In 2008, the production was given special mention in *Perth: A City Again,* a book about the twentieth century in Perth, written by a friend of ours, Jeremy Duncan, and in 2009, the show cropped up again in the *Perthshire Advertiser*'s '25 years ago' feature as a highlight of the time. The audiences had taken Edith to their hearts, and the 'Piaf' experience became the one to which everything else in the future would be compared.

1984, Perth Theatre – Piaf with Cindy Wells.

Unfortunately, Terry had not managed to get a great deal of work done while we were living in Dundee, so ahead of him lay a few months dedicated to our new project, *Judy*. He had done all the research, but John Doyle was waiting to see a first draft, so there was no time to lose. I now faced the prospect of a longish spell back in St Mary's Hospital. I was keen to uncover the mystery surrounding my condition, so had agreed to a five-week stay to give them a fair chance of coming up with a diagnosis. It was a gruelling few weeks, the only plus being that Terry had peace to get on with his play without distractions. My regime was harsh with no food at all, just the required number of calories, all in the form of Nutroxil, a complete food in liquid form.

As time wore on it became very difficult to face that same sickly substance three times a day. At 6am we had the weigh-in, and it's a pity that it had to be quite so early, as it made the days seem even longer. This was followed by the liquid breakfast and a succession of tests that interrupted the boredom of life on the metabolic ward. Some days I was left to my own devices, and I did my best to get on with learning all the Garland songs. Terry would come down in the evenings, often with bits of script for my perusal. Most of the other inmates watched telly all day – anything and everything, and that was pretty mind-blowing. Apart from the ward, there was only the day room to sit in, and I attempted to shut out the noise of the 'soaps' as I sat with my headphones on, listening to music. When it all became too much, I retreated to my bed, but I often found it taken by someone having a biopsy or minor operation, so privacy was hard to find.

I was in a ward with three others, and a mixed bag they were. There was Ginny, with anorexia, who was there to increase her appetite. She was placed, somewhat incongruously, in the next bed to Margaret, a small fat woman, who was hoping to lose five stones prior to a stomach operation. It was ill-judged to have placed Ginny so close to someone who was surely the image of everything she dreaded. Margaret so loved her food that she could not stick to the rules and soon arranged for her husband to bring in lots of goodies for her. She spent her days eyeing the tiny biscuits that we were sometimes given as a treat. "You'll not be wantin' that wee biscuit will ye?" she asked brazenly in her thick Irish brogue.

At night I used to watch the shadow of her hand against the curtain as she moved it surreptitiously in and out of her bedside cupboard, then up to her mouth and back again. The shadow play was accompanied by a variety of noises: burping, belching and hiccuping that proved a total nightmare for Ginny in the next bed. If Margaret did fall asleep she snored like a pig, so waking or sleeping there was always a cacophony of sound. One night Ginny suddenly leapt from her bed and ran out into the corridor. When I found her a few moments later, she was sobbing uncontrollably; it was clear that no cure would be found for Ginny while Margaret was around, but the Metabolic Unit was not a slimming club, the rules were rigid, and Margaret was eventually asked to leave.

I had so many tests I can barely remember them – normal blood tests and venal blood tests, which were the ones that made me weep; for these, they took blood from a main artery in the arm, wrist or groin, and the experience was not a pleasant one. Despite all the tests, the Professor and his team did not seem to be coming up with any answers. I just didn't fit into any category, and I began to realise that I was one of their star guinea pigs. It reached the stage where they thought that if they ever found anyone with identical symptoms, they might have to recognise a new condition, and perhaps name it after me. I thought that the 'Mackie' Syndrome sounded quite catchy.

After five weeks of torture and my body awash with Nutroxil, I was told that there were now more unanswered questions than when I arrived. Professor Wynn was still itching to do a biopsy. "I'd love to get a piece of that kidney", he said with relish, but I didn't see the point unless I felt ill. I think they would have kept me there for as long as I was willing, but I wanted to get on with my life. As time passed, the doctors accepted that, genetic or not, my case might well be unique, allowing me to survive at a lower level of potassium than what was considered the norm, although I was now taking large daily doses of the stuff. I'd been told that I had to mention the 'condition' if I ever had to face an anaesthetic because, if the level was too low, the heart might be put under too much strain. Although it may have caused me a lot of unnecessary worry at that time, it was probably best that I was made aware of the risks. I wonder when I would have found out had it not been for the family row about politics in August 1983. I left the hospital with a promise to return when I felt that I could spare another couple of weeks to undergo more tests and bloodletting.

On the bright side, Terry had made a good start to the play, and we were now free to go to the cottage and immerse ourselves in the project. We spent most of the summer at *Wild Thyme*. I read biographies, watched videos and listened to tapes of Judy, while Terry got on with the often painful and laborious process of writing the play. There were days when he came downstairs clutching two, three, or even four pages of dialogue. On others he was lucky if he even managed half a page, and that invariably ended up in the waste-paper basket.

Judy Garland was such a complex and many-faceted creature, and her behaviour so inconsistent, that understanding what made her tick was a major obstacle, both for Terry and for me. There were times he found her so infuriating he could hardly bear to spend another minute in her company, and occasions when he felt so moved by her story he found it impossible to write about her with any objectivity. Had we but known her we may well have felt the same – one moment intolerant and the next bewitched. She came across as a warm and vulnerable woman who had never quite grown up, a victim of the Hollywood system who never found the end of her rainbow.

While Terry was battling with his problems, I was having a few of my own. There were times I felt I was getting nowhere, that the only thing Judy Garland and I had in common was a shared birthday! Terry's breakthrough came when he finally realised that it was her very inconsistencies that made her who she was; in playing the part, he said, I should start from the premise that if I played two consecutive scenes as if she were the same woman, then I had probably got it wrong. This was a much more daunting prospect than playing the earthy and straightforward Piaf, who remained essentially the same person throughout her life. Even Garland's voice was more complex, demanding a more subtle approach and a greater variety of tone; neither did it escape my notice that it would be no easy task to sustain the vocal quality on a nightly basis, particularly as the play would be full of hysterics and shouting, often followed by a quiet song. We were also aware that gaining sympathy for Judy would be more difficult, as she appeared to have been given the keys of the kingdom and wilfully thrown them away, whereas Piaf, on the other hand, was disadvantaged from birth, and consequently could be forgiven almost anything.

By a small stroke of good fortune, Cathy Jayes met Ken Sephton at a book fair, and he happened to be a major player in the *Judy Garland Fan Club* and gave her his contact details. The club met twice a year, usually in a central London hotel, and spent a few hours watching films and TV 'Specials', gossiping, swapping memorabilia and generally wallowing in nostalgia. We were invited to these meetings, and it never ceased to amaze us that, although the lady was long gone, they kept digging up new snippets of information and trivia to share with each other. At our first meeting, some of the members – and especially those sitting in the front row – whooped with joy and clapped their hands every time Judy opened her mouth. Most of them were gentle, charming, and keen to help. One of the most helpful was Brian Glanville, who was the projectionist and keeper of the films and archive material, and he invited us to his little flat in Ealing to see some of his treasures, and we went regularly throughout the summer.

There was so much to see that we had to cram a lot into each session; we saw Judy with the *Meglin Kiddies* when she was still little Frances Ethel Gumm and barely seven years old, we saw her as the newly created Judy Garland at 14, fooling about with the other child stars in LB Mayer's swimming pool, and we even saw her Wardrobe Test for *Valley of the Dolls*, which took place towards the end of her life and career. Brian had it all, and back then that material was not readily available elsewhere, so without his help we would have missed out on a lot. His flat was a shrine to Judy with photos in every nook and cranny, and he even had yellow Judy Garland roses on his veranda. His image of her was very precious to him; he didn't even read the biographies for fear that they would shatter his illusions, and we knew from the outset that we would have to tread a very gentle path. He wanted to come and see the play, so we arranged for him to stay overnight with our lovely Worcester landlady, Bette Lewis, and he was looking forward to it with great excitement. We did try to warn him that our play would not be simply a tribute show with Judy forever in the 'Dorothy' mould; although a celebration of her life, it would be a full-blooded portrayal with the 'ups and the downs' – and there were quite a few 'downs'. His response to that was that he knew we "would do nothing to hurt Judy", and as we approached the start of rehearsals we began to feel quite uneasy about his planned visit.

We only had two and a half weeks to rehearse the show and much of this time was taken up with cutting and rewriting, a process which went on after we had opened. It was quite a staggering prospect, not only to be playing this gigantic role, but having to cope with daily changes to the script. Songs vanished and new ones appeared, while scenes on which we had lavished so much care and attention were discarded overnight. When we started, the play stood at about three and a half hours with over 20 songs (which we had managed to cut down from our original 33!), and it is something of a miracle that we honed it to an acceptable length in time to open. Such are the trials and tribulations of putting on a new play, but everyone worked their socks off.

Cathy had painstakingly based the arrangements on original Garland recordings in order to create an authentic sound, and as we shared digs with her we were aware that she was scribbling out the parts until she fell asleep over them around four o'clock in the morning. As with *Piaf* we were working on a limited budget, so there were bound to be areas of weakness, but this production was another example of what can be achieved on a shoestring. Although we only had three male dancers, otherwise known as Judy's 'Boyfriends', they played numerous roles, and as we approached the opening night it was wonderful to see how much everyone had achieved in such a short period of time – and what a thrill for Terry and I to see the results of our summer of endeavour, and Terry's first stage play almost ready to open.

After six months of blood, sweat and tears, we finally had a play called *Judy*, scheduled to be given its World Première at the Swan Theatre, Worcester, on September 13th, 1984. Naturally, we had dreams about its future, most of them concerning what it might do for my career south of the border. Terry had been partly driven to write it with that in mind, and being a new play we hoped that it might attract the interest of London producers and casting directors. We knew that it was – and still is – notoriously difficult to persuade them to venture out into the provinces and many a gem never gets the chance to be seen by a wider audience.

Audiences were enthusiastic, the reviews were everything we could have hoped for, and friends and family came to support us. Dad came down with Grant for the opening night, and Mum came later – even Pete D'Souza, my old college tutor, made the trip. Alfie Lynch and Jimmy Culliford, dear friends of Terry, came up from London for the final matinée and, unbeknownst to us, two gentlemen came over from Leicester for that penultimate show. They had been waiting for years for something to come along that might fill the gap left by Judy's death and, as it turned out, our play was the answer to their prayers! They were Reg Needle and David Mars, both members of the *Judy Garland Fan Club*, and the first we knew of their existence was when a *Judy* review, which Reg had written for the Club Magazine, landed on the mat. It was a rave, and all the more exciting for us to have it come from a Judy devotee. I wrote back to him, and it was the beginning of a warm and lasting friendship with both Reg and David.

1984, Swan Theatre – Judy première.

They were destined to see our play many times, and eventually came to visit us in the London flat, where we talked endlessly about the play and about Judy Garland herself, whom they had both met. We had been very nervous about the reaction of the Judy fans, so it was a tremendous relief to discover that most of them were able to accept the play, which showed Judy, warts and all, and it was ironic that the person who had given us the most help with our research, Brian Glanville, was the only one who seemed to be genuinely distressed by the play, although we had suspected this might be the case. After watching the play, he left Worcester the following day, having gone out for a while into the Malvern Hills to be alone with his thoughts. He left us a note expressing his dismay and disbelief that Terry could have written such things about her. There was nothing we could do at that stage to make things better, although Terry wrote to him afterwards to say that he should write his own version and call it 'Saint Judy'!

Although we were well supported by friends and family, the location of the theatre was a bit of a handicap, and no one came from London to see the play – well, no one who could offer the show a future, and in some ways we wondered if it had been worth so much effort. Terry had always felt partly responsible for removing me from the comparative safety of the Scottish circuit, hence his desire to help me gain some recognition in the South; at the end of September 1984, he appeared not to have succeeded. I did find a new agent, but that turned out to be a short-lived affair.

At the end of the two-week run, after all the months of work and study, what appeared to be the final curtain had fallen; but we didn't give up hope. We knew as we left Worcester, that we had a play that had been tried and tested and deserved a future. We also had a set of amazing reviews – including this one from the Evesham Advertiser, 'I fully expect *Judy* and Lesley Mackie to be major stars within a year'. So we still had our dreams.

- 14 -

Better luck next time

It had been another life-changing experience, but disappointing that Terry could not be with me throughout the run. He'd been invited to Perth to direct *Amadeus*, and it was an offer he could not refuse. Having played in the show for 14 months, he knew the play inside out, and he was ready for a new challenge. He did, however, manage to get down for our final performance and, after gathering up all my new bits of memorabilia, we hit the road.

Returning to the cottage could have been a bit of an anti-climax after all the months spent there preparing for a project which seemed to be over, but I had another job lined up, and quite a special one at that. I was to play my first Principal Boy in *Jack and the Beanstalk* with Jimmy Logan at the Eden Court Theatre in Inverness. At five foot nothing, the only Principal Boys I could expect to play were Jack and Aladdin, which I suppose has something to do with the fact that Jack is a milk boy, rather than a romantic figure, and because Aladdin is meant to be Chinese – and the Chinese are known to be a petite race! Anyway, having flaunted my legs a bit as Judy Garland, I was more than happy to go and flaunt them again in Inverness. Terry was asked to play the Wicked Uncle but, being a 'pantophobe', he turned it down. As it transpired, the part also included dressing in a comical striped outfit for the 'Busy Bee' sketch, with a total loss of dignity, which would have mortified him. In any case, he wanted to use the time to get on with Judy re-writes – just in case!

Before we headed for the frozen north, we decided to treat ourselves to a few days in Tenerife. My old friend, David McCalister, had a friend who owned a villa in Los Gigantes, and he gave us a contact number so we could book directly. It was unusual to see Los Gigantes in brochures, so we felt that we had found somewhere a little off the beaten track. Not being part of a package deal, we had no bus awaiting our arrival, so we took a taxi all the way from the airport to our apartment. The barren scenery was reminiscent of our first visit to the island of Kos, but we had come for the weather, and we were very lucky in that department.

When you're abroad, there is something appealing about being miles from home, not knowing a soul, and it can be a bit depressing to see familiar faces, however friendly. On our first evening we went for an after-dinner stroll, and as we wended our way back to our villa, a strangely familiar voice behind said, "Hello Lesley", and I just about keeled over when I turned round to face Jimmy Logan and his current lady, Pamela. We joined them for a nightcap, but even in the short time we were with them we had the distinct impression that Pamela found Jimmy rather tiresome. Although his heart was in the right place, Jimmy did tend to pontificate at length, and it was clear to us that this relationship was destined for failure. After that evening we hardly saw them again, but the following day we walked into another old friend, Jackie Farrell, and his wife; so much for being off the beaten track!

As we drove north at the end of November with our glowing brown faces, *Judy* was beginning to feel like a distant memory. The only real interest had come from a director called Ian Judge, but he wanted so many re-writes for a scaled-down production that we felt that we were talking about a new play, and we weren't quite ready for that. I hadn't heard a cheep from my new agent, but as 'Jack' had been planned for months, she was possibly waiting for my return in January to get things moving. We shared 'digs' with our old landlord-turned-actor, Ralph Riach, plus a few other company members. Ralph took on the role of head of the family and kicked us all into touch, harping on about the use and saving of electricity. I'm a bit of a stickler myself, but Ralph's rules were draconian – although with half a dozen in the house, I suppose we needed someone at the helm. The director was Catherine Robins who I had worked with in Kirkcaldy, but on this occasion she and Jimmy were co-directing, and Jimmy had many years of experience in panto, so she didn't get much of a look-in; at one rehearsal I recall him telling her to sit down and let him get on with it.

The company also included George Duffus, who was to be playing my brother, Simple Simon. George worked for Thorntons Property in Dundee, but he also did 'stand up', was very funny, and had an arrangement, whereby he had time off to do panto at Christmas and the occasional series for Grampian television. He had the best of all worlds, earned a lot of money for his freelance work, with the security of a normal well-paid job. As fellow-Dundonians, we had known of each other for years, although our paths had never crossed. His father and mine had Boys' Brigade connections, and he later told me that he'd dreaded meeting me as he had vivid recollections of a little girl reciting *Peter at the Pictures* and singing *I Saw Mummy Kissing Santa Claus* in St Peter's Church Hall, and feared I might be a little precocious. We had an immediate rapport, however, although our new friendship nearly foundered on our second night.

1984, Eden Court, Inverness – Jack and the Beanstalk with Jimmy Logan.

Jimmy and Pamela were treating us to dinner and it was a little surprising when she started on the subject of male infertility and how desperate they were to have a baby, even considering in vitro fertilisation. It was a subject close to our hearts, so we had that in common with them. In the meantime, George arrived with a few friends from the company, and when Jimmy and Pamela left, he offered us all a drink. He'd clearly had a few already and was a bit overbearing, so Terry declined, but I accepted graciously, and George ordered a round. When the drinks arrived, there appeared to be some dissension about the price of two Remy Martins. George owned a hostelry in Fife called the *Pickletillum Inn*, and the prices here did not compare favourably with his own. The argument got out of hand, and we all began to wish we hadn't accepted the drink, especially those who had ordered the brandies! The atmosphere became uncomfortable, and we left as soon as we could. It was disappointing because I had really taken to George, and it now seemed that I'd just have to put up with him for the rest of the run.

The following morning, he was waiting at the stage door to apologise to all and sundry for his reported sins, which he could barely recall. He was particularly contrite with me – probably scared I'd tell my mum and dad! He offered to take Terry and me out for a meal with a vow not to argue about anything, whatever the quality or price, and a more testing promise was never made.

George chose the venue, a newly opened restaurant in the centre of the town. When he tried to order the wine, the waiter explained that there had been a large party in that afternoon and they only had two bottles of wine left, one red and one white. George raised his eyebrows and ordered them both. As the meal progressed, things went from terrible to appalling. The plates were cold, which was a sin punishable by whipping at the Pickletillum, and the food itself was unremarkable. I was offered tartare sauce with my steak, and at the end of the meal, the waiter was quite nonplussed when we ordered a liqueur. He said that he would have to go over to the bar, which was due to close in two minutes, so he would be unlikely to make it. George kept his cool, simply asking him if he might make the effort. As the liqueur glasses were still on order, we were eventually given our drinks in half-pint mugs. Just before we left, a chap materialised from nowhere, looked at George and said,

"You're George Duffus and you're not fuckin' funny!" It was the perfect end to the evening.

I know that George made a special effort that night, but throughout the rest of the run his behaviour was exemplary, and although he enjoyed a drink, which brought out his sometimes-abrasive personality, we never again saw him 'do a Remy'. One day I came into my dressing room and found a package addressed to Terry and myself. It contained a bottle of Remy and two crystal brandy glasses. He was a most generous man, and we remained great friends for the rest of his life.

The Inverness town centre is not greatly inspiring (as Terry discovered on his daily wanderings), but it is surrounded by sensational scenery and history is everywhere. It is no distance to Culloden Moor where Bonnie Prince Charlie's army was decimated in 1746, and the place is full of atmosphere, especially if you drive there in the winter, and of course you are but a few miles from Loch Ness and the monster.

The show itself was quite good I recall, and I enjoyed playing Principal Boy. However, gossip was rife in the company, and it mainly centred around Jimmy and Pamela, who was clearly having a bit of a fling with a crew member. Jimmy knew about it, and they split up at the end of the season which surprised no one, although a few months afterwards they announced their upcoming wedding, which surprised everyone. Even more surprising was the news that they had come back together because of the discovery that she was pregnant with twins, and Jimmy who had wanted children since his first marriage, was over the moon. He was clearly prepared to forgive and forget and was thrilled at the prospect of becoming a father for the first time at the age of 56.

The summer wedding attracted a lot of publicity and when the twins were born in October of that year there were articles in every newspaper under the sun. There was something quite endearing about the fact that it looked as if Jimmy had had a shotgun wedding! He spoke openly and endlessly about the joys of becoming a father and commented on how his son was the spitting image of his own father, Jack Short. We assumed that the 'in vitro' had been successful, but it was only when Jimmy sent out photographs of his children that we realised how cruel nature can be, as the baby boy bore a striking resemblance to a member of the Inverness panto crew. While Jimmy was singing ditties onstage like 'There's twa bairnies in oor hoose, An' I am their Daddie O!', it appeared that he was the only member of Scottish Equity who did not suspect the truth.

It was sad because he became very attached to these children, and when Pamela eventually left him she took the kids. She went to live with the father of the children, settled down for a few years and had another child. Jimmy was heartbroken, and in the ensuing struggle to get access to the twins, the truth came out. As well as the humiliation and the realisation that he had been duped, he had to face the misery of losing his family. As far as the kids were concerned, he became Uncle Jimmy, but eventually he married his next-door neighbour in Helensburgh, a homely mother and grandmother who absolutely doted on him.

As we strutted our stuff at the Eden Court during that Christmas season, Jimmy couldn't have foreseen what the future held, although he did turn up at our digs on Hogmanay, alone but for his dog, and I still have a snap of him fast asleep on a chair with the animal sprawled on his lap.

We have never had so many late nights before or since – not even in Worcester – and if we managed to get to bed by 4am we considered it an early night, and this was despite two shows a day and an apparently life-threatening level of potassium. I was taking a new potassium-sparing drug, Spironolactone, which I had been given just before I departed for Inverness and it appeared to be working, as my level was steadily rising. I've always been an energetic person, but with my new-found staying power in Inverness I began to visualise a future without sleep! Unfortunately, the drug had side effects, so I went to a local doctor to seek help. He expressed interest and amazement re my condition, and when I told him what my original level had been, he said "Aren't you lucky that you didn't pop your clogs?" Wherever I went I was aware that it was of great interest to doctors, who seemed to think I was something of a walking miracle, so it's not surprising that I was willing to try out different drugs to try and find an answer. After a call to the hospital, it was ascertained that I was on far too high a dose for my build, but I never found out whether it was just carelessness or another example of Professor Wynn's willingness to experiment on me in his quest to solve renal mysteries. I came off the drug and my potassium level returned to my own version of normal.

At Christmas Ralph did us proud with a lovely meal and gave each of us a little present. We managed to get down to Dundee to see the folks, and on Boxing Day we all went for an evening drink at the *Pickletillum Inn* in Fife. I was glad that we went across as George had hired an extra barmaid so that he could spend time with us, although none of us dared order a Remy Martin! We never went again, because the pub became a bit of a millstone round his neck, and it was not long afterwards that he was forced to sell.

Pantomimes up north tend to close a little earlier than elsewhere because heavy snow usually arrives around the middle of January, and it can effectively cut off large areas from the outside world. When the roads become impassable, they shut the large snow gates on the A9 and people can be trapped for days, so we finished on January 6th, all escaping just in time.

After a wonderfully carefree time, we returned to find the flat looking like a building site. To give us a bit more privacy, Sid had managed to get a grant to help with the cost of modernising the two flats and making them self-contained. Upstairs, a wall was knocked down to create a dining/kitchen area and a large partition wall was erected downstairs to block off the open staircase. There was also damp proofing and other disruption in the downstairs flat which caused Sid and Lily acute discomfort. They should really have moved out, because what ought to have been a six-week job extended into months, and they had to put up with constant mess, noise and smells with workmen virtually in residence. At the end of each day, Sid did his best to sweep up the rubble and dust; I don't know how he coped. It was all very well for us, as we arrived, took one look at it and headed for the hills – well, for the cottage, which became a real refuge for us, especially at weekends. It was a relief to escape to Inverness when the worst of the work was being done, but if we had known what we were all facing once the workmen departed at the start of January 1985, we might have settled for keeping the flats as they were.

As we surveyed the situation, we felt that, although Sid and Lily had paid a high price, Sid had succeeded in his primary aim, which was to give us more comfort and privacy. We now had the makings of a modern airy flat, although they now had a home which, blocked off from any light, resembled the Black Hole of Calcutta!

We still shared a front door, but inside we had separate doors leading into our respective flats. Some of the workmanship was pretty shoddy and there had been no effort to clear up any of the mess they had created. It was incredible that the work was passed as 'fit for purpose' by the council, and we wondered if the people handing out the grants were hand in glove with various dubious companies – jobs for the boys, we thought! But there was no going back, and we had to face the daunting prospect of getting out our scrapers and pots of paint. We had nothing exciting on the work front, no money, and all we could look forward to were endless weeks of grime and filth.

There were a few social occasions to distract from the gloom, including an invitation from my new agent to attend her New Year drinks soirée, and I was relieved that she had made contact at last. When I arrived, she said how nice it was to see me, and she hoped that all her clients would turn up because the chances were that she wouldn't see any of them again until the same time next year, which set little alarm bells ringing in my head. Looking around, I was aware that there were a few 'big names' on her books, Julie Walters and Maureen Lipman to name but two. I knew no one and felt very awkward as I stood sipping a drink and talking to the dog. I was ready to pounce on the first person who said "Hello" when I spotted a man standing alone with his drink, so I gravitated towards him.

He introduced himself as actor, Leslie Grantham, saying he was new to the business but had just landed a plum part in a new 'soap' called *Eastenders*! He said he had been in the army, and I discovered later that he had served a number of years in prison for the murder of a taxi driver in Germany. This was probably typical of the gritty, realistic casting on the series under the guiding hand of Julia Smith, whom I recalled meeting a few years before when she was casting the nursing series, *Angels*; she wanted actors of the exact age that it said in the script. When I said I was 26, she actually said "I want a girl of 23 with the mind of a 23 year old". It's a wonder she didn't want a real nurse! Leslie Grantham became famous as 'Dirty Den' and eventually infamous for living up to his name!

I had a pleasant chat with Maureen Lipman; I told her about *Judy* and our hopes for the future, and she in turn talked about her husband, Jack Rosenthal, who had also written a musical, *Barmitzvah Boy*, encountering many pitfalls while trying to put it on.

It was a brief conversation, but strangely prophetic because our next meeting was 18 months later on August 7th, 1986, the opening night of *Wonderful Town* in which she was playing the leading role.

I did not set eyes on my agent again for eight months, but tried not to dwell on that, as we were otherwise occupied with domestic travails and had to get our shoulders to the wheel. If we hadn't found it all so depressing, it might almost have been funny, but it was a hellish spring. Disaster struck at every turn, although we were largely responsible for the mayhem. Under the tutelage of my Aunt Bessie, we started by trying to paper the ceiling in the lounge, which is a tricky job for a decorator, never mind two novices. I will never forget us trying to hold a long piece of wallpaper as we gingerly climbed our respective ladders. We hoped to stick it up in a straight line across the ceiling, but we ended up on the floor like *Laurel and Hardy* with the gummed paper around our necks. After days of struggle and many phone calls to Bessie, we gave up on it and just gave the ceiling a coat of paint.

I took on most of the menial jobs while Terry did the painting and papering, and after weeks of living in my old jumpsuit and woolly hat, Terry christened me Dougie! I stripped the bathroom of its ghastly wallpaper and discovered another ten layers – so that took a fortnight. I then turned my attention to the staircase, as Terry was convinced that the natural wood would look better than the existing red paint, so we borrowed a blowtorch, and it took me the best part of three weeks to burn it all off. It was painstaking, backbreaking, smelly work, and after examining the results we decided that it looked better before, so I repainted it salmon pink!

It was all so dispiriting, and our savings were dwindling fast. Even although we paid no rent for the upstairs flat to Terry's folks in London, it had become difficult, nay impossible, to support two homes and even the simple matter of travelling to the cottage was becoming a luxury we could ill afford. We had no choice, and at the beginning of March, with much regret, we decided to put the cottage on the market, in the knowledge that we would soon have a small, attractive, self-contained flat.

Terry applied himself to putting up shelves, which fell down many times before staying put, and our evenings were often shattered by a crash from the lounge. He took great pains to follow the MFI instructions and construct a wardrobe for the bedroom, but after five days the thing stood before us with most of the pieces facing the wrong way. Terry had been looking at the plan back to front and, while I sobbed, he started all over again. I sobbed a lot during that spring. We finished around the middle of May and the relief was overwhelming; we had slept so long with our furniture piled high around us in our bedroom, that it was wonderful to be able to place all our bits and pieces in their correct locations. We were happy with the flat but had not yet sold the cottage.

Our prospects changed a little when I was asked to do a Scottish tour of *Piaf* under the TAG banner, an offshoot of the Glasgow Citizens Theatre. I had a meeting in early April with the director, Ian Brown, to discuss production details, and although I knew I would have a battle on my hands about whether Edith was to be a Cockney sparrow or a Glaswegian one (cockney being my accent of choice, as the equivalent for a play set in a capital city; London equals Paris). I was on the point of accepting when we had a call from John David, artistic director of the Bristol Old Vic Company. He had seen *Judy* at Worcester and wanted to include it in his Autumn season at Bristol's Theatre Royal. There was no choice to make, so with the usual remorse about losing a job, I turned down the Scottish tour, which went ahead with a somewhat larger Glasgow 'sparrow'! Terry got down to his re-writes with renewed vigour, and I returned to my ritual of visiting Brian and his film footage and re-familiarised myself with Miss Garland.

We had an offer for the cottage on June 23rd, just in the nick of time to sort out our financial deficits. We had drawn the last of our savings from the building society, and although we didn't have an overdraft, as far as I was concerned we were stoney broke. We borrowed money from mum and dad to cover our modest tax bill, but once we had the offer on the cottage we decided to take a chance and book a holiday in Crete. Oh, how we loved our holidays, and much to my parent's amazement we flew off on July 2nd. After a lazy fortnight, we returned to face some irritating delays. There were a few nerve-racking weeks before the date of completion, which was only just before the onset of the Bristol rehearsals. We packed our things, hired a van for the removal and after a double trip on August 23rd, Terry was so weary that he scratched one side of it as he attempted to squeeze through a pair of bollards only a quarter of a mile from the flat in Purves Road. We drove to Banbury to deposit the van, before spending our last night at *Wild Thyme*.

We only had a few days left to unpack in London; we now had two of everything at the flat, although that could be sorted out later. With some of the profits from the sale, we bought our first brand new car, and arrived in Bristol as if we were 'Erchie'! A few weeks earlier we had been penniless, and here we were, not giving a thought for the morrow. At least we now had a fully refurbished and self-contained flat, but the cottage had been our dream, and we'd only had it for three years. Later, we would probably miss it, but at that particular moment we didn't have the time. *Judy* had been given a second chance, and we were determined to make the most of it.

- 15 -

Hello Yellow Brick Road

We started rehearsals on September 2nd, and we already knew that we were going on to Greenwich Theatre after Bristol for an eight-week run over the Christmas period. Our company was strong, and we had a terrific team of young actors, but our biggest bonus was in having Lewis Cowen back on board. He had been one of the 'Swan' company, and once again he took on the two key roles of Louis B Mayer and Sid Luft. Besides being an excellent actor, it was lovely for me to have someone in the company who I knew and trusted. John David did not have the natural flair of John Doyle, although he did have a brilliant flash of inspiration, which got us off to a great start. The play opened with a section of the *Born in a Trunk* sequence from the film *A Star is Born* before flashing back to Judy's beginnings at MGM. He suggested that I start the play with my back to the audience so that when I spun round and the spotlight hit me full on, the audience would be shocked by my apparent likeness to Garland.

Rehearsals were disrupted by a succession of interviews for various newspapers and magazines, radio and television programmes, but we couldn't complain, as this was what the show needed and what we had hoped for. The problem was that I was the one who had to go to all the publicity events, and if I wasn't off doing an interview, I was in the rehearsal room or the Wardrobe Department. Everything was being made from scratch, so there were endless costume fittings; it was a hectic schedule. Luckily, Terry was around for most of the rehearsal period, as he had to be on hand for any re-writes that might be required and to ferry me to and from interviews. One day I was summoned to Greenwich to cavort around in the park whilst photographers snapped away, which was rather fun – especially when one of the tabloid papers referred to me as the 'lovely, leggy Lesley Mackie'! I also did a *Woman's Hour* for BBC Bristol Radio alongside Penelope Leach, expert on child-rearing; little did I imagine that within a year I would be studying her books! One night, Terry and I left Bristol for 137, Purves Road, so that we could be collected at 5am the following morning for a joint appearance on BBC Breakfast Television. That was the worst one, as neither my voice nor appearance were at their best at the crack of dawn; a gruelling schedule to say the least, but we were delighted to be getting so much publicity.

Cathy also had a difficult time because although she would have liked to choose her own musicians, she had little say in the matter as the Theatre Royal used the services of a 'fixer'. As well as his fee for procuring the individual members of the band, the 'fixer' in question appointed himself as bass player, so it was quite a lucrative job. He was also involved in any decision regarding the band or the music, and as far as he was concerned she was only a woman, so she had a problem maintaining authority which was very frustrating for her. She did her best, but the band was not perfect, and if she could have swapped just one of them, I think it would have been the bass player!

We stayed with a lady social worker called Mary Wilkins, who had helped Dawn through the aftermath of Charles' suicide back in 1977. It was a comfortable house within walking distance of the theatre, which was just as well, because Terry was on the point of leaving again for Perth – this time to direct *One for the Road*. He managed to stay for the opening night – and what a night that was! Reg and David came down, and booked into a B&B. They had followed *Judy*'s journey from 'The Swan' and continued to follow it throughout its ups and downs. They were witness to an ever-changing script and seemed more pained by the alterations than we were; they saw the fantasy ending based on *The Wizard of Oz* bite the dust, along with Mickey Deans, husband Number 5. Worst for them was the loss of *Swanee*, which had been the finale in Worcester. We gave it one more try on the opening night in Bristol, but ultimately we all felt that it shouldn't follow *Over the Rainbow*, as we wanted the audience to be left with the poignant image of Judy sitting on the edge of the stage singing 'Why, oh why can't I?', so by the second night *Swanee* had gone.

The opening night was amazing, especially because I was a stranger in Bristol and couldn't count on the support of a familiar audience. Terry spent the entire evening pacing up and down, trying to gauge their reactions and hardly watching the show at all. When they gave us a standing ovation, his legs gave way and he all but collapsed in a heap, or so he said! Everyone was over the moon and the following day the Press were just as enthusiastic. One of my favourite reviews was broadcast on the local radio station, *Severn Sound*... 'If you don't get down to the Bristol Theatre Royal before October 19th', the critic said, 'you will be missing the best British musical for years!' Personally speaking, I loved the review of Eric Shorter, who wrote, 'Miss Mackie is a revelation, a reincarnation, a blazing theatrical personality'.

1985, Bristol Old Vic Theatre – Judy with Lewis Cowen and Michael Gardiner.

He wrote for the *Daily Telegraph* and was loyal to us right to the end, even nominating the play for the London Theatre Critic's Award. After the euphoria of the first night there was no let up, as I was straight to the local radio studio the next morning for a chat about 'the night before'. Fame at last!

Although *Judy* went down a storm, I was suffering from the natural anxiety that comes when playing a major and demanding role; you are only as good as your last performance, and many an actor has gone through agonies with nerves, even Sir Laurence Olivier! I was once again left without Terry to offer support and I've always liked him to be within shouting distance. I had difficulty eating, which I assumed to be a nervous reaction to all the stress and excitement, and I enlisted the help of the theatre doctor, Dr Sluglett, who was very supportive, even driving me to the supermarket to do some shopping on one occasion. My potassium was still rather low, and he was, as everyone seemed to be, very interested in my 'condition'. He thought I was a rare specimen and drove me to the hospital one day to meet some of his friends, who took some blood and asked a lot of questions.

1985, Bristol Old Vic Theatre – Judy.

It was frustrating not to be enjoying my food, as I needed sustenance, not only for the potassium level but in order to make that nightly journey up the Yellow Brick Road, but my adrenalin seemed to be getting me through. After the show, we sometimes went to a lovely little Italian restaurant across the road, although I was unable to partake of much of the cuisine on offer.

Many people ventured down to Bristol, including my new agent. I had not seen her since her January 'soirée', and I had already decided that she and I would have to part company. She was proving to be of little help as far as the Greenwich arrangements were concerned, although she was probably powerless as regards the £125 I was to be paid per week, which was even less than Bristol. I had no experience outside a repertory one, and I didn't realise that around the perimeter of London, most theatres paid measly money.

1985, Bristol Old Vic Theatre – Judy with Michael Gardiner.

Apart from a lack of subsidy, I suppose it was something to do with the fact that actors are desperate to appear in London, even if they have to pay for the privilege. And it got worse, right into the new millennium with thousands of actors working on the fringe for little more than the cost of their train fares. In 2014 Equity brought in their *Professionally Made Professionally Paid* campaign in order to try and address the situation.

What finished me off was a call to inform me that they were unable to provide me with my own dressing room. As well as having numerous costumes to hang up, I needed a little peace before a show, not to mention my reluctance to be in close contact with others at a time of year when there would be a few colds around. The best that was on offer was a corner of the 'Wardrobe', so in the end I had to write to Alan Strachan, the resident director, and put my case to him. After my heartfelt plea, they cleared a room, and I ended up with a reasonable space.

1985, Bristol Old Vic Theatre – Judy.

Before leaving Bristol, Terry had an approach from *Litag*, an agency based in Bremen. They wanted to translate *Judy* for Germany, and this was the beginning of quite a few foreign productions in Sweden, Denmark, Austria, New Zealand and even Japan. The royalties would provide a little cushion for us in the future – but the most exciting approach came from the Henry Fonda Theatre in Los Angeles. Having seen the Bristol production, they sent a letter proposing that *Judy* be part of their season the following spring. The other plays were to include Rex Harrison, Harold Pinter, Claudette Colbert, and they wanted me to play Judy with American actors taking the other roles, but as our hopes were still pinned on the West End of London, we were not able to make a commitment at this stage. I'd hate to have missed out on the chance of a lifetime, so I like to think that we'd have come up against American Equity, which might not have been totally convinced that I was the only actress capable of playing one of their American icons. There would doubtless have been objections from American actresses too – not to mention The Garland Estate, Group V and Sid Luft.

It was thrilling to be asked, but we had no time to worry about it, as during the Bristol run the London producer, Bill Kenwright, came to see us, and afterwards in my dressing room said that, if the timing was right, it might well have a future in the West End. He said that 'Life after Greenwich' would depend on a suitable London theatre becoming available at the end of our Christmas season. It was an exciting prospect, but we knew that we had to pack 'em in for eight weeks at Greenwich to turn that possibility into a viable proposition. He also said that something would have to be done about the band, and I realised he was talking about ditching Cathy. Judy Garland always had a male musical director, but losing Cathy was not something we had even considered, and I felt very uncomfortable getting my head round that.

We already felt bad about John Doyle, without whom Terry might never have written the play – but Bill was talking about 'After Greenwich', so we didn't have to face the problem yet, and it was just exciting to know that the show might have a future. Bristol had done everything we had hoped for, and we'd made the most of this second chance with October 19th, the last night, every bit as exciting as the first. Having just opened *One for the Road,* Terry was there on this occasion, and it was made more special because a family party, including my folks, had travelled all the way down from Scotland to share in the excitement and see us enjoying a bit of success.

There was a short break prior to Greenwich so, as well as a bit of re-writing, we decided to have a few days in Dundee to see the family, but before heading north we had a very important appointment at the Margaret Pyke Clinic. Although *Judy* had taken precedence over everything else for the past few months, we had still been trying and hoping for a baby, but were coming to the end of the road. Our last option was to consider using donor sperm, so we had a meeting where everything was fully explained, and we felt reassured that great care would be taken to find a match for Terry as regards colouring, build etc. They would mix the donor sperm with his, so that there was the possibility that any baby conceived might be our very own. They had to be sure that both partners were happy to take that final step. It was a huge decision, but we weighed things up and decided to go ahead with it, and on December 4th we were put on the waiting list.

The interviews continued, and I was even flown up to Grampian Television to chat to Frank Gilfeather about our 'baby', which was still *Judy*. I recall Frank saying, "It's great to be chatting to someone who's on the way up, as we usually get folk when they're on the way down." I could only hope that he was right! It was a packed few weeks, but despite the various pressures we agreed to go to Liverpool and do a 'Piaf' cabaret for a Jewish organisation. Goodness knows who they were or how they knew about us, but on the Sunday, only a day before we were due to start rehearsals in Greenwich, Terry, Cathy and I drove for four and a half hours up to Liverpool to do our 'spot', and it was quite an ordeal.

The guests were seated at trestle tables in a very long hall and the 'stage' was a tiny, raised dais placed centrally on one side of the dining area. We had guests straight ahead of us and to either side, and in order to play to the entire audience I had to keep my head in perpetual motion, as if at a tennis match. Cathy and Terry were in virtual darkness, so they could barely see what they were doing as regards the music or the narration, and as we waited nervously to begin, one of the organisers came up to us to say that they were not an easy audience and had once booed Arthur Askey off the stage before he had even finished! I think that this was supposed to be some sort of encouragement so that we wouldn't feel too bad if we got the same treatment.

The audience commented loudly on Terry's narration, and phrases like 'Aw shame!' and other sympathetic noises accompanied his tale of Piaf's tragic life. Terry didn't take long to get the message that they were of limited attention span, and he cut his script as he went along, giving me little chance for a breather between numbers! Much to our surprise, we were quite a hit, which was a great relief, as we then had to face another four-and-a-half-hour drive back to London. We chatted about it all the way and still recall that endless day with a mixture of amusement and incredulity. Considering what we were about to face in Greenwich, it was ludicrous that we did it at all and it would be quite a few years before we returned to the cabaret circuit.

It was in Bristol that I met the charming agent, Larry Dalzell, who saw *Judy* and expressed an interest in taking me on as a client, and I'd now made the decision to go with him. I knew that my present agent would not be happy about my leaving her just before we were due to open near London; even so, I did not expect quite the reaction that I got. She was incensed, and in a letter she regaled me with a list of all the friends and dignitaries who she had invited to come along and see my performance, and what a betrayal I had perpetrated. I weighed up the past year, and the lack of a single interview; although it wasn't easy for me, I stuck to my guns and we parted company. I was now with Larry Dalzell, a real gentleman and a genuinely nice man.

As we pondered the future, Terry and I reflected on the content of *Judy*, and felt that we were on safe ground. He had been thorough in his research, and there was nothing in the play that had not been written about elsewhere in some form or another. The events were real, but the dialogue was all his. His most inventive device was in using two Hollywood gossips, Hedda Hopper and Louella Parsons, to comment on the action, and as far as those two ladies were concerned, every line bar one, 'Tempus sure does fugit', was Terry's. Some of the critics credited all the wit to Hedda and Louella themselves, but having read some of those old Hollywood journals I can vouch for the fact that Terry's dialogue was funnier than anything they ever wrote!

Rehearsals were brief, only a few days, and the biggest problem we had to face at Greenwich was the size of the stage. In Worcester and Bristol, the five-piece band played in the wings until the end of Act 1 and were then trucked onto the stage to set the scene for Garland's concert career. It was a wonderful effect, but at Greenwich there was no room for them in the wings or on the stage; there was barely room for the actors! The band ended up underneath the stage, which created all sorts of problems with the sound system, and meant that we had no *visual* contact with them. Our biggest headache though, was the lack of space in the wings. Our Bristol set was too wide for the space available in Greenwich, and it ended up almost flush against one of the side walls. This meant that all entrances and exits had to be made from the other side, where there was all of four feet to spare – and even this limited space had to accommodate all the furniture from the show, which was piled up around us and wheeled out as required. I found myself having to change costume on top of beds, under tables and in cupboards. At one point, I had to clamber over a double bed, crawl under a curtain and enter, looking serene, to sing *Better Luck Next Time*.

1985, Greenwich Theatre – Judy with Adeen Fogle, Paul Jeary, Scott Cherry, Alison Skilbeck and Paul Rattigan.

At the end of a long and difficult day of technical rehearsals, Terry and I went home to Kensal Rise, and I popped round the corner for a couple of fish suppers. On my way back, I suddenly sensed someone behind me, and knew I was about to be mugged; an arm went round my throat, and a husky voice muttered, "Don't scream, or I'll hurt you". Unwisely, I screamed as loudly as I could, and was pushed roughly to the ground; in the ensuing scramble, he escaped with my handbag. I surveyed the scattered remains of my fish suppers and, with a bit of help from a heavily pregnant West Indian woman, I staggered towards the flat to pour out my tale of woe.

After phoning the police, Terry went back downstairs to see if he could find any of the items from my handbag. My specs had gone flying as my assailant ran off, and I knew that they must be nearby. There hadn't been much money in my bag, but there were all sorts of things like my bank card, cheque book, and address book, and their loss was going to cause me a lot of hassle. Terry had just located my specs which were lying in the gutter by the kerb, when a car pulled in alongside him; he heard a crunch, and my specs were no more. After thanking God for His lack of divine intervention, he went off down the road to see if he could find any witnesses to the incident. A couple of blokes said they had seen a boy run into a group of houses just opposite the chip shop, but we decided to go home and pursue our private investigation the following morning.

Meanwhile the police arrived, and I was able to tell them that my attacker was a young man of West Indian origin and wearing a woolly hat. They weren't surprised, commenting that it was 'endemic' in the West Indian population, and as most of the population of Kensal Rise were young West Indians in woolly hats it was not going to help at an identity parade. They were very nice, but they didn't hold out much hope, and we went to bed quite shattered.

Next morning, we went along to the row of houses which had been pointed out and discovered that there was only one West Indian family living there, and I was quite nervous as I approached a young black boy who was cleaning windows outside one of the houses. I instinctively felt that it must be him, but told him the story, and he said, somewhat predictably, that he had neither seen nor heard anything. He was sweating and appeared to be quite jumpy, which might have been a response to our implied accusation, but he said he would look out for discarded bits and pieces from my bag. There was no more to be done, because we had a dress rehearsal to attend. As a postscript to the tale, Sid suggested that we ought to put in a claim for damages to the Criminal Injuries Board; over a year later when we had all but forgotten about it, I received compensation of over £400, which more than covered all the items I had lost, including the fish suppers!

Uppermost in my mind throughout the ordeal had been the thought that he might squeeze my throat too hard, and I would be unable to sing at the first performance, but despite a sore neck I managed the dress rehearsals, and the opening night went surprisingly smoothly with the help of a lot of adrenalin. Our euphoria evaporated somewhat on the second night when things seemed to fall apart. Terry rushed backstage during the interval to express his dismay and said that if something was not done to improve the sound, the curtain would not go up on the second act. Whenever a mike was supposed to be on, it was off (and vice versa), the radio mike crackled against my various frocks, but we struggled through the rest of the show after Bill Kenwright gave us his word that a sound man would be in the following morning to sort it all out. Gradually things improved, and although it was never easy working in such cramped conditions, I had my own dressing room, the show was a success, and we opened to the best reviews yet.

Everyone came to Greenwich, and we played to packed houses for the entire run; we began to wonder if there would be anyone left to see it if we did find a West End Theatre. Even Benny Green came in one evening, and Terry joined him for a drink before the show. Benny was an old friend, master of many subjects, with an encyclopædic knowledge of American popular music and little faith in the Brits where American musicals were concerned. Terry watched with trepidation as Benny headed for the auditorium. He was never a man to mince his words, and at the end of the show, Terry went back to meet him, expecting the worst. He was astounded to find Benny in tears, overwhelmed with the experience, and the review that he gave us was more thrilling than any other, because we knew what it took to win him over. He confessed to us later that he didn't know how he would have faced us if he had hated it, but because of our friendship he wouldn't have written a review had it not been favourable. His review said: 'Judy contains the most startlingly accomplished musical-dramatic performance I can recall by any actress not world famous' – and it made my year!

Terry and I concentrated on the show, and only the show. There were no productions in Perth or elsewhere for him to direct, so it was third time lucky as I had him around all the time. I was able to laze about during the days, writing cards and preparing for Christmas, but nothing too strenuous that would take an ounce of the energy I was preserving for the performances. I knew that the success of the show depended largely on me keeping fit and well, and in an effort to avoid colds and infections, I became quite extreme in my precautions.

1985, Greenwich Theatre – Judy.

Travelling down to Greenwich by train one afternoon for an interview, I sat with my coat collar up so that it was covering my mouth and nose, just in case there were any germs floating around. As I left the train, a lady approached and asked if I was Lesley Mackie. "I thought it was you," she said, "Were you afraid you might be recognised?" Chance would have been a fine thing. It transpired she was the journalist I was on my way to meet, so when I explained my reason for looking like a member of MI6 she used my 'cold phobia' as the main thrust of her article.

Bill was in and out of the theatre, always talking about which West End theatre was the current favourite for a possible transfer, but nothing was certain. We had heard quite a bit about Bill and his ways and means, and there was one story, told by Bill himself that, in his early days as a producer, he had, at one stage, reached rock bottom and couldn't even afford the cost of stamps to send out important mail. At this point he had a brainwave, removing and re-using all the stamps from the many enclosed envelopes sent by actors applying for a job! Ruthless, but it was about survival, I guess.

As things began to hot up, a transfer to the West End became a distinct possibility and we realised that Bill was keen to make some changes to the show; for a start, he was still determined that Cathy had to go. But he was right, we had to have a male musical director (as Judy had always done) and the band would be onstage and visible in London so there was nothing we could do about it. We were all in the dark about possible transfer dates and by the time it was official, Cathy had accepted another job. If only we'd known that Cathy was destined for a very successful career, we needn't have worried so much. It was a surprise to us that a few of the younger actors playing Judy's 'Boyfriends' and numerous other roles, decided to call it a day after Greenwich. They didn't want to be tied down for a year, but we were disappointed because they were great lads. Bill was now speaking about a 20% improvement in all areas for the West End, but we knew it would be hard to replace the boys.

Throughout the run, and in preparation for a possible transfer, I did the usual batch of interviews, the most important one being *The Gloria Hunniford Show*. Surprisingly, I found her a little intimidating, and this, coupled with the height of the guest's chair, which towered strangely above her own, made me feel quite anxious, and I think I spoke even faster than usual. At the end of the interview my 'Piaf' was mentioned (I was already laying the ground for a revival), and a snippet of *No Regrets* brought things to a close. Not realising that my microphone was still open, I blurted out, "Oh sorry Gloria, I was like a hen on hot bricks!" – and I have it on tape for posterity!

Just before we ended our run on February 8th, we received the news that we had been waiting for, and heard that the Strand Theatre was going to be our next home, and with a bit of luck, our home for some months to come. On our way down to Greenwich one day, we decided to go via the Strand, where we parked the car, and in the heart of London's West End, we looked up at the theatre, picturing my name in lights, and dreaming about long runs, fame, and untold wealth – all just around the corner.

1985, Greenwich Park.

- 16 -

The road gets rougher

It was an extraordinary situation. This was my first West End job, and instead of serving an apprenticeship I was facing the prospect of playing a huge leading role, possibly the biggest part I would ever have in my entire life. It was as if all my years in repertory theatre had paid off in one fell swoop. It was exciting of course, but the excitement was accompanied by a stomach-churning sense of responsibility. Frank Gilfeather up at Grampian Television was quick off the mark again and Terry and I were filmed walking down the Strand and chatting inside the theatre.

Facing the prospect of a long run, we decided that it was now or never as far as a short holiday was concerned, so we booked a week in Los Gigantes. Rehearsals were scheduled to start on March 3rd, but there were still many details to hammer out, and it was not plain sailing. My new agent, Larry Dalzell, and I had discussed what we considered reasonable terms, and he came up with £850 per week and my name up in lights! Bill offered £750 and Judy Garland's name up in lights! He justified this by saying that I was an unknown and wouldn't put bums on seats, but from our point of view I would remain so if I didn't have prominent billing. Larry said that we should hold out for our terms, and we trusted him, so decided to go along with his instinct. It was a bold and possibly foolhardy stance to take, but as there was no other contender for the role of Judy Garland we thought that we were in a strong position.

Just before we were due to fly off, Larry phoned to say that Bill had called our bluff and cancelled the production. There was no going back now, we had determined our course, and we could not ask Larry to backtrack and accept Bill's original offer, which was a lot more than I had ever earned in my life! As realisation dawned, we took in the enormity of what we had thrown away. Norman Boyack drove us to the airport on the Thursday. He had been with Bill the previous evening and said that he was feeling very stroppy about things: "Who do they think they are?" and so on; we were beginning to wonder ourselves, and Norman seemed as bereft as we were. Although he wasn't a literary agent, he had agreed to look after

Terry's interests; he had become so involved over the months that, not only was he planning to put his own money into the production, he was also named on all documents as Associate Producer. We started our holiday in an atmosphere of despair, but on our first afternoon there was a call from Larry to say that Bill had changed his mind and was now offering £1,000 per week – and my name in lights! We managed to enjoy the rest of our holiday, although we knew there might be other battles to be fought.

As soon as we got back, however, I got off to a bad start in another direction entirely; I had an interview with a chap from the *Liverpool Post*, as he'd heard rumours that the show had fallen through with battles between producer and 'star', and faced with his friendly enquiries I filled him in with a few details. I suppose it was foolhardy as Bill hails from Liverpool and was not going to take too kindly to adverse publicity on his home territory, and when the article was published he sent us a note expressing his anger and hurt. Things always look worse in print, but it was a useful lesson to learn.

We still had a few nagging doubts about other aspects of the production. Priorities were different as director, designer and writer fought to maintain standards, while Bill fought to keep to a tight budget which was £150,000; even back then, this sum was reckoned to be ludicrously low for a musical. Terry had hoped to be at the auditions, but with all the uncertainty before we flew off they were postponed and then took place when we were too far away to be involved. We managed to get three of the original Worcester actors into the show: Lewis Cowen, David Baukham and Paul Milton, but there were still three 'Boyfriends' to cast. Our Bristol lads had been the absolute proof – if we needed it – that Judy's 'Boyfriends', who had to dance, sing and act were best played by actors who could move well, and we were worried that they might go for boys who were, first and foremost, dancers. On our return we were shown a cast list, minus one, and the final dancer/actor was only found in time for the second day of rehearsals.

In the costume department things remained the same, apart from a couple of new frocks for Hedda and Louella, and as for the set, we were still stuck with quite a gloomy Act 1. Terry had specified a soundstage, but the overall blackness of cameras and flats created a depressing effect and was not the Hollywood that we had envisaged. It was not until some time later when Terry had seen the Swedish production, which had a wonderful glitzy set, that we had a clearer picture of how it could have looked. As for the music: before rehearsals started, I managed to do a bit of work with Alexander (Sandy) Faris who, along with David Redstone, was writing new arrangements for some of the songs. They were all good, but although I took a little while to realise it, *You're Nearer* was special, and I always wished we could have thanked Sandy for that, but our paths never crossed again.

On the second day of rehearsals we were invited to one of Bill's opening nights at the Sadler's Wells Theatre. *Jeanne*, a musical about Joan of Arc, had been budgeted at £400,000, which was clearly one of the reasons why we were underfunded. As the show progressed, everyone's embarrassment was apparent; the music sounded derivative, the lyrics uninspired, and the leading lady sported a wig which looked like a cross between a badger and a Davy Crockett hat! In a final tableau, tied to a stake and with flames lapping around her, she sang a song where she pondered on what the future held for her. All this was reflected in the reviews, and the show closed after five weeks, which was tough on the talented cast, but rotten luck for us as well as Bill lost the entire investment, which didn't bode well for the future of *Judy*.

We forged on with rehearsals, interviews and tying up a few loose ends. I had a dozen changes, so a good 'dresser' was of paramount importance, and we found one in Rosie Bentinck. She was a rock, and I certainly needed her support throughout the troubles I was soon to face. The technical rehearsal went smoothly, apart from one little blip; we started with eight musicians, which became seven once Terry blew his top about the synthesiser. It seemed that no show could be without one, but he thought it had no place onstage in a period play like *Judy,* but I was quite sorry for the musician concerned, who quietly packed up his instrument and departed.

Our preview performances went very well, and the opening night was unforgettable. There was a standing ovation, lots of cheering and numerous curtain calls, and the atmosphere backstage after the show was euphoric with so many friends and family there. My memories of it all are a little hazy, and it is one of my regrets that

I didn't manage to see and take note of everyone who had come to support us. Mum and dad were down from Dundee and having a wonderful time, made even more memorable by their taxi journey from Kings Cross. It turned out that the cabbie had been to a preview performance and had loved the show so much that, when he discovered that I was their daughter, he refused to accept their fare – not the sort of story you would normally associate with London taxi-drivers!

1986, Strand – Judy with Lewis Cowen.

After the opening night party at *Stringfellows*, where the mood was celebratory with Bill and I dancing to '60s music, we moved on to *Le Privé*, an exclusive nightclub which had recently opened, to round the evening off. As part of its launch, they had invited several

West End performers to join for a year, free of charge; Terry and I were delighted to take advantage of the offer – although no one else seemed to have done so as the club was decidedly quiet. The service was overwhelming – white glove treatment, and as we were usually the only people there, we always had the undivided attention of the host, David Cunningham. He sat with us, not allowing us to pay for anything, which became embarrassing, rather than relaxing.

On the opening night, as we arrived, David came over with a cake which had been specially made for the occasion, and a copy of a rare vinyl album of Judy's as an opening night gift. He did us proud that evening, plying us with smoked salmon sandwiches, making us feel like celebrities and the folks were suitably impressed. By this time I was feeling nauseous; I had been aware of it earlier in Stringfellows but had put it down to first-night nerves. When I awoke the following morning, I was still feeling under the weather. I had a couple of radio interviews lined up, but all I wanted to do was spend the morning in bed. I had no choice, however, as our show was now up and running, and it was going to be a roller coaster ride from now on.

The reviews for *Judy* were excellent in the main... 'not recently have I witnessed such a spontaneous reception... if a star isn't born here, then there's no justice'. Unfortunately, there weren't enough of them; almost every newspaper had reviewed the show at Greenwich and getting them to come back again proved difficult. An added factor was that our opening had coincided with Easter, and many critics, as well as their readers, appeared to have gone off for a long weekend.

We expected Sheridan Morley (critic, biographer and playwright) back to haunt us, and he didn't fail us. He'd seen the show in Bristol and Greenwich, and had, apparently, been none too complimentary on both occasions. He was writing for *Punch* magazine at that time but, not content with that, he also sent one of his reviews to the *International Herald Tribune,* which gave it a wider audience. I even had a letter from the man who was unlucky enough to land beside him in Bristol, warning me that he feared a bad review, so restless and irritating had Morley been throughout the show. When he turned up again at the Strand Theatre, a friend reported that he sniggered childishly throughout, seeming to be more interested in watching his companion work on amusing cartoon sketches of myself and others in the cast. Although I never saw any of his reviews at the time, many years later I was thumbing through a library book which contained all his notable reviews of the '80s, and there it was; while it grieved me to see it in print, it wasn't as bad as I had feared and certainly not as personal.

The reviews were the least of my worries. As the days wore on, my health deteriorated, and my nausea was constant. My stomach was severely upset, and I was eventually unable to face food at all. Because of the constant interviews I suffered it for far too long, and by the time I went to the doctor my weight had dropped dramatically and I felt sicker than I have ever done in my life. Dr Coffman came to the flat one Saturday morning when I was so ill I could barely sit up in bed. He thought I had severe gastroenteritis, but I still dragged myself from my bed and headed in to do the two shows. After further investigations, food poisoning was diagnosed, and I was told to stick to fluids until the bug had left my system. The hospital was keen to know the source of the infection, but by this time I had been suffering for almost three weeks, and I couldn't remember where I had snatched that lethal sandwich just prior to the opening night. I knew I had to go on at all costs, as for some reason best known to the management (probably a financial one!), I had no official understudy which was normally unheard of in the West End.

My biggest regret was that we never managed to complete the album of the show, and we came so near. We made a start in the week leading up to what I came to know as 'Black Friday'. On the Monday, Terry and I made our way to *Redan Recording Studios*. The band parts were to be laid down first, but a throat infection was brewing so I just croaked my way through some of the numbers to help set the tempi. I recall that Monday vividly because, after an emergency appointment with Norman Punt, the famous throat specialist, who gave me a massive dose of antibiotics (which, in my opinion, had the added effect of killing off what little resistance I had left), Terry made an announcement about my infection before the evening performance; whether it was sympathy or what, I got a wonderful standing ovation at the end, which was a great morale booster.

The following morning Terry went on ahead to the studios as I could barely rise from my bed. He filled in until I arrived, and I stayed until all the instrumentals were 'in the can'. All that remained was to get the 'vocals' and the piano down, but I knew it would be a few days before my voice was in any fit state to record, so we decided to fix a date once things improved; by the following Monday, Bill had pulled the plug on the album. He was jittery about the poor business we were doing, and didn't want to pay the costs of releasing an album if we only had a few more weeks to run – so near, yet so far. To try and salvage something from the whole affair, I asked Jon Millar of Redan studios if I could have a copy of the backing tracks as a memento. It crossed my mind that one day I might get together with a pianist and add the missing parts to what we had, which would have given me a lovely souvenir of the show. He went to enormous trouble to get a tape together, but when I heard it I couldn't believe my ears; not only had he included my croaky rasping, but Terry's vocal contributions as well, which shattered any hope I had of adding my voice at a later date. At the end of the run, all we had was a tape recording done on a random evening and not representative of the quality of the show. I still feel sad not to have a professional recording of our performance at the Strand.

As the nightmare week progressed, I vividly remember the Thursday evening. I was playing the most demanding role of a lifetime and feeling fit to drop. Twice I had to stop during the show, once during a song, and in the middle of a long speech to the audience, recounting Judy's early days at MGM studios, I found myself telling them about my own plight and how bad I was feeling. I managed to stagger through the rest of the show, comforted by the fact that at least the audience now understood what I was going through. Afterwards our old friend, Benny Green, came backstage. He had already seen the show and given it a glowing review, and I could hardly believe my ears when he said he had enjoyed it even more on this occasion as I had charted Judy's downfall more dramatically. I suddenly realised that as I had stayed in character while I told the audience about my dilemma, they had probably assumed it was all part of the play. I was beginning to think that maybe Judy's life and mine were growing too close for comfort!

On 'Black Friday', I was to appear on the *Wogan* TV show, and I arrived at the studios so dehydrated that my tongue was virtually stuck to the roof of my mouth. I lay down in my dressing room, feeling so ill I could barely function. As I sipped cup after cup of water in an effort to hydrate my system, Sue Lawley came in to ask if I was going to be able to make it; I couldn't even reply. Doctor Diamond, a friend of Bill's, miraculously appeared and gave me an injection, as a result of which I managed to rise and stagger through to the make-up department. I have only the haziest memory of sitting there with George Chakiris on one side, someone from *Dallas* on the other, and thinking, 'This should be the most exciting time of my life, and I'm missing out on it'.

1986, Strand – Judy with Paul Milton.

Geoffrey Boycott chuntered on for his allotted six minutes, and suddenly I was standing in the studio, knowing that I was about to appear 'live', although only just, in front of ten million people and praying that I wouldn't fall over. The lights came up, the band started to play, and I sang 'Forget your Troubles, C'mon Get Happy!' That old theatrical adage, 'The Show Must Go On', should never have been carried so far but, thanks to the amazing powers of 'Doctor Theatre', I got through the number, although I will never know how I made it through that Friday night performance. By the time Terry drove me home I was beginning to hallucinate, my body went into spasm, and he finally phoned the Metabolic Unit at St Mary's Hospital. When he described my symptoms, they thought it sounded like a severe case of flu and suggested that he bring me in the following morning if I showed no improvement. This was no flu! He had forgotten to mention that I was still suffering from the effects of a severe bout of food poisoning, which was entirely responsible for the state I was in. All I recall is lying in my bed overwhelmed by waves of nausea and desperate to be released from the agony; I knew that I was dying and the last thing I remember saying was that I wanted to be cremated. Early in the morning I managed to throw on a few clothes, and Terry helped me out to the car. I still remember what I was wearing – my green cord cloak, bought back in the early '70s, and which I still have.

We reached the hospital where I was immediately put on a drip; I had suffered a great loss of minerals, was on the verge of coma, and even 'Doctor Theatre' could not sustain me any longer. As I lay there, virtually comatose, I experienced a tremendous surge of relief as the fluid and vitamins started to flow through me. Later that morning, a doctor came into the room and said, "Oh, you're still with us are you, Mrs Wale?" which brought the severity of my condition home to me in no uncertain terms.

It was Saturday, and consequently a matinée day, and Terry realised that he had better phone Bill Kenwright to let him know what was going on. In the absence of an official understudy, a girl in the company who was playing a tiny part, had been delegated to learn my lines – just in case I broke a leg! Having sent instructions for her to prepare to go on for the matinée, Bill came down from Liverpool, probably sacrificing his beloved Everton playing football that afternoon. To give credit where it was due, she had learnt all the lines and all the songs but, more to the point, she bore no resemblance to Judy Garland, neither physically nor vocally. When

Terry went down to the theatre to give her a bit of moral support and see how she was coping, he was very surprised to find a very calm young lady, who seemed to be looking forward to the experience. He was appalled to see that there was no visible notice at the box office, and an announcement was made from the stage just before curtain up, which put people in a very awkward position if they felt like asking for their money back. She came on in costumes which had been cobbled together, a scrappy wig, and it was more than he could bear when she ran on for *Zing Went the Strings,* crammed into my little sailor suit and wearing short white socks – and that was the least of the problems. I had spent months honing my performance – how could an inexperienced young performer take on this enormous role with only a few hours rehearsal?

He saw his play crumbling in front of his eyes, and he raced back to the hospital, came straight to my bed and, leaning over my prostrate form, begged me to return for the evening performance. "She can't do it, it's not possible" he implored. "You cannot let her go on – not on a Saturday night!" The doctor led him away and told him, in no uncertain terms, that I was out of the game, and if he wanted to see me collapse onstage, he was going the right way about it. Terry always felt guilty about that irrational appeal, but *Judy* was our baby, and we both knew that, unless I made a quick recovery, the show would close. I was too far gone to rise from my sickbed; I had finally given in, and I had no more resources to fight back. There is no denying the fact that both Terry and I had become blinkered; we couldn't bring ourselves to believe that an illness would put an end to our dream, but as I looked up at him from my hospital bed I think we both sensed that our journey up the Yellow Brick Road might soon be over.

He headed back to the theatre and found a very disgruntled company, one of whom was on the point of refusing to go on for the second show, as he had found the experience of working alongside a virtually unrehearsed 'understudy' totally embarrassing. But he was persuaded, and on that Saturday evening she was allowed to perform in front of the biggest audience of the entire run, and it certainly did our show no good at all. I knew that if I did not get back on the Monday, our dream would be over, so despite the doctor's warning that I needed two weeks to recuperate, I came off the drip after 36 hours, and with a few false starts, forced myself to return to the theatre, where I was greeted by a large bunch of bananas! As I lay on my little sofa contemplating the evening ahead, the phone rang. It was Lucille, Bill's bold and brash production assistant, who was sorry to hear that I had been ill but cheerfully intimated that the Kenwright office would be sending a bunch of bananas along each day to help build my stamina; if only it had been that simple. As I prepared to go back onstage, mum was already on her way down to look after me and help me through the next fortnight. Bowed but unbroken, I managed to get through the show and faced the prospect of regaining my strength over the next few weeks.

Terry headed off at once to direct a play at Cheltenham, although he commuted regularly to spend as much time with me as possible. I had to conserve all my energy for the show, spending most of the day in bed and travelling to the theatre each evening by taxi. As we drove towards the Strand and I saw my name glittering down at me, I experienced a feeling bordering on panic. I almost wished we hadn't fought so hard over billing, as it made my task even more daunting, and each night brought new terrors. My reactions followed a pattern; I was very nervous at the beginning, but as the act gathered momentum my adrenalin started flowing and I usually came off at the end of Act 1 on a 'high'. By the time the interval was over I was scared to go back again, and it was left to mum to cajole and encourage me; I don't know what I would have done without her. She stayed in my dressing-room all evening, and occasionally sat in the front row of the stalls, from where she egged me on. I was managing, but only just, to keep body and soul together. She was also trying to encourage me to eat again, starting with gentle foods, but having been on liquids for so long I found it difficult. So many times I sat down to a plate of food and ended up in tears, unable to face more than a mouthful; it was some time before I was able to take any pleasure in eating.

Once the dust had settled, the doctors filled me in about how lucky I was to be alive, although I had more than an inkling, knowing how ill I had been. I couldn't have done anything about the food poisoning, but there was no doubt that Terry and I had ignored all the warnings. We had been so busy I didn't even think of going for a blood test, which would have undoubtedly revealed that something dramatic was happening inside me, and I could have been put on a drip – days, if not weeks, earlier. Although it was implied that my potassium deficiency may have exacerbated my condition, I have always believed that the reason I survived was due in no small part to the fact that my body had adjusted to living on a much lower level of potassium than the norm. Whatever the finer points, I should have done something sooner, because there is no doubt that even when the 'bug' had left my system, the damage had already been done and hospital intervention was the only option. I don't think that I was even taking potassium during that period, and with a body which leaked the stuff, there was no way I could replace what I was losing. I knew I was meant to take the supplement with food – and I wasn't eating food – so it was a Catch 22 situation.

As I began to feel a little stronger, I decided to face the underground, but when mum and I alighted at Covent Garden we discovered that the lift had broken down, leaving us no option but to climb up 193 stairs. I had to stop before we were even halfway up, and when we eventually reached the dressing room we called a doctor, and the now familiar Dr Diamond turned up and checked my heartbeat, pulse and blood pressure. I decided to fill him in on the details, as I was aware that he had just been told to keep me going without any knowledge of what had been wrong with me. He called Dr Abraham to get more information, and I think he was rather shocked to discover what I had been going through, not to mention my rare condition. There was little he could do to help as I was still running on 'almost empty', but Doctor Theatre got me through again.

On another occasion when Lewis was onstage with me, I suddenly found that my breathing was very shallow and fast, and it went out of control, almost to the point of being unable to speak or sing, but I comforted myself in the knowledge that the audience might not notice, as Judy was often breathy in her delivery. Never having suffered this before, I didn't realise that what I was experiencing were the symptoms of an anxiety attack. I had returned to work too soon, and my body was saying 'Enough!' I still believe that Lewis and Philip were the only two of my fellow actors who had any clue about the extent of my malady, and I'm sure that some of the others just found it irritating because of the 'understudy' factor, never mind a positive risk to their own job security. As I was still managing to give a good performance, they couldn't possibly have known what purgatory it all was.

To make matters worse, the show was in deep trouble. Mrs Thatcher had allowed the Americans to use Britain as a base from which to bomb Libya, and suddenly the streets of London were deserted, as foreigners, and particularly Americans, stayed away in their droves, fearing vengeance around every street corner. Only long-running shows were able to weather the storm, and with no money left in the kitty for the publicity we so badly needed we began to feel distinctly uneasy about the future. As it was, it took the publicity department quite a few weeks to get our reviews and production photos put up outside the theatre, and if you approached from the side it looked like a derelict building with only a couple of posters in evidence, and even the promised glitzy Hollywood foyer was bereft of décor.

We were made even more aware of our predicament by Annette Cook, a young fan who had grown very attached to the show. I spotted her early in the run, sitting in the front row, and she became a talking point once she had been in a few times. She stayed behind at the stage door, and after collecting my autograph and taking a few photos she asked for nothing except friendship. She was a great source of information, and it's a pity she wasn't working with our publicity department. She kept us up to date with ticket sales and told us which tube stations had our posters up and which did not. She spent hours at the half-price booth in Leicester Square, buying her own *Judy* tickets and suggesting to other undecided theatregoers that they ought to do the same. One evening she came to see me in a state of alarm because the rain had washed the *Judy* title off the board, so people weren't even aware that the play was available at half-price; she was convinced that people just didn't know about the show, and I think she may have been right.

As time moved on, I discovered that she had a rather sad background and was almost alone in the world. She loved the theatre and seemed to find a new family and a sense of belonging by visiting and re-visiting shows that she admired, getting to know a few of the performers, and I certainly felt comforted to know that she was out there rooting for me in that front row; she could probably have prompted if required! And she made us very conscious of how dire things were in the West End at that time, and not just for our show. Bill had taken a gamble based on the reviews and the packed houses we had attracted at Bristol and Greenwich, that *Judy* would take off without too much trouble, and that's one of the reasons the production was under-capitalised, leaving us with nothing to fall back on – but there was no doubt that the main reason for the minimalist budget was that he had just lost a small fortune on *Jeanne*. Of course, neither he nor anyone else expected a Libyan political crisis to put such a spoke in our wheel. He called us in to discuss a 'nine-point plan' to save the show; I can't remember all the points, but the two that affected us most were that Terry should forego all royalties, and I should go onto half salary. After all the hassle of negotiating my contract, this was indeed a hard pill to swallow, but we agreed.

During all the efforts to save the show, I was still trying to return to strength, and although I would have done anything to avoid missing a performance, I was finding the matinée days quite an ordeal. I was just not ready, physically or vocally, for two shows a day, but without an appropriate understudy, I was aware that it was not a happy situation for the rest of the cast, not to mention the audience! Ironically, I had a clause in my contract which stated that after the first six weeks of the run, my understudy would perform on one of the matinée days, but without an understudy it wasn't worth the paper it was typed on. Once the poisoning struck, I tried to hold out for my rights, and the 'understudy' was allowed to play on a couple of midweek matinées. She invited her family and friends to see her in the play and probably still has on her CV: 'Played Judy Garland at the Strand'. Well, you would, wouldn't you? Under pressure from all sides, Bill did start to look for a proper understudy, and although I know it is not an easy part to cast, covering such a wide age and emotional range, not to mention finding someone with a physical and vocal resemblance, little effort was made to find the right actress; I don't think that Bill had any intention of paying an understudy until he knew that the show was going to run.

We were plagued with all sorts of other problems too. Our opening had unluckily coincided with Liza Minnelli's appearance at the London Palladium. She was staying in the Savoy Hotel, just a stone's throw from the Strand Theatre, and on leaving the hotel she was confronted with a huge 'cut-out' of her mother in the *Get Happy* costume. She was pestered by the press, who were determined that she should come and see the play. Although it would have generated some much-needed publicity, we never expected nor encouraged her to do so; after all, why should she want to watch a total stranger playing her mother? We were soon having to deal with her lawyers. Liza represented the Garland estate, and although we felt sure that there was nothing in the play that she could pick us up on, we had to respond when her lawyers wrote, expressing her concerns.

I think that she had been misinformed about the last scene of the play which showed Judy alone in a hotel room on the telephone to Liza, who eventually hung up on her drunk and incoherent mother.

After a sad scene with the hotel bellboy, Judy fell to her knees and said, "Give me back my life", but there was a lighting change to signify the passing of time as we heard the strains of *Rockabye my Baby* before the final rendition of *Over the Rainbow*. It was certainly not meant to be taken literally, suggesting that Judy died after Liza had a row with her on the phone. There are times when theatrical licence must be taken in the interests of the play; time had to be telescoped, and although Judy died sitting on a toilet, I don't think anyone would have wanted to see that!

Norman Boyack came to the rescue and found a lawyer to represent us. As we hoped, it all came to nothing, and both sets of lawyers ended up good friends, communicating long after the run was over; we heard that Liza's representatives had invited ours over to California for a vacation. Her lawyer had become so familiar that, at one stage, he used the word 'paranoid' to describe his client, which was indiscreet to say the least. Terry wrote to Liza to apologise about the press intrusion and to state that it had nothing to do with us, but she never did reply, although the letter may not have found its way past all the minders and personal assistants. Months later someone sent us a cutting from *The New York Times* which had a snippet about 'Liza's worst nightmare' being that the play, *Judy*, might find its way over to New York, so it was obviously on her mind for some time. Our play was mentioned in other faraway places; we received a cutting from the *South China Morning Post*, and in the Quotes of the Week section, I was quoted as saying: 'There is no such thing as a Happy Legend', which I suppose has quite a Chinese feel to it. My name was at the bottom of a list which included President Reagan and Colonel Gaddafi, the man who, in tandem with Maggie Thatcher, had caused the recent political storm which had emptied the West End.

Judy's other daughter, Lorna Luft, was also in London, and was quoted in a tabloid headline: 'It Will Be a Cold Day In Hell Before I Go To See That Play!' It was suggested that Lorna and I have a 'face to face' on Breakfast TV, but she refused, and I certainly didn't have the strength for such an encounter as she is a tougher customer than her sister. In the play, apart from being an invisible presence on the other end of a phone, Liza only appeared as a baby in her cot, and Lorna and Joe were only mentioned in passing, so they had no real axes to grind. It was all quite extraordinary; we had gone from great previews, a fabulous opening night, excellent reviews, to a situation where a political crisis had caused audiences to disappear. I had gone through a personal crisis, the Garland family were now on our backs – and we were only five weeks into the run!

Throughout it all, I managed to give a performance each evening, although I was unable to take advantage of many publicity opportunities. I had to turn down an invitation to take part in *Night of a Hundred Stars* and I was also asked to contribute to a Leonard Bernstein Tribute evening, singing *I Feel Pretty* alongside other West End 'stars', but after a couple of rehearsals I had to pull out. I was even asked to open a new Indian restaurant, but the thought of the overpowering aromas and the inevitability of having to partake of the many dishes, brought on fresh waves of nausea, so I also bowed out of that one. And so it went on, but the show had to come first. Although I didn't know him personally, I managed to attend a *This is Your Life* for Denis Quilley, as all the 'stars' from West End musicals were invited along to greet him at the end of the programme. Lewis came along with me, and it was nice not to be a one-man band for a change.

I found a diary entry, written only a few days after my collapse: 'Must get a grip on myself, there's so much at stake', so the desperation to succeed, not to mention the guilt, never left me. I tried various things to try and hasten my recovery; I even started sessions of the Alexander Technique to try and find inner peace and relaxation, but I've never really understood nor appreciated the value of this therapy; it was pleasant enough and I liked the therapist, but it didn't help, and to be honest, I didn't have the time.

And then there was Sid Luft, Lorna's father and Judy's third husband. The flak we were getting from the girls paled into insignificance when Sid appeared on the scene. There had been endless rumours about Sid being in the audience, but none of us had taken it very seriously. One evening as I left the stage door, I was accosted by a couple of large men, who said that they were from *Group V*, an organisation which had something to do with Judy and Sid's financial affairs. I immediately recognised the name, having spotted it in one of the many books I had read about Judy's life. The men were mildly threatening and informed me that Sid was not going to be happy when they reported back to him about the way Judy was portrayed in the second half of the play. I said that I was sorry about that, but I hadn't written the play, and bade them goodnight.

But the hen had come home to roost. Terry was in the middle of his dress run in Cheltenham when Lucille called and asked me to come into the theatre for a meeting with her and Bill. He had received a call from Sid's representatives, who were about to issue us with a writ, listing various matters that had come to his attention. He wanted cuts and changes and he objected to certain words and phrases used to describe him in the play. Bill had tried to explain that it was the character of Hedda Hopper, the gossip columnist, who described him as 'a gangster, a mobster, and a low-down bum' – and as she was quickly discredited in the play, no one took what she said seriously. Sid was not for listening, and it was ironic to say the least, as Terry had gone out of his way to present a sympathetic picture of him. "He should be suing me for flattery", was Terry's response.

Sid also demanded that we removed all our publicity posters as he owned the rights to the image we had used, which was the cover of the *Miss Showbusiness* album. Bill was under pressure, as there was also a call from Warner Brothers, a call which opened with the immortal line, "Have you ever had a lobotomy Mr Kenwright? Well, we're about to give you one." It was gangster talk, and Bill was unnerved by it. They demanded that we omit the song *Born in a Trunk* which, in partnership with Sid Luft, they claimed to own. This was the bitterest pill of all, not only because what I sang was merely an extract, but because our notice had gone up; the show was due to close in ten days.

We had been on heckle-pins for some time, waiting and wondering, and I was hearing one thing from Bill, and another from Nigel, the Front of House Manager. He often came into the dressing room for a chat, and he told me that Bill wanted to bring *Judy* off, although the Strand management were willing to sustain the loss for a little while longer. He said that *Cabaret* was waiting in the wings, but insisted that the management had faith in *Judy* and wanted to give us a few more weeks. On the other hand, Bill was saying that while he was doing everything to keep the show afloat, the Strand were desperate to bring in another show. He also added that, if and when our show went down, he would be the last man to leave the ship, and he'd still be singing *Mammy!* Whatever the truth, the notice went up on May 9th. It all seemed so unfair; we had little time left to run, and here we were discussing alternative openings. Bill, Lucille and I hammered it out in my dressing room before a performance; Lucille suggested *Better Luck Next Time,* and when I showed little enthusiasm for that, she then tried *Over the Rainbow*, a truly desperate notion, which would have ruined the opening and the end of the play. There seemed to be no answer; we knew we had the best opening, but under pressure from Sid and Warner Brothers, Bill insisted that we lose *Born in a Trunk.*

We called Terry, but all he could suggest was that the curtain rose on the scene with Ethel and Frank Gumm, scrapping the musical beginning altogether and consequently losing the lovely onstage transformation sequence, taking us back in time from *A Star is Born* to appear just a minute later as a fourteen-year-old. It was a downbeat solution but thus it remained until the end of the run. By the time that Lucille and Bill left the dressing room, my legs were like jelly, I felt very uneasy, and to make matters even more stressful there was a crazy guy in the stalls. Early in Act 2, he suddenly rose from his seat and sauntered slowly towards me. He was wearing dark sunglasses and shouting, "Sing Chicago Judy!" There was something almost threatening about him, and it flashed through my mind that I was about to be shot, but I tried to placate him (in character of course), and he eventually sat down in the front row. Throughout the run there had often been shouts of "We love you Judy", which I found very flattering, but there were a few fans who seemed to believe that I was a kind of reincarnation, which was none too healthy. The guy with the glasses just crossed that border, but that night we had another standing ovation, so perhaps he added something to the proceedings!

I found the gay community very supportive, and it was always a comfort to spot small groups of men near the front of the stalls. The 'Legend' of Judy did attract unusual interest, and despite our efforts to keep my illness as private as possible, word got around like wildfire; there was even something in one newspaper saying that I had heard the voice of Judy coming from beyond the grave, and it had completely floored me, making me unable to go onstage. I also had a contact from a medium, who wanted me to book a session so that I could talk to Judy herself but, although always attracted by the bizarre, I felt it was too dangerous a territory to enter.

While Bill was receiving threats and intimidating calls from Warner Brothers, my agent also had a call from them asking for photos and reviews of the show, as they were considering me for the movie they were soon to be making about Judy's life. But if that was true, why were they so keen to put a spoke in our wheel? We sent them a batch of photos, but Larry then received another call which ended with the guy saying, "But perhaps your client won't be interested in playing the part when she hears we're gonna sue her husband!" I lost a lot of photos at that time! It was all such a load of codswallop, that if we hadn't been under so much pressure from all sides we might just have ignored the lot of them. The run was almost over, and it was unlikely they had any real grounds for a libel suit, but they were a big organisation, and we were phased. Strangely enough, there had been no sign of any of them in Worcester, Bristol or Greenwich, but now that we were in the West End, they smelled money – fat chance!

Mum went home for a few days to recharge her batteries, and returned with dad in tow, to stay with me until Terry opened his play in Cheltenham because I was still struggling to cope alone. During that penultimate week I made an appearance on *Pebble Mill at One*, and mum came with me to Birmingham. It was a bit of an ordeal, being live, but it went very well, and I was aware that I was on the mend, although it was too late for the publicity to do us any good.

Despite my own problems, I was very sorry for Terry, who had been coping with directing, commuting and worrying about me, and he was very frustrated not to be on the spot to help deal with the many problems that kept cropping up. He would sometimes arrive at the theatre just before the show to find dad pacing outside in a state of panic, muttering "This show is going to kill her." Mum and dad found it hard to witness my nightly pre-show nerves, and the situation now was in such stark contrast with their previous visit on our wonderful opening night when the world appeared to be our oyster. Despite all the trauma, Terry had a successful opening down in Cheltenham, and he was at last able to return to London for the final week of the run. Mum and dad were released back to the north, and although it was but a token, I gave mum a Sony Walkman as a gesture of appreciation and a souvenir of our time together. She was always at her best when needed, a wonderful mum.

Sid haunted us for the last days of the run and we still have his lengthy telegram as a treasured souvenir. It reminded us of a quote from one of our 'Judy' books when Liza asked 'Papa Sid' what he did for a living. He replied: "I'm in the suit business", and what he meant was that he sued people!

To give Bill Kenwright his due, he did make sure that every member of the Olivier Awards Panel came in to see the show before it came off. The panel was made up of seven professionals and six members of the public and it was supposed to be a secret vote with no discussion between judges. On the face of it, it seemed like a fair system, although we were all aware that shows still running stood a much better chance of winning than ones which had been closed for months. The awards were six months away, so we didn't give them too much thought, but we were grateful not to be denied the opportunity of being considered. Even after the notice went up, there was hardly a night passed when I wasn't informed that there was another member of the panel out front.

The final week went well, and on the last day we drove by the Strand before the matinée so that I could see my name in lights for the very last time. There were two standing ovations that day, and at the end of the final show a couple of men ran down the centre aisle and handed me bouquets of flowers. I reached down and shook their hands, and for a few moments I felt that surge of love that Judy herself must have felt so often. My faithful fan, Annette, who had sat in the same seat for no less than 53 performances, also handed me a huge bouquet. I think Bill was as bewildered by our closure as we were. Those who saw our show seemed to love it, but there had simply been too few of them to keep it going, and our run had not been long enough to have the effect on my career that we had both hoped for, and when would I get a chance like this again?

There had been times during the past three months when I would have given anything to escape from the nightmare I was living through, but on that last night I felt immeasurably sad as I was only just beginning to feel I had the strength to carry on and I had missed out on all the razzmatazz of simply being a part of the West End scene. I knew that Terry and I would feel bereft and a little cheated for some time. One of the actors did a pencil drawing of a boat sinking with the entire cast of *Judy* on board; rowing away from the scene of the tragedy was a lone figure wearing an Everton scarf, singing *Mammy*!

As Terry and I left the Strand Theatre that night on our way to *Joe Allen*'s for a farewell meal, and the lights that illuminated my name were plunged into darkness, we felt that we had come to the end of an era. It had been such a long journey from the Swan Theatre back in September 1984, and here we were at the end of May 1986 at what appeared to be the end of the Yellow Brick Road. Well, thanks to *Judy*, I would at least have a decent table at *Joe Allen*'s, should I require one, for the foreseeable future! Of course, 'Joes' had a pecking order with their tables which related to your current status in the business, so we might not have a table for long. As we sat there enjoying our last meal of the run, we had no idea that, within a few short months, our world would be turned upside down.

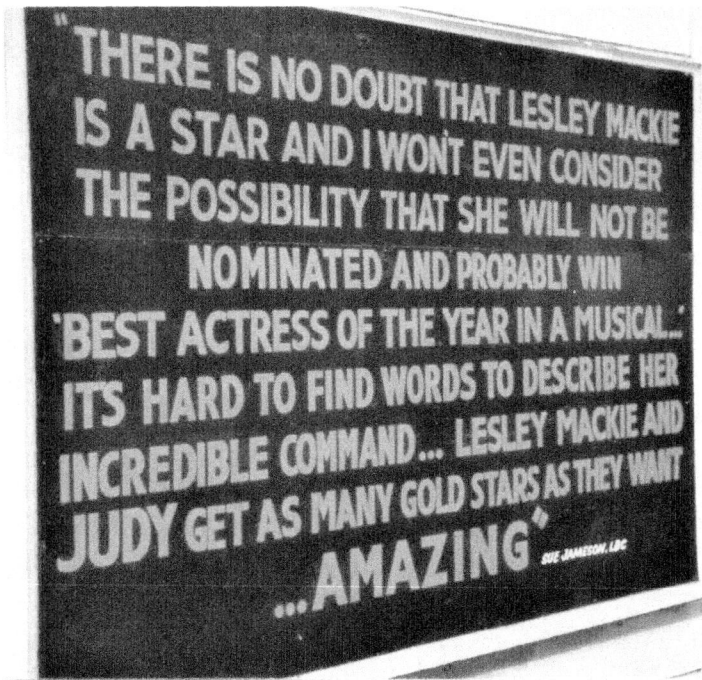

- 17 -

Aches in Provence

After all our trials and tribulations, we wanted the whole 'Judy' saga to end on a sweet note, so we took both Bill and Norman out for a meal just after we closed. I made my private peace with Bill, as we'd never had an opportunity to sit and talk. He was cuddly and warm, and I felt that we cleared the air. Bill would always be a tricky customer, but he did have winning ways. We chatted about *Piaf* and my dream of doing the revival. Edith Piaf was a natural choice for me after Judy; the role was of the same magnitude, but she was a very different character with little vocal resemblance to Garland. It was the ideal part to consolidate what I had achieved with *Judy*, and Bill seemed interested. We agreed to talk again later, and this was the start of a long personal struggle to get *Piaf* off the ground. A couple of nights later we met Bill again when we were among his guests at the Savoy Hotel. He said that he had invited his ten closest mates which made us feel that we were still included in his 'Inner Circle'. As the months passed, we were gradually squeezed to the outer perimeter.

Now I needed a little time to get over the whole experience and look to the future. There had already been quite a bit of interest from various sources, and even as I left the Strand I was being considered for the part of Sally Bowles in *Cabaret*; for some reason they were thinking of replacing Kelly Hunter, who had been on tour with it until the West End transfer. Just before we closed, Gillian Lynne, the choreographer, got in touch, suggesting we do a workout, just to see if we could work together, but for one reason or another that never happened, which was a bit of a relief as I didn't really have the energy to spare until the run was over. I received a card from Gillian, explaining that in the end they felt it was only fair to stick with Kelly, and when I eventually saw the production, I couldn't quite understand why they had reservations about her in the first place.

The job that got my agent most excited was the possibility of the soubrette in Weber's *Oberon*. Although it was grand opera, Frank Dunlop wanted an actress/singer for the role. I still had a reasonably trained mezzo-soprano voice, although I wondered how he could possibly have known that from seeing me in *Judy*; more surprising, he requested that I send a rough tape of the show to Seiji Ozawa, an estimable Japanese conductor, based in Paris. I did just that, but as I expected, Ozawa thanked me kindly and asked if I could learn an aria from the opera, tape it and send it so that he could hear something in the appropriate vocal range.

So, the day after our show closed, I was over at Callum McLeod's flat (our *Judy* MD), so that he could put the accompaniment on tape to enable me to start practising the aria. It was a weird and wonderful piece, but I duly recorded it, sent it off and awaited the verdict. I was daunted by the prospect of working alongside trained opera singers like Benjamin Luxon but it was a wonderful opportunity, and it was only scheduled to play for three nights at the Edinburgh Festival, followed by a week in Frankfurt and finishing with a few days in Tanglewood in the USA. It would have been different and exciting with a relaxed schedule, compared to what I had just been through, and for a while it looked as if it was all going ahead. It was then discovered that Luxon and another cast member had recording commitments, which was going to cut the rehearsal period to ten days. Frank Dunlop felt that this would be inadequate for a non-opera singer, so I was bombed out, and I think Larry was more disappointed than I was.

He was an elitist, and although I had every respect for him as an agent and as a lovely human being, we began to feel that he was almost too much of a gentleman for the market place our business had become. He always had my interests at heart and thought that I should wait for the right job to come along; trouble was, what was the right job after playing Judy Garland? Parts like that come along once, maybe twice, in a lifetime – and for many actors, never at all. I was sent a script of *The Blue Angel*, which was to have a try-out in Bristol before a possible West End transfer. I had to laugh as, prior to *Judy*, there was little chance that they would have considered me for a part made famous by Marlene Dietrich. Who was it that said, "You're wrong for everything until you're right for something, and then you're right for everything!" You don't have to look far to see the truth of this, as once someone becomes the 'flavour of the month', they can be cast in the most inappropriate roles. In my opinion, the script was poor and the score was worse, so I tactfully declined, and Stephanie Lawrence was cast in the role. As it happened, things went very wrong for the production down in Bristol, but I heard that Ms Lawrence received financial compensation when the show failed to transfer, although she must have had a tough agent to have that clause in her contract.

There were other offers around, but Terry was very keen that, after all the trials and tribulations, we should have a holiday so that we could reflect on the situation. I wasn't at all sure, as I hadn't entirely recovered from the food poisoning and eating was still a bit of a problem. Nevertheless, I let him go ahead with the plans, which were to sail from Dover to Calais, and then motor down to the South of France and into Italy.

Just before we were due to leave, I went into town to meet Larry for lunch. I was nauseous throughout the meal, and I finally had to tell Larry that I was unable to eat. He was very sweet and walked me in the direction of the underground at Piccadilly Circus. He wanted to take me right to the entrance, but I insisted that I would be fine. Almost as soon as he walked away, my legs all but gave way, my heart was pounding, I was gasping for breath, and I thought I might be having a heart attack! I had chosen an unfortunate place to collapse, as people were so used to seeing drunks and drug addicts slumped around Eros that no one offered any assistance and my efforts to elicit help were probably incoherent. I felt totally helpless, looking in vain for a taxi, and finally, in desperation, forced myself to go into the underground. After a few false starts I stumbled onto a train where, gasping for breath, I sat down with my head in my hands; I seemed invisible as no one even asked what was wrong.

I alighted at Paddington and despite my jelly legs, I ran along to St Mary's Hospital. After climbing four flights of stairs to avoid using the lift, I staggered into the familiarity of the metabolic ward and gave them a breathless explanation. Someone gently suggested that I'd had a panic attack, and it dawned on me that I'd already experienced lesser versions of what had just been a full-blown one. I now understood what my father had been going through for years. We had always sympathised with his condition but had never really appreciated the extremity of the physical symptoms that accompanied the panic. It reminded me of a story he had once told when, thinking he was dying, he had run from the Sinderins in the

West End of Dundee to Roseangle (almost a mile away) to get help from our family doctor who had looked at him quizzically, and when he discovered how far dad had run, gently assured him that he had a few years left in him yet.

I went home, wondering how on earth we could contemplate a holiday abroad, and we decided to postpone the trip for another couple of days, eventually starting out on June 8th. We'd only reached south-east London when I asked Terry to stop as I just couldn't face the prospect of venturing any further; in fact I was suffering another anxiety attack and it was to be the first of many over the next few weeks. Had I been able to fully recover before returning to work it probably wouldn't have happened. The trouble with anxiety, which I would learn as the days went by, is that once your body learns how to react with feelings of panic it becomes 'sensitised', and the fear of an attack brings on the symptoms – a vicious circle – and the holiday was already becoming the stuff of nightmares. Now that the play was over and my defences were down, a whole new set of terrors had arrived; being away from home and my doctor was just one of them.

After a brief respite at Bernie's flat in Blackheath, I was persuaded to carry on. The first few days were the worst; I experienced an overwhelming sense of relief driving into even the smallest of French towns, and something akin to dread as we left it behind. I became quite an expert on the French pharmaceutical system, and quickly realised that the chemist with the cross outside was of no use to me, there being no trained pharmacist within. It was only the one with the 'snake' insignia that held out any comfort, and sometimes we just sat outside one of those, with me unwilling to move on. The problem got worse as we approached the mountain ranges of southern France, which are not famous for chemist shops of any description!

Then there was food; hunger made me nauseous, eating made me nauseous. The cycle often began in the early evening when we were searching for a restaurant; if we took too long to find one, I was unable to face the food when it arrived. I also found it difficult to eat in front of people because of the length of time it took me to struggle through a plate of food, so we always sought tables in secluded corners. I learned to deal with things to some extent by always carrying some bread with me in the car, and Terry always had vivid memories of glancing across to the passenger seat as I rummaged in my bag for a chunk of bread to gnaw, and thinking, 'Here we go again!' One day in Menton, I was so anxious that I was unable to leave our hotel room, so Terry went to find a 'snake', explaining to the pharmacist, "Ma femme a peur". When he asked what I was afraid of, Terry had to give a long list, finishing by saying, "Tout!" He returned with a packet of tablets, but they were worse than useless; they were probably some herbal concoction, and I put them in my toilet bag where they languished until binned. I had been given some tranquillisers towards the end of *Judy*, but for some bizarre reason had failed to bring them with me. Crazy, as they could have made a vast difference to my enjoyment of that holiday.

The weather took a while to brighten up, but once we crossed into Italy and the sun appeared, the warmth seeped through me and I felt something approaching relaxation. It was a relief, nonetheless, when we crossed back over the French border and began our homeward trail. As we drove through France, the sun emerged from time to time, and we could almost believe that we were enjoying a normal holiday. Cannes was lovely, and we wished that we could have afforded the time and money to stay a little longer.

Terry's patience only ran out once, when we drove into the town of Aix-en-Provence and discovered that all the hotels were full. It was around seven o'clock in the evening and I was hungry. "Let's eat first," said Terry – but I knew I wouldn't feel relaxed enough to eat until we found somewhere to stay. "Okay, we'll find a hotel first," he persisted. "No, I can't wait, I'm too hungry," I protested. It was a Catch-22 situation and Terry finally blew up, which only upset me more. For the record, we found a motel with a restaurant just outside the town and both problems were finally resolved under the same roof. We had a meal whilst watching the World Cup and finally collapsed into bed. Things took a turn for the better after that night.

We travelled through pretty countryside, having lunches and drinks at roadside cafés, welcoming the sun when it appeared until we eventually reached Paris. We took the opportunity to do our 'Piaf Trail', and we started by visiting her grave in *Père Lachaise Cemetery*. What a fascinating place – like a Who's Who or, more accurately, a Who Was Who! So many famous people buried so close together, and many of the graves unkempt and uncared for. Someone had put a tiny posy at Oscar Wilde's grave, but they were withered and forlorn, and there was something poignant about such a tiny tribute at the grave of such a talented and famous man.

1986, Père Lachaise Cemetery, visiting the grave of Edith Piaf.

Piaf's grave was the star attraction. A small man we assumed to be a cemetery employee was arranging mountains of flowers all around it. We only wanted to place a few carnations and take a photograph or two, but his task seemed interminable. When we eventually spoke to him, we discovered that it wasn't his job, but a labour of love; he was a devoted fan of Piaf's and had been performing this ritual every week since her death in 1963. We moved on to 72, Rue de Belleville and saw the plaque above the spot on the pavement where, legend has it, Edith was born on a policeman's cape. We also spotted our little friend from the cemetery, who obviously made a weekly pilgrimage to Edith's birthplace as well as her place of rest. We went to her paternal grandmother's home where she had lived in the brothel with the prostitutes until she was old enough to sing on the streets with her father, and then onto the streets of Pigalle, soaking up the atmosphere of all her old haunts. We did it for fun, but we also took photos everywhere, in the hope that they would come in useful for publicity purposes should we ever manage to mount a London production of the play.

We came into our own in Paris, and although I was unable to sample the delights of French cuisine I coped with the easier option of Chinese food. We went to Versailles, the Left Bank, and on our last night we even fitted in a whirlwind visit to Opéra, where I stood, as I had done three years previously, over the air vent at the side of the main road and Terry took another 'Marilyn Monroe' photograph with my skirt billowing over my head, looking like I hadn't a care in the world.

We headed north, and on the last day of our journey, as the rain poured down, we stopped at one of the war cemeteries and our own worries were brought into perspective for a little while. There were only about ten people and two cars on the boat going back across the Channel, so of course we were searched at the Dover Customs. It was tedious at the end of a long day, but we continued north to London and arrived home in the early hours of the morning.

On our return, I was invited along to Battersea Park where, along with Peter Ustinov and Juliet Stevenson, I made a short speech and released some doves as part of UNICEF's campaign on behalf of refugees. We had missed quite a bit on the work front; Larry told me I had been asked to take over from Anita Harris as Grizabella in *Cats* but thought that an umpteenth take-over in a long-running musical was a bit of a comedown, and he advised me to wait for a better offer. Terry went along with his judgement, and I think we regretted that decision more than any other, because what I really needed was to keep my name alive in the West End. I had come from nowhere, been around for a short time, and then disappeared. It was a grave error of judgement.

My immediate priority was a few days respite at the metabolic ward in St Mary's Hospital. I was keen to go in, because I needed some reassurance that my body was returning to something approaching normal. I had a private room in the Lindo Wing this time, and I prepared myself for a few more weird and wonderful tests. My periods were overdue, but after the trauma of the recent weeks I was not at all surprised. In view of the nature of certain tests, however, I mentioned this and they decided to do a pregnancy test. I never did get the result, but in any case they said there was little more they could do, and I was released without any plans to return. I do recall our old friend Gordon Griffin coming in to see me during that week and commenting on my increased bust size, but nothing really registered.

Terry and I then prepared for a return to Worcester to take part in a concert, celebrating the 21st anniversary of the Swan Theatre. John Doyle was no longer around, but we were still part of the theatre's history, so we headed up to Worcester to start rehearsals. We were to be staying for the week with our dear old landlady, Bette Lewis, and I was feeling very much better, so much so that I found myself enjoying a few pickled onions. I've loved them ever since I was a small girl hurrying along the Hawkhill in my lunch break to knock on Benedetti's door to buy a penny pickle! I hadn't been much inclined to indulge in any during the past few months, but the craving for them now returned with a vengeance.

I also noticed that I was putting on weight as my little black dress was on the tight side, but although I was now daring to dream, it still didn't quite sink in; well, we'd been trying for so long, it was not surprising that I wasn't 'counting my chickens'. It was all explained when, a couple of weeks later, I discovered I was pregnant. People like to tell you, when you have been waiting and trying for a baby, that it usually happens when you stop worrying about it. Nothing could have been less relaxing than the holiday we had just taken; I was recovering from food poisoning, I was underweight, I was suffering from anxiety symptoms, yet here I was just after my 35th birthday, and expecting my first baby. Maybe it had something to do with the magic of Paris, or even our 'Aches in Provence'! We were filled with wonder and trepidation as the reality of it sunk in. Amazingly enough, almost as soon as we heard the good news, I had a call from the Margaret Pyke Clinic to say that we were finally at the top of the list and could now proceed with the donor sperm. I was delighted to be able to say that we had landed lucky and someone else could take our place.

Everything came to a sudden halt, including my anxiety attacks! Any work that I was offered had to be turned down, although I thought long and hard about joining the Scottish Theatre Company to play Maggie in *What Every Woman Knows*, directed by Tom Fleming. I worked out that I would be around 26 weeks pregnant by the time the tour was over, but as this was my first pregnancy I had no idea how big I would be or how I would feel. I was nervous about something going wrong, and although Tom went to great lengths to try and persuade me, with much regret I turned the job down. But I didn't get huge until the last three months, and as Maggie was described as 'a little brown hen', a small chubby hen might have been perfectly acceptable, but my loss was Maureen Beattie's gain. I lost a lot of work at this time, and although Larry was always like a kindly uncle, once I was pregnant he was even more protective and positively discouraged me from doing anything, including *What Every Woman Knows*. Tom asked me at one stage if Larry and I were related, as he seemed so concerned about my state of health and well-being. He had also been emphatic about my not doing *Cats,* but as my pregnancy advanced I felt extremely robust, and with no work whatsoever, I continued to feel vexed about turning down Grizabella.

We went to numerous shows, courtesy of my fan-friend, Annette, who knew every box office manager in London. She seemed able to get complimentary tickets for most of them, and as she had adopted me as one of her surrogate family, I was the lucky beneficiary. I saw many shows with her, some better than others, but it made me feel as if I was still in the swing of things, even if only as a spectator.

As the weeks passed, Terry and I began to look for another suitable subject for us to work on together. He was always attracted to American subjects, so we looked at writer Anita Loos (*Gentlemen Prefer Blondes),* but quickly moved on as her life did not seem to have enough of dramatic interest. We did quite a bit of work on Gladys Aylward, who went to China in 1930 as a missionary, transforming the lives of many, and eventually leading over 100 children across the mountains to safety from the advancing Japanese, something we saw in technicolor glory in *The Inn of the Sixth Happiness*. It was a highly successful film despite the glamorisation of the story and the casting of Ingrid Bergman – well, possibly *because* of these two factors! Gladys was, in fact, a little London chambermaid, so it was an ideal subject for us. We even got as far as travelling to meet Alan Burgess, author of her biography, *The Small Woman,* and with his approval, Terry made a start. We felt the world was ready for *Gladys, the Musical!* He finished the first 15 pages and sent them off to Cameron Mackintosh, but his timing was dreadful as *Miss Saigon* was already in the pipeline, and the West End could not play host to two Oriental musicals at the same time. We did not feel inclined to try elsewhere, as our subject matter required an elaborate, expansive and expensive production, with the tremendous crowd-pulling appeal of all the little Chinese children. We were disappointed, although Terry was already finding it difficult to empathise with the central character. She was courageous, leaving her friends and family in Dundee to head for a distant country in order to become a missionary and help the needy, but he did not easily relate to Gladys, mainly because of her unwavering religious fervour. So he laid it aside, and it became another of our unfinished projects, destined for the trunk of memorabilia.

It was a healthy pregnancy, despite a chronic addiction, particularly in the early stages, to anything pickled. At one point I was getting through two jars of pickled onions a day, plus the vinegar. On another occasion when I went for my ante-natal appointment, my urine sample was so pink that I was ashamed to hand it in; it looked alarming, but I had consumed a whole jar of beetroot the night before! I was eventually told that although the pickles were unlikely to harm a baby, which was a well-cocooned little mite, they might damage my kidneys, so I tried to ease off a bit. It was at this time that Tim West and his wife, Pru, invited us to join them for a day out on their narrow boat on a canal trip in Warwickshire, and I remember Pru advising me to get a nanny, as she had done, as soon as the baby was born, in order to stay in the fast lane! That was not going to be easy, as *Judy* hadn't altered our financial status one little bit, and nannies did not come cheap, but my most vivid memory of that boat trip was disembarking to go in search of a jar of pickled onions!

Out of the blue a sudden burst of real excitement, when I was notified in November 1986 that I had been nominated for a Laurence Olivier Award for my performance in *Judy*! I was delighted, but as the show had been closed for almost six months and two of the other contenders, Elaine Paige and Maureen Lipman, were in shows that were still running, the prospect of winning seemed extremely remote. I had seen both Elaine and Maureen's performances, so I had a fair idea of what I was up against, but I remember sitting there in the packed auditorium at the Prince Edward Theatre, wishing we'd had an iota of the hype which surrounded *Chess*, not to mention a fraction of the budget! Maureen was pretty sparky in *Wonderful Town* at the Queen's Theatre, but she seemed somewhat miscast. The part required vulnerability, and she didn't have that in spades. I knew in my heart that I ought to be a strong contender, but unless the panel had long memories I didn't have much of a chance. Life was exciting again and we looked forward to the awards with anticipation.

There was a bit of a 'do' for all the nominees where we all mingled, collected our framed certificates, and had our photos taken for the papers and the television news. I think that Maureen was the only one of our group to be interviewed, but she was definitely the flavour of the month at that time. A few days later we went to lunch with Benny and Toni Green, and I was amused to find that not only was Maureen one of their guests, but Julia Mackenzie was also there, and she was a nominee in the *Best Performance by an Actress* category. The conversation was a little stilted, with Maureen and I both insisting that the other would win, and Maureen making the point very strongly that she didn't stand a chance because she had been so outspoken with the press about the futility of awards.

Bill Kenwright was also the producer of *Wonderful Town,* and although he said that he thought I deserved to win, he also admitted that it would improve business for him if the gong went to Maureen. All I knew was if that were to happen, no one would remember I had even been a nominee. In the unlikely event of my winning, there was just a chance that it might make people stop for a moment and say "Who?" But to the event...

If I had to choose the absolute highpoint of my career, I would have to say it was the *Olivier Awards* Ceremony, which was held on the evening of December 7th, 1986, at London's Royalty Theatre. I was heavily pregnant by this time, and mum had warned me not to jump up too suddenly if I won, in case I hastened the arrival of the baby. I told her not to hold her breath, as the odds were stacked against me; I was under no illusions, I was a rank outsider and I knew it. I was just thrilled to have been nominated, and to be part of such a prestigious event. We slipped into the theatre, totally ignored by the press who were flocking around the more famous nominees. I bumped into Julia Mackenzie in the ladies' loo just before curtain up, and she very sweetly told me not to be disappointed if I didn't win as these events were often politically motivated, and the panel would give preference to shows which were still up and running. I told her that I didn't expect to win, and Terry and I headed into the auditorium and took our seats in the front of the stalls.

Our innate knowledge that we were not in the running was compounded by the fact that I was the only nominee who had not been invited to sing in the show. I was told that they would try and include me, but priority would be given to the other musicals. I suppose that no one was really interested in publicising a show that had closed six months before. As I sat there with butterflies and a baby in my tummy, I was a little relieved not to have to participate in the evening's entertainment. Maureen said afterwards that she would never put herself through such an experience again. She had to sing before our category came up, which is probably the lesser of the two evils, as it must be tough to get up there and sing if you've just heard that you haven't won. Whichever way you look at it, it must be preferable just to sit there and watch the show. Having said that, Terry and I were so nervous that we were unable to concentrate, and afterwards could remember very little of the events onstage. Thank goodness an old friend had the wit to record it for us; it hadn't even occurred to us, and we were thrilled when she suddenly turned up at our door and presented us with the souvenir video.

It was indeed a star-studded night; Lord Olivier himself was there, although he was old and frail and had to be helped to his feet by his wife, Joan Plowright, to acknowledge the plaudits of his fellow-actors. As he waved graciously from his box there was no doubt that, as far as the theatrical world was concerned, we were in the presence of 'Royalty'! Numerous awards were handed out and we were treated to excerpts from various shows. Finally, Alan Bates came on to read out the nominations for *Best Performance by an Actress in a Musical*. He made a couple of little jokes, mentioned his own desire to be in a musical, and then read out the names of the four nominees: Elaine Paige, Maureen Lipman, Angela Richards, and me. Miss Paige and Miss Lipman had already sung songs from their respective shows as part of the evening's entertainment, and Miss Richards was due to sing something a little later. As the four names were announced, the camera flashed onto each one of us, and even though I knew I wasn't going to win, I felt tense as Alan Bates opened the dreaded envelope and read: "And the winner is... Lesley Mackie!"

1986, Royalty Theatre, London – Olivier award winners.

Ignoring my mother's advice, I shot up as though I had been scalded, finally putting an end to the myth that winners know in advance. Thankfully, I had heeded advice to write an acceptance speech – just in case! I also remembered to kiss my husband before waddling up to the podium where I collected my award, made my speech while choking back floods of emotion and waddled off in the wrong direction. We had been given strict instructions to exit stage right if we won, but by this point I was overwhelmed, and Alan Bates had to chase after me into the auditorium to get me back onstage. By the time it was transmitted only a short time later they had edited my false exit, but kept Angela Rippon's comment, which was, "Well, what can possibly follow that?", which I took as a compliment. Michael Crawford won the male equivalent for *Phantom of the Opera*, and it seemed as if every newspaper in the world wanted a picture of us together. I think he was as emotional as I was! I spent the rest of the evening in a complete and utter daze.

After the ceremony, we all went off to the *Grosvenor House* for the meal and I was able to eat and enjoy it without any problems. The only minor irritation was that the seating arrangements had been altered. We saw on the seating plan that Terry and I had been moved from our original table, (No 50). As we sat down at No 49, we joined a few of Bill's relatives, staff and friends. We saw that our original table had Bill, Julia Mackenzie and Jerry Harte, Pauline Collins and John Alderton, David Toguri and Tim Goodchild (Choreographer and Set and Costume Designer of *Wonderful Town*), Jack Rosenthal – and Maureen Lipman! We put two and two together and worked out that Bill had wanted to make sure that Maureen and I were no longer at the same table; would he have done the same to spare my feelings if Maureen had won? I also wondered why we'd been put at the same table in the first place – unless, of course, he had assumed that Maureen would win, and knew that I would take it on the chin! Strangely, this all flooded back recently when I was poring through memorabilia and found the official printed seating plan, and the evidence was there to see; we were indeed part of the celebrity Table 50 and Bill was the one who was originally at Table 49 – so he'd abandoned his family to keep his other 'star' sweet.

Nothing could dampen our spirits, and at the end of the evening we decided to pay a visit to *Le Privé*, inviting Lucille along to introduce her to our 'club'. We hadn't been there for some time, but it seemed appropriate to let them know that I had won, as they had been so generous to us during the run. We were mortified to find it closed and the evening ended with a bit of a fizzle; in fact, it appeared to have closed down completely, so we said goodbye to Lucille and made our way home.

The extraordinary thing is that when you are involved in a televised event like that, you really do believe that you are at the centre of the universe, and that everybody in the country is witnessing it. The truth is that most people haven't a clue that it's happening, but judging from the telephone calls we received the following morning, there had been quite a few people up and down the country who had been rooting for us. In Dundee, mum had wept as the result was announced, and dad had done a jig around the living-room. I think that they received nearly as many phone calls as we did. Cathy Jayes was on a train that morning and heard the following conversation between two women: "Did you see the Awards last night?", said one. "Yes", said the other, "we must get along to see *Judy*". Too late! We really had been the best kept secret in London.

1986, Best actress in a musical!

Still, we were over the moon. Terry and I felt as if we had climbed a mountain, reached the top, and despite all the setbacks, our efforts had finally been rewarded. We thought that it would change our lives forever, although we didn't reckon with the fickle finger of fate! Whatever happened, nothing could take away our joint achievement on that wonderful memorable night. We seemed to have it all, a baby on the way, and even though we only had a three-month run, recognition for *Judy* in the shape of a very heavy object, which would sit on our bookcase for the rest of time. Perhaps our luck wasn't so bad after all.

Part Two

- 18 -

Fruits of labour

Grampian Television were quick off the mark and, having interviewed me prior to our *Judy* opening, they now invited me up to Aberdeen to show off my award. I packed my trophy, although its shape and weight caused a slight delay at the airport check-in, as it looked like a very offensive weapon on the radar screen. I'm not sure if it occurred to us at the time, but over the years Terry and I often pondered about the nature of the award design, as we'd both love to have had the head of Sir Laurence as our prize. I looked into this quite recently, but no one seemed to have any memory of who designed the award or what it signified, although we'd wondered over the years and many people had asked me about it. I decided to contact SOLT (Society of London Theatres), and they said that they didn't know. 1986 was before their time, but they promised to investigate, and look in their archives.

To cut a long story short, I put my query on Facebook and many people responded. We all had a great time, throwing ideas into the ring, and the result was that the first design (1976-1979) was a decorative, blue urn, followed by a statuette (1979-1984), then there was the depiction of the sword of Henry V by Tom Merrifield, which is the one I possess, and which existed for the shortest span of all – from 1985-1987 – until the bust of Sir Laurence by Henry Marchetti replaced it in 1988. Perhaps we possess something extremely rare.

I enjoyed the interview, chatting about my baby and the future, and it made me feel I was back in the swim; in fact, the Olivier Award kept me going throughout the rest of my pregnancy and kept my name alive for a little longer as far as the profession was concerned. We felt it was a kind of compensation for the premature end of the show, but the downside was that any interest that had been generated by the play and now the award had to go on hold while I had the baby and for a while after it was born, so I was unable to strike while the iron was hot. I missed out on a lot of opportunities at that time, and people in our business have very short memories. It was strangely ironic that, after waiting so long for a baby, it should happen just when things seemed to be taking off for me in a professional sense, but is there ever a right time?

We read baby books by the dozen and went through many names, but I grew so convinced it was a boy that we almost settled on Oliver Barnaby; I called him Nollie B for short, and thus he remained until the last lap of the pregnancy when we started to take more interest in girls' names – just in case. After dismissing Katharine, which along with our surname Wale had the sound of a spinning firework, we put Katy on the list; an old and timeless name, which would appeal to all the family should the baby turn out to be a girl! After *Judy* closed, we had come across various articles which tried to equate my life with Judy's, and as my 'due date' had been calculated as March 12th, which just happened to be Liza Minnelli's birthday, the press had latched onto this; combined with the fact that I shared a birthday with Judy Garland, the coincidence would have been a bit spooky to say the least. Of course, the odds against the baby arriving on time were remote, and the 12th came and went. I finished my spring cleaning, filled my little freezer, and played the waiting game.

Our lives were about to be changed forever, not by the Olivier Award, but by the arrival of our baby. Coincidentally, my cousin, Mandy, in Dundee went into labour at the same time, but it was all over for her in a few hours and Jane was born on March 17th. Mine was a lengthy and painful experience, but Terry was a tower of strength, supplying ice cubes to suck, wet sponges to cool me down, and gentle encouragement. He didn't have time to feel squeamish and only managed the odd brief respite to grab a sandwich, make a phone call or have a fag! Mum told us afterwards that she felt very anxious and helpless stuck up in Dundee, and she feared that we might lose the baby; I think we did too. Thank goodness women are kind to each other. "It's a pain you forget," they say. What they really mean is that it is so excruciating, it's impossible to remember. I recall a joke which said that if you wanted to recall the pain of childbirth, just take your bottom lip and pull it over the top of your head! The best thing you can say is that it's a productive pain, and with the aid of the epidural and forceps, Katy Violet Wale finally emerged at 5am on March 18th, 1987.

Now we were three. We wept as I was handed this little seven-pound bundle with dark hair and a wee button nose, but even as he looked at her, Terry said that he would never allow me to go through such an ordeal again. When mum came down to visit us at St Mary's, she was appalled at the conditions. She had just been to see my cousin in Ninewells Hospital where there was not only more space, but a view of the River Tay. But this was London, and mum couldn't get over the fact that I had to eat my meals while perched on the bed as there was no room on either side to place a chair. Looking at the state of the floor, she had to be restrained from offering her services as a cleaner.

It's not a pain you forget, but time is a great healer. As the days passed and we looked at all our cards and gifts, the memory of the agony of the birth began to dim, although I was sitting on ice packs for about three weeks. Along with the many messages and well-wishes, there was a massive bouquet from Bill Kenwright which said, 'Welcome to our World, from Uncle Bill'. After a few days, Mum, Katy, and I returned to Purves Road, and when Katy was barely a week old the *Dundee Courier* came and took a photograph of us all together. She was a wee star, and I swear that even at that tender age she had a tiny smirk on her face. When dad saw the photo in the paper, it was his first sighting of his new grandchild.

People tell you that a baby changes your life, but no one can really prepare you for the reality, and the growing realisation that your own life must take second place to this demanding little creature. It was more difficult for me to accept this concept, because I'd just had a little taste of success and what promised to be the start of a new era as far as my career was concerned. Now everything had come to a standstill because of the long-awaited pregnancy and the subsequent birth. The star of *Judy* was up to her knees in nappies!

So it was with some excitement that I ventured out one day to record *Over the Rainbow* for a slot on a *Highway* programme, which was to be featuring Dundee. I met the singing presenter, Harry Secombe, at that recording, but I never saw him again until I watched the show when it was transmitted. I still had to do the filming in Dundee, so we decided to have Katy christened at the same time, with mum seeing to all the arrangements with the minister, church and guests.

On June 9th I went up the Law to film the sequence, although it might have been the middle of December. There was not a soul in sight, apart from mum and Aunt Nan, who had come along to be supportive, standing shivering on the sidelines. As I sang along to my pre-recorded tape, the camera searched the sky in vain for a glimmer of light, never mind a rainbow. Not that I cared too much. As far as I was concerned, it was a job, and I was part of the human race again. I was now impatient to return to work and discover the joys of being a working mother.

1987, Cheltenham – Bells Are Ringing with Nick Kemp & Simon Coates.

Katy was five months old when I went back to work, and the invitation came from our old pal, John Doyle. It was to play the lead in the 1960 musical *Bells Are Ringing* at the Everyman Theatre in Cheltenham, and then for a season at Greenwich. There were some lovely songs in the show, including *The Party's Over* and *Just in Time,* and the part of Ella Peterson, which had originally been written for Judy Holliday, was great fun to play. It can be daunting to play a part which has been written for someone else, because the passage of time tends to enhance people's recollections, and thus it was with Terry, who recalled it being a wonderful film. By chance, the television transmission of the original cropped up to coincide with our production, and although Ms Holliday had her own quirky style, it wasn't quite as good a film as he had recalled.

We rehearsed in London, which was extremely convenient, and my leading man was none other than Bernard Lloyd. I was delighted to be working with him, not only because he was an old friend of Terry's, but because I admired him enormously as an actor. I was also curious to discover whether he was as difficult as his reputation led me to believe. We had a talented team, with Kenn Oldfield as choreographer, and he and John assembled a super, energetic group of actor/dancers who contributed enormously to the show. We had dear Cathy Jayes again as musical director, and she was always lovely to have around. I still had my old energy and threw myself into rehearsals with enthusiasm. It wasn't long before Bernie started to cause problems; on one occasion when he dismissed yet another of my ideas as "just crap darling", I thumped him on the shoulders in sheer frustration. He apologised at once and announced to the assembled company: "It's all my fault, I've driven her to this", and I then felt sorry for him.

It's admirable to stand up for production values and what you believe in, but there was little doubt that Bernie went too far. There was something in him, probably his own insecurity, which made him cantankerous; he couldn't seem to help it. The strange and endearing thing was that because his method of working was par for the course as far as he was concerned, he just moved on and looked back fondly on the whole experience. He was surprised and a little hurt that John took many years before asking him to work with him again. I'd have taken the risk, because I was always willing to go through a certain amount of fire to achieve results. Although he tended to imbue the comedy scenes with an intensity that they did not truly merit, you can't beat Bernie for romance, and singing duets like *Just in Time* and *Long Before I Knew You*, were an absolute pleasure.

1987, Cheltenham – Bells Are Ringing. With Bernard Lloyd and company members on the 'subway'.

Being a working mother with a young baby had its downside. Throughout rehearsals, I was up at least three times a night to feed Katy and soothe her back to sleep, and by the time we opened in Cheltenham, the work schedule had taken its toll and my milk supply had almost dried up. With some regret I decided to forfeit the breastfeeding and encourage her to stick to the bottle, which was more satisfying for her and gave her better sleep; in fact, she took to it with an enthusiasm which bordered on hurtful and hung onto it until she was seven! It was a gentle little 'comeback'; reviews were good, and we knew that I had more work in the not-too-distant future with 'Bells' slated to run in Greenwich for an eight-week season at Christmas.

On October 24th, Terry flew to Sweden to help with the first foreign language production of *Judy*. When he was approached by the German agency, *Litag*, after the Bristol production, he could not have imagined how many productions would see the light of day over the next 30 years. The Swedish one was the only one he was involved in, and he found it a fascinating experience. He had to make a few changes and cuts, one being the big speech out front which, apparently, the Swedes would not be able to handle; such intimacy between the actress and the audience was not comfortable for them. Fortunately, there was a translator around to assist with the re-writes. The actors had the kind of support that we could only dream of: eight weeks rehearsal, the security of a full-time job with a permanent acting company, based in a theatre with its own costume and wig department – and they were well-paid into the bargain!

More to the point, they were creating a colourful and imaginative version of *Judy* with novel ideas which we would have welcomed at the Strand Theatre. On the negative side (in our opinion), they had two 'Judys', and although it split the burden of the part, there was so little age difference between the two actresses there was no theatrical point to be made; in any case, we felt quite strongly that one actress should make the entire journey, so that the emotional impact was undiluted. Quite bizarrely, both actresses took ill before the opening night, and the production was postponed until they were fit to return.

It was disappointing, but we weren't complaining, and nor did we about any of the future productions. There was little chance of us travelling to see them, and the language barrier would have made it impossible for us to know what they had done to the text. We felt sure that ignorance was bliss, and were happy to let them all get on with it. The royalties from the Swedes, Germans, Danes, and even the Japanese, helped us through a few barren patches, although we were never paid for a second run of the play in Tokyo! The leading lady in that production got involved with a 'toy boy' and her fans stayed away in droves as a kind of moral protest. *Judy* was the final nail in the producer's coffin, and he went bankrupt shortly after the run.

I was now preparing for my return to Greenwich, but just before I started rehearsals I was invited to participate in a charity performance at the theatre. With my dream of reviving *Piaf* still in the back of my mind, I thought I might lay the ground for a future production by singing a couple of Piaf songs. By chance, a researcher from *Wogan* was in the audience that night, and I was asked to sing *Hymne a l'Amour* on their show the following Friday when Lew Grade was to be a guest, Edith Piaf being one of his favourite singers. Paul Daniels was another guest, and as we waited in the wings, he tried to help me relax by suggesting that I pretend I was singing just for him in his living room!

1987, Greenwich – Bells Are Ringing with Ray Lonnen.

I was nervous about following *Judy* with 'Bells' as it was a much more lightweight proposition; *Judy* had been such a success in Greenwich, it would be a hard act to follow. The obvious choice after the Olivier was most definitely *Piaf*, but maybe we'd have a chance with 'Bells'. On this occasion, Bernie was not free, but I was excited when I heard that Ray Lonnen had been cast in the role of

Jeff. I had seen him in a television thriller called *Harry's Game*, and remembered him as being excellent and extremely attractive, so was delighted at the prospect of playing opposite him. I was not the only lady looking forward to meeting him. He was indeed very good-looking, but without a flicker of flirtation; in fact, he wore shades for the first rehearsal, which seemed a bit pretentious on a dull day – and indoors – but it was probably just shyness.

There was the usual round of interviews for radio and newspapers with the emphasis on my 'comeback', and after only one week's rehearsal (poor Ray!), we opened. Ray did not have Bernie's sense of the romantic, but he did bring other things to the role – not, I hasten to add, a pair of nimble feet! Fortunately, the reviews were good, bar one, written by Jack Tinker, critic from the *Daily Mail*. Mum was travelling down to London by train to stay with her sister, Bessie, and was looking forward to seeing the show again; by sheer chance she landed opposite a woman who just happened to be reading the *Daily Mail*. As they chatted, and snippets of lives were exchanged, the woman suddenly came across the review of our show which she proceeded to read aloud. She had to stop halfway, as the contents became increasingly embarrassing. There was not much Jack liked about the show, and he even made a grudging reference to my award, although we knew that he hadn't even seen *Judy*. You can't please everyone all the time, but he was unnecessarily cruel to a rather charming, harmless little show.

Actors must learn to take it on the chin, but it's always hurtful to read a bad review, which would explain why some actors never read them, be they good or bad. It's not that we really care whether one individual dislikes a show, but a critic can put an unrepresentative opinion into print, where it can be read and believed by friends and strangers alike. Actors have to continue giving a performance, so it's probably best to read reviews – if you must – at the end of a run. Terry and I have only ever responded to critics on two or three occasions, but if your letter is printed, you run the risk of drawing attention to your bad review, which most readers might not otherwise have noticed or remembered.

As for the 'Tinker' business, Aunt Bessie, having seen the show, was so incensed that she wrote to the Daily Mail (assisted by that champion letter writer, Terry Wale), but it wasn't printed, and she never received a reply. But there were many positive notices, and Michael Billington, the reviewer from *The Guardian* gave us a wonderful review. We had expected a rough ride, but he found it 'delightful' and went as far as to suggest that it deserved a transfer.

We were a happy company, and the only little setback we suffered came in the form of a spate of illnesses. Vicky, one of our dancers, went down with bronchitis, and was off for a few nights. I had recently spent an evening with her, and I succumbed with the same. A nasty tummy bug hit Petra Siniawski, so she was the next to go, and John Levitt was suddenly rushed to hospital with gall stones. So depleted was our company that we had to cancel two performances, but at least no individual felt that it was entirely their fault. I imagine that it must have been disappointing for the understudies, but there were just too many of the key actors missing to go ahead. Alan Strachan said that he rarely got through an eight-week run without cancelling a couple of shows, and had been amazed that we didn't lose any with *Judy*.

I had great fun with Ella, although I might have gone for a zanier approach, and instead of trying to merge Ella's personality with mine, I could have hung onto the daft, blonde wig I so willingly discarded before we even opened back in Cheltenham. At the time, I felt I was being steered into the Holliday dumb-blonde performance, but it might have worked too. Katy, of course, has no memory of this time, her introduction to the theatre. Terry would often stand with her in his arms at the side of the auditorium (in the area known as the vomitory), watching the occasional song. She loved the atmosphere and, at only nine months old, was developing a love of musical theatre, which she retained as she grew up.

Somehow or other, the show didn't have quite the right ingredients for a West End transfer. Even John Doyle admitted afterwards that he would have loved to have been the director who brought *Judy* into town and had always considered *Bells Are Ringing* a poor substitute with little chance of a West End run. We'd been looking for an opportunity to exploit the Olivier Award before it became ancient history, but this hadn't been the right one. Alan Strachan, the director at Greenwich, was as keen to launch *Piaf* as we were. He arranged to meet and discuss it with the writer, Pam Gems, but she cancelled at the last minute with an excuse so implausible that we began to think there was more to the Piaf business than quite met the eye.

1987, between shows at Greenwich – Neil Patterson, Petra Siniawski, Simon Coates holding Katy, and Elena Ferrari.

With the situation unresolved, I turned my attention to the immediate future and settled back into the domestic routine of meeting mums and babies in the less than salubrious environment of Kensal Rise, but within a few weeks I was devastated to discover that I was pregnant again. Despite the craving for pickled onions, I could barely credit it; we had been led to believe that Katy was 'a little miracle', and this time we weren't even trying. When the local chemist gave me the result, I gasped, "Oh no" as I ran from the shop. Having felt so fortunate to have conceived one child after so many years of trying, we were dismayed about the possibility of a second so hot on the heels of the first. I had visions of myself, exhausted and struggling, with a double buggy as I trailed around the supermarket, and I firmly believed that the timing of this second baby would finish my career prospects with a vengeance. We decided to have a week in Tenerife with my mother, so that we could talk through it all in a warm and relaxing atmosphere.

If it hadn't been for the usual chaos and delays at the airport on the way back, I think we'd have all agreed that we had enjoyed a rather jolly holiday, although we still hadn't come to any kind of decision. I knew that whatever route we chose would not be easy, but my natural instincts told me that I would never forgive myself if I had a termination. I wanted another child, it had just happened too soon, but I told my friends that I was pregnant and reconciled myself to the future.

I was invited to take part in a *Night of a Hundred Stars* at the Adelphi Theatre, and the song they chose was, predictably, a Garland number, but one of the lesser-known ones from *I Could Go on Singing* which I rather liked – *Hello Bluebird*. During *Judy*, the food poisoning got in the way of such occasions, so it was good to be given a second chance, and I was delighted when Callum McLeod agreed to be my musical director for the evening. I rehearsed the number at his flat and had a brief run-through at the theatre on the Sunday prior to the day, but there were so many participants that we were only allowed a few minutes each to work out entrances and exits. It was fun to meet up again with old chums like Matt Kelly, who was doing a turn with Agony Aunt, Claire Raynor, and my favourite little critic – Jack Tinker!

During the week I bumped into my pal, Mandy, who told me that she and baby Max had just had an appalling sickness bug but were both well on the mend. I said that if they were both fully recovered, they should come round to celebrate Katy's first birthday, which they did. Unfortunately, we discovered that the bug was still alive and kicking, and on the Saturday evening when I got home after a rehearsal with the band, I was sick as a parrot. I wouldn't have thought it possible to throw up 16 times in one night, and on the Sunday morning I felt wiped out, and Terry was now affected as well. Katy wasn't struck down, toddling around our bed, as we both lay there almost unable to move.

Callum arrived to take me into the Adelphi Theatre for a final run-through, and I don't think he could believe his eyes at the vision before him. He had seen me the previous day, so he must have had a real touch of déjà vu, remembering those *Judy* nights just a few months before. I really began to wonder if there was some kind of 'Judy's Revenge', as the curse of Judy Garland seemed to have struck again. We managed to get through the number, and he dropped me back at the flat, where I had another few hours of lying around before he returned to take me in for the show. We decided that we would leave as soon as my number was over, as I would not be up to meeting any royalty afterwards. We arrived to scenes of total chaos; all the ladies, bar a couple of mega-stars, were crushed together in one dressing room; I just slumped on the floor against a wall and tried to put on a semblance of make-up, although I couldn't attempt to socialise.

The evening was under-rehearsed, and at one point Robert Kilroy-Silk introduced all the American stars in one fell swoop; suddenly the stage was littered with 'icons', which all but killed the event stone dead, as the idea had been to introduce them one at a time to keep on thrilling and surprising the audience. They shambled off in disarray and tempers were beginning to fray. I made it through my song, but it was all a bit of a disappointment and Callum drove me straight home, where I found a rather poorly Terry, who was not looking forward to leaving for Cheltenham the following morning.

Just after he left, I was feeling a little better, but later in the day I began to feel very strange with a heavy sensation inside. In the middle of the night I woke up with what felt like bad period pains, and I rushed to the loo, where it was over in a flash. I briefly held the tiny sack; I even saw little eye sockets. I screamed in horror, apologising to lumps of blood as they disappeared down the loo, and I almost felt as if this was my punishment for not having welcomed the news of this second baby; at that moment I wanted it more than anything in the world. When Katy woke up, I was still bleeding profusely, so I called for Dr Lucy, who gave me a brief examination, then called an ambulance to take me down to St Mary's, where I had a small operation to clear out what remained of my pregnancy.

Although depressed about the loss of the baby, my immediate decision was whether to go to Glasgow to take part in a programme called *Friends*. Viv Lumsden was hosting a weekly show where she introduced and chatted to a few of her old 'friends'; the fact that we had only passed each other in the corridor at drama college was irrelevant, and I had been looking forward to the job. I had already been north to rehearse with the pianist, and although the recording was only a couple of days away, I decided to go. I felt a bit wobbly, but the chat went well and the songs were passable, if not my best. As it was Easter, they requested *Easter Parade*, followed by *I Love a Piano* and a song of my own choice, which was *Summertime*. It was a light-hearted show, and everyone was supportive and sympathetic.

There was a little surprise, however, awaiting me in the shape of Miss Elspet Cameron who was in the studio audience. Old Elspet (she had always seemed old!) had kept in touch since our first meeting in *The Thrie Estaites* back in 1973, but this was one occasion when I could have done without her. I had planned to have a quick drink before heading back to my hotel for a night's peace and contemplation prior to leaving the next day, but she was waiting for me in the foyer as I left the BBC studios, with her 'rain mate' already tied round her head, well-prepared to face the ghastly weather outside. Without a 'by your leave', she hopped into my taxi and came back to my hotel for a cup of tea. I had no choice but to let her come up to my room, where she produced the usual array of photographs and asked my advice re the one she should use for her *Spotlight* entry, not to mention myriad programmes and snaps for my perusal. She was a great lover of theatre and trailed around the country to see her friends and acquaintances in various productions, and had even turned up with her overnight bag back in 1977 in Birmingham to see me in that rather obscure musical, *The Duenna*. She was an eccentric old soul and didn't understand my need for privacy at this time, eventually leaving around midnight to wend her way homewards; however annoying, she was an incredibly resourceful and adventurous lady, who never failed to supply me with entertaining anecdotes.

With no immediate prospect of another baby, I wanted and needed to focus on my career. It was nearly two years since *Judy,* and I was itching to get back into the swing of things. Larry had been far too relaxed since the show closed and seemed happy for me to wait around for what he considered an appropriate offer. But things rarely happen to those who sit and wait, except for the very privileged and lucky few, so I started to put a little pressure on. I called Joan Knight to tell her of my miscarriage and she came up trumps very quickly; I accepted her offer to play Mary Magdalene in *Jesus Christ Superstar* up in Perth later in the year, followed by Dandini in *Cinderella*.

I had also heard through the Annette Cook grapevine that Gemma Craven was about to leave the London cast of *South Pacific*, so I asked Larry to check it out. I fancied the part of Ensign Nellie Forbush, even if she really did have to 'wash that man right out of her hair' on a nightly basis. As it turned out, the grapevine had got it wrong, although on this occasion it did bear fruit of a different kind. The same management, Ronald S Lee, in collaboration with Stoll Moss, were in the process of casting a revival of *Brigadoon* and asked if I would be interested in the role of Meg Brockie. The production would rehearse and open in Plymouth before touring to the Palace Theatre, Manchester, but contracts for a West End run would depend on how well the show was received in these two cities.

I met Ronnie Lee in a hotel in Central London, and it all went swimmingly. I learnt Meg's two numbers, sang them for the show's director, Roger Redfarn, and I was offered the part, which I was only too happy to accept. I called Joan to say that I was no longer available to go to Perth – but it was still months ahead, and she would have no trouble re-casting. As expected, she took it very well, and only demanded a large bottle of gin from her old friend Roger Redfarn by way of compensation.

Things had become very cramped in the flat; it was not ideal, and we had started to think about a move back to Scotland, or down to Brighton, which was an old dream of Terry's, but knowing that this was not the right time, we decided to put any thought of a move to the back of our minds. We managed a final meal at Benny and Toni's before leaving London – on this occasion, meeting Michael Denison and Dulcie Gray, quite a starry duo! I was looking forward to the exciting new job on the horizon.

- 19 -

Out of the mist

There was a lot of advance publicity down in Plymouth, where we were to be based for around ten weeks before heading for a month's run in Manchester. There were four principals, and we flew down to Plymouth in a tiny plane, which was quite an adventure. We did interviews, had photographs taken, and from the outset we felt that we were in safe hands. We rehearsed the songs well ahead of time so that we could do a 'Presentation' in London for the press and friends as a taste of what was to come. It went well and I had my first impressions of the cast, who all seemed very friendly. Naomi Sorkina Tate, a very striking Jewish lady, was playing Maggie, a dancing role with no dialogue, and at a first meeting she struck me as a bit of a diva – a Jewish princess indeed. She treated her part as an acting role, as she had a dramatic funeral dance to perform. As time passed, she and I shared a great deal of time together and formed a firm friendship.

It was summer, and a lovely time to be on the south coast. We moved into our little flat in Plymouth, where we had an awful first night. Katy made a lot of fuss and noise, and I was aware that Kiki Dee was in the adjacent flat, having just finished the run of *Blood Brothers*. The last thing she needed was a squawking toddler to disturb her sleep before she set off on the next leg of her tour; at least she only had to cope with it for one night!

Brigadoon was my first real challenge as an actress and a mother. I had Katy, now aged sixteen months, for the entire ten-week stint, and with Terry soon to be working with the students at Guildford, I had to call on the aid of my parents, who arrived at the onset of rehearsals and stayed for a fortnight. They were not available for an indefinite period, so various other childminders had to be enlisted from time to time.

I was only let down on one occasion during rehearsals when the stage door-keeper's daughter didn't turn up because she had period pains. She obviously knew little of the world of theatre and had certainly never heard of the motto, 'The show must go on'! With no one else to turn to, I had to take Katy with me to rehearsals. I was nervous about it, but she was amazing; with nothing more than a couple of bottles of juice, a few biscuits, and a bit of help from the girls in the cast, she sat there watching the singing and dancing all day long without a murmur. I had to seek more reliable assistance, and that eventually came in the shape of Corinna, a student with whom Terry had worked in Guildford, and who lived in Plymouth. As soon as college broke, she returned home for the summer, and I had my 'mother's help' for the rest of the run.

1988, Plymouth – Brigadoon with Robin Nedwell.

It was certainly a lavish production, with a cast of 40, a 25-piece orchestra and lovely costumes; the beautiful kilts alone must have cost a fortune. The management was also keen to make sure that the accents were as authentic as possible, so there were at least a dozen genuine Scots in the company, and I didn't feel any need to apologise when family or friends came to see the show. Our choreographer, Tommy Shaw (another Scot), had been one of the sword dancers in the 1949 production at His Majesty's Theatre in London, and he recreated many of Agnes de Mille's original routines for our production and they had stood the test of time. Our producer was the lovely Ronnie S. Lee, and Stuart Calvert (a Canadian) was our experienced and very capable Musical Director. There were no star names in the cast, apart from Robin Nedwell, so the salaries were quite modest by West End standards. We graduated from rehearsal pay to a kind of touring pay in Manchester, and by the time we reached London I was earning £800 a week (less agent's commission!), which I considered an extremely healthy amount, especially if we managed to get a decent run.

The only sadness was the death of my Gran Mackie. I had always been close to her and went to see her as often as I could when I was in Dundee. She never lost her cheery personality and sociability, and even when she was in her nineties, she would answer her door, humming as she came. She was strangely unemotional and able to talk with ease about the daughter who had died from a bout of measles at the age of six, her two brothers who had both lost their lives in their early twenties during the First World War, about nearly losing my own dad when a leech embedded itself inside his nose and almost finished him off in India during World War 2, and most bewildering of all, about David, born in 1913, who she always referred to as her youngest brother; we only discovered after her death that David was her illegitimate son, brought up by her mother as her own 'late' baby. David did not hear the truth until he was an adult, causing him a great deal of pain when he found that every relationship in his life had been based on a lie, and that his three sisters were in fact his mother and his two aunts.

But we're talking about a different time when being illegitimate was a dreadful stigma to carry and people had to cope as best they could. Dad was with her near the end, and she asked him to sing a little song for her; he managed a chorus of 'Here we are again, happy as can be, all good friends and jolly good company', a song she often sang. At the age of 97, she slipped away. Sadly, I had to miss her funeral as I prepared for the opening night. My stalwart mum returned for her second stint of baby-minding the day after the funeral.

1988, Plymouth – Brigadoon.

The most exciting day in Plymouth came when we met the orchestra for the first time; it was exhilarating. Terry brought Katy along, and I could sense her excitement at her first big musical experience. There was a great buzz and a new feeling of anticipation as we began to look forward to the opening night. On the day prior to the opening, however, Leonard Maguire, who played the old Dominie, had a minor heart attack and was replaced by a local actor/ newsreader, who just happened to be Scots, and was with us for the first week. Leonard was a lovely old actor, but he smoked heavily, and it was amazing that he was able to return so soon; although he often struggled for breath, he remained with us until the end of the run. Despite Leonard's absence, we had a great opening, and my Uncle Allan and Aunt Marie came along with mum, making it a memorable night.

Meg Brockie, the giggling, man-chasing wench, was a lovely character to play, full of fun, and with a couple of smashing songs, but although it was not the most demanding part in the world, I still found it quite difficult to cope once the show opened. After an early morning start, and a long day with a toddler, it was quite a daunting prospect to head to the theatre to get into the right frame of mind to perform in a musical comedy. Katy didn't take too kindly to it either, and her screams of protest as I left the flat were still ringing in my ears when I arrived at the theatre.

People in other walks of life can work all day and flop in the evening, but we must be at our best at 7.30pm, and it's difficult to conserve energy during a busy day. I was very strict with myself during *Piaf* and *Judy*, always fitting in a rest, but I did not have Katy Violet then! Fortunately, Meg Brockie did not come into the 'Legend' category, so I survived, and after we finished we returned to London and made the cast album before we left for Manchester. This management were doing things in the right order, and it was great to have a proper show recording before we reached the West End.

Sadly, the weather up north was dismal, audiences at the Palace Theatre were poor, and we began to have doubts about the future of the show; even at this stage we were wondering how the set was going to survive. It looked marvellous, but it was heavy and cumbersome, and as the major noisy scene change was executed behind the curtain during my big number, I was growing less than fond of the Brigadoon hills and mountains.

The other drawback in Manchester was that it was no joke trying to feed a picky toddler in a hotel room, and I was reduced to heating her food in the kettle; on one occasion I attempted to boil eggs in it! Terry was about to open *The Crucible* at Webber Douglas in London and was unable to help, so the folks came down to help me through the technical week, stayed for a few days and then took Katy away for a while, easing the pressure and giving me a little bit of freedom; I recall a shopping spree when I treated myself to two of the best coats I have ever owned – coats which I still possess. It was such a thrill to have a decent income and to be able to splash out on the occasional luxury item, although they were, of course, bought in a sale! Even at this stage we had no guarantee of a long run.

Anna Pajak, a young fan whom I'd met in Greenwich during *Bells Are Ringing*, turned up in Plymouth clutching a little bunch of flowers, but within a few hours of her arrival, she was mugged and had £50 stolen. I invited her back to my flat, and that was the start of getting to know Anna. She then came to Manchester, booking herself into a small B&B for a couple of nights. Although I never hit the heights of mass adulation, I have been fortunate in my two special 'fans', Annette and Anna, who were always a pleasure to know. They kept in touch, and Anna even came up to Perth to see our final production of *Judy* in September 2012. Sadly, Annette died of a heart condition in 2022.

After our month at the Palace Theatre, we got our transfer, opening at the Victoria Palace Theatre on October 25th, 1988. The preview Gala Night was quite an occasion, our royal guest being Princess Michael of Kent, or 'Princess Pushy' as she was then known – apparently nicknamed by Princess Anne! I had already decided, as a matter of principle, that I would not curtsey, but as she stopped to talk to me, I realised that my little protest was quite in vain. She was so tall that it must have appeared to her that I was stuck in a permanent curtsey, and she was probably delighted to find such a humble servant; despite her reputation, she was rather charming. The following night was our actual opening, and although there wasn't an official party, we organised one ourselves, and Annette, fan extraordinaire, did the catering. The vibe was good, and we felt optimistic about the future of the show. Most of the reviews were favourable, although some did find the whimsy a little hard to swallow. Even Jack Tinker enjoyed the evening, although he managed to finish his review with a little jibe at me, which probably passed unnoticed by most – something to do with my giggle.

My main disappointment was that the noisy scene changes were even noisier. In Plymouth I was told that the noise would go in Manchester, and in Manchester I was told to wait until London, and once there I was informed that nothing could be done about it. The set was showing signs of wear and tear before we got to the West

End, so things could only get worse, and it was frustrating to play my one big scene with a major change going on behind. On some nights the noise was horrendous, and on others it was just irritating, but I had to learn to live with it. At least the scenery looked impressive, although I'm sure that by the end of the run, it was only fit for the bonfire.

1988, Victoria Palace Theatre, London – Brigadoon opening night with Terry.

Now that we were in London, we all had our own dressing rooms on different floors and Katy had a ball. She was our little *Brigadoon* mascot, and at 19 months was such a chatterbox that she knew most of the company by name and regularly visited them in their dressing rooms between shows on a Saturday. It was part of her life for well over a year, and she was quite bewildered when it all came to an end. With the run under way, Terry and I began to feel that we were back in the swing of things; we were invited to the *Evening Standard Theatre Awards* in November and were delighted to be part of the glitz and glamour again. It was around this time that a small theatre in New Zealand mounted a production of *Judy,* and from the reviews that we saw, we had the impression that it might have been rather good. We never managed to see it of course, but the royalties bought us our first colour television and video recorder. We also bought a video camera which provided us with a wonderful record of our children growing up.

When the camera arrived on the scene, Terry couldn't leave it alone, and on one occasion when I was out, he decided to film Katy dancing on top of the kitchen units to the strains of the *Brigadoon* tape. She had often done this before, but never unsupervised. After a few minutes, she bent down to put her bottle of milk on the surface, misjudged her footing and crashed to the floor. There was a beat before the screaming, and although Terry did stop filming as she fell, it's still painful to watch. When I arrived home, I was treated to a viewing of this excruciating piece of footage, but at least I was able to watch it in the knowledge that she had survived the accident.

We were still thinking about a move, and in November something happened which, in a way, accelerated things and prompted us to get our skates on. I had never been happy using the Underground, but I was forcing myself to make the daily journey from Queen's Park to Victoria because the journey was relatively simple, involving one change at Oxford Circus. I always managed to get a seat at my starting point, so I was fine until I had to change trains, but there were only two more stops after that, so I usually coped. Unfortunately, they were the tricky ones because, travelling in the 'rush hour', there was no chance of a seat.

On one unforgettable afternoon I changed as usual, but after a couple of minutes the train came to a standstill in the tunnel. I have no idea how long we were stuck, but it felt like forever. I was jammed between a pole in front of me and what felt like the population of London behind. I was trapped, and as my heartbeat increased, my breathing went out of control and I panicked, breaking down in uncontrollable sobs. I might have expected London commuters to be indifferent to my plight – they were, after all, in the same boat – but they could not have been more helpful. One man offered a mint, another a handkerchief, and one lady even offered her seat. I declined all the kind offers, but when someone asked if there was anything they could do, I suggested they might talk to me. "Where are you going?", one said. "The Victoria Palace Theatre." (loud sobs) "Are you going to see a show?" "I'm in it." (even noisier sobs!) "What are you playing?" "The comedy part." (maybe even registering the irony!) "Is the play suitable for children?" "For about eight-year-olds and upwards." (more hysterical chokes, splutters and tears!). One man offered to alight with me at the next stop, but when the train finally jerked into action I decided to stay put for fear of being late. We had another stoppage before our destination, but with the help of fellow travellers I was able to cope until I said my goodbyes. I staggered across to the theatre where I took a tranquilliser and prepared for the evening performance. This experience had a lasting effect and I rarely ventured into the London Underground again on my own, preferring to use the No 52 bus!

Faced with the agony of travelling in and out of Central London, we started to house-hunt in earnest, and decided to forget about Scotland and focus our attention on Brighton. We opted for the south in the belief that *Brigadoon* had revitalised my career and could be the start of many shows to come. Property prices were still rising, and there was nothing to suggest this boom might burst. It was a tough decision though, as with Lily gone into care, it was going to be hard to leave Sid on his own in the downstairs flat, especially after all he had gone through to make the flats self-contained. With a toddler now a permanent fixture in the only bedroom, and our large bed in the lounge, we needed a home with a second bedroom, but decided not to mention our plans until we had found somewhere.

In the early days of the run, we were very involved in publicising the show, and in December a few of us headed to Birmingham to take part in a *Pebble Mill* television programme. The three male dancers were to perform the Sword Dance, Maurice Clarke was singing a solo, and I was to do my big number, *Love of My Life*, with Robin offering silent support beside me. As we travelled north together, the dancers had already started to knock back the booze. I got the impression that Ronnie Lee was none too impressed with the tone of the conversation, which was decidedly risqué.

On our arrival at the hotel, Ronnie suggested that we all have an early night so that we were fresh for our live appearance the following morning. As soon as he was out of sight, the boys headed for the gay bars and didn't stagger back until around 4am, but they paid the price when they had to get up a few hours later. They looked very fragile under the glare of the studio lights, but with the aid of a few paracetamols, they made it through the lengthy sequence. I was very fond of a couple of them, especially Ian Mackenzie Stewart, who hailed from Dundee and was a pupil at Linlathen School where my mother was a music teacher. Life for a young male ballet dancer was no picnic in Dundee, and once he escaped to a wider world, he rarely returned, except to visit his mum. Mark Freeman lived in Brighton, and after we moved I often shared car journeys with him. Sadly, both he and the third member of the trio, Stephen Lübmann, died only a few years later from the AIDS virus, which was just beginning to enter our consciousness towards the end of the '80s. Ian died in his early fifties with liver failure, which may well have been related to his lifestyle.

Robin and I were interviewed before I had to sing, and that went well enough, but just before going on, Stuart, the MD, told me that my musical intro was going to be slightly longer, and although I understood what was going to happen, when it did, I was completely thrown and missed my entrance. The band were unaware of the problem, although Stuart, who was conducting, could hear the vocals through his headphones, and managed to convey to them what was going on, but we didn't get together until the end of the first four-line stanza. I didn't panic, and we completed the song in good style; I could barely believe that most people hadn't noticed the *faux pas*, as it seemed mega to me – such is the nightmare of live television!

At the end of January the company were invited to take part in the 1988-89 *Olivier Awards*, so a musical sequence was worked out that involved most of the cast. Robert and Jacinta featured in a duet, and Robin and I entered as the other two principals, joining in the end of the number with the rest of the chorus; although we didn't have much to do, we were both in the same boat, so we agreed to take part. At the last minute, Robin decided to back out, because he felt that, as the only character with a non-singing role, he was going to look like an 'extra'. I was vexed because as he was 'my other half', I was left without anyone to relate to and had to tag on to Robert and Jacinta like a spare part. But it was quite a jolly night, and as Robin and I had become good friends by this time, I quickly forgave him for letting me down. As I watched Elaine Paige singing a number from her upcoming musical, *Anything Goes*, I didn't envy her; when we had a brief chat beforehand, she was uneasy and trembling with nerves. I don't think that many performers find it easy to participate in these glitzy live occasions, especially when so much is riding on your performance, West End managements being keen to use the exposure to attract future audiences.

The following day I was invited to take part in a Grampian television panel quiz show called *Shammy Dab,* which I accepted with a little trepidation. I had been feeling quite a bit of anxiety, so Dr Coffman prescribed tablets, which he assured me would have a calming effect. I took one and woke in the morning with my head spinning and my balance badly affected. He clearly thought that my condition required drastic action, but the pills were strong and, knowing that I had to go onstage, he should have warned me of possible side effects. I ended up in Casualty, but it was ironic that, having gone for weeks without missing a performance, after just one pill prescribed by my doctor, I missed my first show. It was a Saturday matinée, and although I was back by the evening I found it hard to accept that one of my two understudies had gone on in my place. Come what may, I was determined to get by from then on without medical intervention.

There were two teams on the Grampian quiz show, the West Coast led by Glasgow comedian, Andy Cameron, and the East Coast by my old friend, George Duffus. It was a relatively simple format with all sorts of local questions, and being from Dundee, I was invited to be on George's team. Terry agreed to come up with me so that we could collect Katy, who had been in Dundee again to give me a break; we arranged for the folks to bring her to our hotel in Aberdeen so that she could fly back down with us. Before the recording, we were given a few pointers about the sort of questions we would be faced with, and we were each given a word, around which we had to weave an entertaining tale. My word was 'wabbit', and I had great fun with that descriptive old Scots word, meaning 'totally shattered'. We recorded two episodes, changing our frocks between the two, and I think that the final score was a win for each team. Despite my feelings of anxiety, I was gay and lively on the show, and it was good to see old friends again. The following morning when mum and dad arrived with Katy, she ran and jumped into my arms, and I was so choked that I thought that I would burst.

It was in March that I finally decided to seek alternative help for my nerves, which I firmly believe were a legacy from the food poisoning trauma at the Strand theatre. Hypnosis sounded like a good idea, and Dr Coffman suggested someone he knew at the Synergy Centre near Sloane Square. I should have steered clear of Dr Coffman's suggestions after the previous fiasco, but I was desperate to find a solution. At our first appointment, during the 'getting to know you' bit, the therapist became quite abusive and reduced me to tears with suggestions that my mother forced me onto the stage against my will, and goodness knows what else. I think I was hoping to be 'put under' and find a quick fix for what ailed me. He seemed quite happy to have upset me and said that it was all part of the breaking-down process. I was not at all sure that I wanted to continue, because as well as his aggressive manner, he had a very irritating Australian accent which did not bode well for the hypnosis sessions.

He was about to go on holiday, and as I left, he presented me with one of his relaxation tapes, adding an extra £5 to his £50 bill. The tape was useless, and I really don't know why I bothered to return. I saw his partner for my second appointment and, eternally optimistic, I probably had hopes that he might be better. I had already been introduced to him when, in a veiled way, he suggested that he would be able to offer me sessions at a vastly reduced rate, because he was interested in the world of theatre. Perhaps it was the thought of a bargain which tempted me, but he turned out to be a bigger balloon than the other one.

As the man wittered on, it took a lot of self-control to remain in the room. I stayed out of a misplaced desire not to be rude, and because I was under the impression that it wasn't costing me very much. When he also presented me with a £50 bill, I reluctantly paid up and hurried to the theatre in a mild state of shock. I had paid over £100 for a lot of codswallop and aggravation, and when I got home I wrote a little note to the gentlemen, explaining that I would not be coming back, as the whole experience, and their fees in particular, could only serve to increase my state of anxiety. Strangely enough, meeting those two charlatans was probably the kind of shock treatment I needed.

I was struck down with a little tummy bug at the beginning of April, and it kicked in the day before I was due to sing on the *David Jacobs Show*. He was doing a special tribute to Judy Garland, and I was to be singing three songs. I struggled into the *Victoria Palace*, and I would have gone on if Marge, our Company Manager, had not insisted that I go home. I didn't argue as I was desperate not to jeopardise my performance on the radio show. The following morning I was slightly husky due to dehydration, but the show was not going out live, and after one false start on *Zing Went the Strings*, it was plain sailing. A few from the *Judy Garland Club* were in the studio audience, leaning down from the balcony, willing me to do well. I returned to *Brigadoon* that evening, but although I only missed two performances through illness during the entire run, I hated missing any.

Not everybody felt the same; it was my first experience of a longish run, and I was shocked at the number of people who habitually missed performances. It was understandable that the dancers suffered from various injuries, but that did not explain their numerous absences. Some just missed the odd show, but there was one dancer who took the occasional Friday, Saturday and Monday off – just to enjoy a long weekend. When he finally reached the upper limit of around 48 absences, he was given a warning. I discovered that you could miss quite a few shows before they docked your pay, but there was a magic number beyond which you must not go, and it was interesting to note that most of the company managed to stay just within that boundary. Naomi came close; she was forever pulling muscles and twisting ankles, and I can still picture her with some limb or other strapped to a bag of ice. Jacinta had to miss a couple of weeks due to sinus trouble, and Ian Mackenzie Stewart had a severe tummy bug for over a fortnight – so severe that his mother came down from Dundee to look after him. The worst hit was our leading man, Robert Meadmore, who was off for three weeks with Salmonella poisoning. He suddenly felt sick one evening during the show, and by the time he reached home, he was violently ill. On one of his many trips to the loo, he tripped in his haste and cracked his nose on the toilet bowl; ironically, it was the broken nose which kept him away for so long. Robin Nedwell never missed a performance, although it is a trifle easier to carry on if you don't have to sing! Poor Robin died only ten years later at the age of 53.

To live in London, you must be able to use the Underground, and because I struggled with it I had never been ideally happy. Even after replacing the tube with the bus, I found that they weren't much better; they were either full up, running late, or both, so I was delighted when our offer on a house in Brighton – well, Hove Actually – was accepted on April 1st. Our decision was totally justified in the knowledge that the journey from Hove to Victoria Station, just across the road from the theatre, took less time than the trip across London.

As the summer approached, there was a big Underground strike, which rendered the buses as crowded and claustrophobic as the trains, so our move could not come soon enough. Property prices were still booming, and our modest house cost a daunting £86,000. We spent a very busy couple of months going up and down to Brighton, planning the décor, measuring up for curtains and the numerous other things that had to be considered. It was comforting to know that there was no pressure on us to clear our things from the flat, and we did the move on June 20th.

'And her mother came too'; always willing to help, mum came for a few days to help with Katy as we got on with cleaning, shopping and getting our bearings. It was a delightful little terraced house with three bedrooms and our first en-suite shower in an area known as 'Poet's Corner', which was about a 15-minute walk from the seafront, so Terry's dream had finally come true. It was so convenient for me to catch a train to Victoria and cross the road to the theatre, although our first few weeks were complicated by a rail strike. I was able to share lifts with Mark on strike days, so we coped. We also had a heatwave in July, and everyone suffered under the weight of the tweeds and kilts in Brigadoon; I could only imagine how the sword dancers felt at the end of their exhausting routine! It was amazing to watch those strong-looking, hairy Highlanders, knowing that underneath the manly attire lurked the odd pierced nipple! They were certainly more at home at Madame JoJos, but there was no denying the skill, strength and stamina required to perform that incredible dance.

Down in Hove we were happy with our new neighbours,

especially Christa, a German lady who had a dog, two cats, and various students who rented rooms from time to time. On the other side was elderly 'Auntie' Win (as she asked Katy to call her), and her very introverted daughter, Jane. Win was a bit of an old battle-axe, but we invited them in one Sunday just to break the ice. A few days later, on the day before *Brigadoon* closed, Jane took her life by jumping from a high hospital window. Win pushed a little note under our door to tell us of her death, and it cast a shadow over our early days in Molesworth Street.

LERNER & LOEWE'S
BRIGADOON

JACINTA MULCAHY   ROBERT MEADMORE   LESLEY MACKIE
MAURICE CLARKE   IAN MACKENZIE STEWART   SORKINA TATE   JO-ANNE SALE
ROBIN NEDWELL
ALAN JAY LERNER   FREDERICK LOEWE
AGNES de MILLE   TED ROYAL
CHRIS ELLIS   RICK CLARKE   STUART CALVERT
MARTIN JOHNS   ROGER REDFARN   TOMMY SHAW
VICTORIA PALACE THEATRE

So many people came to see the show. I had never been in a long run before and I lost count of the number of friends who turned up: friends from my school days, friends of my parents, work associates of dad's and many family members. After Uncle Arthur died, Aunt Bessie came on a few occasions, and I think that she found the show a comfort; I certainly found it a comfort to have the support of friends and relatives, because as *Amadeus* had shown with Terry, the repetition can affect your equilibrium. Despite a few hiccups along the way, I was happy to find that I was still giggling convincingly by the time we reached our 400th performance! Sooner or later *Brigadoon* was destined to disappear back into the mist, and shortly after this milestone we learned that the management had decided to call it a day and close five weeks earlier than planned. No one was particularly happy about this decision, especially as the show that was due to follow us was bound to be a disaster and wouldn't last five minutes. It was a musical called *Buddy: The Buddy Holly Story*; 'Buddy' was a smash-hit and ran for over 12 years!

ONCE IN EVERY HUNDRED YEARS...

I will always have fond memories of *Brigadoon;* it was my own little bit of Scotland right in the heart of London. But all good things come to an end, and after our final two performances on August 5th, 1989, I caught the last train from Victoria Station and headed off for my new life by the seaside.

- 20 -

Look for the silver lining

Things were quiet on the work front after *Brigadoon*, and we were both delighted when Joan Knight invited us back to Perth for *Born Yesterday*; Terry to direct, and me to play the part of Billie Dawn, another kookie blonde made famous on stage and screen by Judy Holliday. It strikes me that, for a brunette, I've played quite a few dumb blondes, but I remember my agent being rather negative about accepting the role, as never having seen me play such a part, he couldn't easily visualise it. Thankfully, Joan asked me well in advance of the March rehearsals, so I had plenty of time to prepare. Gone were the days when just two-and-half-weeks rehearsal would suffice; with my time no longer my own, I rarely had long periods to get on with learning lines and had to grab the moments when I could. But it was good to know that there was a job lined up, albeit a few months away.

Part of the reason for going north ahead of schedule was that our Piaf cabaret was to be given another airing. We had been booked by the *Law Society* to perform at their Annual Dinner at Gleneagles Hotel; the evening had a French theme, and Norman Robertson, our solicitor friend in Dundee, had persuaded us that we had the perfect entertainment for such a night. We contacted John Scrimger, the 'Tayside Maestro', and re-created the cabaret that we had done with Cathy on that strange night in Liverpool over three years previously.

Terry was particularly anxious because narration can be the least rewarding task, especially if the audience has been drinking. In the event, the guests had their meal and dancing before our cabaret, so by the time we were called upon to interrupt the proceedings to perform, it was almost 11pm. Before taking to the stage, we peeped through the door and were greeted by the vision of a wild and inebriated mob doing *Strip the Willow*. As the guests were all in French fancy dress, there were a lot of revolutionaries wielding swords, and we were a little apprehensive as they halted the dance to announce our 'spot'. Despite a bit of heckling, the night was a great success, although Terry vowed that he would never put himself through it again! After that interlude, it was down to work, and both

Terry and I welcomed the opportunity of working together again on such a lovely, heart-warming play as *Born Yesterday*. It was the ideal, him directing and me playing the lead!

1990, Perth – Born Yesterday with Lesley Moore and Martyn James.

Over the years Joan offered us many opportunities to work together, and many of our happiest experiences have taken place at Perth Theatre, well, at least back in the '90s. We had our usual interview with Graham Fulton, the local critic, and on this occasion he wrote: *Meeting Lesley Mackie and Terry Wale isn't so much coming face to face with a theatre pair, but more meeting a torrent in full spate. She drenches her hearer in words with a rapidity that would defy the best of shorthand writers. He backs up with an honest earnestness that makes them a double act that is nothing short of formidable... Perth audiences will get full value for their money. It is the hallmark of everything that Lesley Mackie and Terry Wale are associated with.* The headline of his review read: 'Lesley Mackie gives value for money.' Praise indeed! I was delighted to find that, despite the reservations of my agent, I was able to add Billie Dawn to my list of all-time favourite roles.

1990, Perth – Born Yesterday with James Telfer.

Just before we closed in Perth, I was sent the script and music for *Anything Goes*. Elaine Paige was leaving the West End production, and they wondered if I would be interested in taking over. I wasn't particularly enamoured with the script or ideally suited for the part, but it has a wonderful score by Cole Porter, so of course I was interested. I did a bit of work on the songs, and it was confirmed that I would meet the director as soon as I returned to London; on my return I was immediately informed that they had offered the part to Louise Gold – who <u>was</u> ideally suited and became known as the English Ethel Merman! Apparently, the director met her in the States, and decided there and then that she was perfect for the role.

Another possibility had collapsed, but we were happy with the way *Born Yesterday* had gone and we left Perth fired up with the desire to mount the play elsewhere. Stirring up enthusiasm in others was the usual problem; Bill Kenwright didn't think that the play would go well in London, and when we approached the director at Bristol, he was positive about the play having a revival but was somewhat negative about my suitability for the role. When he suggested Sandra Dickinson as a more likely contender, presumably because she had blonde hair and a squeaky voice, we knew where he was coming from. Typecasting has long been prevalent in television, but it's disappointing when theatre directors can't see beyond the colour of your hair. There was nothing we could do on our own, so passed on that idea.

Our other dream of reviving *Piaf* in the West End was also proving to be an impossible one. We had tried every avenue back in 1988 after *Bells Are Ringing*, when Alan Strachan had been keen to get it up and running in Greenwich. Despite his efforts he never managed to meet Pam Gems, and once he left Greenwich he gave up on the idea. Shortly afterwards, the new director approached me about doing the play, and I told him that if he could secure the rights, I was desperate to do it. He tried, but the door was still firmly closed. It was frustrating, as I knew *Piaf* was the role I needed to consolidate what we had achieved with *Judy,* but we were determined not to give up.

I was delighted when Joan informed me that she wanted to revive it during her 1990 autumn season, until I heard that she also had been unable to get permission to do it in faraway Perth. There was something brewing, and we didn't like the smell of it. She had been given a hint that the rights had been bought by an individual, and suggested that I write to Sebastian Born, agent of Pam Gems, to see if I could glean any information from him. When we returned to Hove I did just that, and when he eventually replied, he told me (confidentially) that plans were afoot for a production with a 'big international star' – namely Miss Elaine Paige (who he also represented). It was quite a body blow, but looking on the bright side, we felt that she was not entirely right for the part. I had to bide my time – after all, she might change her mind.

Two weeks after *Born Yesterday* closed, I wrote in my diary: 'Must leave Larry', and that was the start of a painful departure from a man I had grown very fond of. I recalled a charming lady who had come backstage after *Judy* one evening and had been most complimentary about my performance. She subsequently wrote to me to say that if I was ever looking for representation, she would be interested in taking me on, so I unearthed her note and decided to make contact. It was just a shot in the dark, but I went along to meet her, and we hit it off straight away. The only drawback was that she was small-time and inexperienced, although she was working for a large successful agency.

I also went to see Jean Diamond at *London Management*. I had already met her during *Brigadoon* as she was around quite a lot, which was not surprising as she represented half the company! She was friendly and enthusiastic, and a very experienced agent. On the minus side, she had numerous clients, including a lot of 'star names', so didn't have much time to promote the smaller fry. She was very positive, however, and told me that if my current plan did not work out, I could join her later; I could have my cake and eat it, in fact.

I think my main problem with Larry was that he did not see me in the way I saw myself. He had grandiose leading roles in mind, whereas I knew that I was a character actress who could play all sorts of parts. Perversely, I knew that part of the problem stemmed from the very role that had brought me recognition in the first place. I had played Judy Garland from happy-go-lucky childhood until her death at 47, by which time she had changed completely. It was an all-encompassing role, covering the entire gamut of emotions, and had been like playing half a dozen different people in the same play. Some casting directors seem to struggle with versatility and like to categorise you as a wide-eyed innocent, a *femme du monde*, a hopeless romantic or a dipsomaniac. The fact that Judy Garland encompassed all these elements made it difficult for them to pigeonhole me. Judy had been a huge leading role, and certain people had it in their heads that I would only be interested in more of the same. Apart from the fact that such parts do not grow on trees, I have never been one to sit around waiting for them to turn up.

It was after a phone call to Larry that I finally realised our situation was hopeless. He told me that he had just had lunch with a female casting director, and he had asked her why she didn't use me on the telly. She said that my height was a problem, because it was difficult to cast me in a romantic lead opposite a tall man. Apart from the fact that there were numerous small men on the telly, why on earth was she only thinking of me for romantic leads, and more to the point, why was Larry going along with this? It was only when I put the phone down that it really hit me, and I called him straight back to ask why he had not put her right. In truth, he was thinking along the same lines, and I was in a no-win situation. Because of *Judy*, anyone who thought of me at all, thought of me as a leading lady, but I was too small! Terry was at a party some time later, and told this story to television casting director, Tony Arnell. When he finished, he was dismayed when Tony said, "Well, I feel awful now, because I'm afraid that I've always thought of Lesley as a leading lady but haven't found it easy to cast her because of her height!" To be fair there are many leading roles that I wouldn't consider myself for, but I think that comment says a lot about the attitude towards casting women at that time.

Whatever the reason, Larry had not done enough to cash in on the Olivier Award when things were still hot. His taste was so refined that he thought it was tacky to mention my award underneath my *Spotlight* photograph, but who was going to remember I had won it if we kept it a secret? I needed someone to put the momentum back into my career, so I went in to see Larry, and we had a very civilised parting. It was only after I left him that I fully appreciated the ease with which you could get through to him on the phone, and I recalled with great affection the times we had shared. We even went together to see Bernie Lloyd (another of his clients) in the rock musical *Time* when I was heavily pregnant with Katy. I feared that the excessive decibels might harm my baby, but it was a worse ordeal for Larry, who found the experience quite agonising, being an ardent opera buff.

After Lily's death, Sid put the London house up for sale. Once the sale was complete, we discovered that we were still liable to pay the Community Charge for the previous few months when, to all intents and purposes, we had not actually been living in the flat. The new system, commonly known as the 'Poll Tax', was introduced by Margaret Thatcher. It was having gigantic teething problems and people were rioting about the injustice of it all, with many of them prepared to go to prison rather than pay up, and it became one of the most hated taxes ever introduced. It was a rating system designed to tax individuals and not property, which was going to benefit a single person living in a large home, but not five people living in a council flat! Somehow we had assumed that we'd only pay our two poll taxes for the house in Hove as, apart from a few bits and pieces of furniture, we had left an empty house in London. We didn't require the services of Brent council, so were astounded to discover that, as well as the two Hove taxes, we were also expected to pay another two for the empty flat! 'People not Property' had been the Tory Party boast! It was ridiculous that if we'd been (or even said we'd been!) living apart, one in the flat and the other in Hove, we would only have paid one tax for each property.

It dragged on until they finally issued a summons. We were busy at the time and unable to attend the hearing, so in our absence it was decided that we had to pay the tax or risk having our belongings removed from our Hove home, so we finally caved in. It wasn't until 1993 that the Poll Tax was abandoned for a fairer system, which was called the Council Tax. After the sale of the house, Sid lived with us for a while until he could find alternative accommodation. It's no easy thing to leave a parent in a care home, and it was a sad day when Terry eventually took him to London to take up his place at Kenbrook, a residential nursing home for retired London Transport employees.

An interview – and with David Hare, the illustrious playwright! The play, *Heading Home*, starred Joely Richardson, and I was up for the part of a 'feisty little chambermaid', so I went up to London to meet David and we had a nice chat. I was a little surprised not to have to read for him, but he didn't think it was necessary, and gave me the impression that the part was mine. I left feeling confident and was delighted to hear later in the day that I had indeed landed the role. I awaited the script with anticipation.

I was astounded when Terry came up to the bedroom the following morning to deliver it. Only one scene had arrived because

I was only in the one scene; in fact, my character only had three lines. As I lay in bed, still half asleep, Terry read me the immortal lines. Such was his outrage that he thought I shouldn't do it, but my old agent, Larry, assured me that actors were now tripping over each other to get a three-line job on the telly. Perhaps I should have been grateful that I was being offered a little character role and not a leading role, so height was not an issue – small maids were ideal! I decided to take the money and run; with a bit of luck, no one would even notice I was in it.

1991, BBC – Heading Home.

I was looking forward to my night down in Bristol. You hear stories of actors hanging around for days during filming, and I was hoping for a bit of that, so that I could feel the benefit of being away. Well, the least I could hope for was a night of uninterrupted sleep, a delicious, cooked breakfast, and a relaxing visit to the hotel's pool and leisure suite. I arrived early at the hotel, swimming costume at the ready, only to find that the pool was out of bounds due to maintenance work. I found something to eat and returned for a relaxing evening at the hotel. In my room there was a note awaiting me with details of my morning call, which was 5.40am! So, no swim, no sleep, no breakfast, no nothing! This was the glamorous life and no mistake – a couple of hours filming at the crack of dawn, followed by a quick visit to Dawn, Terry's ex, before I headed home later in the afternoon. But I was very feisty, extremely plain – and true to form, I had more calls about this minuscule little role than I would have had if I had been playing the lead! I was just miffed to have been recognised. I was, however, paid £500 for my efforts, and shortly afterwards it was repeated, so I had no regrets.

I have always thought of myself as an actress who sings, rather than a singer who acts, so I was a bit apprehensive when Benny Green asked me to take part in a concert, featuring the songs of Judy Garland and Deanna Durbin, with Maria Kesselman as Deanna. I caved in and agreed to do it, simply because it seemed foolish not to. I took refuge in the fact that, although it wasn't a play, I was still pretending to be Judy. We rehearsed with Don Innes, a wonderful simpatico pianist, supported by his duo of musicians, appropriately called *The Don Innes Trio*. On a freezing November evening, we had a warm reception for our first performance of *Two Smart Girls* at Clacton-on-Sea. While it was a daunting prospect, it was something of a breakthrough, as I had launched myself into a new area of work.

As Christmas 1990 approached, other things were improving on the work front. A survey had been taken amongst the subscribers of Perth Theatre to assess the favourite ten shows from the previous decade, and our 1984 production of *Piaf* had come a close second to *Joseph and the Amazing Technicolor Dreamcoat*. We didn't mind losing out to 'Joseph' because it had universal appeal, and Terry and I had been in that one as well – and although Joan hadn't succeeded in getting *Piaf* into her autumn season, after a lot of badgering and pleading, we were eventually given permission to mount a spring production in Perth. They must have felt that we could do them little harm up in the wilds of Scotland!

It was scheduled for March 1991, and Terry was invited to direct, so we decided to trail up to Perth *en famille* for the duration. It was a good plan, because the folks would see Katy and we'd have a bit of help. We were beginning to realise that our touring days as a family would be severely curtailed once Katy started school later in the year. As the English system was different from the Scottish one, it was a year earlier than it would have been, had we been living up north.

I had a decent role to look forward to, and it raised my spirits. I had also decided that I was, after all, going to join Jean Diamond at *London Management*. There would be no going back this time as I couldn't go on changing agents at this rate, or it might start to look as if there was something amiss with me.

Still doing my comedy schoolgirl act!

As we raised our glasses to welcome 1991, we knew that after the ups and downs of 1990, things could only get better. We had *Piaf* to look forward to, and the other bit of good news was that a Perth production of *Judy* would tour Scotland later in the autumn. So, after the doldrums of the previous year, 1991 had certainly got off to a great start – in fact, we were about to begin one of the best years of our lives.

- 21 -

Gloria in excelsis

It was in January that Terry first met Gloria Hope Sher. She had called a few months before, having obtained our phone number from Ronnie S. Lee, our New York producer of *Brigadoon*. Had I thought of contacting him at the time, I would have discovered that she was to be avoided at all costs and saved ourselves many months of hassle; I think that he only gave her our details to get her off the phone. So when she rang to say that she was currently producing a show at *Michael's Pub* in New York (a pub where Woody Allen played his clarinet for 25 years), we were bound to be interested, especially as that show was based on an imaginary meeting between Judy Garland and Edith Piaf. She painted a glowing picture of the show and wondered if I would like to play Judy if she could set up a production in London. Instinctively, I would have preferred to play Piaf, or even both, but it was Garland she was after. Although she was a loud, kooky character, we had no reason to doubt her credibility, and as most actors are eternal optimists, always believing that this could be the break they have been waiting for, we agreed to meet her on her next visit to London.

Between her first call and her second, Bernie Lloyd was over in New York, and went along to the venue to give the show the once-over. He reported back that it was dire, although not without a few (unintentionally) hilarious moments. Apparently, Judy and Edith spent the entire evening complimenting each other in a ghastly sycophantic manner; "I love your singing, honey." "Merci Cherie, I have all your records back in Paris." By the time Gloria came back to us, we had her measure, or so we thought. She was in London, staying in Anthony Newley's flat in Mayfair, and Terry thought it best to go alone for the initial meeting. He arrived at the flat, stepped into a lift which went up and opened into the lounge, where Gloria awaited him. She was a woman of indeterminate age, but possibly around 60. She sported a short skirt and had bows in her hair; overpowering was an understatement. For starters, she wanted Terry to read a play, written by a journalist friend of hers from the *New York Post* who just happened to be there that evening.

While Gloria prepared some pasta, Terry made a start on Act 1, but there was no way he could read an entire play with the author sitting watching him, and Gloria popping back and forth to see how he was getting on, so he had to beg leave to take the play home to read it in more conducive circumstances. Her idea was that, if he liked the play, he could direct it and cast me in the leading role; she seemed to have forgotten about the Piaf/Judy show; maybe she'd had her fingers burned at *Michael's Pub* in New York. It was a bizarre situation, considering that she had neither met nor seen either of us in performance, but was prepared to hitch her wagon to both of us because of a recommendation from Ronnie Lee.

Throughout the evening she drank heavily, stroking Terry's thigh at every opportunity, and he eventually left the flat, somewhat relieved to have escaped unscathed. He had promised to look at the script, so he did. It was quite well written, but not very interesting, so when Gloria called for the verdict, Terry tried to convey, in the nicest possible way, that the play was not commercial enough for the West End of London. He winced as he heard Gloria yell: "Terry thinks that your play stinks!" He was mortified, and it was only then that he realised that Gloria and the journalist were an item; well, they were until that moment. Sadly, we had not heard the last of Gloria; she was in regular contact throughout the year, full of dreams and schemes, but although instinct told us we were dealing with a chancer, something stopped us telling her to get lost. In any case, she was not an easy person to shake off.

Another booking for *Two Smart Girls*, and this one was at Croydon. We were now inside the outer limits of London and, on this occasion, quite a few mates turned up. Christa, our next-door neighbour, and Ray Lonnen, my *Bells Are Ringing* co-star from Greenwich to name but two. It was also a lovely surprise to receive a telegram from Deanna Durbin herself, who had long since retired from show business, and now lived quietly with her husband in France. It was a successful evening, and I was growing more comfortable with my new concert singer status.

For the moment though, my attention was now firmly focused on *Piaf*. Although I had been denied the chance to play the part in London, I was now returning to my home ground with high hopes of re-living the excitement of the original 1984 production. We also had confirmation of dates for the *Judy* tour, so it looked as if things were going our way. Most of *Piaf* had been cast by Joan, but she did ask Terry to see a few men in London to make sure that we had a strong, muscular actor in the key role of Marcel Cerdan the boxer, who was the love of Edith's life. He met and chatted to the three actors who Joan had selected, but as she had assured him that they were all good, he felt no need to ask them to read, and he picked the one who, as well as being a lovely singer, looked as if he had stepped off a building site. So, in high spirits, we headed north to start rehearsals on April Fool's Day.

1991, Perth – Piaf publicity shot with Bob Grant.

The read-through was a little disturbing because, although Marcel did look ideal, I was rather taken aback by his high-pitched giggle! My fears were confirmed once we started working on the play, and after a few days' rehearsal, Terry had to take him aside to find out why he didn't seem to be coping with the 'bed' scene. He confided that he felt too big and feared crushing me. Terry assured him that there was no problem, and he should try and relax. He sheepishly responded by explaining that he was not used to small women, only to big men! Part of the problem was that, although a fine singer, he wasn't really an actor, something Joan had failed to mention. After a few private lessons, however, Terry managed to get a performance out of him, and he gave a lovely rendition of *Les Trois Cloches*.

1991, Perth – Piaf with Kathie Whitely.

There were a few positive changes; the set was an improvement on the '84 one which had consisted of a series of walls; when one was removed, another was revealed. This time we had a splendid evocation of Parisian tenements, designed by Nigel Hook, and the overall feeling was much more 'French'. We started the play with a young Edith singing *Les Momes de la Cloche*, a song which she had sung in the Paris streets; it was certainly more appropriate than the one we had used previously, *La Goualante de Pauvre Jean*, which was not written until a later date. The return of the play was heralded with great enthusiasm, and particularly by the local press: *Florists in the Fair City will be rubbing their hands for the next four weeks … when Lesley last played the part, her performance became part of the town's folklore. In unprecedented scenes, the entire audience were on their feet night after night throwing carnations and roses onto the stage by the dozen!* Well, it's true that a few flowers were thrown back in 1984, but the scenes as described would not only have been unprecedented but, in Perth of all places, unimaginable. That is how myths are made, and the local florists must have been terribly let down by the whole affair, but we had a wonderful opening night, and after a bleak year, it was a tremendous feeling to be back in the limelight again. We had great reviews, and I found I was more relaxed the second time around, reading the lesson in church just two days after we opened, and the following Sunday taking part in a charity concert at the theatre – and I didn't easily give up my Sundays when playing a leading role.

The only little 'blot on the landscape' was when Gloria Hope Sher decided to come and see the show and asked us to book her into a hotel for a couple of days. She sailed over on the QE2 and informed us that, due to some accident on board ship, she had met a retired doctor from Bath, who had become her current 'Beau'. We took all this with a pinch of salt but made all the necessary arrangements for her stay. We found a lovely Bed and Breakfast overlooking the river and Terry picked her up from the station before dropping her off at the hotel. Unfortunately for Terry, he was landed with looking after her and she was a very embarrassing person to be around, telling everyone she met that she was going to take me back to Broadway and make me into a big star. Her fame spread through the theatre, so much so that Joan made herself scarce on the night when Gloria was coming in to see the show, although she did make her office available for Terry to entertain her during the interval.

As it was a virtual sell-out, the seats left for Terry and Gloria were not the best, and throughout the performance Gloria made no secret of that fact, complaining in projected tones. She seemed to expect privileged treatment, and as we sat with her in the bar afterwards, we tried to refrain from being rude, just in case she really was a dotty millionairess who was planning to invest in the future of the Wales. We introduced her to as few people as possible, because all her observations about the play were ignorant and misinformed, and one thing we did know was that if we ever had the misfortune of working with her it would be a nightmare, unless she was only responsible for putting up the cash; with Gloria as our producer, we would have big problems with production values. Having dropped her off at her hotel, we breathed a sigh of relief, and I went and stayed overnight at John Scrimger's house, so that I could enjoy a bit of peace before the two shows the following day.

I arrived at the stage door on the Saturday, just in time to take a phone call from the Sunningdale Hotel as Gloria had left without paying her bill! She had tried to pay by credit card but, being a small establishment, they couldn't deal with that. Instead of coming to some other arrangement, she had disappeared in the early hours of the morning. The landlady heard the taxi arrive, but before she realised what was happening, Gloria had scarpered. There was now no doubt at all that Miss Sher was a hideous creature, and we were livid. Naturally, I promised to cover the bill, but we were determined not to let her get away with it.

A couple of days later, Gloria called us at home and Terry mentioned her little 'omission'. She gave him some blethers about planning to send on the money, but she probably didn't even know the name of the hotel, never mind the address. She eventually sent us a cheque, and we noted that it was signed by her new doctor friend, Fred Evans. We were still mystified as to her own financial status, but were now hearing quite a few snippets from the American grapevine about unpaid debts and disappeared funds – yet still we did not cut loose!

On the last night, the family were in *en masse*, and it was another night to cherish. Although we didn't drown in a sea of flowers, we enjoyed a wonderful sell-out run, and the afterglow left me even more determined to get to the West End with the play. We found time to talk a bit about the forthcoming production of *Judy*, and Callum McLeod had agreed to send the London musical arrangements, so all was going well in that department; to play the two 'Legends' in the same year was quite a coup, and we were excited by the prospect.

We returned to a meeting with the ghastly Gloria. She invited us both for lunch, but this time to a different flat in Mayfair. We decided that this would be our last trip, and if she was her usual awful self, full of ludicrous notions, we would have to be straight with her. We arrived to find what appeared to be the debris of the morning after some seedy party. Fred was there, a rather shy gentleman, who must have been so bowled over by Gloria's pushiness and bombast that he had failed to take in that she was a total fraud. He knew little of the entertainment business, and we wondered if he would eventually blow his retirement nest egg on one of Gloria's hair-brained schemes. She offered us a drink, then discovered that she had been cleaned out the night before, so we had to make do with the dregs from a bottle of red wine. We calmed our hunger pangs with a few stale crisps which were lying around, but as time dragged on, we wondered when she would produce our lunch; certainly not before she subjected us to a video screening of her daughter, Bonnie, 'In Concert' at some nightclub in New York, with Gloria accompanying on the piano!

Terry had already suffered this torture on a previous visit, and we had the distinct impression that Fred had sat through it on numerous occasions, so it was clearly being shown for my benefit. Bonnie was unprepossessing to say the least, and her singing did not make up for her other shortcomings, so it was not easy to find a convincing compliment. Terry made some remark about her being 'rather free with the lyrics', and Gloria's response to that was, "What the hell does it matter?" I don't think Gershwin, Berlin or Lorenz Hart would have agreed with her. Whatever we felt about Bonnie Sher, Gloria was making plans to hire the Palladium to give London the opportunity to see this undiscovered treasure.

I think it was Fred who eventually suggested that we must be feeling rather hungry and, quick as a flash, Gloria suggested that we all go over the road to the pub. We were quietly seething, but as we were ravenous, we meekly joined them for four sandwiches and four beers, all paid for by Fred. As we hastily gobbled our food, Gloria suddenly asked us to look at Fred: "Look at the profile", she said. "Who does he remind you of?" We couldn't come up with anything. "Edward the Eighth", she yelled triumphantly. "He is the illegitimate son of the King." Fred sat in silence, so we never had confirmation or otherwise of this outrageous allegation, but I must add that, only a few months later, when we received an invitation to their wedding in New York, he was named as Sir Fred Evans! Maybe he was as dotty as she was.

Having finished our minuscule lunch, we were on the point of leaving when a young girl came across and said, "Miss Sher, are you ready for us yet?" Gloria told her that we'd be coming shortly, and to wait outside the flat. This was very mysterious, but all that we were told was that Gloria had come across this girl working in a nearby restaurant. She was an actress, and Gloria was hoping to help her and a few friends find some work. When we eventually crossed the road, there were five young people waiting at the foot of the steps leading up to the flat. As we joined them, we felt rather awkward as we really had no clue what it was all about, but as soon as we entered the flat, Gloria introduced us to the group as if we were royalty, making a big thing of my Olivier Award. She then asked them if they had prepared their audition pieces. We were aghast at her sheer audacity, because we suddenly realised that she was expecting them to audition for us. She had put us in an impossible situation, and unless we were prepared to kick up a fuss and walk out, we would have to sit there and squirm.

As the afternoon wore on, we discovered that she was intending to hire the Mayfair Theatre and form the group into a repertory company with Terry at the helm, directing various productions of his choice. It was ludicrous, as we didn't know any of the people involved, and if he was going to form any sort of company, he wouldn't have dragged in a few kids working in local restaurants. They said a little about themselves and sang a song. They all seemed so keen, and as 'resting' actors they had our total sympathy; it would have been cruel to tell them that this 'audition' was a total sham. We did admit that we had no prior knowledge of Gloria's plans, but they obviously didn't know her well enough to realise that they were there as playthings to feed her absurd megalomania, and they would be best just to return from whence they had come. As I sat there, I recalled an occasion when I was at drama college, and an American 'producer' turned up and put a few of us through our paces, and then disappeared off the face of the earth. I hoped that the kids that afternoon were able to put it down to experience.

After they left with Gloria's promise that she would be in touch, Terry told Gloria that this was not the way to go about things, but her response was just, "Didn't you like them? Well, you can choose your own company!" As far as she was concerned, people were there to be picked up and dropped as soon as they were of no further use, and I don't think she ever mentioned these young hopefuls again. As soon as they had gone, she was straight onto *Judy*, and her intention to take the show – and me – to the States. We tried to explain the problems that would entail, but she was unsinkable; she was confident that she knew all the 'right' people and would have no problem dealing with the Minnellis and the Lufts – even the might of Warner Brothers did not phase her. She assured us that American Equity would be easily persuaded that I was the only person who could play the part, and the fact that Sarah Brightman had recently failed to get into the Broadway production of 'Phantom' was dismissed by Ms Sher as a publicity stunt perpetrated by Andrew Lloyd Webber – as if he needed the publicity!

She then called her American lawyer, and before I knew what was happening, she had shoved the phone at me. They had obviously discussed the situation, but I was relieved when he started to explain to me, as he must have done to Gloria on many previous occasions, that it would be no easy matter to get me across to play Garland. We were on the same wavelength, and it was clear that he had the same problem as everyone else, which was getting Gloria to listen. He said that it would take another production of *Judy* in the West End, and if it was a success I might attain the 'star' status necessary to give us some bargaining power. That scenario was not on the cards, and despite her presence in the room, I managed to convey to him that we were totally in agreement that it was an impossible situation. He hoped that I might manage to get that message across to Gloria!

After I hung up, I tried to explain the problems, but all that I got was, "What's the matter with you? Don't you want to star on Broadway?" I finally suggested that she should try to mount a production with an American star, and we left her to ponder that one. I suddenly had visions of Bonnie Sher in the role, but pushed that nightmare to the back of my mind. Yet again, we knew that we had not heard the last of her.

THE SOUTH BANK CENTRE **QUEEN ELIZABETH HALL** THE SOUTH BANK CENTRE

'TWO Smart GIRLS'

LESLEY MACKIE
as Judy Garland

MARIA KESSELMAN
as Deanna Durbin

with the DON INNES GROUP

Devised and presented by
BENNY GREEN

Sunday, 2nd June 1991

Concert Management: SID ECKMAN PROMOTIONS

PROGRAMME £1.00

Benny, Maria and I, plus the lovely Don Innes Trio, now had a prestigious booking for our *Two Smart Girls*. The venue was the Queen Elizabeth Hall on the South Bank. The only problem was that our producer had arranged two shows for Sunday June 2nd but had done little in the way of publicity. It's not easy to persuade folk to venture inside a theatre on a sunny June afternoon, and in a last-minute effort to save the day, he hired a publicity lady to set up a few interviews. Maria and I chatted on *Woman's Hour*, and I went on *The Gloria Hunniford Show*. By the time Sunday arrived, we had a respectable number for the matinée and a better one for the evening, but it would probably have been better all-round if we had just done one show to a packed house. On this occasion, we added a new number, *Americana*, a song from *Every Sunday*, which was a 'short' made in 1936 when both girls were at MGM; it was, in fact, the only song they ever sang together, and a novel way to end the evening. Maria's boyfriend looked after the 'sound', and he even managed to tape the show to give us a memento of the occasion. At the end of the day, it all seemed worthwhile to have had the chance to appear on the South Bank in this rather special venue. 1991 was still going well.

We started to prepare for what we hoped would be the highlight of our year, *Judy* in Perth. Due to the overlap of dates, we had obtained permission for Katy to miss her first six weeks of schooling, but we were aware that this would be our last jaunt as a family, well, at least during term times. Auditions for the Perth production of *Judy* had provided us with a brand-new company, and in no time at all we were back in the Fair City. Terry's only disappointment was that he had not been allowed to direct (Joan rarely allowed writers to direct their own work), but we were more than happy with Clive Perry. Despite his sometimes-perverse behaviour with actors, he had a lot of experience and a great deal of flair. The icing on the cake was a generous financial agreement. Although working in a repertory theatre, Joan was one of the few directors who always tried to give special remuneration if the part merited it. Terry had, as always, done more re-writing and in this, the final version (or so we thought!), I even appeared briefly as Dorothy in Oz – and at 40 years old that gave me quite a kick! He had added a couple of new characters, and in creating Betty Asher he had not only provided Judy with a friend to tell her troubles to, but he had given Karen Pierce-Goulding a decent role to play while she was understudying the massive role of Judy Garland; although she never did go on, it was a great comfort to have an understudy.

Not only that, but we had six 'Boyfriends'! Most of the boys were actors, rather than trained dancers, but they were terrific. Our choreographer was Perth-based Tony Ellis, and although we had worked together on previous productions, we considered his work on *Judy* amongst his most inventive. For the first time we had two genuinely middle-aged gossip columnists; Hedda Hopper was played with panache by my old friend, Anne Downie, and we couldn't have wished for a better Louella Parsons than that Perth stalwart, Janet Michael. On this occasion Michael Roberts took on the 'double' of Louis B. Mayer and Sid Luft.

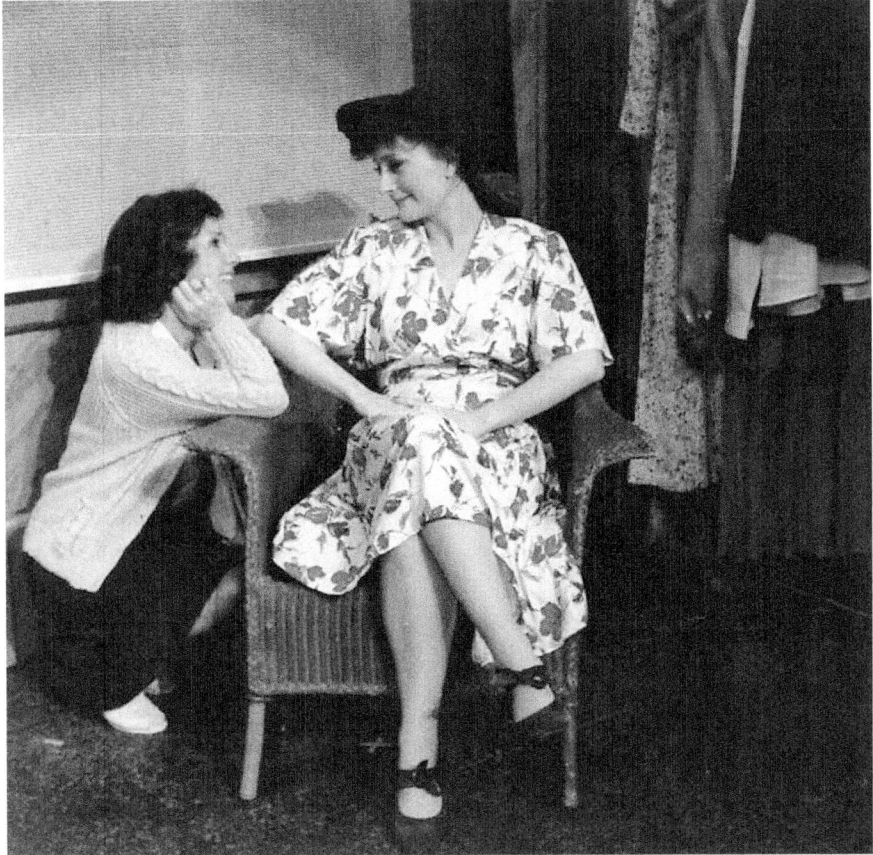

1991, Perth – Judy with Karen Pierce-Goulding.

Clive Perry had a degree of infamy regarding his ability to reduce certain actors to quivering wrecks, and I had been on the receiving end back in *The Wizard of* Oz, but Clive came into our rehearsal period just oozing consideration and charm, and he was a pleasure to work with. This uncharacteristic behaviour may have had something to do with the fact that he had just emerged from a spot of bother up in Pitlochry. He had (allegedly) been responsible for causing a young actor to suffer a nervous breakdown and one of the older actresses had tried to rally the company in his defence. When push comes to shove, actors have a rather strong streak of self-preservation, and it can be difficult to stand up and be counted, so she didn't have the backing of the entire company, but she took the complaint to *Equity* and Clive had been grilled about the affair. It was a brave stand to take and she, along with one or two others, was never invited to work in Pitlochry or Perth again.

Whatever the reason, Clive was on good form, and it was just unlucky for him that one of our *Judy* actors appeared to be going under. I noticed from day one that the young man was very tense and uptight, and even before he introduced himself, he was stressing about Scottish banking hours, and worrying about how he would cope with life in the North. By the end of the first week, Clive, not renowned for his perception and sensitivity, quietly suggested to me that we just go along with his wishes, for fear that he might go over the edge. I recall one scene where I, as a neurotic Judy, was obliged to sit down for the entire time, while the analyst paced the floor because he was unable to keep still. With the double burden of various acting parts and numerous dancing routines, he eventually headed for Joan's office and wept on her shoulder. A real analyst was called in to assess his state of mind, and without further ado he was bundled into a taxi and driven back home, where his family had to foot the £400 bill – or so we heard! We never managed to say goodbye, nor did we hear how he had fared. There is no doubt that he had a nervous breakdown, but it was nothing to do with Clive. We were left minus an actor, and on the day that he departed, it was just by chance that local actor, Ralph Riach, was sitting in the coffee bar and was promptly invited to join the cast; right place at the right time, although there was no question of Ralph putting on his dancing shoes. Tony, our erstwhile choreographer, now had to be Choreographer/Boyfriend, so the whole drama increased our onstage company by one.

After a few days' rehearsal I began to experience several disquieting symptoms, one of which was a sudden and irresistible craving for pickled onions. I felt a growing sense of unease, but I put my suspicions to the back of my mind. By the second week of rehearsals, I had the result of a pregnancy test, and it was positive. I was certainly shocked, and somewhat nervous about playing such a rigorous part in the early stages. I informed Joan, who spoke to Clive, and I was told not to mention it to anyone in the press, and as far as possible, to keep it a secret for the duration of the tour. Terry and I had already decided that we would try for a second baby once 1991 was out of the way, so we were delighted because it was a fait accompli and a genuine surprise.

1991, Perth – Judy with Ian Grieve.

My only disappointment was that I had already agreed to come back in November to play Jane in *Absurd Person Singular* followed by Jack in *Jack and the Beanstalk*. While Joan was happy about a five-month pregnant Jane, a seventh-month pregnant Jack trying to climb up a beanstalk was beyond a joke.

Clive directed with great skill and could not have been more accommodating, even checking that I was happy with what the other actors were doing; he treated me like a star! He consulted Terry about everything and was so solicitous that Terry eventually had to tell him to feel free to direct the piece as he saw fit. We only had two-and-a-half weeks rehearsal before the technical, which was barely adequate for a play with 16 songs, but I had done a lot of preparation. The boys had a tough time because, as well as their acting roles, there were a lot of dance routines to learn, and some of them were also understudying the larger parts. It was some feat, but it all came together and at least we had a few previews to iron out any problems before the opening night.

We hoped that Gloria might give it a wide berth this time, but no such luck, although we managed to persuade her to come before the official opening; we wanted her out of the way so that we could enjoy the rest of the run. On this occasion she turned up with Fred in tow, but she was strangely reticent about the show. I'm not sure what she was expecting, but her main gripe seemed to be what we had considered one of the show's virtues, which was that I had not done an impersonation. I think she would have preferred to see Judy played by a drag artist! Fred had nothing to say at all and we found them both very irritating, so were relieved that they were not overly enthusiastic, as she might now give up on the notion of taking the play to New York. As we saw her off the premises after the show, we almost believed that this might be the last time we would hear from her. And it was.

Many years later I Googled Ms Sher and came across the following: *A wealthy Briton and his Broadway show producer wife were ordered off the Queen Mary 2 cruise ship after an alleged fight with another passenger at a black-tie dinner. Frederick Evans, 91, and Gloria Sher, 82, were told by the captain to leave at the next port, following what was said to be an expletive-ridden row over anti-Semitic remarks. The couple claim they should be given far more regal treatment because of their connections. Miss Sher says her husband is the illegitimate son of the Duke of Windsor, the abdicated King Edward VIII, as well as a British knight.* She died on March 9th, 2013.

Our opening night was wonderful. There was a real company feeling, and everyone seemed to get a buzz out of doing the show.

When you consider that Bill Kenwright had the entire profession to choose from, it was interesting that Clive had found such a fine company with the limited resources of Perth Theatre. It wasn't just the acting company; we had a wonderful set and costumes, courtesy of Nigel Hook and Alex Reid, and we managed to get hold of most of the musical arrangements from the Strand production, so there wasn't a single area that let it down. This was the production we had hoped for, and I wished that Bill could have seen it.

1991, Perth Theatre – Judy with 'Boyfriends'.

Quite a few of our friends from the South came up to see it, including my sweet 'fan', Anna Pajak, who came from London and saw the show on two consecutive nights. David Mars from the Garland Club made the journey from Leicester by coach, and we arranged for him to stay with Ralph Riach. Sadly, his friend, Reg Needle could not leave his ailing sister, Lily, and so disappointed was he to miss the show, that David could not tell him until well after the event that he had come up on his own.

At the end of the first week, Ron in the box office had what he interpreted as a hoax call; Sean Connery wanted two tickets to be reserved in his name for the Saturday evening performance! In fact, Terry had heard that Sean was in St Andrews playing golf and had invited him over to see the play. They went back a long way, to a time when Terry worked for Richard Hatton's agency in London, and Sean was one of their illustrious clients. Terry was not what you would call a close acquaintance and hadn't really expected a response to his note, so he was jubilant when he heard that he was coming. The buzz went round the theatre, and although she couldn't be there herself, Joan arranged for drinks and snacks to be laid out for them before the show and at the interval, and asked Terry to look after him.

I imagine that quite a few of the subscribers were taken aback to be joined by Sean and his son, Jason, in the Dress Circle. I suppose that it's silly really, but we all felt excited about 'Big Tam' being out there. Mike and Aileen (Terry's cousin and his wife) were also in that night, and Terry's favourite memory of the evening was when he found them in the foyer during the interval and escorted them up to the office for a drink. Aileen's face was a picture as she was seated between Sean and Jason, and she talked about that night for many years. Afterwards, Terry invited them to join us for supper so that I would have the chance to meet them. I was seated beside Sean, and although I remember little of the conversation, he did look wonderful, and I was impressed by his stardom. At the end of the evening, just before we left, he went over to enquire about the bill, but he was far too late as Terry had already seen to that, and he always said it gave him quite a kick to pick up the tab for a millionaire!

It was a joy from start to finish. We played to packed houses in Perth, and over a couple of evenings Terry managed to film all the songs from one of the boxes at the side of the stage, plus a few shots from the back of the auditorium. I wasn't mad about being in profile most of the time, and our camera couldn't cope when I was in the spotlight, blotting out my face, but it's lovely to have it, and the sound quality was excellent; at last we had some show footage.

Publicity was now hotting up for our little tour: Glasgow, Aberdeen and finishing in Dundee. Unfortunately, Edinburgh had fallen through, but bookings were going well in Glasgow and

Dundee. Our only concern was His Majesty's, Aberdeen, as their publicity seemed to be non-existent, and we had to trundle up one day during the Perth run to try and stir up a bit of interest. There was the added problem that we were due to open there after a holiday weekend and a lot of locals were out of town.

1991, Perth – Judy with Michael Roberts.

Glasgow came first, and short as this tour was, I was keen to be comfortable and stay fit, so we booked ourselves into nice hotels for the two 'away' weeks. The Grosvenor had a pool and a sauna, and we thought of this as our treat week. I will always be grateful that Clive was considerate enough to get Karen to stand in for me during the run-through of the play each Monday afternoon on the tour, leaving me fresh for the evening performance. On this Monday afternoon Terry and I went to *Radio Clyde* to chat about the show, and my new agent, Jean Diamond, flew up to see us; I was desperate that she would see a good night, and it was one of the best. We could feel the warmth from the audience and the Glaswegians responded audibly during my out-front dialogue. I remember a woman in the front saying loudly to her neighbour, "Look at her bunions", just after I removed my shoes, which rather took me by surprise, and from that night on I tried to position my stockinged feet in the most flattering position!

After the show and in high spirits, we took Jean for a meal, although our determination to take her back to her hotel took a bit of a dent when we discovered that, in our euphoria, Terry had left the car keys in the dressing room, and the theatre was locked. She had to hail a cab, and we spent the next hour trying to attract the attention of the night watchman, but we finally gave up and got a taxi back to our hotel, which was a bit of an anticlimax after all the excitement. The following morning, Terry had to rise early, bolt his breakfast, grab another taxi and head back to the theatre for his keys and his car before he received a parking ticket. The final straw was that he left his specs in the cab so, all in all, it was quite an expensive opening night.

Throughout the week our audiences grew, and by the last night we wished we could have stayed for another week. Ronnie Lee was passing through, and I was delighted that he managed to catch the show. Old Elspet turned up, and on the nights when she wasn't in the audience, she was at the stage door waiting to see me about something or other. On the first visit she brought me a few flowers, on the second she turned up with a coffee jar to put them in, and on the third she had some photographs for my perusal. The stage doorkeeper apologised for her persistent appearances, but as he said, "She's such a sweet old thing!" And so she was – but there were times when we could have seen her far enough! On our last night at the King's Theatre, several people ran down the aisles to shake my hand across the footlights, flowers were handed up, and I felt again, for a moment or two, something of the excitement that Judy herself must have experienced so often. It was a wonderful heady evening, and as well as a week to remember, we had super notices; I will always treasure Mary Lockhart's review in the *Glasgow Herald*:

'*Lesley Mackie's Judy Garland, sometimes sexy, sometimes seedy, always vulnerable, excites, infuriates, delights and breaks the heart.*' It was the kind of review you dream about.

We headed to the 'Granite City' on cloud nine, and on our arrival at the hotel, we nearly left when we discovered that the pool and leisure area were out of bounds due to renovations; they were essential to me, but I made use of the local leisure facilities. I had been so careful throughout the run, with regular steaming of the vocal cords and very little after-show socialising, that I wasn't about to let up now.

1991 Judy tour, Janet Michael and Anne Downie.

Thank heavens that Glasgow came first! If the dates had been reversed, and we had opened in Aberdeen, we would have been convinced that we were in a flop; well, not really, but Clive did warn us on the opening night that if we heard heavy breathing we should feel encouraged, as it was more than likely the sound of the Aberdonians guffawing! It has also been said that it is only on the terraces at the Pittodrie Football Stadium that you can hear the sweetie papers being unwrapped! To add to this diatribe about Aberdonians, my dresser, Janet, who had travelled with us from Perth, informed me that her first husband came from Aberdeen, but she left him when she found a man who laughed!

We ended our tour at the Whitehall Theatre in Dundee, and it was a week to remember with not an empty seat in the house. Initially, the choice of venue had been disappointing because it was just a converted cinema with very little atmosphere, but we somehow created our own. We had bare and very basic dressing room accommodation, the stage had virtually no wing space (shades of Greenwich!), and changes were done in whatever little nooks and crannies we could find, but there was a great feeling of 'Let's put on a show right here!'

1991 Judy tour, with Raymond Coulthard.

I treasured this final week because it would soon be time to head back home where I could give more thought to my pregnancy which, apart from a slight 'letting out' of the costumes towards the end of the tour, had given me no problems whatsoever.

The last night was unforgettable; I felt so choked that I could barely sing *Over the Rainbow* at the end, and once again, we experienced the joy of a standing ovation. We had erased, or at least negated, the bad memories of the London production, and here we were at the end of the tour, very happy and a little bit richer for the experience. Not only was I in my hometown, but I also realised that this was probably my last ever performance as Judy Garland.

1991, Dundee. Backstage with Katy.

- 22 -

Nappy days are here again

Now it was time for ante-natal tests, a scan, and making all the arrangements for the birth, but I only had a few weeks to see to everything before heading back to the 'Fair City' for *Absurd Person Singular*. Having taken on no work at all during my first pregnancy, I was delighted to be working until the fifth month on my second time around.

1991, Perth – Absurd Person Singular. Paul Nivison, Karen Pierce-Goulding, LM, Philip Lowrie, Roger Kemp and Anne Kidd.

I lived in Dundee throughout the rehearsal period for the Ayckbourn, and once we opened I moved into John Scrimger's little 'Granny flat', which had been used by his mum. Although the flat was part of his home, I had privacy, I revelled in the freedom, and spent my days writing Christmas cards, shopping, swimming – and as a bonus I enjoyed being in the play! My five-month pregnant figure suited the part, and although I had played Jane 15 years previously, I believe that my performance benefited from the maturity I had gained along the way. We ended our run on December 7th, and I felt a little bereft because I knew that my old make up box would once again be relegated to the attic. I still consider the play to be one of Ayckbourn's best, and Jane remains on my list of favourite roles.

I had my second scan at Ninewells Hospital the week before we closed, and the nurse said that it looked like a boy. For some reason, Terry and I had always assumed that we would have another daughter, but one of each sounded grand to me. Initially, Terry was disappointed, as he had been looking forward to his little Eliza Lesley, but he adjusted very quickly. Apart from my frustration at not being able to use all the clothes which I had hung onto since Katy was three months old, I was delighted. Being of a frugal nature, it was really the only reason I had hoped for another girl.

I decided to use the remaining months of my pregnancy to monitor all the film that we had taken since Katy was a toddler and transfer the highlights onto a 4-hour video tape. It was a time-consuming process, demanding endless patience and a bit of ruthlessness. I also wanted to transfer the *Judy* footage taken during the Perth run, and that was a two-person job, as the complications of joining up musical moments were intricate and endlessly frustrating.

Although our equipment was basic, transferring film onto video became a favourite hobby during the next few years, giving us a great deal of footage to pass onto the children. I also managed to make a tape of myself doing a few 'voice-overs' with appropriate background music, and I eventually handed cassette copies to my agent. Not surprisingly, I never landed a job from my painstaking endeavours; I should have done what most actors do, which is to hire a studio and make a professional recording, lasting no more than two minutes. With the benefit of hindsight, both Terry and I signally failed to make any proper investment in our careers, always 'having a go' ourselves, and as the voice-over market started to snowball throughout the '90s and onwards, we were fools not to have got around to something so essential. The same applied to my singing; having played *Piaf* and *Judy* on many occasions, we only had recordings made during performances by a sound man who was, undoubtedly, concentrating on other things; *Brigadoon* is the only proper studio recording I possess.

The 'Katy' video was completed, apart from the introduction of the baby, which would provide the closing shots. I tried to pack in a few last-minute outings before my life was taken over by the new arrival, and on Monday, April 6th, we joined our friends, Richard and Jenny Lyon, who were treating us to an evening with Billy Connolly at the Dome in Brighton. Richard, an old boyfriend of mine from the early '70s, was a pilot with British Airways and we'd kept in touch over the years.

We were a little reticent when we first received the invitation to go and see Billy because I was not at all sure that I would feel like going out just four days before the 'due' date, and I might not even still be pregnant – but we decided to take a chance, and we were very glad that we did. I sent a little note backstage before the show just to say 'Hello' and remind him of our 'Welly' days together. I mentioned my pregnancy and requested that he refrain from too much hilarity, just in case! As soon as he came onstage, he strode straight to the front of the stage and yelled: "Where is she? Where's my wee pregnant pal?" Sitting near the front and perched on the seat for all the world like a little Buddha, I had to wave and allow him to locate me. He based the next ten minutes on pregnancy and birth and was hilarious, even though he was clearly improvising; apart from a few notes scribbled on a beer mat, he free-wheeled his way through two-and-a-half hours of sustained mirth. It was some feat, and not only for him, as I struggled to sit there for that length of time without a visit to the loo. I was enjoying myself so much that I didn't want to leave, but I was also aware that, had I left, he would draw attention to my departure, so I had to stay put and exercise my pelvic floor muscles.

At the end of the show he gave me a wave and told me to come backstage and say 'Hello', so Terry and I popped round and spent a few minutes chatting to Billy and his son, Jamie, who I'd not seen since he was a toddler. On the face of it, Billy had not changed a lot, and was still as open and friendly as I remembered him. His marriage to Pamela Stevenson had changed his eating and drinking habits, and all that was on offer in his dressing room was herbal tea –

not that I was interested in alcohol. He put his oar into the ongoing debate about our son's name and came down heavily in favour of Oliver, even though his own son's name was Jamie, the other name on our shortlist of two. Knowing that we might eventually move north, we had almost decided on Oliver, which was still relatively rare in Scotland, and our favourite name since my first pregnancy; Ollie has always liked to think that Billy Connolly chose his name!

The following day I had my final swim with all the pregnant wifies, and on the Wednesday I had my last meal out with Terry and mum, who had arrived to stay with us for a few days, or at least until our son was born. I did not have long to wait; the following day we all went for a walk down by the seafront, and I had my usual attack of Braxton Hicks contractions. Although I was crawling on the ground to cope with the discomfort, I assured mum that these were false contractions which would soon ease off, but she was not convinced, and I was persuaded to head home for a warm bath. It was only when I was in the bath that I realised that this was the real thing. I managed to get dressed, and left the house around 9pm. It was painful, but I was trying not to alarm Katy who was hovering around, both fearful and fascinated by the whole event.

Things were now moving very fast, and by the time we reached the East Sussex County Hospital, I needed a wheelchair to get me up to the labour ward. I was quickly examined and handed a machine called TENS, which was supposed to deaden the pain, but not very effectively I recall! I got onto my old favourite, the 'gas and air', which helped a bit, but the pain was extreme, and I urgently needed an epidural. We had picked a great night for birthing as the staff were run off their feet with only four midwives attending to eight births, one of which was an emergency caesarean. It was General Election night into the bargain, and the hospital staff, already stretched beyond their limits, became increasingly dispirited as seat after seat fell to the Tories.

During all the build-up, Terry found a few minutes to nip outside and film the exterior of the hospital. We had forgotten on the way in (our minds being on more pressing matters!), but we wanted the shot as an introduction to the birth, which was going to be the final segment of the video I had been working on for the past few months. He returned to supervise my progress, but soon realised that we needed a member of the nursing team to help us along. He tried to attract the attention of passing staff, and 'our' midwife eventually returned and took over. I was now begging for an epidural, but it takes 20 minutes to take effect and we didn't have that long. The nurse was only humouring me when she said that an anaesthetist was on his way – and in any case, he was probably assisting at the emergency caesarean. By way of contrast with the interminable labour that preceded Katy's birth, this one was fast and furious and, strangely enough, even worse. They say that when the baby's head appears, a woman has an overwhelming desire to push, but my every instinct told me to keep that baby in, for fear that I might be torn asunder by the cannonball that was trying to emerge; this was definitely the real deal. As the midwife yelled at me to push, I recall hearing, as through a mist, a radio commentator announce that we were well on the way to a Conservative victory, but by that stage I wouldn't have cared if he'd said it was a military coup! I must have eventually 'let go', because Oliver Duncan Wale was born at 1am on Friday, April 10th, 1992, and on the same day, John Major was duly elected as Conservative Prime Minister.

Oliver was weighed and examined, and I do recall a nurse saying, "Oh, he's a placid little fellow", words which often popped into my head during the following months as I paced the floor, trying to calm him down or tried to hold a conversation above the noise of his screams. He was seven-and-a-half pounds and pronounced fit and healthy. The nurse disappeared to get on with her other duties, whilst assuring me that someone would soon be along to attend to my wound. She took one last look, and muttering, "Looks like there's been a war in here", she headed back to see what was happening in the emergency room. After a couple of people arrived to attend to my stitching and were dragged away before they could even get started, I began to feel rather anxious. At one stage, someone got as far as getting my legs into the stirrups, and I was stuck in that unseemly position for what seemed like an eternity. At 5am, four hours after the birth – by which time, nature's own anaesthetic had completely worn off – a male nurse arrived to stitch me up.

His ministrations were even more excruciating than the birth! He was, in retrospect, a good needle man, who left me with no long-term after-effects, but the actual procedure was a nightmare. I was given a local anaesthetic, but he didn't wait for it to take effect before he began his handiwork, and I felt as if I'd suddenly been caught up in the Crimean War, expecting at any moment, to look up and see Florence Nightingale hovering over the bed. I can barely describe the pain, and there was nothing I could do but scream. In a strong foreign accent he told me to lie still and be quiet, as he was unable to concentrate on his task, bringing to mind an image of an evil Nazi doctor experimenting on some helpless victim in Auschwitz. Terry sat at the other side of the room rocking Oliver in his arms and trying to block out the noise. I was shouting, "Somebody help me", and even "Mum!" at one stage. A large black nurse, who had helped earlier, appeared on the scene, took my hand and murmured words of comfort, while a young male student observed the whole sorry business. I became aware that the pain was easing off, and realised that the anaesthetic was finally kicking in; as the pain diminished, so did my screams. The ordeal was almost over, and I vowed that I would never willingly go through pain like that again; two children would be lovely, thank you very much!

Later that morning the student observer came round to the ward, and he came right out with it and said that he thought that the 'stitcher' had not waited for the anaesthetic to work, and asked if I would be reporting the incident. He said that he had never witnessed anything like it, and if I had not been so relieved to have a healthy baby, I might well have put in a formal complaint – and with the benefit of hindsight, I most definitely should have done! My next visitors were mum and Katy, and we took a little bit of film of them with Ollie, which added the finishing touch to the family video.

With Katy now at school and a new addition to the family, it was time for a major re-think. We enjoyed living in Hove, but our work was always elsewhere and, significantly, most of it had recently been in Scotland. Besides, mum and dad had been travelling the length and breadth of the country to be of assistance ever since Katy was born and would not be able to keep that up for much longer. It had been a wonderful experience for them (I hope!), but with Oliver on the scene, my touring days were over for the time being, and I was going to need the folks even more if I was going to be able to work at all. We were also aware that they would like their grandchildren to be closer at hand. So a plan to move to Scotland began to take shape, although it would be almost a year before we finally said goodbye to the Sussex coast.

During all the broken nights, nappy changing and breast feeding, I received a call, quite out of the blue, from Catherine Robins, who was still director at the Eden Court Theatre in Inverness, where I had last played Jack in *Jack and the Beanstalk* back at Christmas 1984. She wondered if I would be interested in playing Dorothy in *The Wizard of Oz*! I laughed, although I was extremely flattered that she thought it conceivable that I could still get away with playing a child. I suspected that I might be pushing my luck, but it was a big theatre with the audience some distance away, so I finally accepted her offer. As it happened, her theatre board overruled her desire to do a Christmas play and insisted on the usual pantomime. *Aladdin* was her choice, and it gave me another chance to play Principal Boy; knowing I had a job for Christmas got me through the rest of the year.

There were a lot of arrangements to be made as Ollie would have to come with me, which meant finding a local childminder and suitable accommodation, bearing in mind that Terry and Katy would be joining us for Christmas. I was put in touch with Moira Lacey, an old primary school friend, who was living in Inverness and happy to accept the part-time job of looking after Ollie, so once I found a suitable house, I felt well prepared for Christmas. I was going to have another opportunity to don my fishnets and high boots!

Time was drifting on, and we were still keen to move north. Earlier in the year, Terry had been shortlisted for the post of Artistic Director at Perth Theatre and his interview had gone well, so we had tentative hopes that he might just land the job, which would make the move essential and take the decision out of our hands. Chris Dunham, the Director at Westcliff, had also been shortlisted, and he and Terry were in regular contact with each other as the months passed with no word.

When word finally did come, it was to say that Joan had been invited to stay on for another year to ensure the smooth running of the theatre in the absence of David Bonnar, the General Manager, who had been ill for a while and was going to be absent from work for the foreseeable future. It would have been tough for an incoming director to settle in without support if the theatre was in a state of turmoil, so all the shortlisted candidates were told that they would be reconsidered the following year, possibly along with a few others, as the post would have to be re-advertised after such a long gap, but all hope was not lost! It was disappointing but it certainly didn't alter our resolve to move back north, which was based on more than landing the job, although that would have been a definite bonus.

I then had an offer over which I agonised for some time. On the face of it, the chance to play *Shirley Valentine* up in Perth, directed by Terry Wale, was irresistible, but when Joan Knight asked me to do it, I almost turned it down because, quite simply, I didn't know when I was going to learn the lines. Shirley is alone onstage for two hours, and she never stops talking! Fortunately, Joan had foreseen the problem, and had asked me well in advance of the production, which was scheduled for the following spring. She asked Terry to direct it, so that we could organise rehearsals around our domestic arrangements, which was Joan at her very best.

So I decided to go for it, and spent two hours a day, the two hours being Ollie's daily nap, for the next four months, learning the script. Taking it on was as much a test as anything else, as I wanted to find out if my brain was still capable of responding to such a huge task; it certainly wasn't a financial decision – I mean, you don't get paid for learning the lines, the most laborious, boring and thankless part of the job (in my opinion). Job satisfaction can only happen once the lines are rock-solid.

Aladdin at the Eden Court was fast approaching, and Ollie and I flew up to Edinburgh, where we were met by the folks, who drove us up to Inverness, stayed for a few days, and saw us settled in before leaving us to our fate. My old friend, Moira, quickly became part of the family, and we established a routine. Rehearsals were reasonably smooth, except that there was no Jimmy Logan around this time to impart his 'panto' wisdom. My main problem was lack of sleep; Ollie was still breastfeeding and woke up regularly for a drink during the night. As he tended to feed from alternate sides, there was the additional problem of lop-sidedness, which resulted in Aladdin looking a little misshapen!

The weather was bitterly cold, and just after we opened, we had a lot of deep snow, which made getting to and from the theatre, especially with a buggy, a bit precarious, but it all looked very pretty, and I was hoping for a white Christmas to add a bit of magic to Katy's trip north. Ollie had forgotten who they were of course, and he was quite disorientated when he was left alone with virtual strangers.

1992, Inverness – Aladdin with Iain McColl.

Before I left, I contributed to an article in a local Inverness paper, expressing my three wishes for the coming year. One of my wishes was that we could sell our home and return to Scotland. It still seemed the right thing to do; my folks needed grandchildren, the kids needed grandparents – and I needed help. I remember someone telling me that 'two children are as easy as one because one child takes up all your time anyway!' It's not true. The simplicity of having Katy on her own was now a dim and distant memory, and most of our work during the previous two years had come from the north, so north we were still determined to go. With only a few days left before the predicted snow arrived and roads were closed, I was keen to finish the panto run and head homewards. The folks came to collect us, and we said fond farewells to the cast and to Moira, who had been such a support throughout. We managed to reach Dundee before the snow appeared, but our Dame, Iain Stuart Robertson, stayed on for an extra day in Inverness to dally with his new amour, Rachel Pittman, our Principal Girl, and was snowbound for a week!

We stayed overnight in Dundee, and on the Monday morning we prepared to head for Edinburgh Airport. Terry was eagerly awaiting our arrival as he was due to start work the following day, and my services were urgently required. A blizzard was blowing up, and dad was not keen to embark on the journey, but I managed to persuade him that it was worth a try. We made it to Edinburgh, only to be told that the plane was already on the runway. I was devastated, because not only was it essential that I get home, but I had no extra supplies with me, and to travel light, I had – rather stupidly – only brought one spare nappy. The weather was deteriorating, so when the airport announced that all flights were cancelled we were advised to head back from whence we had come.

Conditions were now horrendous, and as I sat in the back of the car with Ollie latched onto my breast, I began to wonder if we would escape with our lives. To help keep dad calm, mum sang *Grandfather's Clock* in time with the movement of the windscreen wipers. We couldn't see more than a few inches ahead of us, and suddenly we were confronted with a police roadblock and informed that the A9 was now closed. In a way, it was a relief to know that at least we would not end up stuck on the motorway for the night in a snowdrift, but what was the alternative? By a strange quirk of fate, we were at the turn off to Dunblane, and the police suggested that we slide in there and try and find somewhere to stay. As we skidded up to the Stirling Arms Hotel, the only hotel in sight, we entered the bar like refugees and bagged the only room left, which we had to share. With mum and dad in one bed, and Ollie and I in the other, we had no choice but to stay in the hotel for the next two nights. Quite apart from our trauma, Terry and Katy had been waiting for us at Gatwick Airport, and when we failed to materialise, headed home and waited to hear what had happened – no mobile phones back then. Terry was on heckle pins with the uncertainty of it all.

On the first morning, I trudged through deep snow to find nappies, Ollie having managed (but only just!) to get through the night on the final one. As mum didn't have her asthma medication, it was not a happy state of affairs; there was a scary incident when she had a choking fit, and we knew that she would be a lot safer at home with her nebuliser. We took what meals were on offer at the hotel, and on the second day we were sitting in the bar when a man burst in, looking like the Abominable Snowman. He was a reporter from *The Sun* who, having landed in the middle of nowhere, was determined to make the best of it. "Anyone got a story here?", he burst out. As we appeared to be the most interesting, I wrapped Ollie in a blanket, and he took us outside, where we had a snowy photo taken. They never used the photograph, but the story merited a couple of inches, with the heading 'Actress Out in the Cold'. After leaving us at Edinburgh Airport, the folks crawled back to Dundee, having most certainly been called on to give support above and beyond the call of duty. I think that they both took some time to get over it.

As 1993 got underway, we moved on with our plans to sell our lovely little home in Hove. We found a buyer, and although she seemed a bit of an oddball, it looked as if things were going ahead. She had chosen not to have a survey done which, although strange, was entirely up to her. We knew that the property was in excellent condition, and she was getting a bargain at £60,000. It still pains me to think of that figure, and the enormity of the loss, but the market was disastrous in the south, and we'd been assured that it was not likely to improve for many years to come, so we had to be philosophical about it.

We wanted to try and coincide our move to Scotland with rehearsals for 'Shirley'. From over 500 miles, with a bit of help from the folks, we had short-listed eight properties, four in Dundee and four in Perth, and we decided that we'd go for our favourite house, wherever it turned out to be. In the normal way of things, a move north might have meant a move upwards with the possibility of finding a better house from the proceeds of a sale in the more affluent south, but prices in Scotland had not slumped in the same way and finding the home we wanted was going to cost a lot more than £60,000!

In February we went up to look at a few properties; what a frantic week we had, but we found the house that we wanted in Bridgend, Perth. Bob Bywalec had built all the houses in Croft Court and was living in one of the semi-detached properties with his wife and baby, and this was the one he was selling. He was a bit of a character, pointing out various features as he showed us around. As he told us the price of the wallpaper in the hall, he added, "It's no' shite!" Once we had the survey done, we were delighted to discover that the property was indeed in great nick, and the insulation was as many inches thick as he had said. Before returning south, we checked out the local school, hoping that our own sale would go through with no hitches; we were in for a few hellish weeks.

On the week that we had arranged to exchange contracts, our buyer, Miss P, changed her mind and decided to have a survey done after all; we felt very vulnerable, knowing that she was aware of the urgency of our situation and she continued to drag out the process until we were nervous wrecks. Our future was hanging by a thread: not only were we losing a small fortune on the Hove property, but we had to find the extra cash to buy a £90,000 house in Perth – and learn my lines for 'Shirley' into the bargain.

The one thing that caused me more anguish than any other, was when I was sent a few pages from a tabloid, which showed Miss Elaine Paige posing in all the Piaf 'haunts', the very ones that both Terry and I had visited just a few years before. As I looked at the picture of her at Piaf's grave and read about her decision to play the part at last, something in me died, because I knew that my long-held dream of playing it in the West End would now never come to fruition. If it went well, it would not be done again for years; similarly if it died the death. Although I have never been a stranger to the injustice and vagaries of our business, I wept that day. Any lingering doubts I may have had about the wisdom of leaving were quickly dispelled.

All that remained for us to do was to arrange the 'cut-offs' while Miss P continued to dither. Terry called her to say that we couldn't hang around any longer and were about to withdraw the house from the market, and on the Friday we exchanged contracts. We made our offer on the Perth house and collapsed in a heap.

As the removal men were in full swing, Katy, Ollie, and I left Terry to supervise the final stages and headed for Gatwick Airport. He would drive up and join us the following day. It was all too sudden, and I hadn't managed to say a proper farewell to our lovely home; no time to look backwards at all. It was Goodbye Hove. Hello Perth.

- 23 -

Trying it on for size

It was a strange time to arrive in Perth, which was just beginning to recover from the Great Tay Flood which had occurred in January, with the loss of 1,000 homes and £10 million damage. As we surveyed our new home filled with boxes, down in Dundee mum was not at all well. She had been ill for a few days, but we had no idea how serious it was, and she was deteriorating by the day. Dad had called the doctor, who didn't think the situation was serious enough for hospitalisation, but her breathing became so bad that dad had no choice but to call him again, and on this occasion he agreed that she had to get to Kings Cross Hospital as fast as possible. As she was wheeled up the path with an oxygen mask over her face, she managed to whisper to me that I wasn't to worry, and she would still be able to look after the children. That had indeed been the plan, but we were due to start rehearsals immediately, so other family members mucked in to give us a hand for the first few days. We then enlisted the help of a childminder, and with a lot of juggling we managed to make some inroads with the boxes, see to the kids, and rehearse the play as well; thank goodness I had learnt most of the script in advance.

I've mentioned line learning in repertory theatre and repertoire earlier in this book, but a one-woman show involves a different approach. People often ask actors how they learn their lines, but I remember seeing the play in London and wondering myself how on earth the actress managed it. Well, I was finding out. There is no easy route unless you have a photographic memory. It is hour after hour of reading the text aloud, starting with one line and building up, scene by scene, covering the script, repeating over and over, perhaps even putting it all on a tape cassette – or nowadays on a mobile phone – to listen whenever you get the chance, and adding to your memory store as the days go by. If you're lucky, you might have a partner or friend willing to hold your script and prompt. There is the occasional actor who is known as being a 'quick study', but there is no easy way to learn a 90 minute, one-person play, knowing you won't have cues from other actors to help keep you on track. The 'business' would become very important; when I'm peeling potatoes or frying eggs, I'm onto one subject and when I'm buttering the bread I'm onto another.

Mum was in hospital for two weeks and came home just before Ollie's first birthday. She was still very weak as she'd had a severe bronchial infection, complicated by pleurisy, and her lungs suffered irreversible scarring, making her much more vulnerable in the future. It always troubled me that our recent horrendous journey through the snows might have contributed to her condition. With all the stress, something had to give, and once we opened I had to give up breastfeeding; well, it was about time, although I was sorry to lose something I had enjoyed so much and was not likely to experience again.

1993, Perth – Shirley Valentine.

Shortly before the opening night, someone at the theatre had the sweet idea of booking me into a hotel for the night prior to the opening, just to ensure that I had a good night's sleep. As I arrived at the chosen place I was stopped in my tracks by the loud ringing of bells. The hotel was situated just opposite St John's Kirk, and not only did the bells ring on the hour, but they rang on every quarter and all through the night. I had experienced a similar nightmare in Bath in the past, and I was panic-stricken, as I was a poor sleeper at the best of times. The man on reception seemed less than interested in my predicament, but after a change of room so that I was not facing the bells, Terry left me to my fate. I couldn't even look forward to a cosy breakfast because there was no cooking on the premises, and I was told to go to a tea room along the road. The building itself was quite unnerving as there was no obvious way back to reception; on one trip when I tried to find a route, I put faint pencil marks on the walls in case I lost my bearings. Despite my earplugs and sleeping tablet, I had a ghastly night and arrived for the photo call feeling even more shattered than usual.

1993, Perth – Shirley Valentine.

Fortunately, everything went like a dream. It was a challenge to face that audience alone every night, but Shirley is a warm, funny character, and as well as the humour there are some very touching and poignant moments which help to make it a richly satisfying experience, both for the actress and the audience – and I had a wonderful, sympathetic director with my interests at heart. I had never been in a play with so much 'business', but the novelty of cooking egg and chips onstage never failed to engage the audience; people often commented on the aroma wafting over the stalls.

1993, Perth – Shirley Valentine.

It wasn't long before Elspet appeared on the scene. She turned up one Saturday to see the matinée, and then, by mentioning her close friendship with me, also managed to wangle a free ticket for the evening performance! She sometimes managed to wangle a lift, by saying audibly during an interval, "I don't know how I'm going to get home to Glasgow tonight" in her distinctive 'old lady' voice. On this occasion I managed to dissuade her from showing me her entire portfolio between shows, with the vague promise that I would spare a few minutes at the end of the second performance. I valued my rest after a matinée – especially in a one-person show – and was loath to let anything or anybody get in the way of that, even a sweet old lady. When I found her waiting at the end of the night, photographs at the ready, it was not as easy to escape as I had hoped, and we missed our booked meal in the theatre restaurant. As we walked Elspet through the rain, back to her digs near the South Inch, Terry would have happily throttled her, but I think we made an old lady very happy!

I was disappointed that Elaine C Smith took her own version of the play out on tour at this time, as it effectively put paid to any plans we had to do the same. It was even more disappointing because it was a totally different experience – not so much a play as a 'stand-up' performance – she didn't even cook the egg and chips! But I had found another favourite role, which I dearly wanted to play again, and not just because it had taken me four months to learn it.

After we moved back, taking part in local activities, such as opening the occasional charity shop, became quite a feature. I was also invited to give a talk about my life to the *Ladies Inner Wheel Club* in Dundee. I resisted at first because it was many years since I had been involved in public speaking, but I started to write a speech and became so immersed in the past that it was the prelude to many years of getting my entire life story written down. I'd kept diaries since 1967, so after taking notes from each one, I wrote my story down in longhand before copying it onto the word processor, eventually transferring it to the computer; it was a laborious time-consuming job, and it has undergone endless rewrites, but it has been tremendously satisfying.

I gave my 30-minute speech, and as time moved on I received a few invitations to do the same elsewhere. On one occasion at a men's rotary club in Perth, they titled it: *A Life in the Spotlight*, and I altered it slightly to *A Life in and out of the Spotlight*, which made more sense. I privately renamed it, *A Cup of Tea and a Biscuit*, which was my usual payment! I never minded, particularly if it was for a charity, and it was always understood that in the unlikely event of a professional job cropping up, I might have to let them down. I knew that they could always call on Mrs McTavish to show her holiday snaps if all else failed!

Our return to Perth, having coincided with Joan's imminent retirement, was beginning to look a little foolhardy because we had hoped that our local theatre, even without Joan at the helm, would keep us gainfully employed until we found our feet – wishful thinking indeed. After 'Shirley', things went very quiet on the theatrical front, and we began to realise that you are never appreciated quite so much if you live around the corner.

Terry signed on with Pat Lovett, one of the Scottish agents, and waited for the interviews to pour in. As Jean Diamond had no objection, I followed suit, because it seemed sensible to have representation in the country where we were based. On the positive side, although Joan was now about to take it easy and watch from the sidelines, we were well acquainted with the man who was soon to be her successor – our old friend, Andrew McKinnon – so all was not lost.

Once Andrew had been back in Perth for a while, we took him out for a meal; we owed him that, as when we were married in 1977, we were totally broke and couldn't even afford to give him a present as a token of thanks for his very able services as our Best Man. Over the years we lost touch but we had an enjoyable evening and felt that we were back on a good footing. Terry and I made a private pact that we would do our best to be loyal to Andrew and try and support him, because we knew what a daunting job it would be for anyone to follow in Joan's footsteps.

At that time we didn't know what had happened regarding Andrew's appointment. It was much later we discovered that after the first round of applications and subsequent interviews, the theatre Board had decided to let Joan stay at the helm for another year until Andrew finished his contract at the Actors Centre in London, so that he could take over – in other words, a fait accompli. It was true that David Bonner was ill, but I believe that was used as an excuse in order to postpone the appointment until Andrew was available. After the process of applying and all it entailed – the preparation, travelling up for the interview and getting shortlisted, it was a bit disheartening, but Joan obviously considered Andrew a safe pair of hands. She was lovely about inviting certain actors to direct the occasional play in her theatre, but did not think an actor should be allowed to run it!

We knew little of this back in the summer of 1993, when Terry was invited by John Doyle to be in *Charley's Aunt* down in York, which was a nice treat, especially at that time of year, and we were all able to join him in that lovely city for a few days. After York, I went down to London to do a little job of my own, taking part in a sketch on *The Alexei Sayle Show* – I didn't even have to go for an interview. It was a spoof on the old-fashioned, starry, American Christmas Specials. Alexei was waiting in his lounge, alone on Christmas Day, only to be surprised by three of his old 'friends': Sammy Davis Junior, Bing Crosby and Judy Garland, all dead stars! My verse went like this: 'It's tough being dead at Christmas, no toys strewn around the floor, RIP that's my initials, So yes, it's official. Horizontal that's me for evermore.' At first we were aghast, and Terry strongly advised me against it because of loyalty to Judy's memory, but after advice from my agent, I decided to do it. And it was a hoot, very good-natured, no malice intended, shown on late night TV, and if I'd turned it down I would have kicked myself. It only took a couple of days, but I had two nights in a hotel with a pool, took in *Crazy for You* at the Prince Edward Theatre with Bernie – and even managed a quick 'Hi' to Terry on the station platform as the train passed through York on my way back to Perth.

The House Among the Stars was the beginning of a tortuous relationship between Andrew and the Perth public, which went on deteriorating until his departure less than three years later. Despite his past connections with Joan and the theatre, he chose to take little heed of what had gone before and bombarded audiences with a string of plays which alienated them, decimating the subscription scheme and destroying what Joan had built up over many years. Sadly, it also destroyed his relationship with Joan, and as far as I know they did not keep in touch after he left Perth, never to return. We tried not to dwell on it, but always felt some regret that Terry hadn't got the job. It's easy, of course, to look at this with the benefit of hindsight – and it was still early days. On the bright side, we were now settled in our home, the folks were happy, and the kids loved it.

Before the year was out, *Piaf* finally came home to roost. Elaine Paige had embarked on a tour prior to a West End opening, and although I had known for some time that it was going to happen, when the tour edged nearer it was a bitter pill to swallow. Terry decided to go and see it, and I still remember his call after the show, when he said that it was better than he'd expected, but he found her hard as nails, leaving him unmoved. She sang most of the songs in English, and when singing, it was very much 'Elaine Paige in Concert', which made it difficult to have any emotional involvement with the character. I was almost relieved when it finally reached the West End in the spring, suffered mixed reviews and closed soon after. It was indeed Bill Kenwright who had produced it, and I wrote to him soon after it closed, because I couldn't resist reminding him of the many conversations we had shared about the possibility of me playing the part, how disappointed I had been when he had cast elsewhere, although I fully understood his reasons for doing it; with Elaine Paige in the title role, and Peter Hall directing, it should have been a perfect 'bums on seats' recipe. Bill did reply, and I will always keep that letter, because in it he said how unhappy the production had been, and how he wished it had been me! Cold comfort, but I welcomed it. Whatever happened, it was clear that it would not be mounted again for some time, and probably when I was too old for the part. Over the years, I've met many people who went to see the West End production because they'd loved ours so much; one man was so disappointed he said he didn't think he was seeing the same play.

Towards the end of the year mum heard of the death of wee Tommy, and she went to his little flat just in time to see it being emptied. We felt bad about it, as it seemed that he must have had a 'pauper's' funeral (now known as a public health funeral), when the deceased has no family to take care of the arrangements. A simple wee man, not quite 'the full shilling', but one who had somehow become part of our lives.

On New Year's Day, 1994, we went to watch the annual tradition when foolhardy souls jump into the River Tay, and spotted Henny King, a lively lady we had recently met, rigged out in a penguin suit. From there we went to mum's yearly family get-together, where only wee Tommy was missing; it was the end of an era, and New Year at Nairn Street wouldn't be quite the same again without his 'Laughing Policeman'!

- 24 -

Swimming against the tide

As 1994 dawned, we were both aware that not enough was happening on the work front. We were in a vulnerable situation, living in a small town, with two young children, without much opportunity to mix in the mainstream theatrical circles in Edinburgh and Glasgow. Terry was doing a little better than I was, which was not what we had expected at all. After some prompting from me, he had landed a production at my old Alma Mater, the RSAMD, and was soon into rehearsals for *Sweet Charity*. This boded well, as he wanted something to replace the work he had been doing at Webber Douglas Academy, and he was now recording regular audio books for a company called *Soundings* in Whitley Bay, so he was ticking over. I was soon invited to play the title role in *Elizabeth Gordon Quinn* by Chris Hannan, although it was a bit of a double-edged sword. Andrew had opted for a slightly more accessible season than his previous one, which had alienated many of the local audience, but 'Elizabeth' was a complex piece. Although I sensed that it might empty the theatre, I loved a challenge, and it was a brave choice of play with a strong role for a woman.

A few weeks before rehearsals began, I was approached by Hamish Glen at Dundee Rep to play a part in *Toshie*. It was written by a friend of ours called Stewart Brown, and it was a play about James Mackintosh, the only survivor of a whaling expedition to the Antarctic. I was delighted to have another job offer, although the women's roles were subsidiary, but when Hamish called to fill me in on the details and to let me know that it was to be a community project with amateurs playing some of the key roles, including the lead, I began to have second thoughts. There was also talk of evening rehearsals to accommodate the amateurs who had day jobs, and because of the 'equal opportunities' philosophy behind the whole approach, everyone was to be paid the same. Apart from all that, it would have meant commuting to rehearsals in Dundee during the latter part of the run of *Elizabeth Gordon Quinn*, which was a daunting prospect. Had I known that only a few years hence, Hamish would form a permanent repertory company based in Dundee

336

(Dundee Rep Ensemble), a company which is still in existence over 23 years later with some of the original actors still there (effectively reducing the possibility of leading roles for other Scottish-based actors), I might have had second thoughts about accepting the job – or maybe not!

At the time, and after so many years away from Scotland I felt, perhaps misguidedly, that I should return to my hometown with a decent part in a strong production. Having only been back in Perth for about a year, it was perhaps surprising that I felt able to say "No". When we went to see *Toshie*, my fears were well-founded as there were a few weak links – not all of them amateurs, but the set, which consisted of the large whaling boat, was amazing, although we felt that the overall production did not do full justice to the play.

I launched into the Perth rehearsals and stayed on good terms with Andrew throughout, despite the five days we spent improvising and playing games, which was not my style at all. Perhaps he thought we would achieve a greater understanding of the text if we held hands and 'passed the pulse'. As part of our process, we all had a go at playing the piano – just for fun; although she couldn't really play it, the piano was Elizabeth's pride and joy, as it was to many working-class families at that time.

The play was written in Hannan's highly idiosyncratic voice which sometimes bore little resemblance to normal speech. It was set during the Glasgow Rent Strike of 1915 with a stage design which depicted the poverty of the home, except for the piano centre stage, which was 'a symbol of quality which cannot be degraded into an object of utility', as Perth poet, William Soutar, once described it. It was the only recognisable piece of furniture on the stage, although it was never actually mentioned. When the piano is eventually poinded for rent arrears, that 'living presence' is gone, leaving her filthy house empty. Her defiant final line was 'I refused to learn how to be poor'.

Challenging as the piece was, some of it was bewildering. Terry and I spent hours discussing it at home, and I gave it my full commitment. I made every effort to create the enigma who was Elizabeth, this woman who kept her feelings locked away behind a sad and misplaced pride. It was different from anything I had ever played, and for that reason was a worthwhile experience. I remember a night when I had a ticklish cough and was forced to leave the stage in the middle of a scene. I returned just before I was due to utter, and carried on, but the play was so strange that anything could have happened, and no one would have questioned it.

1994, Perth – Elizabeth Gordon Quinn.

My strongest memory from the run was of one performance when Elizabeth, having been such an immovable figure of stone for the entire play, finally runs after her son who has been arrested for desertion from the army, and probably taken to be shot. I ran towards the door screaming, "Aidan!", tripped over his coat, and went all my length on the floor. Totally winded, I dragged myself up to continue the scene, glanced across at Joanne Bett who was playing my daughter, and found her in a state of barely controlled hysteria; she was shaking with laughter, but somehow the drama of the scene kept me focused. After the show, Edith MacArthur came backstage and said that she had never seen a stage fall like it! As I said, you could get away with anything. We had excellent reviews from the national newspapers, which was lovely from our point of view, but it was not a success as far as the general public or the local critics were concerned; they were just puzzled. In his programme notes, Andrew described the play as 'one of the classics of modern Scottish theatre' but, personally speaking, I sometimes felt that Chris Hannan had written the play and then removed every other line so that we could spend hours working out what it all meant. Having said that, I enjoyed the experience as we were a very happy company, including old friends like John Yule and Jane Nelson Peebles.

1994, Perth – Elizabeth Gordon Quinn with John Yule.

We were soon invited back to do Alan Ayckbourn's *Taking Steps*, with Terry directing and me playing one of the two rather unrewarding female roles. Although we did our best with the piece, and it had an excellent central performance from Michael Tudor

Barnes, it was not one of Ayckbourn's best. We finished the play with feelings of some frustration, because we were still hankering after something a bit more stimulating.

We did, however, have a lovely treat lined up, and just after we closed, Terry and I headed off to Paphos in Cyprus. Mum and dad had agreed to have the kids for a week, and although we missed them, we treasured those few days, knowing how unlikely it was to happen on a regular basis. The most memorable event in Cyprus, if not exactly a highlight, was on the day when I persuaded Terry that we ought to try paragliding. He didn't have my spirit of adventure, but lying on the beach, it had looked so idyllic, peaceful yet exhilarating, that when we saw a cheap deal one afternoon, I persuaded him to have a go. Quite apart from the fact that the sea was choppy, the crew took far too many on board, so there were insufficient life jackets, but I didn't realise quite how much terror Terry was going through. As we sat in the boat waiting for our turn to fly, I was taken aback when he volunteered to go first, mistaking his keenness to get it over and done with for enthusiasm, and when he was brought down after about two minutes in the air, I complained to the guy on the boat. I knew that we were supposed to get about eight or nine minutes, but Terry was quick to reassure me that he was quite happy as he'd had enough – more than enough as he said later; in fact, he hated every moment of it.

As I heard the wires creak and spotted holes in the parachute, I found the experience quite nerve-wracking, but I was determined to say that I had done it, and almost convinced myself that I had enjoyed it. Our flights over, we still had to watch while the others had a go, and to get through the large number of people, they started to put them up in pairs; I can still see a rather large Russian woman clutching her small son as they briefly rose into the air, only to fall unceremoniously down into the Mediterranean. I am still glad that I did it, and we do have photos to prove it, but I wouldn't have considered it, had I seen the television programme we saw when we got home. Two people had recently died in Paphos doing that same sport, and simply because certain unscrupulous companies were breaking the safety rules, one of which was most definitely the one we were with, so we had a lucky escape.

It had not taken us long to get acquainted with the ebullient

Henny King, a dynamic Canadian who had been signed up by the Dundee Council to take charge of the *Dundee 800* Celebrations, and who had decided to make Dundee her home. Henny was a driving force with lots of ideas and we went on to work with her on various projects. Earlier in the year we had performed our Piaf cabaret, now titled *Toujours l'Amour*, at the Queens Hotel in Dundee as a Valentine's Day fundraiser in aid of *Operation Shipshape,* which aimed to preserve Captain Robert Falcon Scott's tall ship, the *Discovery.*

1994, Dundee – Operation Shipshape.

We did another on our return from Cyprus, and on that occasion we did the Judy cabaret, titled *A Garland for Judy*. It was held at the Marryat Hall in Dundee and was absolutely packed, but in her desperation to make money for the charity, Henny stinted on the food; a chicken wing, small tub of coleslaw and a Mr Kipling apple pie did not constitute an 'American Picnic', especially when people have paid £15 a ticket. She had also caused havoc by selling numbered reserved seats from one office and unreserved 'first come first served' tickets from another. This caused the people queuing with what they thought were pre-booked tickets, quite a lot of discontent as the 'unreserved' people sailed past them to bag the best seats. Despite the irritation this created, we had a great night, and it left us keen to pursue the cabaret world.

During the summer, having failed to mark Joan's retirement in any kind of personal way, we decided to have a lunch for her at our home; nothing too elaborate, but including a few of her personal friends: Clive Perry, Roger Kemp, Alex Reid (Designer), Clare Richards, Jane Nelson Peebles and Richard Baron, a young director who had just appeared on the scene. It was a sunny day, and we were able to sit outside and listen to tales of Joan's recent trip to Russia, whilst sipping on glasses of wine. Although we could never have imagined it, that was the last time we would ever meet Joan on a happy social occasion. A few days later, on August 19th, Terry and I marked the 20th anniversary of our first meeting in Perth with a Chinese meal, which was very appropriate; when we met, we would have been lucky to have found any other kind of restaurant in Perth.

Widening our net a little, I had been asked to do a couple of good plays at the Byre Theatre; one was *The Steamie*, in the role of busty Margrit (which would have entailed digging out my big, padded bra!), and *Mary Queen of Scots Got Her Head Chopped Off*, playing Corbie, but St Andrews was not an easy place to get to without a car, and I was still dependent on Terry to get me around. With the kids still so young, moving into theatre digs out of town didn't feel like an option, so I had to decline. It says a lot for how little else was on offer that I did a rehearsed reading at the Netherbow in Edinburgh for nothing more than basic expenses. By drawing attention to the wealth of talent which existed in Scotland, the hope was that if the 'movers and shakers' took notice, they might want to support a campaign to give us our own Scottish National Theatre, but it was another 12 years before that happened.

Being in Edinburgh, I took the opportunity to stay overnight with old friend Thelma Rogers. This was the only time I stayed with her, but I was aware that she was losing touch with reality. There was very little food around, and it was almost as if she wasn't planning to eat, never mind expecting a guest. I put it down to poverty, but that was only one aspect of her problems. She had a tiny black and white television set, which she watched with the sound off. After she put on a programme to see an old acquaintance, opera singer Donald

Maxwell, I suggested that it might be more enjoyable if she turned up the volume. She looked aghast and said that she was fearful of disturbing the neighbours, and so we watched him sing in silence. Her worsening glaucoma and increasing isolation were alienating her from the real world, and I was witnessing the start of a dreadful deterioration. She had no one to look out for her; her ex-husband, Robert Robertson, had long settled with his new partner, she had no children, no close relatives, and being a very private person, she had few friends. I should have spotted the signs of dementia, but living in Perth with my own young family, I was unable to keep tabs on her.

After reading for young Richard Baron, the 'Great White Hope', Terry was offered a part in Tom Stoppard's *Rough Crossing* at the local theatre, so he now had a role to get his teeth into. Richard was working on a training scheme at Dundee Rep and was 'on loan' to Perth for the duration. He had seen me in various productions over the years, and one day when I bumped into him in the Perth coffee bar, he asked if there was anything I would really like to do as he would love to work with me, so this boded well for the future.

Something then occurred which put us in a very difficult situation. Shortly after our move, we both had 'getting to know you' meetings down in Dundee with Director, Hamish Glen, and Terry had expressed a wish to direct *Amadeus*. Hamish seemed enthusiastic and asked Terry to badger him over the following year in order to remind him, which he had duly done by sending a couple of notes. Hamish failed to respond, and Terry had just about given up on the idea, when I mentioned it to Richard Baron one evening in the Perth bar. To my surprise, he said that Hamish was planning to do it in the spring of '95, and Terry should get onto him right away. Although we couldn't understand why Hamish hadn't been in touch, Terry dropped him a line, simply enquiring if there was any news re the play, and on this occasion he received a letter back by return of post. It said that a spring production was indeed on the cards, but he hoped that Terry would not be too disappointed because he had invited a trusted friend to direct, someone who had asked him about *Amadeus* even before Terry, and that person was Richard Baron!

Terry was outraged but decided to speak to Richard before responding. Richard confirmed our suspicions, which were that he had never approached Hamish regarding the play, but had just been invited to direct the piece. He insisted that when I had spoken to him just a few days before, he had no knowledge of this and it did seem unlikely that he would have told me to suggest that Terry make contact if he already knew he was to be doing it. All very mysterious, but even although there was nothing we could do about it, Terry felt that he had to write to Hamish to clarify matters – not about asking someone else to direct it, because that was in his gift, but for trying to pull the wool over his eyes. If it was true that Richard had approached him with the same idea, why didn't Hamish make that clear to Terry from the outset? Terry felt that he was, at the very least, entitled to honesty and courtesy, and we wondered if Hamish would have let him know at all, had it not been for my chance encounter with Richard.

Hamish riposted, but was adamant that he had told the truth about Richard asking to do the play first, but if that was the truth, why did he ask Terry to keep in touch – and if it wasn't the truth, that was unprofessional. Whatever the details, we had blown our resolve, and had already started to 'burn our boats'. I was concerned that the whole affair might affect my own chances of working in Dundee.

During all this trauma, Katy was enjoying an active social life. At seven, she was still a little dot with a very determined nature, and from an early age we referred to her as the 'unsinkable Molly Brown'. Nothing seemed to daunt her, and however much she was reprimanded, she always bounced back as if nothing had occurred. She did take a little advice re Halloween, and on this second attempt, Croft Court and Kincarrathie Crescent had the best 'guisers' they had witnessed in many a year, with the Sword Dance thrown in for good measure. We quite enjoyed the whole 'guising' experience, because it was such a walk down 'Memory Lane' for me – Tait's Lane to be exact! Of course, you could no longer let them out on their own, and for the next few years Terry and I took turns to sit in the car and, Fagin-like, gather up all the goodies between houses!

Her life was full and busy and was almost beginning to seem more interesting than ours. She was in the Brownies, the Sunday School, the *Fair City Singers* and *Annie,* which occupied us for most of the autumn as it involved a lot of driving up and down to Dundee. She had succeeded in getting the part of Molly, the youngest orphan in the *Downfield Musical Society* production, but although I managed to catch some of a dress rehearsal, I never managed to see a performance because I was playing Nursie McCuddles in *Sleeping Beauty* at the local theatre.

Our rehearsals were fun, although Andrew seemed in thrall to our Dame, Walter Carr, who did a lot of the directing; Andrew did have the grace to ask him one day if he would like his name on the programme as co-director! Experienced and talented as Wally was, like a lot of the old comedians, he could be quite stuck in his ways. Most of the jokes in the script were his, and some of them were antique. On one occasion, when I tried to get rid of a dreadful joke which was a play on the words 'potty' and 'cannabis', I said that I didn't think it would work. Wally retorted with: "Of course it will. I've done it a hundred times!" I duly kept it in, it died the death, so Wally 'suggested' that I cut it! When it came to 'cuts', Andrew usually did what Wally suggested. I had a tiny 'spot' which seemed quite modest, but when it came to the trimming, Andrew was prepared to take a couple of jokes from my two minutes, to avoid having to cut a word of a lengthy, tedious, Boy Scout routine. That was the only time I voiced a strong opinion, but the following day, in order to keep the peace, I apologised for interfering.

The only other 'fly in the ointment' was that there was a little bit of bitchiness. I was oblivious for much of the time, and it was only when an actress was openly hostile in the bar one evening that I realised that she wasn't a fan. I recall her saying quite early on, "It's all right for you. You've had it all." That wasn't quite the way I saw it. Silly really, because we were all in the same boat up in Perth, away from the possibility of any big opportunities and bright lights, just trying to earn a living.

One little postscript to the panto was that I started to do the occasional Radio Tay advert for Robertson's furniture shop in Dundee. Brian Cram, one of the partners, had liked my Nursie's voice, and decided that was the voice he needed to sell his beds! We were slowly opening a few small doors, but not always where we really needed them, which was in the television world and in the few productive Scottish theatres. Terry had rather bombed us out as far as Dundee Rep was concerned (and my turning down *Toshie* can't have helped!), but following on from Terry's *Amadeus* tale, I decided to swallow our joint pride and approach Richard Baron to suggest myself for the lovely role of Constanze, Mozart's wife, in his upcoming production of *Amadeus*.

So when I bumped into him backstage at Perth one day, I brought the subject up and he said that he thought it a great idea, but he would have to clear it first with Hamish Glen and get back to me. Little alarm bells did ring, but I hoped that Hamish wouldn't hold his recent fall-out with Terry against me. Time passed, and I was wondering what decision had been taken, when a local actress suddenly announced in the bar that she had been upstairs in one of the offices, reading for the part of Constanze, along with half the female members of Equity! I couldn't understand why Richard hadn't at least let me know that, for whatever reason, Hamish had clearly said "No." Actors are used to this kind of treatment, but it's a small world in Scotland, and I felt that to hold his auditions in the theatre I was working in, without informing me that I was no longer a contender, was a bit thoughtless. And I knew it must be down to Hamish, as Richard had seemed keen, and would surely have allowed me to at least read for the role along with the world and its mother.

So I wrote to him, expressing regret that he hadn't kept me informed, especially when he had expressed such interest in working with me, and had said he would let me know. I also said that it was disappointing after 'Hamish's shabby treatment of Terry'. It was weeks later when he bumped into Terry in the street, that he said how awful he felt about it, but was too nervous to make contact. Shortly afterwards Richard and I did meet up for coffee, and we got on famously, although I don't recall getting to the bottom of the issue; I think Richard was already well trained in the art of skirting round things – Hamish didn't call him 'Tricky Dicky' for nothing! The footnote to this sorry tale was that Terry went to see *Amadeus* at Dundee Rep and thoroughly enjoyed Richard's interpretation and wrote and told him so.

We both knew, however, that we now had a problem with Dundee. Nothing daunted, Terry wrote to Hamish and suggested that we hire his theatre to put on a show of our own. Hamish responded, but although he expressed an interest, was surprised that Terry had come back to him after his 'shabby treatment'! It was clear that Hamish had seen my letter to Richard, but we wanted to put it all behind us, as a Dundee week would be very important to us. We were already looking ahead to the following year, as it would take a lot of preparation before we were ready to go.

The show we had in mind was one we decided to call *Legends*. Having done our Judy and Piaf cabarets on a few occasions, we felt that we should put them together and form an entire evening about the two ladies. I had initially resisted because the thought of singing over 20 songs in two different voices in one evening was daunting, but we knew it was a good idea, a tremendous challenge and the ideal way for me to make a comeback at the Dundee theatre after a gap of 20 years! Terry would narrate, and all we would require was a pianist.

1995 also saw the start of a yearly booking at the Dundee-Orléans dinner, held in aid of sending schoolchildren to study in France, and they wanted an hour-long cabaret after the meal. We started, of course, with *Toujours l'Amour*, and as John Scrimger seemed to have many other strings to his bow, he suggested that we approach George Donald of *Scotland the What* fame. As he lived very near us, we introduced ourselves, and he became the obvious choice for *Legends*, so we began working with him and putting the evening together.

In the spring of 1995, Terry and I headed off to Houston, Texas, for a holiday with my brother, Grant, and his wife, Celeste. They both managed to organise time off work, and we did a great deal in our ten days. We went to places of interest in and around Houston: shopping malls, the Imax Cinema, (which I had never experienced before and loved), Galveston (although not as appealing as Glen Campbell's song had led us to believe!), a day in San Antonio where we saw the Alamo and mosied along the wonderful River Walk with its many open-air restaurants and jazz bands, plus a guided tour round Rockall, where both Celeste and Grant spent their working days. A highlight was a trip to the Westheimer Festival, which was full of extrovert gays, eccentrics, people with weird, exotic pets, and quirky little shops. I purchased a pair of lovely fruity earrings that became favourites for as long as they lasted. If I had to choose one favourite thing, I would single out the food. We made many outings to a variety of restaurants, and in each one we sampled new tastes, with the food abundant and delicious. We were glad that we had been able to spend some time with Grant in the place he had been living for so long.

We returned to little of excitement on the work front and another Pitlochry season under way without us. Looking at the planned programme for 1996, there didn't appear to be much for us in that one either, and without the seven months' work that Pitlochry could offer, there was little else around. It was crunch time, and Terry began to think about applying again for the post of Artistic Director at Perth Theatre. Even as early as the spring of 1995, it was clear that Andrew was not the right man for the job. In the space of two short years, the theatre had gone downhill, and people were being openly antagonistic towards Andrew, which must have been very difficult for him to deal with. Terry thought very carefully about applying, but after a lot of persuasion from me, started to give serious consideration to how he would approach the matter this time round.

After two years in Perth we had a mixture of feelings; happy to have time with mum and dad and to see their pleasure in sharing the kids, but when I look at a little diary entry at the beginning of May, which says, 'We've come to the conclusion that there is just no room for us here!', we were clearly having second thoughts about our move, at least from our work and careers point of view. I remember Terry saying at one point that he felt under sniper fire and was scared to go outside and put his head above the parapet; once his application had been submitted, he might just be lucky this time round and we would have a real reason, apart from being near the family, to stay. Little did we know what torment, pain and anguish lay ahead throughout the rest of that year.

- 25 -

A sea of troubles

We were hardly back from Texas when I had a call from the *Dundee Courier* who were keen to take a photograph of me with Lorna Luft, younger daughter of Judy Garland. Lorna was appearing in concert that evening at the Dundee Caird Hall, but I knew from experience that Lorna would not easily give her consent to such a suggestion. I was informed by the Courier that, although they had not managed to make personal contact, her agent had assured them that as so many years had passed since *Judy*, she would be fine about it. I had my doubts.

1995 with Lorna Luft and Katy Wale.

We all headed down to Dundee, where I met the photographer on the steps of the Caird Hall, and was disappointed to hear that they had not managed to make direct contact with Lorna, but we were to meet her inside after she had unveiled a commemorative plaque. We waited around until her manager appeared, and when he started with, "Unfortunately...", I knew what was coming. She didn't want to meet me and was appalled that her agent had agreed to a meeting without her permission. She felt that if she had a photograph taken with me, it would legitimise any others who were writing plays about her mother, and the floodgates would open. This seemed somewhat over dramatic, but what could I say?

She suddenly appeared in a glamorous evening dress and said that, although she wouldn't pose with me for the newspaper, she'd be happy to have a casual photograph taken, should I want one for my personal collection! I said I would be happy to do that – just for fun! As we stood together, she in her glittering show dress and me in my dark navy trouser suit (How I wished that I had dressed up!), she hauled Katy into the picture, holding her possessively in front of her, and as Bill Brown flashed his camera, she said, "You print that, and I'll sue!" – like father, like daughter. She then muttered something to me about the press trying to exploit us, which I thought was an over-reaction – this was a local paper and not the *New York Times* – but I didn't offer any opinion, having no wish to upset a member of the Garland family. She asked where we were to be sitting, and with no prior knowledge of her appearance in Dundee until that very afternoon, I hastily explained about having just returned from Texas. She kindly arranged complimentary tickets, and Katy and I found that we had no choice but to stay overnight in Dundee. I was impressed with the way Lorna chatted so easily to me just before she had to go on and perform, as I would have been in the dressing room knocking back the Rescue Remedy!

Bill sent me copies of the photos, and as I feared, I looked like the dowdy friend and was glad they didn't appear in the paper. I then received a letter from Lorna's publicity agent, warning me against using the photographs to promote my career; had I thought that was even a possibility, I might have been tempted! As for the Courier, they did manage to make a story out of the meeting and placed a 'Judy' shot of me on one side of the article and one of Lorna on the other, which seemed like a good compromise. The headline was 'Stars Heal Rift', and although there had never been a rift to heal, I was pleased to have been given equal billing.

Soon after, I was invited down to London to take part in the Greenwich Theatre 25th Anniversary Gala. 'Stars' who had worked there over the years were invited to take part at the Duke of York's Theatre, and it was to be a glittering affair with luminaries like Dawn French, Jennifer Saunders, Joanna Lumley, Ned Sherrin, Susan Hampshire and hundreds more, and I hoped that it would give me a little taste of the high life again. A couple of things occurred, however, which turned our plans upside down.

Aunt Bessie, my mother's oldest sister, died in the middle of May, and it meant that mum and dad would be going to London for the funeral at the same time as I was heading down, and therefore be unable to help on the babysitting front. We'd hoped to leave the kids with them so that Terry could come with me to the Greenwich concert and then stay on in London for rehearsals of *Travels with My Aunt*, which was to be playing at the Theatre Royal in York. He was looking forward to the production, as it was to be directed by John Doyle and his old friend, Bernie Lloyd, was also to be in it. Without my parents around, we had to adjust our plans and look elsewhere for help with the babysitting.

Matters were further complicated when Ollie took ill on the day before I was due to leave. He had a severe tummy bug with vomiting and diarrhoea, and it was clear that Terry would have to hold the fort until I returned, or until Ollie recovered. Although I felt very uneasy, I caught the Saturday morning train, leaving Terry to cope. I stayed overnight with Gordon Griffin in Ealing, and when I phoned home at night, I was horrified to hear that when Mike and Aileen popped in, Ollie had lain inert on the sofa throughout their visit, and it was Aileen who had realised he was lying in a pool of poo, quite oblivious to his surroundings. Terry didn't want to bother the doctor so late in the evening, but from 500 miles away, feeling totally powerless, I begged him to call him out. In the middle of the night, Terry phoned back to tell me that Dr Auld had come to the house, and Ollie had been taken to hospital and put on a drip. Had I realised how ill he was, I would never have left him, but I was now in a quandary; should I pack and return first thing in the morning, or should I go ahead with the show and leave as soon as it was over the following evening? Feeling sick at heart but reassured by Terry that there was nothing that I could do that he couldn't, I decided to stay.

I rehearsed my 'spot' with my old friend Cathy Jayes, but the gloss had been taken off the whole affair. While everyone was buzzing around in a state of anticipation before the concert, I just felt guilty. Gordon came along because he always loved glitzy occasions, and Bernard was there because I was going back that night to stay with him in Blackheath. My 'Judy' bit went well, but I didn't find it easy to socialise afterwards, and I left with Bernie while the party was in full swing. It could have been so different; I should have been able to renew a few contacts and make the most of such a rare occasion, but once again there seemed to have been a touch of 'Judy's Revenge'; not my tummy this time, but my three-year-old son's.

On the Monday when I met Terry at Swiss Cottage after his rehearsals, I discovered that he had booked a meal in a smart restaurant, and I kicked up a bit of a fuss, as I'd been hoping to just flop in some quiet little place and catch up on the past traumatic couple of days. Despite my protests, and a few tears if my memory serves me well, he persuaded me to go. As we entered the restaurant I couldn't believe my eyes, for sitting there at a big table was Ronnie Lee and his entire family, and I hadn't seen him since Brigadoon! He invited us to join his party, and after calming down and allowing myself to relax a bit, we spent a couple of hours with them. He said that he spent most of his time in New York and had virtually given up as a producer. He'd had his fingers burned a couple of times and preferred the security of his theatre ticket agency. It was lovely to see him again after so long, and, true to form, he treated us to our meal.

The following day, Uncle John picked me up at Perth station and took me straight to the hospital. As we reached the ward, I rushed across to Oliver's bed, but he looked straight past me and said, "Uncle John!" as if I didn't exist. Who knows what goes on in little minds? Perhaps he was punishing me for my absence in his hour of need, but I took him home and cosseted him for a few days. The gastroenteritis had taken its toll, and he looked like a skinny little rabbit but he quickly regained his strength.

Looking back, I can't imagine why I didn't try and catch a sleeper or a plane and head straight home as soon as the concert was over. Over the years, Terry and I often mulled over this incident and always got emotional as we pondered how differently things might have turned out. Terry could have asked John about joining the rehearsals after I came home, and John said afterwards that he would have worked round him for a couple of days, but 'the show must go on' goes so deep that we sometimes don't think straight. I guess Terry must have felt sure that Ollie was not in danger, but the little mite was lying in a hospital on a drip, and I wasn't there! I must have tried to block it from my mind, knowing that Aunt Betty and Uncle John had come to the rescue and were spending hours at Ollie's bedside, and we will always be grateful to them for that.

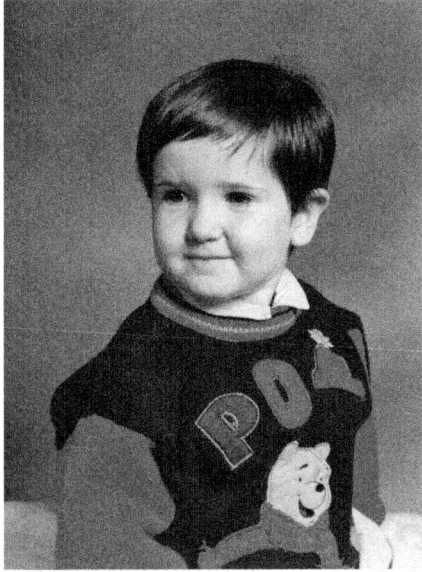

Ollie, back to robust health.

With life almost back to normal, I arrived in Whitley Bay to record my first audio book, an important little job, as I had finally managed to break into the privileged group of readers at *Soundings*, and this was to be the first of many books; God knows what we would have done without them. It was comforting to have that little oasis of security which always made us feel as if we were employed; when there was a book in the pipeline, all was well with the world.

On June 9th, I received a bottle of champagne from Andrew McKinnon. Attached to it was a brief note, which said that he was unable to join us for a meal as planned, but he hoped that Terry and I would drink his health with the bottle. I was puzzled by the tone of the note and sensed a troubled soul, so I sat down there and then and wrote him a letter. It was just to say that if he wanted a chat, I was available, but I never got a reply, and assumed he was not in the mood for socialising. I also remember that date, because it was on that day that the rejection letter arrived, saying that Terry's application to take over Andrew's job as Director of Productions had not been successful. Terry had spent so much time on it that I knew he would be disappointed, and he was due back from York that evening, so I mentioned that in my note to Andrew, saying something about the champagne being a lovely treat, not only because it was so near my birthday, but because I was about to break the bad news to Terry.

When Terry arrived that night we chatted about his letter from the theatre board, and his disappointment quickly changed to relief that he could still have a life! I think it was John Doyle who said that not getting the post was a mixed blessing, because running a theatre is such a total commitment, that it would only have worked for him if he didn't want to see his family again! The strongest contender, and the man who eventually got the job, was Michael Winter, who was experienced and had a long history of running repertory theatres. We decided that we had to put it behind us and get on with our lives.

Only a few weeks later I headed to Pitlochry with Jane Nelson Peebles to see *A Chorus of Disapproval*, totally unaware that something was about to happen which would affect my life and state of mind for months to come, and make me recall the year 1995 as an annus horribilis. After seeing the show, I decided to nip to the loo before the company appeared in the bar. As I was walking down the stairs, I spotted Joan Knight coming towards me. I smiled broadly, but it only took a couple of seconds for me to realise that something was very wrong. Was she ill? Was her vision impaired? Whatever it was, it was clear that she wasn't about to give me her usual welcoming, "Hello Darling!" As I got closer, the look on her face was quite chilling. I was puzzled, and touched her arm, saying, "Joan, it's Lesley". Her look was icy as a rather disembodied voice said, "And how are you?" She almost pushed me away as she continued making her way up the stairs. I couldn't make any sense of the incident, but as soon as I returned to the bar to relate the story to Jane, I started to cry and had to disappear downstairs again in order to compose myself.

All the way home I analysed and debated this turn of events, but could not come up with any answer. I had only seen Joan *en passant* since the lunch that we'd held in her honour only a few months before, and she had recently sent me a postcard acknowledging a message I'd left on her answering machine. It was a total mystery. Terry and I talked, cogitated and worried but came to no conclusion. I knew that I'd done nothing, and despite Joan's perversity with many, she and I always had a good relationship, and I had little reason to say a word against her. Terry had an inkling that it must somehow concern him, but we were grasping at straws, so I decided to call Joan and ask her what the problem was; unfortunately I got her answering machine, which had Andrew McKinnon's voice relaying a message, but I left my garbled thoughts after the beep and awaited her response.

Not a word, but knowing that she was not good at anything technical, and to be sure that she was aware of my concern, I wrote to her. I simply said that whatever imaginary slight she thought I had perpetrated, I was not prepared to let a 20-year relationship fall onto the cutting room floor without knowing what it was that was troubling her. The ball was in her court, but I cared too much to ignore it. I mentioned it to a couple of people, although no one seemed to be able to throw any light on the situation. I decided that the only course open to me was to write to Andrew; if he had Joan's ear, he might be able to help. Andrew himself was now going through a bad time, even more than I was aware of, and by contacting him I was about to open another can of worms.

I didn't give him any details, except to say that something had occurred which had left me puzzled and upset, and as he was close to Joan I hoped that we might meet for a coffee to see if he could provide some enlightenment. I had no idea that letter would spark off the second half of the nightmare. In contrast to the brief but friendly note which had accompanied the champagne, I now received a very formal letter, which expressed regret about my concerns, but said that he would not be available until after August 15th, which was some way off. The tone was quite different, and I knew it was intentionally so, because Andrew did nothing without due consideration. I had the distinct impression that he would prefer it if I did not call him at all.

When you really don't know what's going on, the danger is that you begin to write the script, and we now began to link Joan's attitude with Andrew's, and deduced that they had both been affected by whatever it was that I, or we, were supposed to have done. We became convinced that it must be connected to Terry's application for the job at the theatre, and although he had given a Joan a glowing report, he'd been quite outspoken about the current regime. He had steered clear of directly mentioning Andrew by name, but it was implicit. We'd been told that all applications were confidential, but we realised that we would be naïve to assume that they really were! Further investigation proved that not only had Joan been invited to help with the applications, but Andrew, as departing director, also had the right to look at them. We tormented ourselves over it, but it looked as if no one was going to tell us what the problem was.

This affair was to cause me a lot of heartache and sleepless nights in the months to come, and I wished that I could have Terry's attitude, which was to regretfully push the episode to the back of his mind. Everything was surmise, and after an initial burst of enquiry, I was aware that I would have to let it rest. A meeting with Joan in Tesco confirmed Terry's involvement. She gave him the glacial treatment before hastening off with her trolley, and I had the same a few weeks later in Safeway. It left me with a feeling of isolation and the growing realisation that this could make our lives very difficult in the coming months. Joan didn't have a theatre anymore, but she still had the power to influence others. We were concerned that we might not be able to hang around for long enough to be accepted back by the 'Scotia Nostra', our nickname for the 'powers that be' throughout the acting fraternity in Scotland.

We kept things ticking over with audio books and the odd cabaret, some more odd than others! The worst I can recall took place at the opening of the new *Pierre Victoire* restaurant in Dundee. We had eaten many times at the smaller branch in Perth, and when the restaurateur, David, said that he was about to take over a large property in Dundee, we expressed great interest. We were delighted when he invited us to perform our two cabarets on the opening night, and because George Donald wasn't available, we enlisted the help of Ian Strachan, a very capable accompanist and fellow Dundonian. We were there for photographs during the day, and the atmosphere was fraught. As the buying and refurbishing of the old David Winter shop had been a joint financial venture with the town, David had invited 150 councillors. He had been led to believe that around 50% would accept the invitation, but the figure had been nearer 100% (since when did town councillors refuse a freebie?), and not only that, most of them were planning to bring their wives or partners!

We checked the tiny stage, realised that there was no proper lighting, and having tested the sound system, knew that we would have our work cut out. The ceiling was so high that the sound just went up in the air, and as the massive room was divided by a staircase, it was unlikely that we would be heard or seen beyond that point. I guess we were lucky that they'd managed to borrow an old piano! We had to make the best of it, so having arranged to eat in the restaurant after our cabaret, we went off, leaving them all to prepare for the onslaught.

Later that day, as we arrived at the foot of the stairs, the noise of the crowd hit us. Our hearts sank as we entered the space and were almost deafened by the hubbub. The place was mobbed, the waiters were tearing around in a frenzy, and it became clear that the customers were not entirely happy. We disappeared to our changing area, which was a small disabled toilet – not an ideal arrangement because it only left one other small loo to cope with hundreds of folk, who we assumed would be drinking rather heavily.

When someone went on to announce our first 'spot', we were aware that no one was listening to him at all; it did not bode well. Terry was filled with dread, because he had all the talking to do. We were almost invisible on the darkened little dais, and at one point, I remember someone trying to shine a torch in my direction. Half of the diners, the ones who were behind the central staircase were not even aware that there was a cabaret, and the audio system battled with the high ceiling which absorbed most of the sound – except the roar of the crowd, which was directed mostly at the waiting staff.

Due to the large numbers, the food disappeared fast, and there were many who never saw a starter, never mind a main course. We soldiered on, although Terry was cutting his dialogue as he went along, and I was losing the odd slow number. I kept turning round to let Ian know what was happening – no one else could hear me anyway. We completed the 'Judy' spot and I headed for the disabled toilet to change. Not surprisingly, I walked straight in on a lady with her knickers at her knees, as there was no sign to say it was a changing area for the 'Artistes'! Just before we ventured back to face the throng, Calman Cathro, a Tory MP from Broughty Ferry, and an old acquaintance of the family – indeed the lady who had stood in for me at a Harris FP Burns Supper only a few years before – poked her head 'backstage' to say, "It's like Fawlty Towers out there!" She gave a brief, hilarious account of people not getting what they ordered, and of strawberries falling all over the floor, before heading back to her table. Sadly, that was the last time I saw her, as only a few weeks later she passed on after a very sudden illness.

As we returned to do our 'Piaf' spot, I knew it would be a little easier because the songs did not require so much subtlety, and it was encouraging to note that quite a few people had come forward to listen to us at closer quarters. It was still a relief to finish and escape to a table to partake of a much-needed meal, only to find that there was not a morsel to be had, and we had to settle for a small glass of champagne. When I went to the bar to order a second, the barmaid burst into tears as she was so stressed out. We were weak with hunger, so we got our things together and prepared to scarper. Having been advised to collect our cheque before we left, we located David, who was by this time a little the worse for wear and had mislaid his cheque book, but I gave him our address and we left the place, still heaving with people. Now we had first-hand experience of what club singers and comedians face on a regular basis, but it was not for us.

We had to pursue our fee, but at least we got it, and we were about the only ones who did. So many people were paid nothing, including some of the furniture suppliers. The opening night had been strangely prophetic, because things continued to go wrong, and the restaurant eventually went bust. David had a severe breakdown, left his wife and four children and disappeared back to North America. It was then discovered that he owed money to all and sundry, including customers from the Perth restaurant who had been persuaded to invest. Despite valiant efforts to keep it afloat, the Perth one soon closed as well; he had been too ambitious, and everybody else, including his own family, paid the price.

Like a black cloud lurking overhead, the Joan/Andrew situation was still unresolved. As the year ended, I was still suffering agonies over it all, so I decided to drop another note to Andrew, asking him to meet me for a coffee, just to clear the air before his departure in the spring, but I received no response. When I eventually received a note, it simply said that he couldn't meet me because certain things would have to be talked about which he was not prepared to discuss. That was the end of the matter as far as he was concerned and, for the time being, we would just have to live with the mystery unresolved.

1977 - Happier days with Andrew McKinnon at our wedding.

For his last few months, Andrew chose to withdraw from all social activity, and I learned later that he had also become completely estranged from Joan. She had been his mentor during the '70s and had been partly responsible for getting him the job of Artistic Director, but because of the path he had chosen to take she had taken him to task and their relationship was severed. Andrew left Perth, vowing never to return, and he kept faith with that promise, not even returning for Joan's funeral; it was a sorry and confusing affair. I was sad that he had gone; Andrew and I had always got on well, he'd been our Best Man, and once again he had disappeared from our lives. I was never allowed closure on this.

It had not been a great year from a family or a work point of view. Apart from Bessie's death, Ollie's illness and our personal frustrations, Uncle Arthur Johnstone, my mother's brother, underwent a very disturbing assault in the summer when he had gone with his partners to collect rent from a tricky tenant. As they stood outside the door, Mr Baikie suddenly appeared with a hammer and Arthur had to undergo a vile and frenzied attack. His skull was cracked in four places, and he was left in a pool of blood. The man was apprehended, charged and sent to prison but it took a long time for Arthur to recover.

On a brighter note, over 20 years after passing my driving test, and never having driven since, I took a few refresher lessons and got back behind the wheel. Having two children who had to be walked or buggied to here, there and everywhere, I finally realised how daft it was to have a car and a licence but let Terry do all the driving.

It was wonderful to finally feel confident enough to do it, as it gave me a new independence, and I've never tired of driving. From 1996 onwards, I was a driver, with a wee Peugeot 206 all to myself. It would really change my life.

- 26 -

Every day's a school day

1996 saw us preparing for our own little show, *Legends*. We had already done both cabarets with George Donald, but Terry would have to do some interweaving of the two scripts so that they hung together as a whole, rather than two separate entities. The most unnerving prospect for me was having to sing so many songs in such dramatically different styles in one evening, and because of the strain that Piaf songs put on the voice, we opted for singing the Garland songs in the first half; although they required more skill and variety, they were slightly less taxing. Terry had the bigger pill to swallow, because as we were now preparing to perform the show in theatres instead of halls, he felt that he could no longer read from a script. It was a lot to learn, but at least I was not the only one who was nervous. We took it upon ourselves to organise every aspect; there was the hiring of pianos, the printing of leaflets and posters and their distribution – even buying gels for the lighting rig! But at this stage we only had two definite bookings: two nights at the Byre in St Andrews and a week at Dundee Rep.

As well as performing, Terry was also directing, so he had to light and 'tech' the show before the opening night in both venues, which was a lengthy process, as he had devised a lighting plot which had over 70 cues. George didn't take part in the business side of things, and as *Legends* was the beginning of getting to know George, I have to say that was probably just as well.

February offered a brief distraction in the form of a trip to London to attend a *This Is Your Life* for Benny Green. We were part of the group of friends who sat on the set to welcome him as he arrived, although we didn't have to make a personal contribution. Benny's life encompassed so many different aspects that there were people there from all walks of life. He had written on subjects as diverse as jazz, cricket, P.G.Wodehouse – and even boxing! The programme overran and they had to do some ruthless editing; what a pity that they chose to cut Michael Feinstein's contribution, which came via satellite from New York. Benny had taken us to a concert a few years before where he introduced us to Michael, and so entranced were we that evening that we became devoted fans, but perhaps it was assumed (maybe correctly!) that, at that time, few would have heard of him! I have a brief memory of tripping over the leg of an elderly gentleman in the hospitality area, only to discover later that it was the leg of Dennis Compton, the famous cricketer, who didn't mean a lot to me, but caused Terry some excitement as he had been Terry's cricket hero.

Benny Green

Sadly, that spring will be remembered for one of the greatest tragedies in living memory. I was down in Whitley Bay when I saw on the news that a crazy man with a gun had burst into the Dunblane Primary School and shot dead over half of the Primary 1 pupils. His name was Thomas Hamilton, and having done his dreadful deeds he shot himself. It was a black day in Scotland, and many dark years ahead for the bereaved families in Dunblane.

Legends premièred at the Byre Theatre on Saturday, March 23rd. Although we realised that we weren't going to make big bucks out of it, it was a good little show and we hoped we might take it round and about over the next few years. After our two nights at the Byre we enjoyed a few days at Dundee Rep, and despite the short run, we managed to cover our expenses and make a bit of money into the bargain. Terry found the dual roles of actor and director quite taxing, so we were keen to avoid the added strain of being producers in future. It was no fun having to 'count the house' to make sure we'd be paid; we preferred to be employees.

Quite apart from the organisational burden, we had an area of concern regarding George. Naturally enough, he was fussy about the quality of the piano and had gone in person to Edinburgh to select the instrument, so we reckoned that we didn't have to trouble ourselves with that aspect. On our arrival at the Byre, he said that he was not at all happy with the tone and feel of what looked like a very attractive white Baby Grand, but as he had chosen it, we assumed that he would live with it; we assumed wrong.

1996, rehearsing Legends with George Donald and Terry Wale.

On the Sunday, he went back to Edinburgh to book a new piano for the week in Dundee. This was not typical of George, who was usually happy to leave the organisation to others, but he clearly dug his heels in over certain issues. He told us that the man at the piano shop had been difficult to deal with but had grudgingly accepted the complaint. We were alarmed that there might be a charge for a second piano, but George assured us that the fee would remain the same. Sure enough, the second piano arrived on the Monday morning and was taken across to Dundee Rep where it remained for the rest of the week. The lovely white Baby Grand was duly collected by the company on their way back to Edinburgh.

It was not long before George expressed his disappointment with the second piano. We didn't understand his problem, but we had endless tunings, and on the last night the piano tuner dismantled the whole keyboard to try and improve matters. It was alarming to see all the black and white keys scattered over the floor, particularly as it was 7.40pm, and the audience were waiting to come into the auditorium.

Despite the piano business the show went well, and when a second bill for the piano was presented to Terry, we just assumed that there had been an error. On investigation, we found that the firm in Edinburgh was indeed expecting us to pay twice over and were not taking 'No' for an answer. Terry had a dreadful row with them over the phone, but George remained adamant that there had never been any question of us having to pay a second time.

The engagement over, Terry and I were heading off for a few days with the family at Alton Towers, so we left strict instructions with Dundee Rep that they were under no circumstances to pay for that second piano, and should the firm give them any hassle, they should get in touch with George. We duly told him that in the event of anyone getting in touch, he was to insist that we were not paying another penny, and he promised to deal with it; all very clear.

On our return, we were astounded to find a financial statement from the theatre, which included a fee for the second piano! We were livid and checked with George to make sure that no one had been in touch with him, and having had his assurance, Terry wrote a very angry letter to the theatre, castigating them for not following our instructions. We were astounded to receive a letter in return, saying that as the piano firm was adamant about the bill, they <u>had</u> called George, who had told them just to go ahead and pay it! We still thought there had been some mistake, but as the truth dawned, we realised that we were now dealing with a very sensitive issue.

Terry went round to see him, and after much probing, George recalled that Dundee Rep had called him one day when he had been giving a piano lesson in his lounge and, yes, he thought he might have told them to pay up. It was the easy option at the time and meant that he did not have to face any hassle from either the theatre or the Edinburgh company. It was bewildering that he didn't, at least, stand firm and tell Dundee that the bill was not to be paid until we returned from our holiday, which would have passed the buck very firmly to us and absolved him of any further responsibility. But he preferred to say whatever he thought would keep him in everyone's good books. That was all very well but we were now in Dundee Rep's bad books and Terry was left with the task of explaining why our pianist was behaving like Walter Mitty! George did offer to write a letter of apology to the theatre, but we instinctively knew that he would never get round to it.

So Terry wrote the letter, and in it he said that the misunderstanding had arisen because our pianist was suffering from stress and had, initially, forgotten about their phone call, which had resulted in Terry jumping the gun and blaming the theatre. It all left a bad taste in the mouth, and we also realised that there might be more to it than quite met the eye. Perhaps there had never been any question of us not having to pay for this piano, as George may have assured the Edinburgh firm that they would be paid. Whatever the finer points, it was clear that there was no chance of reclaiming the money.

Shortly afterwards, I was thrilled to take part in a cabaret with old friend, comedian George Duffus, at the Invercarse Hotel in Dundee. Having put the hiccups of *Legends* behind us, we invited George Donald to make up the threesome, and the evening was especially successful because George, as well as accompanying, also performed his own *Scotland the What* songs, giving the cabaret a lot of variety.

It was now three years since our move back, and although I had also joined Pat Lovett's Agency, we rarely heard from her. One day in May, when Terry was down in York, I did hear from her, and about a rather bizarre job. A photographer was looking for three couples of varying ages to go on a ten-day P&O cruise on the *Oriana*, the newest of their fleet. The trip was called *The Italian Affair*, and would take in Palma, Cannes, Livorno, Elba and return via Gibraltar. All we had to do was to pose in the many areas of the ship, and in return for this 'modelling', we would have a free cruise. The reason they had approached Pat was because they didn't want people who looked like models, but would represent a cross section of the people who might want to go on a cruise. She wondered if Terry and I would be interested; I was more than interested – I was desperate.

It was not easy to find photos without the children, but I ferreted around, cut up a few holiday snaps by way of an 'audition' and sent them off to David Darling, the photographer. I didn't really expect that we would be chosen because, with the difference in our ages, we were not a typical couple, so I was absolutely over the moon to hear that we were due to embark from Southampton docks on June 15th, which was less than a month away; it was like winning a prize.

Pat asked me to make all the arrangements, because she realised that she couldn't take 10% commission from a free holiday, but we sent her a bottle of champagne for putting the trip our way. The company was covering most of our expenses, but there was still quite a lot to buy. There would be a couple of photo shoots every day, so a variety of clothes was essential, not to mention a specific new outfit for the 'Black and White' night, a photo that eventually went into the brochure as publicity for their POSH Club. The only moment of panic was when I found that my passport was out of date, but once that was resolved it was all plain sailing. Mum and dad took the kids, and we headed down to Southampton to stay overnight in a hotel prior to our departure the following day.

It was exhilarating to be played off by a big band at the quayside, to the tune of Rod Stewart's *Sailing*. It was a new experience; the ship was like a massive floating hotel – the lift worked on 14 levels and had every facility you could possibly hope for. So extensive were the amenities, that there was even a small operating theatre plus surgeon, who did have to deal with a couple of broken limbs on this voyage, although a helicopter was called in to airlift a heart attack victim from the top deck to get him to a hospital in Lisbon. We heard that there were a couple of coffins on board, which I suppose was not surprising when you considered the ages of some of the passengers; even at this time, it was a way of life for the elderly wealthy, and it was entirely possible that they might end their days on the ocean. It wasn't long before ships got even bigger, and the *Oriana* would be considered one of the smaller vessels.

1996, POSH Club.

Despite the two or three photo sessions each day, we had plenty of free time to sunbathe and visit the ports, although it felt odd to don our makeup and our full evening dress at 9am in order to have photographs taken in the empty casino or ballroom, when other passengers were occupied elsewhere.

The food was good, always available, and despite the five meals a day, people still queued up at mealtimes as if they couldn't wait. Perhaps if we had paid for the cruise, we too might have been stuffing ourselves to get our money's worth. The only 'flies in the ointment' were the other models, with whom we had little in common, but that didn't spoil my own enjoyment – even although it was uncomfortable having to eat with people who were rude to the waiters and boorish in the extreme, particularly a couple from Glasgow called Kenny and Maggie. Her behaviour with our waiter, Denny, was typical. She started off by greeting him like a long-lost brother, but once he gained in confidence and started to respond in kind, she was aghast at his lack of respect. It changed very quickly from, "Denny Darling" to "Will you hurry up and serve us please?", and this after only a two-minute wait.

Despite the extensive menu, she and Kenny rarely found anything that they liked, and having looked at an elaborate and varied menu, they would order a mushroom omelette – or because Kenny was addicted to soups, he might order three soups and a pudding, which was designed to throw busy chefs dealing with 1,800 passengers into a frenzy. Even the soups elicited complaints, as he preferred *Baxters*. Maggie ordered champagne as if it was going out of fashion, simply because we could buy drinks at crew rates, and we were 'saving so much money!' Because of all the antics with the waiter and the food, our evening meals, usually our favourite time of day, were somewhat undermined. On the odd night when they disappeared into a port, it was bliss to have the table to ourselves. It was a small price to pay later in the evening, when we had to listen to a description of a "truly authentic Chinese" that they had enjoyed in Gibraltar and an "authentic pizza" in Cannes!

Fortunately, we didn't have to spend our days with them. When we had time off from the modelling, we would look at the information in the cabin, before heading for some old and picturesque site of interest while they headed off to pursue their favourite hobbies of shopping, scoffing and swilling. Elba was the highlight for us with its hilly network of pretty, little streets, and we always hoped to return one day.

None of the group ever asked for our opinion about the on-board entertainment, or anything else for that matter, but they certainly regaled us with theirs. If we had enjoyed a show, you can be sure they walked out in the middle. There was just no meeting point, and despite all their spending sprees, at the end of the cruise not one of them gave Denny a tip! One of the most irksome moments for us was when I mentioned tipping, and overheard one of them say,

"Tip him, I'll tip him over the side!"

Whatever the setbacks, we had an experience that we could never have afforded and probably would not even have contemplated. I loved sitting on the deck, looking out at the frothy wake of the ship, knowing that we were miles from anywhere. We even coped with a Force 8 gale that struck one night, not in the Bay of Biscay as anticipated, but in the usually more tranquil Mediterranean; even Terry, who did not think that he had great sea legs, found the *Oriana* experience remarkably smooth – and I remember the man who suffered from tinnitus, who derived so much pleasure from standing on the top deck during the storm, because it was the only time that the noise outside his head was louder than the noise within.

I have memories of so many people and so many electric aids, and it was a sight to see them all zipping around in the ports. There were those who lived from one cruise to the next, those for whom cruising was just a way of life. We said farewell to the ship, and headed back to collect our car, only to discover that some vandal had removed a couple of hubcaps, the battery was flat, and we had to call out the AA, but we didn't let any of that lower our spirits. We had one more day of freedom before collecting the kids from Dundee. It was straight back into family life with a vengeance, because the school holidays had just begun, and we were about to start the Summer School at the Whitehall Theatre in Dundee.

A well-connected lady in Dundee had left money in her will to help the children of Dundee, and Norman Robertson, our solicitor friend, had decided to use some of her legacy to run a summer school for a period of five weeks on a four-day week, six-hour day basis, and we had been invited to run the school, take the classes and devise a project for the kids to work on. He was part of a trust who owned the Whitehall Theatre and was very keen to put the space to good use. We asked Tony Ellis to join us as choreographer, and Jack McGowan, an ex-student from Queen Margaret College, as musical director. We were all to be paid a weekly salary, although the children wouldn't pay a penny for the course.

We were inundated with applicants, and we spent a full day in April holding auditions. David Strachan, who had Whitehall connections and was a colleague of Norman's, was appointed as administrator, and he was responsible for setting up the auditions and the day-to-day running of the school. He seemed very efficient, but despite all the official-looking computer charts and spreadsheets, the auditions were quite tricky. About 80 young people between the ages of eight and fourteen arrived at the same time, and the only way we could cope, was to see them in small groups, starting with the youngest. By the time we reached the older ones, we felt that they'd been hanging around for so long that we had to accept them all, and then felt guilty about the few we had turned down earlier in the day. David had taken the decision to tell the children there and then if they had been successful, which was guaranteed to cause much weeping and wailing, and gave us no opportunity to change our minds. This meant that we now had to face 75 kids, instead of the 60 that we had planned for. With four tutors, we could only have four classes going on at any one time, and almost 20 pupils per class was more than enough, especially as very few of the children seemed to have any background in theatre, let alone discipline. There was no doubt that some of the parents had sent their offspring along, regardless of talent or inclination, because it was a great way to keep them occupied during the summer holidays.

We arrived full of enthusiasm on the first day of term, and much to our surprise only one child failed to turn up. We'd done a vast amount of work in advance, and I had devised voice classes and improvisation exercises based on ideas gleaned from books by Augusto Boal and various other experts in the field, but we knew that whatever we did in the classes, we still had to devise a project that would give all 75 something worthwhile to do. We had agreed to produce an 'end of term' show, which put a lot of pressure on us, because time was short, and the kids were extremely difficult to control. They were just about manageable in a class situation, but after the first week when we had to move on to rehearsals and deal with larger numbers, it became virtually impossible to exercise any authority. We started by projecting, then shouting, using whistles and ended up with microphones! When working with a large group, anyone who we weren't directly addressing, just started chattering to their neighbour. They were, without doubt, the worst audience we had ever played to. David was very confident about his powers to control them, but I will never forget the background roar as he tried to read out the register each morning.

My main feat in those early days was in memorising the name of every pupil and labelling them with a 'characteristic'. From this information, Terry and I worked round the clock to devise a play with music which would give every child something to do. No matter how hard we tried to be fair, it was inevitable that one or two would end up with only a line or two of dialogue. A few, whose verbal skills were poor, had other gifts, and we endeavoured to allow them to display their dancing, singing, gymnastics and baton twirling talents.

David maintained that extra volunteer help (which had been offered) would not be necessary, but we four tutors ended up dealing with sore tummies, twisted ankles, bulimia, and children who had other psychological problems. 'Dr' Strachan endeavoured to soothe injuries with bags of frozen peas, and the delinquency and bad behaviour with counselling and words of wisdom; he even started handing out yellow cards for misdemeanours, like yawning during one of his pep talks.

And there were others who willingly voiced their opinions about how we should go about things. Some comments were well intentioned, and we were assured frequently that we shouldn't worry so much because the mums and grannies would love it whatever we did! There were many willing folk who helped us cope during the final week of dress rehearsals and performances, all of whom were invaluable, and especially Betty Wood, who found all sorts of bits and pieces of costume to give the show a bit of colour, and that was some feat with 75 in the cast.

There were amusing incidents which kept us going, like Chris who came on the day of the auditions to accompany his sister and ended up participating. According to him, "Eh wis jist standin' there, an' a man said, "Follow them", so eh did!" By the time we realised that he wasn't part of the official group, it was too late. We let him through, and he turned up trumps. On the other hand there was cheeky little Steven who, although amusing to have around, was impossible to control. He didn't know when to stop the banter. He meant no harm, but after one of Terry's explosive reactions to a piece of extreme behaviour, Steven would say, "Bit stressed out are you, Terry?" As well as embarrassing many of the girls with his personal remarks, it was when he finally started locking them in the toilet, that David justifiably decided that he had to go; it was a shame because he was one of the most talented.

Then there was Becky who kept disappearing from rehearsals to head for the toilets to comfort kids who were in despair because their romances had broken up. The list of problem kids was long, and some just craved attention; one girl spent so much time volunteering for things, that one day when she had me virtually pinioned against the wall, regaling me with her, "I can walk on stilts, I can scream, I can do cartwheels, I can do this, I can do that", I lost my cool and said with no small degree of sarcasm, that she should get her mother to hire the Caird Hall to provide a showcase for her unlimited talents!

A few mothers got involved, and I can still see Mrs M. in tears because we had taken away her daughter's part, but we thought we were doing her a favour, as she always looked so bored and unenthusiastic; we quickly wrote another scene, and she seemed much happier when we cast her as deadpan Crystal Gowk in what we thought a hilarious sketch. Mrs H. also had a complaint, and that was over a line in *Little People* from *Les Miserables;* being a fervent Catholic, she was not happy with 'A flea can bite the bottom of the Pope in Rome', which she took to be a slight against the Pontiff! After a reassuring chat, she left, satisfied. And there were all the lost items, forgotten bus fares, juice spilt on floors or cartons burst inside bags. There were mini revolts by children who wanted bigger parts, and those who didn't even know that Act 2 followed Act 1!

By the final week we had a show which seemed to be in reasonable shape. Tony had choreographed some amazing routines with a troupe of about 20 girls. Jack had done sterling work on all the songs, and Terry and I managed to get them to speak loudly and almost clearly, but we still had to face the technical rehearsal and a stage manager called George. Throughout rehearsals he would barge onto the stage without a 'by your leave' and start lecturing or shouting at the kids. We had to stand there until he was finished, and sometimes he would ask the kids to change things we had directed them to do.

Terry tried not to undermine his authority and told them that George was The Boss backstage and they had to do what they were told; it was almost a relief to hear somebody else shouting! On one occasion, when some of the girls became overheated, George told them that they couldn't go outside for air. Terry intervened on their behalf and elicited the response, "I'll give them some air with the back of my hand!" We knew that letting them leave the building was a risky proposition, but Terry insisted that George either let them go outside for a short break, or at least open the dock doors to let some air circulate and cool the place down. The 'register' included a few prima donnas, and we had witnessed enough fainting and swooning not to take any chances.

We had to run a tight ship, and we'd told the kids that, whatever happened, they were to come onstage when called, unless they were too ill to move. George overrode that as well, and instructed anyone complaining of feeling ill to leave the wings at once. We had been working with this bunch for five weeks and knew that if they were allowed to make this sort of decision, there would be a succession of missing people as they all headed off to the toilet to deal with their period pains or to nurse their broken hearts. On the plus side, he did show a great deal of enthusiasm about dressing the stage and making it all look good – but he could have done with a course at the Charm School!

We made it to our opening night, and we could not have been prouder of our mob as they rose to the occasion for both performances. We'd been told that we were trying to achieve the impossible, and I hope that we did. Few would have been aware of how great a journey had been made by the children, and perhaps there were those who had hoped for *Oklahoma,* but anyone watching the kids strutting their stuff in *One Singular Sensation* could not fail to be impressed; we certainly were! Thanks to Gary from Linlathen, we managed to be topical and include *Wannabe*, which had just hit the No 1 spot and launched *The Spice Girls* on their path to fame and fortune. Katy adored it, but she was always in her element with older children, and she saw a real slice of life as she was mixing with so many different types. We were lucky she had just reached the age for acceptance on the course, enabling us to take her along each day. Ollie was juggled between family and a children's nursery.

After the second and final performance we were given 'Thank You' gifts from the band of children, and it was a happy night for everyone. Over the years I spotted several of the kids appearing in local shows, so some of them went on to develop their talents. I looked on the summer school of 1996 as a worthwhile, learning experience and would have considered doing it again because of the positive feedback from the children, parents and audience. When I asked Terry what he felt about it, his response was, "Do it again? I'd rather have a major operation!" I wouldn't have wanted to do it without Terry, so we turned our minds to other things, one being the possibility of getting to know Michael Winter, who had recently started at our local theatre as the new Artistic Director. A new era had begun.

1996, Dundee – Summer School with Jack McGowan, Terry Wale & Tony Ellis.

Just another winter's tale

I spotted that Michael had *Tartuffe* planned as part of his Autumn Season so, knowing there was an ideal role for me, I quickly dropped him a line. When he called to offer the part, he said that he could only afford to employ actors who were willing to do more than one play, but the only drawback was that all he could offer, along with Dorine in *Tartuffe,* was a minuscule part in *Having a Ball.* I was reluctant to do this because it had been some time since my last appearance in Perth; to return as a patient having a nose job in one tiny scene was a bit of a let-down, especially as that play would come first. But Michael was the new director so, in order not to rock the boat, I decided to bite the bullet and do it. At least I didn't have to stay for the curtain call, which was a welcome concession. I was then invited to do a couple of episodes of *High Road*, and although STV were willing to juggle my filming schedule around my theatrical commitments, Michael was adamant that I had to be available for all rehearsals; he said that he didn't approve of actors having more than one job at a time, and never looked on any such case with compassion. This was very different from the regime under Joan Knight, who was more sympathetic towards actors when they had an opportunity to boost their meagre earnings – but she was a bit of a one-off.

It would have been so easy for him to have released me with little or no disruption, especially when it transpired that I was not even required on one of the two days that I had requested, and the other was taken up with National Poetry Day, on which we each performed a piece of poetry in the Perth bar at lunchtime, which had nothing to do with our rehearsals. I rode the storm, but it was already clear that he was not going to be an easy man to deal with.

Actors sometimes tend to make excuses for directors, as if they are not quite of the human species, and that's how I was with Michael. He was not a great communicator and could be quite antisocial. He found it difficult to mix with actors outside the rehearsal room, and no one could bring up the subject of work without a negative response, yet I was strangely taken with him and found myself saying to people how much I enjoyed working with him, and that his reputed rudeness was simply shyness. Directors shouldn't be excused such behaviour just because of the position they hold or the power they wield, but I think that Michael had taken a bit of a shine to me, hence my willingness to excuse his eccentricities.

Having A Ball was painless, but once we were onto *Tartuffe,* there was an issue because he refused to let Liz Lochhead, Scottish poet and playwright, attend any rehearsals. Liz had adapted Moliere's comic masterpiece into a rollicking Scots version, and Michael may have felt insecure about directing such a Scottish piece. When he came to my dressing room on the opening night and asked if he could accompany me to the bar, I knew he was nervous about meeting Liz for the first time, especially as he had denied her access to the rehearsals, but she was very complimentary, and he managed to stand still for a few minutes before he scuttled off home. She said after he left that she thought him one of the rudest people she had ever met – but I still managed to complete the run with a bit of a soft spot for him.

Shortly after we returned from a break in Tenerife we heard that Joan Knight had died; it was the end of an era, and we were doubly saddened because we had never managed to heal the rift that had inexplicably come between us. When I realised back in the summer that she was dying, I wrote to her, making no mention of her strange behaviour towards us. I simply said that I had heard that, just as we had settled in Perth, it seemed that she might be leaving. It was the gentlest way I could find of saying 'Goodbye'. I thanked her for her friendship over the 20 years we had worked together, reminisced a little, and expressed the wish that she, like myself, could say 'Je ne regrette rien.' I heard nothing, while her many friends and acquaintances were invited to her home to spend a little time with her. A few chosen people were given gifts, and I did eventually receive a note which, although not couched in her old warm style, was friendly enough, and I had the feeling that she might have wanted to make amends.

The year ended with her funeral, which we attended on December 30th. It was lovely to see so many faces from the past. Andrew was conspicuous by his absence as, sadly, he had not managed to patch up his differences, despite his long association with her; whatever had occurred, it obviously went deep. I feared I might not be moved, but a tear did spring to my eye at the end of the service as her coffin was brought back through the church to the strains of *Westering Home*. It had always been her party piece, badly sung and out of tune, but played that day by John Scrimger who had known her for so long. When I was asked to sing at her memorial concert a few months later, I knew it was the right thing to do. I wanted to remember the good times, and there had been many of them during the years we had worked together, so I gave my *No Regrets* and hoped that she would have approved.

On checking the Perth spring brochure, I spotted a role that I fancied and dropped a line to Michael to suggest myself for Prossy (Miss Proserpine Garnett), a delightful cameo in Shaw's *Candida*. Michael called immediately, wondering if I would consider another two plays, one on either side of *Candida*. There were good parts for me in all three, and of course he was thinking of his budget. The family were still young, and gone were the days when I wanted to play and rehearse for weeks on end, but it was some time since I had nine weeks of continuous work, not to mention my desire for the old familiar taste of working in the repertory system.

Lucky Sods was first, and it was a beast to learn. I spent a lot of time on holiday in Tenerife trying to break the back of it, but with a cast of four and a lot of 'one liners' you couldn't take your eye off the ball for a second. It was a play about winning the lottery, fun to do, and I was happy to have the female line that incorporated three different roles. I was a wife, an old woman and a rather tarty mistress. The other actress, Monica Gibb, played the lottery winner throughout.

I arrived on the first day of rehearsals, and was happy to find that Monica was only slightly taller than myself, and the two men playing our husbands were massive – clearly a good recipe for some humour. One of them, Ray Gardner, had recently done an advert for Tango, a sparkling drink, and he was very keen to pass his video round so that we could all have a look. As the days passed, it became increasingly difficult to tolerate his enormous ego. He had brought many of his cuttings and reviews, and the publicity department had pasted them outside the theatre. When he came into rehearsals one morning and said, "It's like a shrine out there!", my mouth dropped open. He even managed to get hold of a large cut-out of himself in his Tango shorts to place in the St John's Centre, a rare treat indeed for the shoppers to feast their eyes on! He expected Monica and I to take turns at working with him in the evenings, and we had to keep throwing his cues at him until he had learnt it; apparently it was the only way that he could get the lines to stick. Although I had other methods of line-learning – and a busy life at home – it was indeed tricky stuff, and the repetition probably helped us all get it into our heads.

1997, Perth – Lucky Sods with Ray Gardner.

By the time we opened, his company was extremely challenging; in the middle of a conversation, particularly with a lady, he would pick up a book, just to show how bored he was. He talked about his 'Tango' at length and one evening before the show, he plonked a large cheque on my dressing table – to show me his repeat fees! "I'll be able to buy you a drink this evening", he gloated. Trouble was, when I shared my feelings with Monica, it gradually became clear that she and 'Tango Man' got on rather well, so I had no one to have a giggle with. On the positive side, all four of us were very well cast, and it was quite an entertaining evening – although I was somewhat at odds with the rest of them who thought it a masterpiece.

Ray was rude throughout the run; if I was chatting to a friend in the bar, he would saunter over and say something like, "Is she sending you to sleep?", which was the pinnacle of his wit. When you didn't fall about, his repartee was, "Lighten up" or "Get a sense of humour!" Once the show opened I was straight into rehearsals for *Candida,* so I only had contact with him in the evenings, which was quite enough.

One sunny day, Monica and Ray went out on one of their country drives and came across a little shop selling various bits of memorabilia. They bought a replica model of the Drury Lane Theatre and a little doll, both of which they discovered had belonged to Joan Knight. They wanted us all to chip in and give the ornament to Michael on the opening night. I didn't think that he would be enamoured, but as there were only four of us in the company it would have been churlish not to put in a few quid. As he received it, he looked extremely taken aback, said that he couldn't accept it and would have to donate it to the theatre.

Once they had all departed, I was sorely tempted to parcel up a pair of bloomers and send them to Michael with a little note saying that I had found them in a rural lingerie outlet, discovered that they had belonged to Joan, and knew he would love to add them to his Late Knight Collection. I got as far as procuring a pair of knickers from the wardrobe, but I lost my nerve and never got around to delivering them to his office.

Richard Digby Day was charming and a pleasure to work with on *Candida*. He was the long-term partner of Michael Winter and known by some in the business as 'Richard Giggly Gay'! On the preview night, we all delved into the 'comments box' to find out what the punters had thought, and it was poor Sue Edmonstone, playing Candida, who came out of it worst. She already felt that she was too old for the role, but she was hurt to find it mentioned in the 'reviews'. The following morning when we had our final 'notes' session, she asked if she could change the age of the character to make her feel a bit more comfortable, so when the play opened that evening, Shaw's Candida had gained ten years. It was not long after this that the infamous 'comments box' was removed from the bar before the actors could get up there and sneak a look.

1997, Perth – Candida with Alec Heggie and Justin Harvey.

The final play was the toughest. Colette O'Neill had great faith in the piece *When We Were Women* by Sharman MacDonald, but it was written in such a strange style that it was almost impossible to learn. There were a few tears shed over that one because I had little time to get the lines into my head whilst playing in *Candida* in the evenings. There were five in the cast, and my very small husband and I had been given a very tall daughter. In one scene, while we fussed around her as she tried on the wedding dress, which was the one I had (supposedly!) worn to my own wedding, there were audible titters! Patrick and I felt like a couple of Munchkins attending to Dorothy. I eventually added a line about having taken down the hem, but when you're talking about a height difference of around nine inches, it was a bit far-fetched. Directors sometimes used the 'casting' argument as an excuse if they wanted to cast elsewhere, and actors were often frustrated by being told they were too short, tall, fat or fair to balance up with others in a family, so I didn't really mind because it showed Michael's spirit of adventure. Nowadays this is less important, because with the prevalence of diverse casting, directors can't be too specific in case they discriminate under the Equality Act. The only real argument has to be that they consider their chosen actor to be the best person for the role.

1997, Perth – When We Were Women with Patrick Hannaway, Neve McIntosh and James Murray.

But audiences didn't really take to the piece and, in a way, felt misled. It was an atmospheric, poignant, poetic drama, but a fragmented portrayal of family life in Second World War Govan, with constant, chronological cross-cutting. It had been billed as a wartime romance set in Govan, which rather led folk to believe that it would be a cosy piece for the 'oldies' to relate to. It was anything but, and although we were a strong cast doing our best, it was not a great choice for Perth.

At the end of my stint, I was keen to get back to a normal life and spend a little time with the family. The irony of it was that, despite the hard work, we were in deficit by the end of the final play. It was hard to live on £250 per week, and when you're working round the clock with a couple of kids at home, there is little opportunity for your partner to work either. It rankled a little that Michael had said he wanted actors to do more than one play to balance the theatre's books, but I was the only one who did – and I was in all three!

The two 'Legends' still held us in their thrall. Despite lessons learned the year before, we decided to go ahead with our short tour of four one-night stands. We took Gillian Beard, friend and dresser at the theatre, along with us as our Lighting and Sound Technician and Stage Manager, and that took a bit of the pressure away, but after this series of gigs, we vowed, once more, that we would never take on the organisational aspect again. When you only have one night, publicity is crucial or people will barely notice that you've been before you've gone, but how much money can you risk spending on posters and leaflets when you're in a small venue, sharing box office takings, with no idea what business you'll do? On the other hand, you're not going to do any at all if you don't publicise. Had it not been for the rather decent fee from the Webster Hall in Arbroath we might have come out of it with barely enough for three fish suppers.

It was galling enough to hear that a Scottish tour of *Piaf* was in the offing, starting in the city of my birth, Dundee, but to have the Glasgow producer, Robert C. Kelly, call us and tell us that he had the rights to all the Piaf songs and didn't want us to appear near Glasgow with *Legends*, was just too much to bear. We checked this out, and he did indeed have the rights for north of the border, so it was only through his 'goodwill' that we were allowed to go ahead with our final show in little Cumbernauld. But he still forbade any publicity, so we had to pull an interview we had arranged with a Glasgow evening paper, which kind of scuppered us and explained the tiny audience. Nothing could save Robert's show, however, and it lost him a fortune.

There was no doubt that we needed a producer or company manager to look out for us, to take care of finances and the choosing of venues, so that we could concentrate on the artistic side of things. After our last night in Cumbernauld, we packed up our costumes and assorted bits and pieces and headed home for a brief night's repose before re-loading the car for our departure to London the following morning, where we had quite a busy schedule planned for the next few days during the kids' Easter break.

On arriving in London, we deposited the kids with relatives, then headed straight up to Oxford where we had a cabaret booking for my old pilot friend, Richard Lyon, and his wife Jenny. They were hosting a seminar connected with child psychology, which related to Jenny's work, and Richard had set the weekend up, inviting about 200 eminent people from around the world. George Donald came down from Perth, we did *Toujours l'Amour*, stayed in a nice hotel, and it was a very civilised occasion. The following morning I took a train to London where I was taking part in a radio play, written by and starring Mark Eden; it was about the last days of Shepperton Studios and I was playing Judy Garland, who was only a peripheral character, but it was great to be able to incorporate a tiny bit of work into our short break.

I was straight back into *Cat on a Hot Tin Roof* at Dundee Rep, and at last I was to be directed by Richard Baron. I had been in the play back in 1974, and on that outing I was Dixie, eldest of the 'no neck monsters', and Janet Michael was Sister Mae. This time round, Janet was Big Mama, I was Sister Mae and some of the kids from the Whitehall Summer School of the previous year played the 'no-neck monsters'. I dug out my 1974 cuttings and the Courier covered the story.

The only unfortunate thing about the show was its timing, as it clashed with brother Grant's wedding. He and Celeste had invited me to be Matron of Honour, and the wedding day clashed with the first preview of the show. It was such bad luck; if it had been a week earlier during rehearsals, I could have done it, but when a performance is involved, there's no option; although it was an uncomfortable decision I had to go with the job – although I did manage to get along for the last half hour of the wedding!

We decided to have a summer trip to Disneyland in Paris,

driving all the way. We split the journey so that it wasn't too painful for the kids, stopping in London to see Grandad, who was becoming increasingly frail. After Ollie sang a verse of *Doh a Deer,* we departed, and I had a feeling that we might never see him again.

On Saturday 2nd August, I had a call from Kenbrook to say that Sid had died. We had been aware that he was failing, and for the previous few weeks he had been unable to come downstairs to the phone box to make his weekly call to us. For many months, he had put a coin in the box on a Sunday evening, and Terry had called back and chatted for a while. We were told by the matron that, as Sid was deteriorating, she had tried in vain to contact Pete and Annette. I was surprised that Kenbrook were unaware that they were off on holiday in France and not easily contactable, but more to the point, why had they not called us? We were stunned. They said something about us being so far away, but I've never understood why they didn't realise that Terry would have wanted to head down to be with him during his final days, and we felt very aggrieved and sad that they hadn't kept us informed.

Terry went down to London to make the funeral arrangements and to sort out his dad's belongings; it gave him the chance to be in the room where Sid had spent his so many years. He had few possessions, and Terry returned to Perth with a biscuit tin full of papers, cards and snaps. That was all there was – a whole life in a biscuit tin; such a tidy end, and so like Sid to leave us with nothing to do.

We were not comfortable leaving him for so long in the funeral parlour, but we had to wait patiently for the return of the Wales. By the time they set foot on British soil, another death had hit the headlines, that of Diana, Princess of Wales. The nation responded with an extraordinary grief, and the news of her untimely death in a car crash in France with her boyfriend Dodi Al-Fayed swamped all other news for months to come. Was it foul play? Was it the fault of the paparazzi pursuing her? Was she on the point of marrying Dodi? Was she pregnant? The questions were endless, but the real tragedy of it all was that she had left two young boys who now had to deal with the intrusive glare of publicity as they coped with the loss of their mother.

I shed a tear when I heard the news, but the public outpouring of grief was beyond belief and ultimately almost irritating. Her funeral on September 6th was watched by an entire nation, and the mounds of flowers outside Kensington Palace had to be seen to be believed. Elton John sang a version of his hit song, *Candle in the Wind* (originally written about Marilyn Monroe), at the funeral service, and it was broadcast into the local park to be shared with the mourning thousands. She had been the darling of the press – and sometimes the victim – for many years, and who would they train their lenses on now that she was gone?

Sid's funeral by contrast, and only two days later, was a simple affair. Terry and I travelled down on the Sunday when things had begun to quieten down after the royal event, although the train still managed a three-hour delay. We went to the funeral parlour on the Monday morning and said our private farewells to Sid. I had never seen a body and had hoped to touch him or perhaps even kiss his forehead, but there was something forbidding about the wax-like visage that greeted us. The cortège left from Kenbrook, which had been his home for the past seven years, and a couple of elderly residents joined the mourners. There were hardly any flowers, because every flower in London had been bought for Diana.

So that was Sid gone, and I'm sure that he would have considered his long, hard-working life a good one. He had outlived all his eight brothers and sisters, and all of Lily's too. He derived such pleasure from his family, especially his five grandchildren. A few years previously, my sister-in-law, Annette had suggested to Sid that he write down his life story, and although he had initially been reluctant to do so, we knew that he had spent quite a bit of time on the project. Terry found the manuscript in a drawer of his bureau after his death, but Sid had only managed to get as far as the '60s. Annette decided to take it upon herself to get his work typed through so that we could all have a copy of Sid's Unfinished Symphony.

- 28 -

Take the High Road

As time passed, Terry and I felt less connected to the local theatre. Back in the '70s it had been like a second home, and even in the early '90s when we did *Judy* and *Piaf*, it was always a pleasure to step into the building. One evening, however, on an outing to see *A View from the Bridge*, I received a surprise bit of news from Lizzie, the publicity lady, who had just heard that I had been nominated for a TMA Award for Best Supporting Actress. I was so taken aback, that I had no idea which of my recent roles it could be for. They had all been supporting roles in a way, but it transpired that my nomination was for Miss Proserpine Garnett in Candida, and although it was unexpected, I was delighted. When you go through the years giving some of your best performances in provincial repertory theatres, it's reassuring when a small cameo role is spotted and taken notice of. Never mind the 'Piafs', the 'Judys' and the 'Shirleys' – I had been honoured for my 'Prossy'!

The ceremony was to take place in Norwich, and although I had a feeling that the part was not big enough to stand a chance of winning, we decided to go. At the end of October, we drove the circuitous route down to Norwich, and stayed overnight before a lunchtime ceremony the following day. I didn't win, and we joked afterwards that it was a long way to go for lunch! I did, however, return with a commemorative plaque for the wall.

As it was our 20th wedding anniversary, Terry wanted to do something special, and our destination was New York. Terry had waited so long to see the 'Big Apple', had so many movie images in his mind, that he was moved to tears as our taxi drove through the streets on the way to our hotel, which overlooked the south side of Central Park.

On our first day we suddenly spotted the Theatre Guild in West 47th Street, and after going inside to find out if Ronnie Lee was in his office, we were thrilled to discover that he was. He gave us a great welcome, took us to Sardis that evening and organised a couple of free tickets for *Barrymore,* written by William Luce, and starring Christopher Plummer, who won a Tony award that year.

We loved Greenwich Village, where we enjoyed exploring and shopping at quirky little market stalls and observing the colourful characters around, but the highlight was our anniversary meal, which we had in the World Trade Center at the top of Twin Towers, in a restaurant called *Windows on the World*. The quality of the meal did not justify the extortionate price, but it was justified by the incredible view and the overall experience. It was impossible to even imagine that it would be blown out of existence on September 11th, 2001.

The only aspect which we found tricky was the 'tipping'. It's so much a part of American life, that you almost feel you should tip everyone – just in case! Cousin Mike had told Terry of a time he was chased down the street by an angry waiter, who was mortally offended by the size of the tip, saying sarcastically, "Is this all for me?" On our return, Terry wrote an extended diary in the style of Damon Runyon which, as well as reminding us of happy times in New York, was something that he hoped to sell to a travel magazine. Clever as it was, there aren't many magazines that will find the space for an article of 16,000 words!

I had one little job in the autumn which cheered me no end. John Temple, my contact at STV, had finally found a part for me in *High Road*. I was only offered three episodes to start, but as they were the final three of the current batch, I had hopes that my character would continue when filming re-commenced in April. It was only shown once a week, so they could film enough episodes for an entire year in four months at the rate of three each week. It made continuity tricky, as when the cast returned after a lengthy break to take up where they had left off, you could find that half of them had dramatically changed their appearance; from a viewer's point of view, it appeared to have happened overnight.

Further incongruities arose because they were never sure when episodes would be transmitted, so there were no references to important days in the calendar, like Mother's Day – or even Christmas! There was no mention of major world events or catastrophes, and Glendarroch took on a 'Brigadoon' quality, where a week later you watched the events of the following day, and a new baby would only seem to age four months in episodes spread over a year, unless they remembered to re-cast the baby! The strangest aspect was that because most of the filming took place in summer months, the observant viewer might occasionally spot leaves sprouting from trees in January!

I'd been cast as the mother of one of the main characters, so I wanted to know all about her. I gathered that my daughter, Sarah, was 20 years old, and had recently gone through a very traumatic time. Her husband had been murdered by her lover, who had then shot himself, which is just what you expect in a sleepy little Highland village! She had a new baby, and Maureen, my character, was arriving to give her a hand.

I wanted a character profile, but no one seemed to have a record of her past life. Apparently the research team were running around like headless chickens trying to find someone who could remember how and why Maureen Gilchrist's children came to be fostered in the Scottish village of Glendarroch. All they could tell me was that she lived in Rugby, she'd had two nervous breakdowns and a brain tumour, although I wasn't to let that influence how I played the part so that they could change her story if they felt like it. I wasn't even told whether she was a divorcee or a widow, but for some reason or other she'd been unable to look after her two kids and had them fostered in the Highlands when they were young teenagers. Sarah had made her home there, got married, although her mother hadn't shown up at the wedding – the production team probably just forgot all about her! That was fairly typical; the barmaid in the village had recently had her 'girlfriend' to visit, and the actress in question had no idea she was a lesbian until she read the upcoming scripts.

The cast seemed to be a happy family, and there were a few stalwarts amongst them, like Eileen McCallum who played my mother-in-law back in the 1972 *Play for Today*, and Mary Riggans, who had played my mother. My three episodes centred round the baby's christening. The organist was hired, the minister cast, the hymn was chosen (*The Lord Bless Thee and Keep Thee*), but no one checked whether any of the actors knew it; I think I was the only one who did, as at the church service, attended by about a dozen people, I seemed to be the only one who was singing. When they showed the episode, they did a big fat close-up of one of the leading characters, and my voice suddenly featured, so it sounded as if it belonged to another character – a touch of *Acorn Antiques*, the fictional and very funny spoof 'soap', created by the late Victoria Wood.

Eileen suggested that I, being a newcomer, try to organise a few props for rehearsals, because the regulars had given up asking, but despite my efforts, the actors were still handed their props – including a live baby Sadie – for the final rehearsal and actual 'take'. I was given a dirty wee basin instead of the large baby's bath I had been expecting, and told that it was big enough to 'top and tail'. The notion that any responsible adult would wash a new baby in such a grubby receptacle, was absurd. To top it all, Mary Riggans disappeared just before the scene was filmed and forgot to return. After a lot of hanging around, her lines were shared out, and just as we started the final rehearsal she raced onto the set, blethering her apologies.

We were so far behind with the day's schedule that, when we finally reached the scenes with my daughter, we'd nearly run out of time, and I was told there was no room for error. We completed them without too much trouble, although there was a moment when I 'dried', and I just sat still until the lines came back into my head. At the end of the scene I asked if we could do a quick retake, but was assured that it was fine, and to save going back they would just remove a few seconds from my pause! I had a feeling that I might have had a look of panic in my eyes, which they would be unable to remove. I should have just stopped and said, "Sorry about that", giving them no choice but to go back over the scene. I got away with it, but I had witnessed other moments when the editing made the actors look decidedly 'eggy', with a reaction held just a trifle too long for comfort.

Having come in at the end of the year's filming, I attended the last-night party and was delighted to hear that, when they resumed in April, I had another 18 episodes lined up. The initial three episodes had revealed Maureen as something of a control freak, taking over the organisation of the christening, allocating little tasks to all the locals, and generally being a bossy pest. I would have to wait until the spring to find out if she was a lesbian into the bargain!

Following a chat with Ron Thompson who wrote a regular column for the *Dundee Courier*, I was contacted by Sandra Monks, the fiction editor, about the possibility of writing my life story for the paper. I had been working on it for around four years and was already onto a second draft, but I had gone into so much family detail that there were screeds that would not be of interest to the general public. I decided to face the daunting prospect of selecting career highlights and sorting out all that seemed relevant.

The suggestion was that I write up to 30 episodes, each to come in at around 1,100 words. This was no easy task – not to mention leaving each episode with a mini cliffhanger to keep the readers interested, so Terry had to come on board. He was very enthusiastic about the project and agreed to be my editor-in-chief. At the start of the new year, we had no idea just how huge the task was that we had undertaken. It became all-consuming; I often worked late into the night, and although it took months to complete, I enjoyed putting it together and I cannot underestimate Terry's role. I was bringing in each episode at around 1,800 words, and he was not only honing it into shape but losing around 700 words per episode; it was a Herculean task for us both.

Then came the sting in the tale. After I had completed the first six episodes, Sandra called to say that they liked my style and were looking forward to the next six. It was only then that money was mentioned. I was hoping to receive about £100 per episode, which would have paid us the princely sum of £3,000 for the complete package. When Sandra broached the subject and I heard the words 'three hundred pounds', I was about to say that I was delighted with the offer, until she quickly explained that was the fee for all 30, working out at £10 per episode. On recovering my composure, I said I was unwilling to accept less than £60 per episode, and although she didn't hold out much hope she said she would take my suggestion to her editor, Adrian Arthur. His response was quick and final. £300 was the fee, and that was all they could pay.

It crossed my mind that perhaps the *Dundee Courier* was in dire straits, but I was assured that the Thomsons were the third richest family in Scotland, so there was no penury there. The paper usually featured books which had already been published, and paid a minimal fee for the right to edit a book for their serial slot. That was all very well if you had written a best-selling novel, but I had written my story from scratch, and for a specific local readership; it had been tailor-made for the *Dundee Courier*, and I found it a bitter pill to swallow that I was being offered such a paltry fee. After much debate, Terry and I concluded that we would rather see the story in print than not, so we decided to continue, and *In and out of the Spotlight* took up the best part of 1998.

In April I started my ten-week stint on *High Road*. It was good to escape from the word processor, and with 20 episodes lined up I'd be earning reasonable money. I was disappointed that the story liners didn't really develop my character, but the new writers were not always given character breakdowns, which explained some of the discrepancies that arose. There were sudden changes of personality; having started out as a lively, friendly (if somewhat overbearing) mother, I suddenly became much more 'nippy sweetie' and full of prejudices. I hated lesbians and was responsible for starting rumours about the poor barmaid. I even started to bring God into the equation to back up my reactionary views. As my daughter was a popular character, it was not going to endear me to the public.

Despite the 'soap' and its incongruities, I had a ball and would have been very happy if Maureen had become a permanent fixture. By the time I finished in June, returning to my fictional home in Rugby, a new producer had replaced the retiring John Temple, so I assumed that I would be forgotten, and Sarah would return to her former, motherless status. The series came to an end a few years later and, strangely enough, Terry was in the final episode as a mafia man with plans to turn Glendarroch into the Las Vegas of the North!

Whilst tootling back and forth to Glasgow, I was trying to fit in the occasional rehearsal for a rotary engagement which I was to be doing with George Duffus and George Donald as soon as I finished filming on *High Road*. It was called *Side by Side by Side* – an evening we'd tried out before at the Invercarse Hotel. George Donald was a lovely man, friendly and eager to please, who would always say, "Yes, I'd love to" to any request then, finding that he was unavailable or too busy, leave himself with no option but to back out at the last minute, causing endless frustration amongst his long-suffering colleagues and friends.

And thus it had been with this 'Side by Side' engagement that had originally been planned for the previous year as a two-night booking at Perth Theatre. It was on one of my regular visits to his home just around the corner that George let slip that he was also due to appear as a compère at the City Hall on one of the two fixed dates.

Having discovered that he had double- booked, he had taken so long to own up that by the time he informed the various parties of his mistake, it was too late, and chaos ensued. He said that his loyalty lay with the rotary bookings because they had asked us first, but he somehow ended up doing the other gig at the City Hall, which was a shame because he could easily have been replaced as compère, but was irreplaceable as the third member of our trio. If he had acknowledged his faux pas sooner, there might have been time to change the dates; as it was, we lost a nice booking. So when they decided to go ahead again the following year, I was asked to take on the organisation. They even suggested that we find a different title for it, so that people wouldn't make the connection with the previous year's debacle.

1998, Side by Side, with George Donald and George Duffus.

So here we were in the spring of 1998, and little had changed. It didn't matter what time we had arranged to meet; you could be sure that if he didn't cancel at the last minute, I would arrive to find him either in the shower, shaving, or supervising some of the many workmen who trooped in and out of his home. Even if he was ready to rehearse, I usually had to wait while he located the music, and when we eventually did get down to some singing, we were usually disturbed by the constant ringing of the phone, which the friendly George happily answered. As I sat in his lounge while the clock ticked on, I remember one call where I could almost feel my blood pressure soar as he enquired after the caller's entire family.

On one classic morning, I was surprised and happy to have had no phone call to say that he had forgotten he was judging the Auchenshuggle Women's Rural Flower-Arranging Competition, so I headed for Kincarrathie Crescent. He invited me in, whilst explaining that the builders were in the lounge, but he hadn't let me know, as he thought it would be nice to see me in any case, which was quite endearing really. It never occurred to him that I might also have a busy life to lead with arrangements to make, places to go and people to see. He left me with a newspaper, and an hour later the workmen departed. I was about to jump up and get down to work, when he said that his fingers were a bit sore because he had helped the workmen with their heavy lifting, so could I come back at 3.30pm? Choking back tears of frustration I went home and rallied again in the afternoon. I arrived to find no one at home. I left a note, which said curtly: 'You said 3.30pm!' He called shortly afterwards to say he had suddenly remembered that his sister was coming, and he had raced out to Safeway to buy something for her tea!

On another occasion which also involved George Duffus, who had taken time off work to come up from Dundee, the pair of us were left standing outside his house until we were greeted by the sight of G. Donald arriving in a jazzy little sports car, calling cheerily "Come and see my new car!" He had just been through to Glasgow to pick it up, but had not thought to let us know. I did go to his wife, Isabelle, at one point and ask sincerely if he was suffering from stress. She responded with, "Only the same stress he's been under for the past 30 years!" It was part of his character, and those of us who were very fond of him, coped with it.

During our rehearsals, George informed me that he had double-booked – again! It was hard to believe, but he had suddenly remembered that he was booked onto a cruise, and would be out of the country on the evenings in question. To avoid causing the local Rotarians to commit bloody murder, he had to arrange to fly back from Copenhagen in order to be at Perth Theatre for the two cabaret performances which, incidentally, went rather well.

The King's Theatre Trust presents a

CABARET CONCERT
and Finger Buffet Supper

featuring

LESLEY MACKIE
with

GEORGE DONALD
of "Scotland the What?"

and Master of Ceremonies, Dundee's Own

GEORGE DUFFUS

BONAR HALL, DUNDEE
SUNDAY 18th AUGUST at 7.00 pm
Tickets £12.00 available from the Box Office, 6 City Square, Dundee
Telephone 434940

- 29 -

Great Expectations

One day in August, Katy heard that she'd landed the part of Flora in *The Innocents*, which was to be performed at Perth Theatre later in the year. It was a wonderful part and had particular significance for Terry who understudied the part of the boy, Miles, back in the 1952 West End production, starring Dame Flora Robson. Katy took it all in her stride, learning the lines fast and efficiently, and she gave a very sure performance.

Earlier in the year when we realised that 1998 was the 80th anniversary of the end of World War 1, we decided to compile a programme of poetry and songs for Armistice Day. We applied locally to try and obtain finance for the venture and were delighted to be awarded £600 from the *Common Good Fund*. This covered all expenses, including the hire of the church, the fee for the choir, poetry books, music and other sundry items, enabling us to donate the proceeds to an appropriate charity. We threw ourselves into the project, named *Lest we Forget*, and as well as compiling the programme of poetry, readings and songs, Terry took it upon himself to design and print the leaflets and promote the event. As he was just coming to grips with our first computer, this was a Herculean task and he spent days on the challenge, although I helped a little by designing the poppy.

We booked the church and invited the *Fair City Singers* to join me in singing all the songs, because we felt that children's voices would give the content an added poignancy. There was so much masculine poetry that two contrasting male voices were a necessity, so we invited local actor, Ian Grieve, to be our second actor. The choir had an excellent reputation, led by Martin and Marion Neilson, who instilled a professionalism and discipline into the children that was evident in performance. Marion was a force to be reckoned with and it wasn't always easy to be diplomatic when an issue arose. I recall that they were somewhat overcommitted at this time, and we were aware that the *In Paradisum* section of the Fauré *Requiem*, which was very challenging for a young choir, was under-rehearsed. When Terry called Marion prior to the event to suggest that the choir might give that one a miss, Marion protested about the amount of work that they had already put into the piece and she wouldn't hear of cutting it from the programme, so we complied, as people usually did with Marion.

They also had their own way of punishing absent-minded children, and on the day of the performance, because a few choir members had forgotten to bring their folders, she declared that none of them could be allowed to carry them, insisting on total uniformity. We were far more concerned that they had the correct words in front of them, and I noticed quite a few blank faces in the front row, mouthing a load of nonsense to *King and Country*.

At the end of the programme after our final poem, we had an excellent trumpeter to play *The Last Post*, followed by *The Flowers of the Forest* on the bagpipes, which was a moving finale. It was a great success and we raised £1,000 for the Erskine Hospital in Glasgow and Blesma (The British Limbless Ex-Servicemen's Association).

Still smarting with memories of trying to prepare for the performance whilst running around supplying sweets and drinks for 70 little choristers, we decided that if we ever did it again we would try to delegate some of the tasks – but time erases the memory of the problems, as we discovered in 2014 when we embarked on an even bigger project to commemorate the centenary of World War One.

Having hosted the seminar in Oxford a few months previously, Richard called me in the early autumn to say that he was concerned about an eight-minute section of piano music George had promised to write for a CD that Richard was producing for his wife's business. I had warned him about George's idiosyncrasies at the time, but he didn't take me seriously and decided to go ahead. George, of course, was delighted to be asked, had expressed great enthusiasm, and even insisted on doing it for nothing. Although Richard had been in touch with George, the music was not forthcoming, and as the date for the release of the CD was imminent, he wondered if he should send a couple of boxes of wine to jog his memory. I told him not to, and to leave me to have a word. George expressed surprise about the urgency; he had no idea that Richard wanted the music so quickly and he didn't have the time – in fact, he wasn't going to be able to do it at all! I asked him to call to deliver the bad news, and with his absolute assurance that he would do so, I phoned Richard to say that George would be in touch to explain; even I was surprised to hear that George never made that call.

Terry and I were still very occupied with my story. Towards the end of October we had reached the final episode, although there were still quite a few details to sort out with the *Dundee Courier*. I was pleased to receive a letter around the middle of December, saying that they still wanted to run the story in February 1999. I was looking forward to seeing it in print, and after all the negotiations it was a great relief to be able to put it to the back of my mind.

Busy as we always were, professional work had been scarce throughout the year, and as 1999 approached, I copied from *The Stage*: 'If you want to be a professional performer in Britain, expect poverty, unemployment, hardship, the insult of indifference and a lifetime of disappointment'. Things were certainly never that bad!

Our family get-together at Nairn Street on January 1st had become an annual ritual. As we were free, we joined John and Betty, Nan and Archie and the usual 'regulars'. After eating, it was customary for the kids to do a 'turn', and then we would all sit around in the lounge chatting or playing a game. On this occasion, someone suddenly spouted out the riddle, 'Brothers and sisters have I none, but that man's father is my father's son'. The given premise is that a man is looking at a photograph of another man, and the rhyme is the key to revealing whose photograph he is looking at.

This riddle has probably been responsible for more family feuds than any other single thing in the history of the Mackie clan gatherings, but it didn't stop us all from launching into the usual heated debate. For me the answer is so simple, and there is nothing so infuriating as having to argue with people who are in no doubt that they have the right answer, when they are quite definitely wrong. John and Betty were adamant that the man was looking at a picture of himself, whereas it's quite clear that it's a photo of his son. Amidst a certain amount of bad feeling we had to agree to differ, but I felt exasperated for ages afterwards because they clearly couldn't understand our failure to solve the simple riddle!

February was fast approaching, and with it, the publication of *In and Out of the Spotlight*. I was excited when it finally appeared in the *Dundee Courier*, so much so that I bought the paper for the entire

30 days. Episode One graced their pages on Feb 15th. I had signed the form giving the paper editorial control, but I had been assured by letter that they had no intentions of altering the text – just trimming it to fit the allotted space. In the event, they made numerous tiny changes, but even the addition of one word can alter the entire meaning of a sentence and attribute opinions that the writer (if I may call myself that!) does not hold. The addition of the adjective 'wonderful' three times in one episode to describe people and programmes I had mentioned, made me sound like a real 'luvvie'.

I did venture to suggest that they might use some of the titles that Terry and I had pondered so long over. How could they have left out 'Aches in Provence'? or 'Nappy Days Are Here Again!' As the story wore on, I discovered that if they could use the name of someone famous I had worked with or, even better, the name of anything with a Dundee connection, that's what they went for; understandable in a local paper, I suppose – but I've managed to squeeze in a few of our titles here! As so many people said they had enjoyed it, I wrote to a couple of publishers, but the one who showed the most interest suggested I had done things the wrong way round by publishing an edited version in a local newspaper which, in effect, gave the public my story for nothing. They doubted if people would buy the book if they felt they'd already had the highlights. I decided to put it all away for a while, and maybe resurrect the idea if I ever became a regular in a 'soap'!

Happy Days indeed, as I had just landed a job, and a long one at that. After 21 years, I was returning to Pitlochry Festival Theatre. After all the promises and maybes, Clive had confirmed a season. I was a rather dowdy housekeeper in the Agatha Christie play, *The Unexpected Guest*, a frumpy wife in Alan Ayckbourn's duo of plays, *Sisterly Feelings*, and Mrs Joe in *Great Expectations*. Having a great capacity for enjoyment, I managed to derive some pleasure from all of them. I also had company in the car for *Great Expectations*, as Katy was also in the cast, playing the Young Estella. The actors were quite an assorted bunch, but I grew very fond of Alice Fraser, with whom I shared a dressing room. She was from New Zealand, although she spent much of her time in Britain. She was the granddaughter of the wartime New Zealand Prime Minister, Peter Fraser. Her life had been touched by misfortune, with one disastrous marriage and a couple of unhappy relationships, and her only daughter was diabetic and blind. Alice had recently suffered from stomach cancer, but she was quietly optimistic that she was in remission.

We shared many laughs about the Christie play – the 'Aggie', as Clive always referred to it – as it was a tiresome piece, albeit the opening production and the most heavily booked of the season. Amanda Beveridge had not been due to arrive until rehearsals started for the Ayckbourn plays, but her services were required sooner because of one of the familiar Pitlochry 'casualties'. The young actress who had been miscast as Laura in the 'Aggie' struggled with the role until Clive grew twitchy and started to undermine her confidence. This caused her to panic, and a few days before we were due to open, after a session when Clive refused to let her use her script, informing her that she was 'letting the entire company down', she asked to be released. It was what Clive had been waiting for, and the drama caused him to perk up and occupy himself with getting Amanda ready to take over. "She'll know it by Monday", he chirped, which of course she did; she was a very quick study. The other actress was given the option to stay on in her other roles, and was very relieved to lighten her workload.

A certain amount of friction is inevitable in a long season, and there were one or two irritating personalities. One actor caused quite a bit of aggravation in the 'Aggie', in which we shared the climactic scene. From the day of the 'blocking', it was clear that he was determined to do it his way with little regard for anyone else onstage, and Clive was clearly enamoured enough to allow him free rein. In one climactic scene, we eventually managed a compromise that did not involve me having to chase him three times round the sofa in order to retrieve his gun! He was talented, and gave an interesting performance in the role of Jan, the abnormal boy. It wasn't like any mental affliction I had ever witnessed, but it was very watchable, and he won the *Leon Sinden Award* for *Best Actor in a Supporting Role* at the end of the season.

That award was a bit of a sore point. No one really took it seriously – except they did, because the prize was worth having, being a week's salary, at that time around £300. Each year, audiences could vote for their favourite male and female performance of the season, so it was obvious that it would go to an actor and an actress in one of the more popular plays with the largest audiences. It never crossed my mind that any of my trio of roles could even be in the running, so I was amused to discover that I had pulled in a good number of votes for Miss Bennett in *The Unexpected Guest*.

It's inevitable that in any season with five or six plays it's not possible to give every actor three or four parts, and in this season, Deirdre Davis landed lucky, being cast in only the one play, which entailed giving one or two performances a week, and for the same salary as the rest of us – just the luck of the draw. She had a nice cameo role as an alcoholic in *The Summertime is Come* which was a very popular play, drawing the largest audience figures of the season, mainly because it starred Jimmy Logan and Edith MacArthur, two well respected Scottish actors. When the audience votes were counted, Deirdre had won the coveted *Leon Sinden Award* for *Best Actress in a Supporting Role*.

Jimmy Logan and Edith MacArthur were the two oldest and most established company members, and Clive paid them a lot of attention. Alice and I would frequently exchange glances in the mirror as Clive made a beeline for Edith to ask how her back was, or if she was happy with the costume, or to tell her during technical rehearsals that her coffee would be down shortly. As Alice, Mandy and I weren't in *The Summertime is Come*, Edith was only in the dressing room with us for *Great Expectations*, which was the showpiece of the season and most of the company were in it. It was an ensemble piece, and we expected the curtain call to reflect that. It hadn't been given a lot of thought and it was decided that we would come on in groups of four, and the few larger roles would have solo calls at the end.

That was where the trouble started because when Jimmy Logan, who was a Long John Silver type of Magwitch, discovered that Mike Mackenzie (Mr Joe) was coming on after him, it wasn't long before he suggested that they come on together. I think he considered himself a rung higher in the pecking order, but coming on as a twosome was the lesser of two evils as far as he was concerned. They were followed by Pip, the young leading man, and Edith had the final call with the two children in tow. This was clearly not going to work, as Pip was a huge leading role, and the applause was destined to fade a little if anyone came on after him. It was dotty that the children had the final call with Edith, but to quote Jimmy: "If we show that we love the kids, the audience will love us!" – his background in pantomime coming to the fore! I think that we changed the curtain call four times, ending up with a 'line up', which appalled Clive, who just about blew a gasket and insisted that we go back to the actors taking individual bows in order of importance (the 'who's best?' as he called it), with Edith as the senior member of the company, coming on last. It wouldn't have been so bad if she hadn't taken so long to come on and go into her deep curtsey, as the applause was dying by the time she managed to rise again, causing some embarrassment and suppressed mirth amongst a few of the cast. The guest director, Richard Baron, was long gone and missed out on all the antics.

Time passed, and one evening when Edith and I were sitting in the dressing room, we got talking about the *Leon Sinden Award*, and it was only when I said to her that she might well be in the running for her performance as Miss Havisham, that she ventured to say that she didn't think she would be eligible. I said that indeed she was, as Miss Havisham came into the 'Supporting Role' category. There was a brief pause before she said that she agreed with me, which was why she was so mortified by having to take such an embarrassing curtain call; she even mentioned the dying applause. As she seemed very serious, I suggested that if she was unhappy about it, she ought to get it changed – and she did! After more debate and company rehearsal, it was finally agreed that Pip would take the final call, and everyone seemed to be happy.

And there was Guy, a middle-aged actor who was perfectly cast as my husband in the double bill of Ayckbourn plays, giving a very good performance. We got on well until I started to make suggestions, which he saw as 'notes'. Like most actors, I was keen to improve the odd moment, as well as attempting to prevent myself being hidden throughout by his rather tall persona. One night, he suddenly took me up on something I had suggested, and it worked well, so all went smoothly from then on. I believe that's what acting in a company should be about, sharing and developing ideas, particularly when you're together for a lengthy period, and trying to keep things fresh when directors have inevitably disappeared.

All in all it was a pleasant season, and although there were amusing moments of temperament – like Mike Mackenzie turning to Neville Barber one day and telling him to, "Shut up, you silly old Queen!", the main memories are convivial ones. Strangely, I've omitted to mention Martyn James, a Pitlochry stalwart, who would be returning in 2000 for his 13th season. Clive clearly found him eminently castable, and he was something of an institution. It would have been a strange season without Martyn's presence outside the main door, coffee in one hand and a fag in the other, imparting and receiving the gossip of the day. By the time he died in 2013 at the age of 63, he had done 23 seasons.

Terry had been doing sterling work in his house-husband capacity, although taking an active interest in what was going on up the road. As a fun postscript to this saga, I'd like to add a short excerpt from a 'review' Terry wrote of *Great Expectations*, a production he was not over enamoured with; it was outrageous, quite wicked, and written, somewhat tongue in cheek, for our own amusement. It was only shared with a few, but Alice Fraser told me that she framed it and put it on her wall when she returned home to New Zealand.

1999, Pitlochry - Great Expectations
with Alice Fraser

It ended on a gentle sincere note: *There are a handful of performances that shine out like good deeds in a naughty world, and I wholeheartedly compliment Martyn James, Lesley Mackie and Richard Hollis for having the right instincts and for holding onto them against the odds. Alice Fraser, in the tiny role of Estella's natural mother, manages to convey both suffering and madness in her brief and wordless appearances and it is the memory of her desperate vacancy as she stands holding out the bowl for Jaggers to wash his hands, that provides an indelible image in this otherwise ephemeral production.* Alice was a lovely actress, who died five years later at the age of 70.

I would happily have returned the following season, which was already on the cards. The main appeal for actors was that Pitlochry offered a variety of plays and a substantial period of work, but in the year 2000, due to continuous and extensive building work, they only planned to do two plays instead of the usual five or six, one of which would be a one-person play. It was clear that the actors engaged for the season would only be in one play, with probably a maximum of four performances a week, and the possibility of returning to 'do a Deirdre' was very tempting for us all.

Having discussed *Shirley Valentine* on a few occasions with Clive, I finished in the knowledge that the approaching season of 2000 was still a possibility and 'Shirley' might well be the one-person play of choice. He told me that he was also in discussion with Jimmy Logan about his one-man show *Lauder*, but as that was by no means a definite, he wanted to keep 'Shirley' up his sleeve. I was quite excited until I realised that Clive was just covering himself in case Jimmy broke a leg. When I saw Jimmy staggering under the weight of a load of old costumes one day, I realised that he was already preparing for the revival of his show, and it would take more than a broken leg to stop him. I sensed that 'Shirley' was probably not going to happen.

On the last night, Clive referred to its dwindling prospects, but said that I was probably right for Pauline in *One for the Road*, the other Willy Russell play that he was considering. Over the next few months, Clive seemed to forget his offer (as he was sometimes wont to do), and it was becoming clear that I wasn't going to be part of the season of 2000. There was nothing I could do about it, and the only satisfying thing was that I was eventually able to let him know that I was no longer available because I had been asked to do *Shirley Valentine* elsewhere.

Back in the summer, George Donald had told me that Robert Lovie, Entertainments Manager for the National Trust, had expressed an interest in having me on the next cruise. George had been doing cruises for many years with Isabelle, his wife, as ship's doctor, and he had put in a word for the Piaf cabaret, which would be ideal for the upcoming cruise in May 2000. After a week cruising round the Scottish Isles and the southern Irish coast, the *Black Prince* was due to sail to Bilbao, and then pass by Bordeaux and St Malo when *Toujours l'Amour* would be particularly appropriate, with George accompanying and narrating. Having heard nothing since, I suddenly had an urgent call from George reminding me about the cruise, so it was clear that it was still on the agenda, and I told him to accept on my behalf.

Now this is where it became rather complicated, as I realised on looking at my diary that I had a booking on one of the dates when the ship would be at sea, and the surprising thing was that George was part of that same booking; in fact, he had organised it! Once again, he had double-booked. Having committed to the cruise, he had made another commitment to go up to Banchory with George Duffus and me to perform our *Side by Side by Side* at the small Woodend Barn Theatre. The date was May 12th, the event was organised by a great enthusiast called Graeme Wilson and was to be his annual fund-raiser for the Banchory Scouting Association. In previous years he had featured luminaries like Jimmy Logan and Peter Morrison, and on this occasion, part of the deal was that George Donald, an old friend of Graeme's, would also perform at a charity function on May 11th, and plans for these events were steaming ahead. What George had failed to take on board was that the cruise incorporated both dates – and as I was not involved in the cruise at that stage, I knew nothing of the mix up. Thus it came to pass that Mr Donald had cleverly arranged to be in two places at once, and rather than heading for the wilds of the North, would probably be 'riding along on the crest of a wave' on the dates in question.

We decided that George Duffus and I would go ahead with the

Banchory booking, find another pianist and bring Terry into the equation. George Donald was terribly disappointed because he was looking forward to it, and to make matters worse he had let down an old friend. He really needed a little doggie at his heels, and that dog was usually me, a little yapping terrier! On one occasion he dared to refer to himself as just 'relaxed about time', implying that people like myself had got it wrong – 'all oot of step except oor Jock!'

As for the cruise, I was still keen to be part of it. George seemed sure that I would only be required for the second week, and although I was disappointed to miss all the Scottish islands, once it was confirmed that I could join them at either Santander or Bilbao, I began to look forward to it. But before *The Black Prince* set sail in the early summer, the New Millennium was looming on the horizon.

I've never understood how a decade can finish at number nine, but the whole world seemed to have got it wrong, apart from the few stalwarts who were writing to newspapers and arguing on chat shows and the like. What amazed me was that there were those who didn't know what we were all talking about, but as the world was planning to celebrate the arrival of a 'new' century, we decided that we had better follow suit; at least the year 2000 had a ring to it, and it sounded like the start of a new millennium, rather than the last year of the old one. There was no stopping brother Grant, who loved an excuse for a celebration and went right over the top.

He had been making plans since the previous New Year when he booked his and Celeste's tickets over from Houston, and he did us proud, treating us to dinner and an overnight stay on the 30th at the recently refurbished Carnoustie Golf Hotel; each suite could have housed a family of six. That was followed by a Dinner Dance at the Woodlands Hotel. Terry showed remarkable restraint by leaving for Perth shortly after the 'Bells', to the amazement and disappointment of all present, for whom the night was yet young. The rest of us, overcome with millennium fever, decided to make a night of it. I was under the weather for the next three days, and I vowed to restrain myself when the real millennium arrived the following year.

- 30 -

Family matters

Having recently checked on Katy's tiny height, we were keeping an eye on that, but she was surviving very well in the jungle that was Perth Academy, and was very popular with her contemporaries. Ollie was developing into a real little character, writing his own songs (with a little help from his dad!), and his composition, *Go to It,* became a hit at school in the year 2000. He had a good sense of humour, typified by "Who is the odd man out in this family?" (said to Terry). "You, because you have blue eyes, grey hair and you're the only one who's not working in the theatre!" Ouch! He had recently had his début as one of Fagin's gang in *Oliver* at the Whitehall Theatre in Dundee, and was heavily smitten by the whole experience. I suppose it was inevitable that the kids would be lured by the business, but we went on hoping that they would go on doing it for fun, and not attempt to make a living from it. And although Terry and I wouldn't have changed our profession – it had been an interesting journey, and we'd never have met – anyone reading this must be aware of the insecurities of our business, with so many performers not knowing when or even if there will be another job. At this present time a recent survey showed that only 2% make a decent living from the profession, and 90% are out of work at any one time – surely sufficient to have most aspiring Thespians reaching for the bottle, if only they could afford a drink in the first place! Every actor knows the old adage that if you really need a job, book a once in a lifetime holiday – and the phone will ring as soon as you've paid for it!

Olly was smart, had a lively mind, was an excellent speller, and thought the reason that 'diarrhoea' was quite difficult, was to make it hard for children to spell such a rude word. His interest in language was not surprising, as Terry was a natural writer, and I also loved the English language. I always make notes at the back of a diary, and my comment 'Intrusive r's are more intrusive this year' (a reference to an 'r' that many English-speaking people put in between two vowels as in 'idea(r)of') reminded me that Terry and I were consistent in our obsession with speech and grammar.

My first 'fleepie' of the year was caused by Katy's acquisition of a mobile phone. I was still at the stage of thinking them quite a novelty, an adult toy, and although I had received one the previous Christmas, I still thought of it as something to take with me in the car in case of an emergency. We were aware that many children were acquiring this latest accessory, because there had been endless articles about children phoning each other in playgrounds and even in the classroom.

When Katy asked if she could have one, I laughed, because I believed it would surely end up as an expensive toy, so the answer was "No!". When she walked in one day, having just gone and bought one with her Christmas money, I reluctantly accepted it, but made a few conditions – such as she was not to take it to school or flaunt it in the street. I soon spotted her heading towards Croft Court dancing to the tunes on her phone! Now that everybody owns one, I smile when I remember the furore it caused.

There were more important events, and one of them was when our old friend, Thelma Rogers, was discovered lying on the ground in the early hours of a cold and frosty morning. She had finally been driven by whatever demons she was living with, whether depression or dementia I really don't know, to take her own life, throwing herself out of her bathroom window, which was a few floors above ground level. It's a mystery that she was even able to open it because she kept her windows closed to try and keep some warmth in her little flat. It had been a year since we last popped in to see her, and her life was dire then; her flat was filthy, cold and spartan, and it was clear when we arrived in the afternoon that she had emerged from her bed to let us in. She was dirty and unkempt, with no food in the flat apart from a few old crusts of bread by the side of her bed. We only spotted these because I'd brought an electric blanket, and while putting it on the bed we saw the food debris, as well as the years of grime on her bedclothes. This once smart, pristine lady had lost touch with the real world and had forgotten how to look after herself.

In retrospect, none of us did enough. We were always busy, and she was not exactly on the doorstep. After our visit I contacted her friend, Ruth, as she was very concerned about her. We both wrote to her doctor in Edinburgh, but confidentiality rules stopped him disclosing any helpful information, and all he could say was that they were keeping an eye on her. When, like Thelma, you live alone, are in dire straits, and have no close relatives to help you, surely a doctor should be able to disclose a few details to a couple of well-meaning friends? Although there was mental illness in her family, there is little doubt that her total isolation was the most likely cause of her disintegration. Perhaps all the millennium celebrations and visions of happy families had tipped her over the edge.

She had often spoken of a 'Coffee Club' at Jenners department store, and after her death we decided to check up on that. After I jogged her memory, a waitress recalled Thelma, who she described as looking a bit unkempt. Thelma had indeed gone for coffee in the restaurant, and having arrived there early in the morning, stayed for most of the day. She arrived alone, sat alone, and left alone, and I only hope that she managed to delude herself that she did have friends who she was meeting there.

We were determined that she had a proper funeral, and Robert Robertson, her ex-husband, helped with the arrangements. It was a sad state of affairs. There is always someone who slips under the radar, but after many phone calls round and about to old acquaintances, including her fellow actors in *Take the High* Road, we rustled up enough people to make sure that she had a decent 'send-off'. Robert collapsed and died almost exactly a year later whilst performing *Holy Willie's Prayer* at a Burns supper in the bar at Perth Theatre.

Jean Diamond was still my agent, but in name only, and having stayed with her in case we eventually returned to London, it no longer seemed a good enough reason to rule myself out of what was going on in the north. Finding a simpatico agent was never easy, but as a new one had just started in Glasgow, I decided to drop Maryam Hunwick a line, resulting in an interview in February, which went so well that I thought that I would soon be back in the marketplace. Her only reservation was that she had not seen my work, but with the wonderful part of Shirley Valentine now lined up at the Byre Theatre in St Andrews, that would soon be rectified. In the meantime, I had to prepare for the May cruise and a couple of guest 'spots' for Thomson Leng's *Razzle Dazzle* in June (featuring Judy and Piaf), and *Shirley Valentine* to crack before rehearsals started at the Crawford Arts Centre at the end of June. Although I had done it before, it was seven years previously, so it was a big challenge.

Thank heavens for the audio books. Whatever work we did or did not have, there was usually a book on the horizon so, in a funny way, we rarely felt out of work. All our books came from *Soundings* in Whitley Bay, but at the beginning of May I went down to Leicester to read a book for another company. It's only worth a mention because the other reader who was in the same Bed and Breakfast was Jean Alexander, aka Hilda Ogden from *Coronation Street*, one of the most famous characters in the history of the 'soap'. It had been many years since she'd made her last appearance in 'The Street', but her character had been so popular, and her face so unmistakeable, that in order to get a very elusive cab one morning, I ended up saying that it was for Hilda Ogden! A taxi arrived, and the driver had an autograph book at the ready; Jean was happy to oblige. Our paths never crossed again.

For some time I had been in contact with various 'Wicker Man' buffs about my recollections of the film, and I discovered that, despite my minuscule role as Daisy, my reminiscences were in great demand. I was never paid a penny for them, or for the use of my ancient snaps, but I rather enjoyed the attention. I was amazed that the film had such a cult following, and even a 'Fanzine' (magazine) called *Nuada*. Over the years all sorts of myths had developed around the movie, including tales of lost footage buried under the M1, but whether it was fact or fiction, there was no doubt that the film had preoccupied many people for a long time.

Suddenly, after a gap of 25 years, Robin Hardy, director of *The Wicker Man*, was back in touch. Terry and I met him for dinner at the Caledonian Hotel in Edinburgh, and it was good to see him again, especially after our last meeting back in 1975, when he came to Perth to try and interest me in his film script for *A Billion Women to Lay*. This time he had other things on his mind, the main one being his long-held dream of making a sequel to the original film; his script was, at this stage, called *The Riding of the Laddie*. He was hoping that we might have ideas about casting and finance, and even suggested that I could be casting director on the project.

He had made the original film in Scotland on a small budget, but I hadn't much of a clue as to where he might get the money for the sequel; he wanted it to take place in the Scottish Borders, with

Scottish actors, and he clearly had faith that I would be able to help him to cast it on the cheap. He hinted at a small role for me, so we took the script home, and discovered that there was indeed a tiny part – not much bigger than Daisy – of 'a very attractive middle-aged woman' called Molly, playing the piano in the local bar and singing a few lines, and I guessed that was what he had in mind. When he called to find out what we thought of it, I had not been wrong in my assumption, but I would have happily accepted anything to get on board again. He had been planning this film for years, so I wasn't getting over excited; in fact, it stayed on the back burner for some time.

More immediate was our booking at the barn in Crathes (minus George Donald, who was already on the high seas!), which went very well, and a few days later I headed for Bilbao to join the ship. I had been booked overnight into a five-star hotel, and was able to travel light because George had kindly taken my luggage with him, so it was already on board. We had rehearsed a bit before his departure, so all that remained was for me to meet up with my fellow passengers at the Guggenheim Museum in the centre of Bilbao. It was quite an adventure because it had been many years since I had travelled abroad on my own – 27 to be precise. I changed planes in Brussels and took a taxi once I hit Bilbao. I did feel slightly anxious, because Bilbao was not a holiday resort and very few people spoke English, but having settled into the hotel, I headed off into the city to explore. I located the museum so that I knew how far I had to come in the morning, and then settled into a roadside café to enjoy a coffee and watch the Spanish world go by.

I rose early and, rucksack on my back, I arrived at the Guggenheim with time to spare. I took a bit of film to curb the feelings of anxiety rising inside as the 10am meeting time came and went. I would not have felt too cheerful if I had been abandoned in Bilbao. I was more than relieved when the coaches arrived, and familiar faces started to disembark. The average age on board this cruise was 70, so it was probably not too surprising that there were quite a number on sticks and zimmers. I spotted Ludovic Kennedy and Moira Shearer, both walking with aids, which was a sobering thought as Moira had been such a beautiful dancer in her heyday: the red shoes had become a red zimmer! Safely on board, I was straight into rehearsals with George and the accordionist, because *Toujours l'Amour* was slated for the following evening. Everyone was kept very busy with day trips and excursions which, along with our entertainment commitments, we had to help supervise, so there wasn't too much leisure time.

Whilst sitting at dinner just before our cabaret, and feeling extremely nervous, an announcement came over the tannoy, summoning me to reception. I was not over familiar with the lay out of the ship, but it was a small vessel, so I ran as fast as I could and was astounded to hear Terry's voice on the line, calmly asking me if I had managed to meet up with the ship! Poor Terry, I'd been unable to let him know, and he was worried, but the first thing which came into my head was that satellite calls cost a mint, and the time taken in running to the phone had probably cost 50 quid! After a rather grumpy call, I returned to finish my lukewarm meal; not the best way to prepare for a cabaret, but our show went well and was different from any of the other entertainment on offer.

I was involved in another couple of evenings, one a 'Songs from the Musicals', and the other was a last-night extravaganza in which everyone participated. I was particularly delighted that my Sondheim songs were quite a hit with Ludovic and his wife Moira, who put in a request for *I'm Still Here;* looking at them in their frailty I wondered how long that would be. It was sad to see such a brilliant man so vulnerable, but having started out rather self-consciously, he was happily shuffling into the evening entertainment in a big pair of comfortable slippers. He was officially on board to give informative talks about various ports, but even that was a struggle, and on one occasion he felt so unwell that he was unable to finish his lecture. He was one of a few old-timers who were involved, and was probably the oldest. There was also Jimmy Logan, around the 70 mark, and something of an institution; when you considered the average age of the passengers, the entertainment certainly catered for them, although much of it was geared to the Scottish contingent, and the north-eastern Scots in particular, so for the Canadians, Americans and English, the French songs may have been something of a relief.

Although it was early summer, we were too far north to experience any real Mediterranean weather, but there was little time to sunbathe. Our route took us from Bilbao, onto Bordeaux and St Malo and I enjoyed the excursions and my role in them, although I preferred to see places at my own pace, and not at the pace of the man at the back. I sometimes brought up the rear in order to keep stragglers on course, and to hang around if someone had to pay a visit to the loo. Mont St Michel should have been a highlight, but there were far too many tourists (of which I was one, of course!) to allow any real appreciation of the atmosphere – not to mention the tacky souvenir shops littering the path all the way up to the top, and with half a dozen tour guides shouting in different languages inside the beautiful church, the magic quickly evaporated. You would really have to visit these places in the depth of winter to get any peace, and even then …

We were unable to make our last stop in Guernsey due to inclement weather. I was supposed to be supervising a boat trip to Sark, and we had risen at dawn, but there was little hope of the elderly passengers leaping across a gap in order to land on a bobbing boat to take them to shore. As all outings were cancelled, Jimmy Logan and a few others came to the rescue and at very short notice provided some entertainment to fill the gap. Who could have imagined that less than a year later, Jimmy would succumb to cancer of the oesophagus? After the cruise, he returned to Pitlochry to perform his Harry Lauder play, and while there, he was diagnosed. He spent his last few months coping with his illness, while raising money for charity. He was a real trouper in the old-fashioned mould, and there are few of that old brigade, if any, still with us.

It had been announced that the following year *The Black Prince* was taking a northern route to the fjords, visiting all the Nordic countries which, although not the places we would have chosen for a holiday, was a trip I would love to have been part of. But they tended not to ask singers two years running, and I knew that I had been asked specifically for my Piaf contribution, which wouldn't be quite so relevant in the northern hemisphere. As we docked, the family were there on the quayside in Leith to collect me.

Shortly afterwards, George Donald recommended a book that he had bought on board the ship – *All in the Mind : A Farewell to God* by Ludovic Kennedy. When I read it, it articulated many of my own half-formulated thoughts and affected me deeply. I still have a beautiful copy of the book and often return to it.

After the cruise, it was back to preparations for my spot on *Razzle Dazzle* at the Whitehall Theatre. Now a seasoned member of the Dundee *Thomson-Leng Musical Society*, Oliver was in the show as part of the children's group. I was delighted to work with Michael Ellacott, who had been designated as my accompanist, as he was young, enthusiastic, talented, and he lived in Perth. The show itself was a contender for *The Guinness Book of Records*, with almost 80 songs in the programme. I had two, twelve-minute 'spots', one in each half, and I had the privilege of a solo dressing room. As the others were crammed into the other dressing rooms like sardines, I could not expect to be popular. As for Ollie having the chance to work alongside his mum – well, that was summed up for me one day when he innocently queried: "When are you coming to see me in my show?"

Then there was the onset of 'Shirley' rehearsals. I had waited seven years for another go at the part, and I was nervous at the prospect of climbing that mountain again. Terry had directed the previous production, and although an experienced director, Ken Alexander had slightly alarmed me before we started, by suggesting that I play the part Liverpudlian because Willy Russell had originally set the play in Liverpool. Apart from the fact that it was not my strongest accent, I felt that it was one of those roles which had to become an extension of your own persona, and I imagine that most actresses would want to play it in something close to their own accent. After a bit of discussion, we agreed that Shirley was a universal character, and I went for a gentle, west-coast accent – the same as I did at Perth Theatre back in 1993.

Throughout rehearsals I was careful not to refer to the other production, and although I was pretty sure of what I was doing, I did try to bring something fresh to my performance. Ken often took a back seat, letting me get on with it, and only commenting when there was a technical problem or when he felt it was time to put his oar in. My concern was that he would get bored, but he was probably aware that my having done it before was a plus, and even suggested that we use my recording of *Long Ago and Far Away*. Luckily, Perth still had it in their archives, so we played it at the start of the play before the dialogue, and it still worked very well.

This production was quite a different experience, because the Byre Theatre was in the process of being rebuilt with Lottery money, was behind schedule, and the only available venue in St Andrews was the tiny Crawford Arts Centre, which seated a maximum of 80 people. I discovered to my delight that the play worked perfectly because of the intimacy of the space; the audience were so close I could have reached out and touched them – although it was sometimes quite unnerving having folk just a couple of feet away as I cooked the egg and chips, especially when I heard the occasional spontaneous comment, "Look, she's burst that egg!"

2000, St Andrews – Shirley Valentine.

Our audiences varied in size, and being a holiday town, people tended not to book until the day of the performance, which kept us all on heckle pins. Neither was there much interest in the matinées, and it was quite disheartening in a one-person play to perform for a dozen folk in the afternoon and then start all over again in the evening. But I loved all the '80s songs that were played before 'curtain up' and never tired of hearing them over the tannoy; *Girls Just Wanna Have Fun* always got me in the mood. It was still quite a daunting experience to make my first entrance, knowing that for the next couple of hours I was on my own.

The show had excellent reviews, but like most ventures in our neck of the woods, nothing else would come of it. A fair number of friends came over to see it, but I was disappointed not to see the agent I had met back in February, who had said that she wouldn't take me on without seeing something of my work! On this occasion she was too occupied with the Edinburgh Festival which clashed with our production, but parts like Shirley are rare, so that was frustrating.

2000, Golden Wedding with mum, dad & Grant.

We were now onto the plans for mum and dad's Golden Wedding. They headed off on a luxury cruise on the new P&O ship, the Aurora, and although they found the ports too hot, and dad had little inclination to leave the ship at all, I think that they enjoyed the experience. On their return, we all headed to the Queen's Hotel for a lovely meal and family get-together. Old war buddies of both mum and dad turned up – mum's two ATS pals, Ann Caldwell and Ella Clough, and it was the last time that dad would see Arthur Greenwood and Clifford Linford, his two closest buddies from his days in the Far East. We were allowed one couple, and we invited George and Ann Duffus, who were always great company. Since our first meeting in Inverness in 1984 we considered them amongst our closest friends and it was the last social occasion we spent with them. When the time arrived for the speechifying, George leaned across, took a few notes, and much to our delight, added his own little 'spot'; as always his contribution was funny, short, and appropriate – a night to remember.

Just over a year later, George invited me to reply to his Toast to the Lasses at a Burns Supper in the north of Scotland. His health was not good, and at the last minute, he had to pull out. Just a few weeks later he died of cancer of the oesophagus at the age of 57. Such a sad loss for his family and his friends. One of the funniest men I ever knew.

- 31 -

The best laid plans

Earlier in the year I had been asked to take part in a production of a new play called *The Great Reckoning,* a play that had been commissioned for the Perth Centenary season. Having had a note from Michael, which was intended to tease and excite me about the imminent arrival of this epic on my doorstep, I was disappointed to discover on reading it that it held little allure; the idea of a promenade production through the streets of Perth filled me with dread, especially as it was scheduled for the end of April when woolly vests would still be a necessity – not forgetting a megaphone for the scenes on the North Inch. I honestly couldn't envisage the Perth subscribers taking kindly to a long trail around town, stopping at various historical sites and finally arriving at St John's Kirk, only to collapse in a pew for a couple of minutes before being told by King James, "But up and awa!" And there were other drawbacks; as well as the actors, there were to be around 60 locals to swell the numbers for the *Battle of the Clans*, and who was going to stop random shoppers and a few dogs from tagging along at the back?

I politely declined Michael's offer and hoped that he would come up with something more enticing next time. As it turned out, the show was pulled out of the spring season for various reasons, one of them being police objections to the problems involved in the marshalling of the audience, so I thought we might never hear of it again. The author, however, was asked to do a complete reworking of his script and it was rescheduled for the autumn, but this time it would be inside the theatre and without the 60 amateurs. Although this was a marginally better scenario, I wasn't invited to join the company this time and I did not venture along to see it; come October, it came and went without much ado.

Just prior to this, in June 2000 I decided to write to Michael and find out if he had cast Mrs Darling in *Peter Pan,* a small role and one that could be played by any number of people. I was looking for a little, undemanding job for Christmas, and it seemed sensible to cast it locally to save on subsistence. As always, Michael replied to my note, but added a caustic little comment, thanking me for letting him know which parts I '<u>do</u> wish to play', but still not understanding why I had turned down his previous offer. He said that he would let me know about the Christmas show, but I had the feeling that I was out of favour.

Early in 2001 I went to Jimmy Logan's funeral with George and Isabelle Donald and, true to form, George cut things a little fine, so that by the time we approached the doors of Glasgow Cathedral, we were told that there was not a seat to be had. After looking around we were eventually guided to a side pew, and as we squeezed into the row, I realised that I was heading to snuggle in beside Michael Winter – pure serendipity. I had not seen him for some time, so it was good to meet him under these circumstances, and it was a relief to clear the air. It gave me the nerve to drop him a line about his upcoming production of *Annie*. The spell was broken. I was indeed asked to play Miss Hannigan and was looking forward to a return to the Perth stage.

Just prior to that, Terry and I had our own show to get together. After a gap of a few years, with the help of a fledgling producer, we were about to expand *Legends* into *Born to Sing*. We'd always wanted to do it with a band, and in conversation with one of his Queen Margaret students who aspired to become a producer and was looking for a production, Terry offered him ours – and thus did *Michael Harrison Productions* begin.

Michael was only 21 years old, and had an amazing knowledge of the business for someone so young, but we were lucky that we accomplished what we did with only minor burns. He arranged a 'Première' in his own neck of the woods, at the Whitley Bay Playhouse, although the cost of setting it all up – posters, leaflets, rehearsing the band, bringing them down from Scotland and putting them into a hotel – was going to leave nothing to pay the 'stars'. Michael, Terry and I had all agreed that we three would be the last to be paid but this went without saying because the show was our baby. We hoped there might be future opportunities to work together if Michael hit the big time!

As well as having written the show, Terry was also director and narrator. This effectively meant that he spent the entire day lighting the show and going through it with the in-house staff, and as the time for the evening performance approached, he was almost ready to

418

collapse. Michael took this on board and found a stage manager in Tony Hall, who observed the show at the Playhouse and agreed to come with us on future dates. Although Terry always had to direct the technical rehearsals, having Tony with him eased the burden. As expected, the band was paid, plus expenses, but that was it. We were a bit disappointed with the publicity and the ticket sales, and surprised that Michael hadn't managed to spread the word, living as he did on the spot. That notwithstanding, we had a great night with a standing ovation, and as we signed autographs after the show, it amused Terry and I to think that the audience would have been a bit taken aback to know that neither he nor I had received a penny. We hoped that we would make up for that on our next outing in Perth, which was approaching fast.

It would take pages to go into the appalling treatment we received at the hands of the Marketing and Publicity Department in Perth at that time. We were immediately struck by the fact that no one had informed us that the theatre was closed for refurbishment prior to our playing week, so there would be no coffee bar or restaurant to attract passing trade; not only that, but passing the theatre, there was no sign of any of the posters and leaflets that we had supplied. After a quick tour round all the local outlets, including the Byre and Pitlochry theatres, we were horrified to discover no sign of any of our publicity material.

We called Marketing and were told that all our leaflets and posters had been distributed throughout the area, but they were unable to put a poster in either of the display cases out front of the theatre, as they were just about to come down as part of the renovation process. In effect, this meant that anyone passing the theatre would only see a small notice telling them that the theatre was closed, and giving them directions to go 'round the back' to the studio where they could book tickets for future productions. On entering the dark studio, a potential ticket buyer was greeted with a temporary box office where some of our posters were in evidence, but quite hidden from the world outside. Further pleas finally saw one of our posters in the display case out front which, strangely enough, did not come down until long after our show had been and gone.

Terry and I distributed a few posters round and about and

popped leaflets through letter boxes in target areas. Terry was on the hoof, and I stayed at home or lurked in the car, as I didn't want to be seen pounding the streets to sell my own show. When we were eventually informed that they employed a company called EAE to distribute their material, it was too late for us to do anything. I did ask Anthea in the publicity department for a distribution list, but was told that I would have to send for that. We were entitled to know where our stuff had gone, so I eventually contacted EAE after our playing week was over. I received a vague reply suggesting that we ask Anthea for the elusive list, which they assured us had been sent to her.

After a lot of hassle we finally received it; it contained the name of every outlet used for each production. It was worse than useless, as places like *The Three Bellies Brae Bar* in Kirriemuir and the Kenmore Caravan Site were hardly prime targets! When you are running a show for just a few days, you want locals to come and so you advertise locally. There is no point in taking things further afield, especially when you're clashing with the Edinburgh Festival. It was clear that it had either gone nowhere at all or to outlying areas where it would serve no purpose. We were furious, but powerless after the event.

To pile Pelion on Ossa, when we were desperate for a few more leaflets for our door-to-door marketing, Anthea informed us that there were none left anywhere in the theatre. We were livid, although not at all surprised when, at the end of our playing week, a member of the band found a box of our leaflets lying backstage. So concerned were we just before we opened, that we had a banner made and put on the Perth Bridge, and we were castigated for that by the waspish Anthea. She called it 'interfering in our publicity campaign', but it must have finally clicked that it was quite a good idea, as keen to jump on the bandwagon to market their other shows, they called us a few weeks later to ask for the name of the company who had done the banner for us. Michael Harrison was with us throughout that week, but with a fledgling producer on board, we were still not relieved of much of the hassle that goes with putting on a show – and I am almost forgetting in all this that our entertainment was enthusiastically received.

No time to ponder though, because we were straight into

Annie. It was some time since I'd done a production in the local theatre, so I was really looking forward to it, particularly as Katy had landed the role of Annie and we'd be working together for the first time. We had a jolly company, and I loved playing Miss Hannigan. Despite his idiosyncratic traits, Michael Winter was sweet with Katy, who did very well, although she struggled in the scenes with the dog. It was a short-sighted, good-natured, retired guide dog, and all it craved was food, but at that time she wasn't comfortable with dogs of any creed or colour, and always felt that it ruined her rendition of *Tomorrow,* throughout which it either wandered blindly round the stage or scavenged in her pockets for grub.

2001, Perth – Annie with Katy Wale.

Michael's eccentricity rose to the surface over the doll, whose Velcroed head I planned to rip off at the end of *Little Girls*. After witnessing it in rehearsals, Michael made sure that the doll's head was stitched firmly on, because he assured me that the children in the audience would be crying and the mothers writing letters of complaint if they witnessed such a violent piece of carnage. There was no point in arguing, as once Michael has dug his heels in... although I dug mine in over the 'Silent Scream', which he wanted during a little scene with Daddy Warbucks' secretary, Grace. The comedy depended on holding back a scream until I left the room, closed the door and let rip, before returning as if nothing had happened. The idea that it would work if I just mimed, was beyond belief, and Michael eventually gave in, allowing me one of my best moments. Apparently the actress playing Miss Hannigan in a previous production of his would not scream before her big number which is understandable, I suppose.

2001, Perth – Annie with Vanessa
Clarke & Phillip Arran.

2001, Perth – Annie.

My most abiding memory from the run is of sitting in the green room on September 11ᵗʰ during the technical rehearsals, watching

422

what we thought was a horror movie; in fact we were witnessing the destruction of the Twin Towers in New York, an atrocity known forever as 9/11. It was made even more poignant as we recalled our wedding anniversary meal there 14 years earlier.

Annie came between our two *Born to Sing* bookings, the second at The King's Theatre in Glasgow, but we were already having doubts about the future of the project, as our main objective was to make a happy, hassle-free living, and that rarely seemed to be an option. We had reached a crossroads of sorts. Here we were with a strong piece of our own devising, and where were we to go with it? *Michael Harrison Productions* had no money in the kitty, and we were faced with the prospect of trying to find a venue down south without a CD or video of the show for marketing purposes, and we knew how difficult it would be to persuade anyone to take it on board sight unseen. We were getting weary of the constant problem of having to create our own work. We'd have been happy in the smaller Scottish pond, but the work wasn't abundant, and we couldn't get away from the fact that, in the eyes of the world (our own small world it must be said!), we appeared to have recklessly left the bright lights of London far behind, on the bedrock of putting the family first.

I recall one evening when I was attending a *Fair City Singers* show, and a woman approached me and said that she had followed my career and wondered what I had been doing lately: "You just suddenly disappeared. Did you decide to return to a normal life?" she asked. Sitting in the local theatre one evening, I overheard a woman behind me pointing out that she was sitting behind the seat which Terry and I had bought when the major alterations were done to the theatre back in 1983/4. "You don't see much of Lesley Mackie these days", she said. "Oh, she'll be down in London doing something!" said her companion – which was strangely comforting, but it did make me ponder over what we could do, now that we had made our bed on what seemed to be infertile soil. As far as Scotland was concerned, after nine years, we sometimes felt as though we were still on the outside looking in. We would almost rather have been down south struggling amongst the big boys than constantly seeking employment up here. We were in a Catch-22 situation. With the huge loss that we had sustained in Hove in the early '90s, and the subsequent soar in house prices during the next few years, we heard that our old home, like other properties down south, had risen in value by a crazy 500%, whereas the Scottish market was solid but slow, so a return south was out of the question. In any case we were rather attached to our Perth home – and I found the prospect of leaving my elderly parents impossible to contemplate.

As 2002 dawned, we pondered all sorts of possibilities, and I started doing a few hours a week in primary schools, taking drama classes with children in P6 and P7. Terry and I were also toying with the idea of starting a company devoted to improving communication and presentation skills. *Stand and Deliver* had been germinating for some time, and we read endless books and made copious notes. We even went to talks at the *Small Business Gateway* to get advice on a business plan. We'd reached the stage of printing the cards, designing the leaflets, and booking a website. The only thing we hadn't done was arrange a launch, and this was partly to do with our unwillingness to fully commit ourselves, but a few people had heard of our plans, and we were asked to host a couple of events which we said 'Yes' to, and then had to face. It struck me as funny that you could try and sell yourselves as actors 'till a' the seas gang dry' and still face obscurity, but when you're not really trying because the commitment isn't there, you can be sure that people will somehow hear about you – Sod's Law I suppose. After an engagement with a group of doctors, where we felt a little out of our depth, we decided that running a company was not really what we hankered after. We preferred to be employees – when the opportunity arose. It was hard to be hopeful that things would change, but like most actors we had an eternal optimism, and it didn't take much for us to bounce back and see the light at the end of every tunnel.

Suddenly I had a Pitlochry season lined up for 2003, and being a long season, it was much to be desired, so that was a great morale booster. Apart from a brief mention by Ian Grieve (holding the fort now that Clive Perry had departed) that it might depend on my ability to tap-dance, I didn't foresee a problem. *Stepping Out* was only one of about four plays in which I would participate, and it was a heart-warming tale about a bunch of hopeless hoofers who manage against all the odds to put on a show at the end of their year's classes; simple skills would be required.

So when Ian called to say that all those slated for his season had to attend a 'Tap Workshop' on October 1st, 2002, with Rita Henderson, choreographer of the piece, I was happy to attend. I managed to fit in one tap class before the session, encouraged by my old friend Amanda (wife of director Ian Grieve), who had already started training for her role in the play.

I went to the class, and two and a half hours later returned home feeling a little puzzled. There had been routines, double time steps, triple time steps, even spinning across the room whilst doing time steps. When we were finally asked to perform in pairs, we were instructed to execute some of the steps we had been shown previously. I removed my shoes, which Rita commented on, and I explained that I was just giving my feet a break from shoes I hadn't worn since 1983. Her response was, "Real dancers dance until their feet bleed!" The girl beside me was asked to execute a triple time step, and when she asked if she could see it demonstrated once more, was told, "No, because this is a memory test" – yet the season was six months away, and there would be four weeks rehearsal. I did my double time step in reasonable form – possibly with a tap spring short – but I still thought that, come next April, I would be heading for the 'Theatre in the Hills'.

The letter came, saying that of all the ten people at the audition, only one came up to Rita's exacting standards; unfortunately, that one was not me. Rita was clearly planning to finish with an ending worthy of *42nd Street!* I couldn't fathom why the casting seemed to be at the sole discretion of the choreographer, when her requirements were only for one play out of six in the repertoire season and her cast would also have to play roles in at least two or three of the other plays; ours not to reason why. When Julia McKenzie was directing, she invited me to join the cast – and didn't even ask about my tap skills; no chance of resting on my laurels up here though! After an initial bout of frustration, I accepted the inevitable and turned my mind to other things.

Always nervous at the prospect of booking a holiday in advance, we were on the point of doing so, when Mandy dropped me a hint that, although I had been told that my services were no longer required up in Pitlochry, Ian was planning on coming back to me, because he was pretty cheesed off with the situation. I was greatly boosted by this news and decided not to book the holiday.

Having given me this snippet of information with the proviso that I mustn't let Ian know that she had broken his confidence, I was then put in the position of waiting for someone to make contact – and I waited, and I waited. Christmas came, and despite my ongoing tap classes, there was no word. Sometimes loyalty has its price – and although I had appreciated her flagging it up for me, I think that as the months went by she probably forgot she'd ever told me. She and Ian had their own problems at that time in coming to terms with the news that Ian had not been appointed as Director of Productions of Pitlochry Festival Theatre beyond 2003 – something they had both been hoping for, and had been led to believe might be on the cards.

I knew now without a doubt that I'd lost the imminent Pitlochry season – one of the most valued jobs in the area with eight months continuous work. Then Michael Harrison, who was on an upwards spiral, offered me the Wicked Witch in *Sleeping Beauty* at the King's Theatre Glasgow, one of the leading panto venues in the country, a job which I would have loved to do. I went through to Glasgow to meet the MD, but Elaine C Smith, who was the star name in the show, insisted that one of her actress friends play that role. Michael then discovered that he didn't have full casting approval, so that fell through as well – but his time would come!

The year became very much about mum, who took ill in April and deteriorated over the next few months, but there were a couple of events which brought a bit of fun to the summer. On the 4th of July I headed to Edinburgh to participate in the presentation of the Duke of Edinburgh Awards. Terry was with me, and a favourite moment was when we arrived at Holyrood Palace, showed our pass and were able to drive straight into the VIP parking bays. That was the beginning and end of the special treatment, because there was nothing else laid on, not even a cup of tea and a biscuit. I was slightly disconcerted to discover that I was expected to say a few words, as I had not prepared anything. I was representing the group of young people from Perth and Kinross, and after the Duke came through to address them and shake hands with us all, I took a deep breath, gave my short spiel and handed out the certificates. They took a few photos – and the Duke didn't even put his foot in it, although he sympathised with Terry about being an Englishman in

Scotland!

As mum seemed to be recovering, we had no qualms about heading to London for a little engagement planned for 10th August at the tiny theatre in Jermyn Street. We had looked at the venue the year before, but had been more than a little daunted by the £2,200 weekly rent. Suddenly, we had been approached about doing an evening in their summer cabaret season, called *Jermyn Street Jewels,* and after I realised that I wouldn't have to pay <u>them</u> for the privilege, I accepted with grace. In fact, they were able to pay the sum of £100 to me and the same to my accompanist, who turned out to be Mike Ellacott, the only talented pianist I knew who would travel to London for a one-night stand for that ludicrous sum. The fee had to include our numerous rehearsals, but there's no end to what we performers will do to be seen near Piccadilly Circus. We were only required to perform for one hour, so Terry re-wrote *Born to Sing* so that it was a condensed version called *Songbirds.* The hardest bit was that in the re-jigging, the songs were no longer divided into one half Judy, one half Piaf, and I now had to switch back and forth from one lady to the other; with the difference in vocal timbre, that was not an easy task.

It had been a warm summer, and London was enduring a heatwave, which was not the best weather to spend a few days in the capital. We were greatly helped by relatives, who put themselves at our disposal. We abandoned our car and Terry's cousin, Mike, took us into London for our technical rehearsal on Saturday afternoon. The next morning, the heat outside was stifling. I didn't want to do much before the performance but knew that we couldn't just sit in the hotel all day, nice as it was. We trailed down to Speakers' Corner, which was entertaining for a while, but we finally had to succumb and staggered back to the hotel before we all passed out from sunstroke; we had chosen the hottest day since records began to give this nerve-racking performance. In the late afternoon we went down the stairs leading to the little theatre with some trepidation, but wonder of wonders, the theatre was air-conditioned, and may well have been one of the coolest places in London on that hot unbearable evening. Backstage was basic and humid, and even the one toilet was virtually onstage so I had to wait for the audience to use it before I could go in for a last visit at the five-minute call.

We sold all 70 seats, and the fact that half of that number were friends and family made it even more special. Our nephew, Steven, had brought his mobile phone, which went off during the second number, but his mortification was worse than ours, and so relaxed was I, that I was even able to smile during the insistent ringing. I was only barely daunted by having to sing straight into the faces of our kids who were plonked right in the front row, although I think that I may have embarrassed them by impulsively looking into their eyes as I sang 'And the dreams that you dare to dream really do come true'.

2003 - With old friends at the Cavendish Hotel after the show.

At the end of the show, some of our friends stayed behind in the tiny auditorium before we headed along to the Cavendish Hotel for a drink and a long chat to try and catch up on all the years apart; we wished that we could have stayed all night. We had brought old friends back together, and were back in the West End, even if only for the one night.

A few weeks later my dear mother passed on, and we quickly discovered that my father had the beginning of Alzheimer's disease, and that fact sealed our fate as there was no question of us ever leaving during his lifetime. Any debate about whether we should stay or go evaporated; 2003 had been an *annus horribilis*, but we were here to stay and make the best of it.

- 32 -

Work of the Wicker kind

The summer of 2004 brought *Oliver* to Perth Theatre, where I played numerous roles, including Mrs Sowerberry, the undertaker's wife, and Old Sal, the beggar-woman, who dies and is dragged offstage by her feet. The show was made special because our Oliver had been asked to be in it, and not just as a member of Fagin's Gang or as a workhouse lad, but as one of the three 'Olivers'. Our kids were lucky to have these opportunities at the local theatre with Katy as Annie in 2001, and then Ollie getting his turn.

2004 – Perth. Oliver. Ollie Wale centre.

Michael Harrison seemed to be riding high, working for Qdos Pantomimes, and I was given the choice of three to celebrate my ten years without one – the most recent being Nursie McCuddles in *Sleeping Beauty* in 1994! Now the world was my oyster: I could go to South Wales, or His Majesty's, Aberdeen to play the Wicked Witch in *Snow White* – which was tempting – but I opted for Mrs Darling and the Mermaid in *Peter Pan* in Darlington with Cannon and Ball.

I was one of eight ladies, the other seven all under 28 years of age. I enjoyed their company but tended to go back to my rather cosy digs as soon as the show was over. Cannon and Ball were Born Again Christians which had, apparently, transformed their behaviour, but as they were two of the most egocentric people I'd ever met, I can't imagine what they must have been like before they found God. We got a fair idea of what we were in for when they both arrived at rehearsals a day later than everyone else. We were rehearsing in a local rugby club, and with only a week's rehearsals to get the show on, we were all focusing on the 'blocking' when the hilarious duo arrived late, Bobby Ball heading straight to the bar at one end of the room. He ordered a soft drink, and although within earshot, shouted constantly into his mobile phone. When he eventually came over to where we were attempting to rehearse, he ignored the company, said he was too tired to work and disappeared until the following day. When they did turn up, they usually only gave us 'And then we go blah di blah di blah', and on one occasion I remember the gentle director saying, "Quiet everyone, Mr Cannon and Mr Ball have agreed to show you a bit of their act" – and this was at a dress run! In fact, we never saw what they were going to do until the first performance!

Over the next few weeks we were treated to more boorish and bizarre behaviour, although there were also a few laughs. We had barely opened when Cannon and Ball were accused in the local press of being homophobic, but they refused to stop their antics. I got a taste of their nonsense when, shortly after the opening, Bobby brought me to the front of the stage at the curtain call to make an announcement. I was horrified, as he'd said something to me before the performance about seeing in my programme biography that I had won an Olivier Award, and I thought he was about to tell the audience. But no, he just informed them that a special award was being given for the best performance by any Mermaid in *Peter Pan* throughout the country, and I had won *Mermaid of the Year*. The audience applauded politely, and I was allowed to return to my place in the line-up.

That was quite amusing – well, certainly more amusing than what he had done to one of the *Acromaniacs* the previous year during the curtain call, when he singled him out and announced to a packed house, which included the boy's parents, that he had 'come out' – and he wasn't even gay! I only came in for one more stunt when he took me by the hand and told the audience that he and I had been having an affair and I had asked him to marry me. He waited for the ripple of applause, then added, "But I've turned her down", and shoved me back into line.

2004 – Darlington. Peter Pan with Lee Brennan.

One major area of irritation was the noise they often made in the wings. When they weren't onstage, they 'forgot' that other people were. After one occasion when I could hardly hear myself speak as I cast my Mermaid spell to magic the children back home, I had a quiet word with the stage manager. I said I was happy to go and speak to the guilty parties myself, but I felt that they might take it better coming from him. From my dressing room upstairs I could hear Bobby yelling furiously from the floor below, and I knew they would want to know who had complained. The next performance was a travesty with no *joie de vivre* at all, and Bobby muttering in the wings about someone spoiling his fun and ruining the show. After a couple of lazy, grumpy performances, they started to interact with us all again – but I do remember Tommy grabbing me in the wings shortly after this incident and, without thinking, I said "Ssh, Tinker Bell is about to do her big number", and he seethed, "Don't tell me what to do. I've been 40 years in this business love, and I'll make as much noise as I want!"

Although I was keen to work over Christmas, it was a long time to be away from home – and, I discovered, from dad who was growing quite needy with his deteriorating condition. I would not be happy to leave him again.

The Oran Mor had recently started their *A Play a Pie and a Pint* lunchtime theatre in a converted church in Glasgow. It was a wonderful idea, as people could go there during their lunch break, see a play, have a pie and a drink – and all within an hour. It quickly developed a following, and became one of the biggest success stories in Scotland. As we approached Christmas 2005, I was delighted (and nearly as surprised as I was when I was offered Dorothy in *The Wizard of Oz* back in 1992!) to be offered the title role in the Oran Mor's version of *Cinderella*. There was a sting in the tail; in this version, Buttons and Cinders were supposed to be so 'over the hill' that they couldn't get into a panto for love nor money. Dave Anderson was Buttons, and it turned out to be one of the most enjoyable Christmas pantomimes I have ever been in – funny and short. Terry, who had a total aversion to the genre, declared it the best he had ever seen. This pantomime became the benchmark for all future Christmas shows.

It also gave me the opportunity to set up *Laughter and Hope and a Sock in the Eye*, a one-woman play Terry had been working on for some time. Having explored many ideas and subjects, we had finally settled on Dorothy Parker, American poet, short story writer, journalist and wit. He had already sent the script to a couple of theatres, but getting a director to read a piece, never mind return it in an enclosed self-addressed envelope, was an uphill struggle. I mentioned the play to David MacLennan, director and founder of the Oran Mor, and he said that if Terry could get it down to less than an hour, he would consider it. This was no mean feat, as at this stage it was over two hours long, so ruthlessness was essential. He pencilled us in for autumn 2006.

2006 brought various interesting jobs, one of them being *The Vagina Monologues*, produced by rising star, Michael Harrison. 'Vaginas' was making its first outing in Scotland, and I had a few minor reservations. As well as a total lack of inhibition, the monologues demand skilled acting, and although 'getting bums on seats' is a fact of life in this business, it can be tricky when a 'celebrity' is brought into this kind of venture because it has to be a team effort. We found that audiences were curious about the show, not a particular individual. The publicity focused on Carol Smillie – not her fault, but Jo Freer and I didn't even have our names on the poster, and these things are important to actors.

2006, The Vagina Monologues. With Carol Smillie and Jo Freer

It wasn't long before Miss Elspet Cameron appeared on the scene. Over the years we had constant, lengthy and often nutty phone calls and meetings with dear old Elspet, but latterly her calls were becoming ever more eccentric. After my mother died, she called to enquire if mum had ever needed incontinence pads, and if any had been left behind. She was only allowed one a day from her care home (she said!), which was barely adequate, and she would appreciate any I could send. At one stage she asked me to come to Glasgow to help her plan her funeral and was talking about Dylan Thomas's *Do not go gentle into that good night,* which did not seem appropriate for Miss Cameron at the age of 93. Right to her last days she told us that she was trying to call Buckingham Palace and the House of Commons to ask them to address issues that troubled her, and on one momentous day she called to tell us she had been given the last rites and a special service had been held for her in the Buchanan House Care Home where she had been in residence for the past few years. We never found out what that bit of confusion was about. Her phone bill must have been immense.

Miss Elspet Cameron

Towards the end of our tour, Elspet called Terry, asking him to book seats for her for the last night of *The Vagina Monologues* at the King's Theatre, Glasgow, on March 25th. She was no longer independent, had no credit card, so was unable to book seats for herself and a few of the other residents who were to accompany her to this potentially inappropriate show. He declined to do so, not just because of the money which he would certainly never see again, but not wanting to pay for tickets which would be wasted, as she would clearly be unable to attend the theatre on a cold March evening. He questioned her ability to get there, but she was determined to see me. I forgot about it until our last night, when I received a call from the box office to say that an elderly lady by the name of Miss Cameron had arrived in a taxi and was wondering if I could arrange a ticket for her, which I duly did, the Company Manager organising a freebie.

Shortly afterwards, there was a call from Buchanan House Care Home to say that she had escaped unnoticed from the home, and was to go straight back after the show. They said that they would see to the payment of her taxis, as she hadn't even paid for the one that brought her to the theatre. At the end of the show, she crippled round to the stage door on her bag-laden zimmer, sporting her distinctive, wee, cosy tammy. As I came to the door to greet her, she said, "It was a wonderful evening Lesley", and then the immortal line, "Your mother would have been very proud of you" which, bearing in mind the contents of the show, I'm not entirely sure about. That was the last time I saw her.

When I think of the *Vagina Monologues*, I always think of Elspet. It was an interesting experience, exciting even, I was glad to have done it, and the following was a review I added to my collection; to give Carol her due, she had seen it herself, came into my dressing room and pronounced defiantly: "Well, she loved you, hated me!"

The star of the show, however, is Mackie, a veteran stage actress. She switches effortlessly between the old lady whose legs have been closed for business since an unfortunate incident in a Morris Minor in 1953, and the survivor of a Bosnian rape camp. And in the voice of an American dominatrix she leads us through the vocabulary of moans. There is The Catholic, The Doggy, The Kids-in-the-next-room, The Machine gun, The Diva, and then for the finale, the one that makes Meg Ryan look like she has inhibition issues. Hair awry, writhing, spitting out water and falling off the chair as red fireworks go off, Mackie has the 90% female audience waving their Daily Mails in the air. Smillie is left to look impressed and lead the clapping. (The Sunday Times)

Being on a roll now and utterly convinced that there was a big female audience out there for all things female, I was ripe for *Mum's The Word* which I was asked to do as a direct result of 'Vaginas'. It had been written by six Canadian friends who had been pregnant at the same time and shared their baby experiences. They wrote it all down, turned it into an entertainment, cast themselves in it, and made a success of it in Canada and then over in Scotland. They got a lot of mileage out of it for many years, eventually writing the sequel – *Mum's the Word 2 (Teenagers)* to keep them in work as their kids got past the baby stage. That was the one I got involved in with a few actresses of the more mature kind. *The Scotsman* review for the show described us as 'a fine team of Scottish actress mothers led by Lesley Mackie'.

2006, Mum's The Word 2 with Barbara Pollard, Carole Anders, Estrid Barton & Amanda Beveridge.

On July 30th, a month later, Miss Elspet Cameron died. There had been a few false alarms, and she often said that she didn't think she would see next August, Christmas or Easter, but there was something indomitable about her spirit and we couldn't really imagine a world without old Elspet. I was asked to contribute something to the memorial service, so I read *Fear No More the Heat of the Sun,* plus a short poem by Willie Soutar, one of her favourite poets. The service was lovely, and we all exchanged 'Elspet' stories. She was a one-off, someone I had always imitated in order to entertain, as I was able to find her distinctive timbre in my voice. Perhaps one day I might find a way of doing a one-woman play about her. She left both Katy and Oliver £100 in her will, which was very touching. A never to be forgotten lady; 'a kenspeckle character', to quote *The Scotsman* obituary.

Out of the blue I had a call from Robin Hardy, and it seemed that things were moving, albeit slowly, on the 'Wicker' front. After a gap of a few years Robin had now written the book of the sequel to *The Wicker Man* and had decided to publish it before making the film. He considered this the right way round in order to raise its profile, which might help secure funding, and it was no longer *The Riding of the Laddie* but *Cowboys for Christ*, although the title was to give Robin a few headaches over the next couple of years, and even caused certain religious groups in America to withdraw their funding.

Robin invited me over to Glasgow for his book signing at Ottakar's Bookshop, where he wanted me to sing a song, which was to be in the movie when it eventually saw the light of day. This song, *Fruits of the Forest,* had been in the film since its first dawning, and was originally a stand-alone item to be sung by Molly in the bar. Robin now felt that the tiny song was not worthy of my talents and had decided to combine the two roles of Molly, the middle-aged floozy in the bar, and Daisy, the cook at the big house. This delighted me, and in his new book lived my new character, Daisy the Cook, who just happened to sing at the bar on her nights off; not only that, but when I read the book, I discovered that she was a fat cook! Although our paths had only crossed on a couple of occasions over the previous 30 years, Robin must surely have noticed my slight form. I called to remind him that I was not at all fat; he said that he remembered me as a 'chubby little thing', but it would not be a problem as they would provide me with a fat suit – solved. So after a gap of 34 years, my film career was about to be resuscitated, and at the very least it would surely supply me with a fund of stories to last another few decades.

It had been 20 years since *Judy* in the West End, so it was time to give the re-titled Parker piece, *Excuse My Dust*, an airing at the Glasgow Oran Mor. It was autumn 2006, Terry was directing, and he enlisted the help of our old friend Charlie Bell, who lived locally, to give us a more objective eye on it. We did a few days' work together at home in Perth and the rest in Glasgow, although I had been learning it for months. It was one of the most challenging scripts I had ever tackled; so precise, and there would be no ad-libbing a la Dotty Parker.

2006 - Oran Mor, Glasgow. Excuse My Dust

If you do go blank onstage, something will usually come into your head to fill the gap. I always felt that I would cope if I lost Shirley Valentine somewhere en route, but if the character is cleverer than you are, that is not likely to happen, and that's what I felt about Dorothy. She was a wordsmith, and I felt sure that any attempt of mine to fill in, might have stuck out like the proverbial. Like Dorothy Parker, Terry agonised for hours over every phrase; not for nothing did she herself say that for every five words she wrote, she changed seven! We opened on November 6th, ran for the week, and had a warm reception and good reviews. I was relieved to find that performing it didn't cause me excessive anxiety, and at a running time of around 50 minutes it felt right.

One thing I did not expect to do again was the Edinburgh Fringe and we were surprised and delighted to hear that we had a slot at the Gilded Balloon in an Oran Mor/Gilded Balloon joint production, which meant that we would be paid a salary of sorts and not leave Edinburgh bruised, battered and broke as most performers had to do. I hadn't been involved in the festival since my first and only other venture in 1973 in *Voyzeck* and *The Thrie Estaites* with the Young Lyceum Company. We grasped the opportunity, although we knew that having done it for a few performances at the Oran Mor and at the Edinburgh Jazz House, we would not be eligible for *The Scotsman Fringe First* awards and might even find it difficult to get reviewed again – and I'd no intention of trailing up and down the

Royal Mile handing out publicity leaflets before the show! I travelled through each day by bus for my lunchtime slot, changed in a virtual cupboard, saw all sorts of other shows – I even wrote an extensive blog. It was a fascinating experience and we acquired a few excellent reviews. We hoped that it would not be the end of the road for Dorothy Parker, as we now had our sights set on the possibility of London. Well, we were still able to dream.

With the dawning of 2008 I met Andrew Steggall, a young, would-be director and impresario, who had gone to great lengths to raise the money for a 'Wicker' project, the long-term plan being to do a stage production of *The Wicker Man*. So March brought the Wicker Workshop, which was a kind of compensation for the movie which, with numerous cries of, "It's on!", "It's off!", just didn't seem to be happening – and in any case it was fun to be back in London. There were ten of us, mainly actor/musicians, and despite a lot of unproductive improvisation, we managed to concoct a short presentation which we performed for friends and producers at the end of the fortnight. Although the script was close to the original film version and barely adapted for the stage, the music seemed to stand the test of time. I invited a couple of friends along, who were quite taken with it and felt that a stage production was a distinct possibility. Robin Hardy, director of *The Wicker Man*, also turned up, and although none too impressed, he did say to me in a conspiratorial manner that at least I had a nice part in his film to look forward to, which confirmed the news I had just received that the movie was scheduled for April. I was quite excited and left London feeling all wickered up.

Robin insisted that I had one of the better deals, because I had a key role and been patiently involved for years; not only that, but there was a deal for Terry as well. It's not often that a film director comes on the phone and says, "Would your husband like a part?" The part was a trade union convenor called Murdoch Renfrew, and although I reminded him that Terry wasn't Scots, this was deemed unimportant. The original film featured every accent under the sun so it was probably not important in the slightest. In any case we had no idea whether the film would ever see the light of day.

On 22nd March, the 14th draft of the script arrived, now called *Queen of the May*, in which I was happy to see my part looking rather fun with quite a bit of dialogue plus the two songs. Things were moving and April/May seemed to be the time. Annan was to be the location in the Scottish Borders, hotel rooms were booked, crew were hired, and it was all appearing on the IMDB site with daily updates. I went through to Glasgow on March 25th, 2008, to rehearse the two songs with Keith Easdale, the MD, and his assistant sound man Stuart, known as Sag. A week later, on April 3rd, we laid down the tracks and I was given a rough CD copy of my recordings, so that I would be able to practise miming to my own voice. As Daisy was supposed to be accompanying herself on the piano, which was to be done in situ, I was more anxious about the piano-playing than the singing. I was assured when I left the studio that Stuart would send the music as an attachment within a couple of days. I never did get it, and still no contracts were coming in.

On April 8th, I noted that I was 'still waiting for the axe to fall', so things were very uncertain. When it did fall, I saw the headline and read the gory details online. There had been 65 local crew hired, 91 hotel rooms booked in Annan, and all were cancelled; the project had fallen apart yet again, but this time at the very last hurdle. So that was it, or so we thought. It had been a pipe dream for Robin Hardy and Christopher Lee.

After we were informed officially that it had been postponed, this time because of the credit crunch and sudden withdrawal of offshore funding, we spent a brief time being very disappointed. The people of Annan, who thought they were going to have a busy summer with employment for many, must have been equally gutted.

Terry and I were suddenly offered a job – and together at the local theatre. On the face of it, not very exciting, but one we became very attached to; so taken was Terry with our job, that he would have been happy to play the doctor in *A Streetcar Named Desire* for the rest of his life. I was the nurse, and he was the doctor, and although we popped up elsewhere in the play, it was a breeze. I didn't have to be in the theatre until the interval, and when we did eventually make our brief appearance towards the end of the evening, it was a key scene. Terry was in his element; he had the longed-for dressing room camaraderie, a brief entrance at the start yelling, "Red Hot" as a street vendor, and his main appearance as the doctor at the end. He was amused by the story of the actor who had played this minute role in the very first production on Broadway who, when interviewed about the play, began, "Well, it's about this doctor!" We have a splendid photograph of our cameo roles, which Terry was tempted to send around to try and sell us for any future productions of the play.

Perth – A Streetcar Named Desire with Terry Wale.

For Terry, the doctor was his *raison d'être*, but I was also contracted to play a crow (Auntie Peck) and Soft Bear in *The Snow Queen* so had the added delight of two shows a day over Christmas and the New Year, which I enjoyed despite the discomfort of the costumes; the bear's costume was so claustrophobic that at the start I didn't think I would be able to 'bear' it. Soft Bear turned out to be a joy.

In Feb 2009, after a year of silence when we had all but given up on it, I received an email from Tressock Films; 'Cowboys' was back on, and now renamed *The Wicker Tree*. They thanked us for our patience as if we should all have known that it would eventually happen. We were not out of the woods yet though. The funding was still uncertain, and what had started as a movie on a normal budget, was now being called a 'low-budget' movie, which was preparing us for our new 'deals'. The spring was punctuated with uncertainty, but I had a couple of calls from Robin, which were positive and made me feel a little more convinced that it still might happen.

We never saw a contract, but were eventually given a starting and finishing date, and so we embarked on the movie in July on a daily, basic rate, mine slightly better than Terry's to reflect my important role of Daisy the Cook! In the film Robin kindly encouraged us to share the screen, singing in the choir, partaking of the feast, and generally enjoying each other's company; he clearly had our best interests at heart, but had failed to take into account that the very last person Murdoch Renfrew would have associated with in the village of Tressock was Daisy the Cook.

2009 – The Wicker Tree with Terry Wale.

Having been furnished with a (totally unexpected) horse and riding habit, Terry nervously awaited the summons to ride out on the hunt, only to discover (much to his relief) that his services were no longer required. Standing in the lunch queue one day, a 22 year-old girl with a grey wig inside her riding hat told me she'd been asked to double for an old man! As for me, suffice it to say that I never had the opportunity to sing, as one song was mysteriously cut and the other was sung by Robin Hardy's daughter – although I heard at one stage that they wanted Susan Boyle to sing it; in a Wicker World, nothing would have surprised me. Even without a song, playing the chubby cook was a hoot.

2009 – The Wicker Tree with Clive Russell.

Sir Christopher Lee had grown too old for his leading role while waiting for it to happen, but despite ill health, he played a small part, which meant that a star name graced the credit list; he and I were the only two people to be in both 'Wicker' films! If the third part of the trilogy was ever to surface, I might be the only person in all three – an idea I found very enticing. As it transpired, the film only ever made it onto DVD, so didn't manage to cash in on the success of the original film. Despite its shortcomings, I wouldn't have missed being in *The Wicker Tree* for anything.

- 33 -

End of the Rainbow

Without a Scottish agent, I was missing out on quite a lot – not hearing about jobs until they were already cast, and various theatre policies added to my problem: Dundee Rep and its long-term resident company had two good actresses in my age range, so there was little chance of my getting a look in. In Pitlochry, just up the road, any line of parts that suited me seemed to go to the partner of the resident director, and in Glasgow, Glaswegians ruled the roost – lovely as most of them were. It was a no-win situation, as by contacting those involved, I was more likely to offend somebody than land myself a job!

After much deliberation, I wrote to the Artistic Director at Pitlochry, just to ask if there was any point in my putting myself forward for any season; I had a bit of a track record and was surprised never to have reached the interview stage. He replied in detail, but with rather patronising and insensitive comments about 'actors taking disappointment on the chin', and about 'each season requiring its own distinctive mix of skills, disciplines and experience' – something his partner clearly had, and not just for one but for every season! Perhaps I have a self-destruct button, but as it was clear that he wasn't going to employ me, I had nothing to lose, so I responded with a bit of mildly sarcastic humour; it gives actors a tremendous feeling of empowerment to say what they think to a director – something many directors are not used to.

In 2009 we had an extreme winter, but the one of 2010 surpassed it in its awfulness. There is always something beautiful about wintry scenes, but the snow began on November 28th, and it was a Winter Wonderland until the middle of January, which was the first time we looked out of the window and saw that the grass was still green. Katy had recently graduated from ArtsEd in Chiswick and was back home with us, sharing the extraordinary conditions throughout those wintry days. At the beginning, people were struggling to get around, and the terrible conditions coincided with the onset of our rehearsals for our first job together since *Annie*, playing mother and daughter – the Empress and Princess Pikaboo of

Pekin, Perthshaw – in Perth's production of *Aladdin*.

The Spirit of the Blitz came to the surface, the roads were thickly gritted, wellies and boots became the norm, and people began to cope with the Arctic conditions. Everyone mucked in to help each other, and we put the musical director up for a few days when he was unable to get home to Edinburgh. Katy and I had a lot of fun, although I was disappointed to lose a scene containing my only number (a comedy version of *Don't You Wish Your Girlfriend was Hot Like Me*) in a last-minute cut, implemented in order to bring the panto in at an acceptable length – the perennial panto problem.

2010 – Perth. Aladdin with Helen Logan & Amanda Beveridge.

It had long been a dream of Terry's to do a show about Harold Arlen, and in April 2011, we finally did *Sitting on a Rainbow* at the Byre Theatre, but sadly the audiences were small, which was probably as much to do with the lack of publicity as the fact that Arlen is not the best-known composer, which is bizarre considering that he wrote over 500 songs including *Stormy Weather*, *Come Rain or Come Shine* and two of Judy Garland's most iconic songs: *The Man that Got Away* and *Over the Rainbow*. Arlen's relative anonymity was one of the reasons Terry had been so keen to celebrate his work. So much time and energy was invested in the project for a two-night run, and to top it off, while walking backwards to get a better look at a screen projection during the rehearsal, Terry fell off the stage, landing in the front of the auditorium. He struggled on despite great discomfort, and took a month to get over it.

It was destined to be the year of the big spend so, after my Big 60 birthday party, and having heard that a two-hander version of *Judy* was about to open at The Kammerspiele, we decided to have a short break and fly off to Vienna. It is a lovely city and we wandered, took trams and trains, and managed a couple of trips to the Prater, where I ventured on a high chairoplane ride which was much more nerve-racking than I thought it would be. As I twirled around, it wasn't easy to deal with the high winds; I hung onto the simple bar restraint with one hand, and my specs with the other, but I could barely look down upon the view of the city.

The chairoplane in Vienna.

On the Sunday evening, which was the last night of the run, we were met at our hotel and directed to the Kammerspiele, which was in the Fleishmarkt and was the smaller sister theatre of the Joseftheater. We met both cast members, Ruth Brauer and Michael Dangl, before the show, and found them utterly charming.

It wasn't easy to follow what was going on because of the language barrier (it had been a long time since I studied German at school!), and Terry, at times, was barely aware of which scene we were watching. They didn't sing the songs that were listed in the script, and Ruth bore little resemblance to Miss Garland, either vocally or in appearance, but she was a good actress – committed, energetic – and the audience loved it. Michael Dangl, who played the piano and all the male roles, was excellent. Terry had a wonderful night; after they had taken their many bows, Michael mentioned Terry's presence in the auditorium, and he received an enthusiastic round of applause as he rose like Larry Olivier and waved graciously to the audience, which was definitely the icing on the cake. We went for drinks with the cast afterwards, when Ruth explained her approach to the role and why she didn't attempt to look or sound like Garland; the Germans and Austrians are not over familiar with Judy and don't demand the kind of detail we had to observe; their intention was just to tell her story.

"Großes Schauspielertheater" (Kurier)

Terry Wale

Judy

Somewhere Over The Rainbow

Ein musikalischer Abend mit
Ruth Brauer-Kvam und Michael Dangl
Regie: Michael Gampe

Premiere: 17. März 2011
Kammerspiele

"Ein Hit!"
"Schlichtweg großartig"
"Jubel, Jubel!"

(Presse, Wr. Zeitung, Standard)

www.josefstadt.org T 01-42 700-300

We wished we'd thought of doing the play with a small cast many moons before, so we returned home and within a very short time we adapted the play ourselves. It was a relatively easy exercise as so many scenes in the original were written for two people, and apart from using the device of a voice-over of gossip columnist, Louella Parsons, to help move the story on, we did not – indeed, could not – copy anything they did in Vienna, as we barely understood a word. Whether we would ever get it on was an entirely different matter, but I hoped that we might succeed in 2012, the year of Judy's 90th birthday – the sooner the better, before I got too old for the part!

We started by adapting the play into a two-hander as it had been in Vienna, and we decided to have a read-through with local actor, Ian Grieve, just to hear if it all hung together. After a rather unsatisfactory session, we began to have reservations. It was a big ask for one actor to play all 13 male roles, and having seen a cast of 12 so many years ago, an audience might feel a bit short-changed with a cast of two, never mind the huge demands on the actors. We decided to introduce another actor to share the burden, and got to work on a three-hander version, which made more sense. My next task was to try to sell the idea to our local theatre.

2011– Perth. Toujours l'Amour with Jim Cleland,
Terry Wale & Mike Ellacott.

As we approached the end of the year, we had arranged a very special night at the theatre – probably our last *Toujours l'Amour*. We introduced an accordionist to give it an added dimension, hopefully justifying hiring the theatre as opposed to the smaller Redrooms, where we had done it for the past two years. On November 12th, we filled the theatre to bursting point, so our faith in the show had been justified, but having sold the tickets under the assertion that this would be a 'possible farewell' to Piaf, I was now swithering. Well, I did say 'possible!' After all the planning and excitement of the evening, I almost hoped that there might be a chance to do it again.

Suddenly our big news was about *Judy*. Having been the protagonist re our adapted, revamped version, which was for three/four actors, just after Christmas Horsecross Arts offered us the finance to produce it ourselves and stage it for five performances at the end of August 2012 – and we were scared out of our wits. It was 21 years since we'd done it on tour up here, and 25 years since the London production. It might be our last joint venture – with myself as Judy, and Terry directing. We had to cast it and get all the preparatory work done so that we could put it on the back burner until rehearsals started on August 6th. It would be very different with a small cast, and we'd barely leave the stage. Costume had to be kept to a minimum and age had to be irrelevant – I hoped! I'd said a kind of farewell to Piaf, and this was to be the farewell to Judy.

With the altered script, we thought of bringing in one of the actors from our London production, because there is nothing more comforting than working with old friends who you know will bring something tried and tested to the show – but it was a Horsecross production, so it was only fair that we cast locally, and budget limitations would not have stretched to importing actors. We decided not to hold auditions, as we already knew many of the Scottish actors. With two male actors, it began to be more feasible that they might be convincing in most of the roles assigned to them – Ian taking on more of the 'heavies', although he was going to have a struggle with little Mickey Rooney! We threw a lot of names into the ring for actor number 2, and after a lot of debate we invited Richard Conlon, who was in America at that time on a lengthy tour.

The idea of having Louella Parsons as a voice-over (which I could have done myself in advance) began to seem like dead theatre, so we did a bit of juggling with the finance and introduced Ann Scott-Jones as a fourth member of the cast. She accepted a reduced fee, as Louella was self-contained and she would not be required at many rehearsals. This was not a normal or ideal situation, but it was the best we could do. We suggested that she use a clipboard as a prompt, which would have been 'in character' for a journalist and made her role easier, but she wanted to learn the lines. We also appointed a designer and a musical director, so we had a full team. It had been quite a journey from our inspiration in Vienna the previous June to being on the verge of starting our own rehearsals as writer, director, actress and producers – and we called ourselves *Wizard Productions*.

Terry concentrated on his lighting plot, props list, meetings with the designer, tweaking and re-writing bits of the script and seeing to all the contracts. I was more involved in sending myriad emails to the cast and friends, doing press and radio interviews to promote the show, seeing to the printing of posters and leaflets and working with the MD.

Rehearsals began on August 6th. We got off to a good start, but Ian, being a director as well as an actor, sometimes found it difficult not to take over: "With all due respect I'm not telling you how to write/direct, but..." Terry has always believed in actors' theatre (having worked under the direction of Peter Hall who, according to Terry, didn't!), but if someone is being obstructive, it must be addressed. So, just prior to the first run through, Terry had a blazing row with Ian over the song, *Happy Birthday to You*, which was sung to Clark Gable, and which Ian had to lead as Louis B Mayer, encouraging the audience to join in. For a few days he had been singing it out of tune – quite deliberately – for comic effect. In the context of the scene, which was not about Mayer's inability to hold a tune, it felt destructive. Terry asked him if he would go back to singing the song as written, but Ian, after assuring Terry that his version would 'go down a storm', dug his heels in.

Terry lost it, I'm afraid, and went berserk. It was unfortunate because the drama was witnessed by a few people, who were probably quite taken aback by the ferocity of the interchange. I tried to explain to Ian that Terry was very stressed out. "Why is he taking it out on me?", he asked. "Maybe because you've caused it!" To lighten the atmosphere, I playfully said that I did recall losing my only song on the opening day of the panto (which he had directed!) not that long ago. "That's below the belt" he raged and stormed off –

then we had to do the run; the trials and tribulations of rehearsing a show. Ian changed after that day, giving good performances in his various roles, and getting the play off to a good start by singing *Happy Birthday* in tune – and the audience did join in.

Stuart Watson, the MD, worked extremely hard, always being the first to arrive in the morning, working on sound effects and coming up with some lovely authentic material; he worked in a meticulous way. He wanted the pace set exactly using a metronome, but as Judy was always free with tempi this seemed contradictory. I'd always endeavoured to emulate Judy's laid-back rubato style, but Stuart was a talented musician taking on a mega task, so we assumed that the somewhat robotic approach to the pace must be something beyond our ken and undoubtedly connected to the inner workings of his instrument. One sophisticated keyboard may not have been the ideal backing for Judy Garland, but he did achieve an amazing sound for a one-man band. Jess, the designer, did wonders with her limited budget and went way beyond anything we expected or requested; the simple addition of a hat or a jacket suddenly became full costumes with everything in period, including shoes, mikes, phones, the lot. Right up until our opening night, she was arriving with shoes for me to try, although I was perfectly happy with what I had. With a cast of four, there was virtually no time for changes, and my main problems in performance came about because of the amount of costume I had to cope with.

Opening night was a mixed bag. I was flying, and got added inspiration out of desperation when things went somewhat awry for poor Ann; after a fall on an early entrance, I think that nerves took over – every actor's nightmare – and a lot of dialogue was cut with long uncomfortable silences. She almost seemed to get away with it; one person asked me if she was playing Louella as an alcoholic! It still astounds me; as I changed in the wings during the silences, heart thumping and feeling that it was bound to affect the evening – but that's the mystery of theatre. We never mentioned what had occurred as everyone deals with such issues differently, and perhaps her way of coping was to block it from her mind.

The other four performances flew by, and friends and family came from far and near. We got lovely local reviews but, as expected, the nationals were too busy at the festival. It felt like quite an achievement at my great age to play Judy from her teen years onwards – and to see people from the past like Anna Pajak, and Alan Strachan from Greenwich, seemingly as moved as they had been over 25 years previously, was very reassuring.

2012 – Perth. Judy with Richard Conlon, Ann Scott-Jones & Ian Grieve.

As producers, we had a few gripes – like where were the three staff we were promised for rehearsals? – something which was in our contract. At his 'Meet and Greet' opening 'spiel', Terry said we would be leaning heavily on the stage management team, and he thanked them in advance for their support, but during the rehearsal period they seemed to disappear into thin air; perhaps Rachel O'Riordan, the new Artistic Director, required their services elsewhere. When we analysed the experience in hindsight, I think our big mistake was not to take on board that employing a dresser was essential – budget or no budget! Never in my life have I had so many changes to do without one – although the two young lads who were assisting did their best to hand me items from the mound of clothes accumulated in the wings during the show. At the end of the interval, I was still placing costume and re-arranging props for the second act – with no chance of a cuppa. Never underestimate the importance of a dresser! It was an immense challenge, and we were grateful for the financial backing from Horsecross, which gave us the opportunity to climb this mountain for the last time.

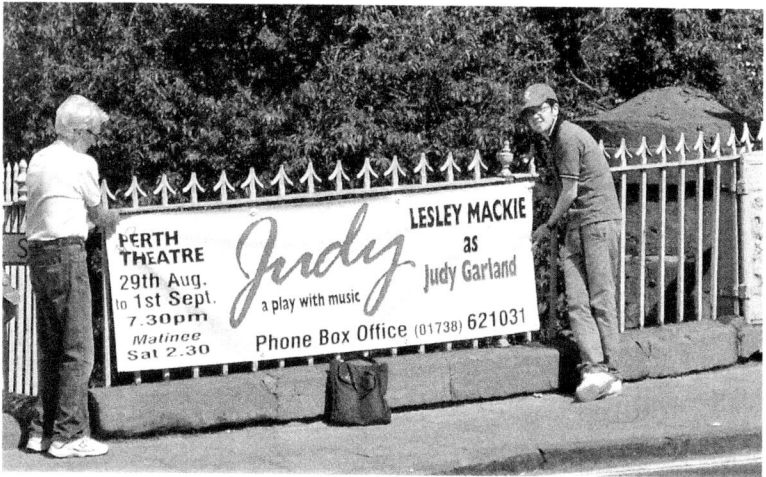

Terry and Ollie helping with the publicity.

It was in the back of my mind that we should really get on and promote the show while it was fresh and new, but having survived this venture, Terry was more than happy to move onto the next one, or even retire. Work had become too stressful, and he was discovering that there is no place quite like home. We had, however, booked a holiday, so flew off for a week on the Danube, the perfect antidote to the stress and strains of being producers.

- 34 -

I'm still here

Terry celebrated his 75th birthday on February 25th, 2013, and the following week we planned to head to London to see a repeat performance of *Merrily We Roll Along*, a musical Terry had adored. But after many years with Alzheimer's and three-and-a-half in a dementia unit, my old dad was going downhill. From the start of his gradual downfall in 2003, he managed to retain his cheery persona for several years, with a song for every occasion. He provided us with many laughs, losing his inhibitions, all political correctness, and said the first thing that came into his head, "Who would have thought someone your size could squeeze into a wee space like that?" And to a lady he'd never seen in his life and who was trying to do up her seatbelt. "I wouldn't even try to get that round you dear!" He was full of it: "It's enough to put a coolie off his rice", and his favourite, "As Mary said to the soldier"! He was funny until he wasn't, and his ultimate decline was the saddest thing to watch. It is such a cruel illness, and to see a man reduced to being spoon-fed liquid meals and lifted in a sling to move him around, was heart-rending: sans speech, sans mobility, sans everything.

As we approached the weekend, I was feeling very uneasy. Grant and I were in and out of the care home, and he was no longer being fed or given fluids. He was clearly nearing the end and we made what plans we could. We met with the minister and the undertaker and had everything in place by Friday, March 1st. We had written our tributes, sorted out an Order of Service, and made all the arrangements for dad's funeral except the date. As I sat with him at midnight, one of the nurses came in, and when I said I was reticent about opening and touching his hands as they had been twisted and painful for so long, she said that as his body was changing, the tension had all gone, and he would feel no pain. I was aware that he was being very well cared for, but I had to make a choice – to go to London the following morning with Terry and Ollie, or stay with dad until he died. I left him around 12.30am, knowing that was the last time I would see him alive, but reassured that my brother, who lived nearby, would be with him. Dad died that day as we travelled down to London.

I began work on a major project which I'd been researching for some time, ever since we realised how important the 2014 Centenary of World War I would be. I was keen to update our previous anthology, *Lest We Forget*, performed back in 1998 to commemorate the 80th anniversary of the end of the war. I was in the driving seat on this one, partly because I felt that I had a special connection due to the loss of three great uncles, two of them from Perth, both mentioned in the Golden Book of Remembrance which was on display inside St John's Kirk – and also because Terry wanted an easier life!

To avoid clashing with any other similar events, I had a meeting with Elizabeth Grant, our Lady Provost who, after an initial resistance to the idea because of her belief that we were <u>celebrating</u>, as opposed to <u>commemorating</u> the anniversary, threw herself into it with great enthusiasm, and within a short time, offered her own services as a performer! By the end of the year we had settled on St John's Kirk as the venue, Sunday November 2nd, as our date of choice, keeping clear of Remembrance Sunday. 2014 was otherwise completely taken up with our daughter's wedding on September 6th, which we followed with a cruise en famille, returning in time for the final preparations for *Lest We Forget*. We chose two charities for the proceeds: Soldiers, Sailors, Airmen and Families Association (SSAFA) and Scotland's Charity Air Ambulance (SCAA), and all the work involved in researching and compiling the script, designing the poster, programme and tickets was now behind me. We had our actors, the Jambouree choir (in the capable hands of Edna Auld), the piper, cornet player, and almost everything else in place, so after all the excitement of the wedding and the cruise, we were ready.

As the day approached, my heart began to sink. It was almost two years since we first had the idea and I suddenly felt very alarmed by the burden of responsibility. Organising rehearsals with everyone involved had been almost impossible, and we only just had time for one complete run before the audience started to arrive around

2.15pm. We had sold a lot of tickets so were expecting a good house. Our ticket helpers: Arlene, Marjorie, Wendy and Jeremy were in place, the audience filed in, the dignitaries took up their places, and the concert began. The little piper started his *Bonnie Dundee*, walking slowly through the kirk, before Lt Col (retired) Andy Middlemiss read the famous Binyon verse from *For the Fallen (At the Going Down of the Sun),* the choir launched into *In Paradisum*, and we were off. The next hour and a half passed with few hitches; any mini concerns were ours alone. I had met Brigadier Sir Melville Jameson a few days before and been a little taken aback when he asked if we would be sticking to the predicted 90 minutes as he had a plane to catch. In the event, he was so surprised by the disciplined nature of it all, that he abandoned his prepared vote of thanks, and positively raved about it, mentioning almost everyone by name – and still managed to catch his plane!

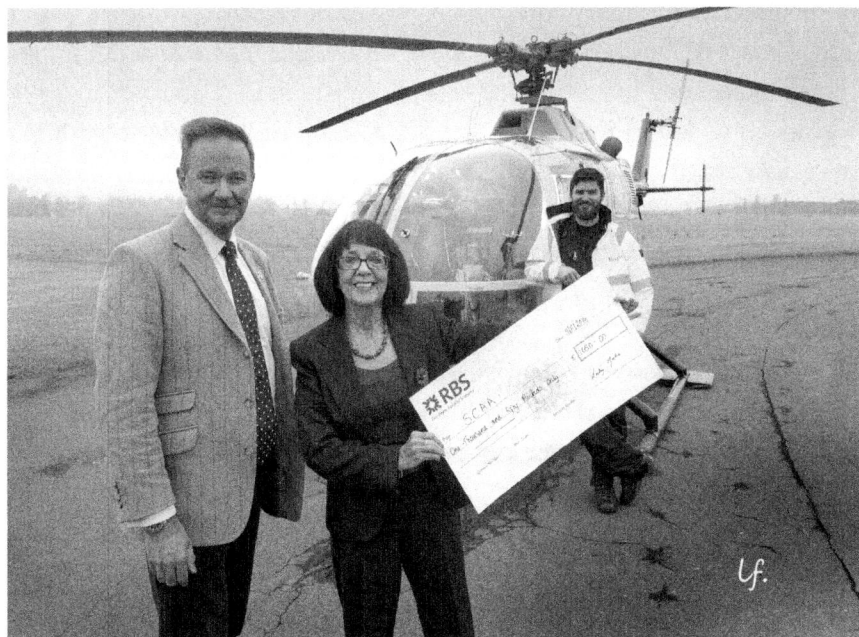

With Gavin Davey.

All in all we raised £2,050 and we set up a press photo with a rescue helicopter from SCAA out at Scone airport, where we handed over large dummy cheques to Andy Middlemiss and Gavin Davey.

We received lovely emails from them both. … *It was a concert that will stay forever in our memory, those lucky enough to have been there. For you to have chosen us as one of the two beneficiaries was wonderful. To also choose a newish charity as co-beneficiary, the Scottish Charity Air Ambulance, which is saving lives in a physical way, was an inspired combination. What an emotional journey you took us on. It was electrifying.*

With the wedding and *Lest We Forget* now but hazy memories, we had another event just around the corner. Terry wanted to support me in my projects, but it was getting to the stage where he was always looking forward to 'the morning after' – the morning after whatever bookings we had in the diary. We thought we had said goodbye to *Toujours l'Amour* towards the end of 2011, but I had been approached by Horsecross Arts about doing it again and all four of our team were keen. It would take place at the Perth Concert Hall on Thursday, February 19th, 2015, was called *An Evening in Paris*, and we were sharing with The Alex Yellowlees Band. Not being part of a tour, we needed a few leaflets and posters, as a one-night gig on a cold Thursday in February might need a bit of help, but they did an excellent mail-out, jointly advertising our evening and Barbara Dickson's – and I was more than happy to share billing with her. After the show we chatted until about 2am, and at last Terry was able to go to bed, dreaming of 'the morning after', which always does eventually arrive.

Later that month I happened to cross paths with Alan Dear one evening at the Bonar Hall in Dundee. He greeted me warmly before asking me why I'd never done the 'Piaf' for him at the Gardyne Theatre, and I said that we'd certainly love to do it one more time – particularly as it was in my home town, and in Piaf's centenary year. So we confirmed a date for *Toujours l'Amour* on Dec 11th, just a few days before the actual centenary on December 19th.

Suddenly, Robin Hardy was back in touch, with news of a movie! Undaunted by the failure of *The Wicker Tree*, he was planning the third part of the trilogy, *The Wrath of the Gods*. This time he was offering me the part of a statuesque, forbidding, nursing sister from a holy order – Sister Firebrace – requiring a huge headdress to give me added height, which would, at least, be a change from a fat suit. It was to be filmed in either Iceland or The Shetland Islands, which was an exhilarating prospect.

The most likely outcome, having read the script, was that the whole thing would bomb, but the website for the film was duly launched and I was quite surprised to find that I was one of the main weapons in their armoury. Their announcement said: *The Wrath of the Gods Ltd. is pleased to announce that LESLEY MACKIE will return for the third and final film, taking on the role of SISTER FIREBRACE in The Wrath of the Gods! She made her film debut in Robin Hardy's The Wicker Man (1973), playing the role of the schoolgirl, Daisy. Lesley then returned to star as Daisy the Cook in the second film in this set of three, The Wicker Tree (2011). In the great tradition of nursing matrons in English films optimised by Hattie Jacques, Sister Firebrace is a woman of 'striking appearance'. Costume in this film is that of her nursing order The Sisters of The Penitents. We are thrilled to welcome Lesley back to complete this set of three films!* A massive build up, and clearly, their film would now take off!

I met Robin on Perth Station towards the end of May, when he talked of various stars he was keen to enlist – Tilda Swinton in particular – and his need to do crowdfunding as a way of raising the budget. Once the 'Wrath' website went up, people didn't seem too keen to donate ten bucks for a signed poster – or even $5,000 for the honour of being an extra – and the situation was becoming more excruciating by the day, as everything came to a grinding halt. I think the total reached was less than $8,000. I put it on the back burner and awaited further developments.

Remembering Loos was a Dundee event in which I was keen to participate. There was to be a concert in the Caird Hall, a Black Watch service and the Lord Provost's special event in the City Square, all to commemorate the Battle of Loos and to take place over the weekend of September 25th, the day the original battle had taken place in 1915, 100 years before. The monument on the top of the Law (Scottish word for hill) was lit every year in memory of the decimated 4th Battalion ('Dundee's own') and other soldiers lost in that horrendous battle. I was invited to be one of the main speakers at the Lord Provost's occasion in the City Square, but was quite anxious about the lengthy tale I was expected to deliver about the battle, as I couldn't imagine how it would hold the attention of 1,000 veterans and dignitaries sitting in the open air. A brief summary of the battle might have impact; a detailed account of the armies, positions, tactics and endless French names might not. There was to be a 'royal presence' so Buckingham Palace was putting its oar in with the Royal Chaplain overseeing the six ministers and their various readings and prayers, and anything military was vetted by some General or other. To my surprise I discovered that the 'royal presence' – the Duke and Duchess of Rothesay – were not minor royals as I had imagined, but none other than Charles and Camilla.

My reading had been specially commissioned and written by Trevor Royle, author of many books and articles on the First World War, so I was not allowed to alter at will. Rev. Jeremy Auld, who was organising the event, had taken my comments very seriously though, and the matter was debated at the highest level, the result being that I was allowed to find synonyms for obscure words, make tiny edits but, to sum it up, I had to make it live by the sheer force of my delivery!

The day dawned and we headed to Dundee and our special parking space under the Caird Hall. We had a sound check once everything was in place although, being a royal occasion, the painting was still going on, and the Rev. Auld got white paint all over his black cassock in his keenness to bring out the newly-painted lectern. He rushed off to find a garage with paint remover and eventually returned with no visible trace. Terry disappeared to try and find a pew in the 1,000-strong throng, and we took up our places in our allotted seats. The royals arrived and we began. It all went well, and the weather held – just. I was aware as I sat down after my lengthy tale that I had (in common parlance) nailed it.

At the end of the service we had refreshments in the Marryat Hall, and the royals came in to shake a few hands and meet a few of the 'great and the good' of Dundee. Terry and I missed getting into the 'line-up' to shake the royal hands, but we watched from the sidelines, Terry clutching a cup of tea. As the royal party began to depart the hall and make their way to another area where all the veterans were waiting, Charles suddenly spotted us, stopped his journey, broke away from his party and came directly to us, where he shook Terry's hand, instigated a conversation about cups of tea, and then took my hand, saying how brilliant the reading had been. He was so warm and sincere that, although I have never been a royalist, at that moment I became a fan. We left Dundee with our souvenir programmes along with our Battle of Loos commemorative mugs. I received another lovely email from Andy Middlemiss, who had been somewhere in the marching regiments on the day: *We all said in my squad how marvellously well you read - how expressively and patiently, quite nerve wracking eh! Sorry to miss you in the scrum, but we had a stunning day. Andy.* I was delighted to have the approval of the military.

Toujours l'Amour turned out to be the major event of our winter, but just ten days before the concert, I caught a throat infection and my voice virtually disappeared. The tickets were going very well, so it would be a total disaster if we had to pull out. A few days before the event, Terry caught the bug and started coughing like a consumptive, and then Mike arrived for one rehearsal, full of the cold. Jim, our accordionist, was the only one still in fine fettle. Things were not boding well, and I was only just beginning to feel as if I might make it when the day arrived. Although Terry's voice had returned, he was still exhausted with the virus and struggled through the afternoon lighting session, but Dr Theatre came to the rescue and our show went as well as it had ever done. I think I compensated for my weaker vocal timbres by acting out Piaf's disintegration in more dramatic detail, and Terry got through on his adrenalin. He got praise for his vocal qualities and lovely singing, and after all the compliments, even pondered on the possibility of doing it again one day!

To walk into the bar afterwards and see so many people that I knew from past and present, was a lovely way to say au revoir to the show, and to bring our cabaret days to an end. Mike was becoming involved in other areas of the entertainment business, and I had no desire to start rehearsing with anyone else, as he was wonderful in our show. Our story had revolved so much around the lives of Judy Garland and Edith Piaf, but it was time to hang up the ruby slippers and little black dress.

But there's a postscript: when you're having an uneventful career far away from the bright lights, it comes as a surprise to be invited to any glitzy occasion! On March 30th, 2016, I headed down to London to take part in a very special one. A few weeks before, I had received a message from Julian Bird who was organising the event – and I take my hat off to him as it was some amazing feat. They were inviting all previous winners of the *Best Performance by an Actress in a Musical* to attend and perform in the finale of the 40th Olivier Awards at the Royal Opera House on Sunday, April 3rd. This was doubly exciting, being the theatre where Terry had played Puck in Benjamin Britten's *A Midsummer Night's Dream* at the invitation of Sir John Gielgud back in 1961.

As time passed I heard that only 16 had accepted and it was mainly the young ones who were coming along – no Judi Dench, no Julia McKenzie, no Virginia McKenna; I would be one of the vintage attendees. Katy was now an agent living in London, and was keen to come to the performance, but I'd been told that tickets were at a premium and I hated to ask – she said I had to learn how to behave like a diva! We were then informed that we could all have one guest who would accompany us on the Red Carpet, have a seat in the balcony for the show and join us afterwards for the party. It should have been Terry who shared such a special occasion, but we knew that the time he would have to occupy himself might be challenging, as he was no longer fit enough to cope alone in the busy metropolis.

It was great to be back in a rehearsal situation with different egos: ladies who seemed extremely confident, those in work, those not, but all friendly and approachable, and a couple of whom, like Sharon D Clarke, have gone on to even greater things, adding more 'Oliviers' to their collections! After a matinee of *People, Places and Things*, I went to Katy's office to shut my eyes for ten minutes, get changed and go for a bite at the sushi bar nearby before attending the press night of *How the Other Half Loves* just across the road. I was delighted to see Bill Kenwright in the foyer. I hadn't seen him for almost 30 years, but he greeted me as if he'd seen me yesterday, gathering a few of his coterie to tell them that I'd given one of the best performances he'd ever seen; typical Bill, but quite comforting; the fact that I might never see or hear from him again was irrelevant. Rod Coton, Bill's former assistant, was just a few rows behind us, and although Facebook acquaintances for some time, our paths had never crossed, so we shared a smile and a wave. I also managed to exchange a few words with Alan Strachan, who had directed the Ayckbourn play that evening, and who we'd last seen at our small-scale production of *Judy* in Perth.

On the red carpet.

On Sunday, the Audi driver arrived to take me to the Royal Opera House. After a short rehearsal, I disappeared to the canteen to get a snack to keep me going until it was time to meet Katy at 5.30pm to head onto the Red Carpet; I was wearing my red, vintage Ossie Clark dress, kept since the early '70s. The crowds weren't really interested in anyone except the stars, although at one point all cameras were turned in our direction – but only because Eddie Izzard was behind us! Katy headed to the balcony, and I was taken to a reserved area with the other ladies, where we found little goodie bags on the seats. We watched the performances before being ushered backstage at the interval when we refreshed our make-up and then floated around waiting for our finale number. I managed to say "Hi" to Michael Feinstein – one of our idols – and then it was our moment.

With Michael Harrison at the after show party.

As I entered I knew that somewhere behind me was my name, the year I'd won and JUDY; it was incredibly moving to be on that wonderful stage in that amazing building singing our hearts out. After the show I got lost in the maze of corridors, but was eventually guided out front, and directed upstairs to the party where Katy was waiting. It was crammed but we quickly relaxed, enjoying the people-watching, chatting if we saw anyone we knew, grazing as the food passed, and knocking back a few glasses of wine. We were on the point of leaving when Ben Stock, an old friend from the Perth *Annie*, and partner of Julian Bird, signalled to us to make our way through the crowds to where he was located at the other side of the room. Our journey led us to a glorious quiet area where we settled in, took a few more photos, chatted to Maria Friedman and had a laugh with the lovely Darius Campbell, musical artiste, sadly no longer with us. We felt sorry for John, our lovely taxi driver, who we'd led to believe that we would be out before midnight, but he didn't seem to mind being woken up when we emerged at 12.45am; a lovely evening – and quite an emotional one remembering a special night over 29 years before when I was pregnant with Katy as I went up to collect my own award.

With Katy & Ben Stock.   *With Darius Campbell & Katy.*

The Facebook and email messages occupied me for a few days, and I received the following: *Dear Little One. It was so lovely seeing you at my opening – and then I did see you performing at the Oliviers on TV. And it did have our image behind you! I send my love to you and Terry. Alongside cherished memories of a truly great performance. God bless you. Bill.*

It was not long before I was invited to another occasion, which was a 40th Olivier Summer party at the V&A. My initial reaction

was not to bother, and then I thought – hey, these parties don't come along too often, and it's another excuse to wallow in a bit of nostalgia. I met a few actors who I'd worked with back in the day, and whom I hadn't seen since: Simon Callow at the Young Lyceum in *Voyzeck* at the Edinburgh Festival in 1973, Patrick Stewart (now Sir) in *The Anatomist* (BBC 1979), and Matthew Kelly in a 7/84 tour of John McGrath's *Bitter Apples* (1979). Katy was my 'plus one' again and made a couple of new contacts herself.

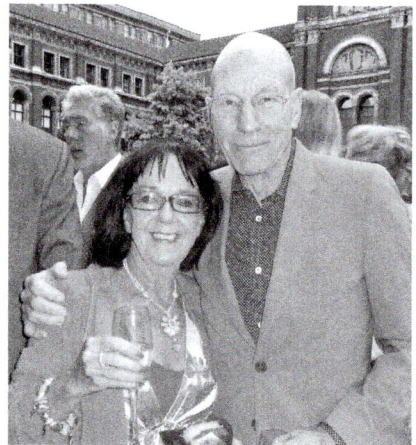

While down there it was sad to hear of the passing of Robin Hardy at the age of 86, only a year since our last meeting on Perth station. He never lost his energy and enthusiasm and had such hopes of completing his Wicker trilogy with *Wrath of the Gods*, but it was not to be. Maybe his legacy was always going to be the original film, but to have been the only one to appear in all three would have been something else. To be connected, albeit in a small way, with such a cult film has been special – and I've met many lovely 'Wicker' people on the way, with whom I keep in touch.

A few years ago I had the honour of opening the *Wee Wicker Man Fest* in the Isle of Whithorn with a few words and a rendition of the Highland Lament that I sang in the film. The Isle is off the beaten track and there were times as we drove down, that we wondered if we would ever emerge from the wilds of the Galloway Hills. But the weather was divine, and we eventually returned to civilisation, stopping for a coffee in Newton Stewart, where I stayed over 45 years before when I was filming. Whithorn was gorgeous, as was *The Steam Packet Inn*, overlooking the harbour. They showed the film in the village hall, and I took part in a Q&A session. Saturday saw the bands, the stalls, the memorabilia and the burning of a wicker man on the beach.

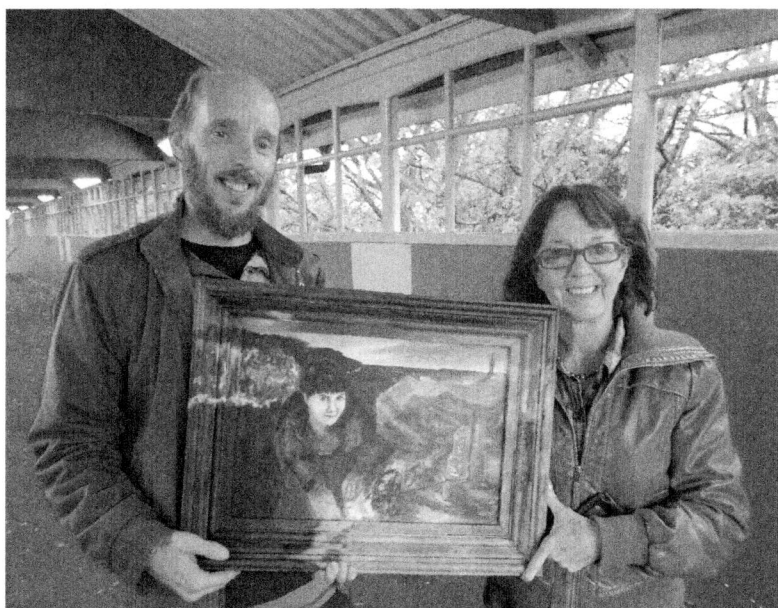

Commemorative painting by Amanda Sunderland presented to me by Ian Thomas, a Wicker enthusiast.

Life was beginning to be more about the past than the present, and at the end of October 2018 we spent a few days in London attending a reunion with some of the cast from *Brigadoon* – 30 years after the Victoria Palace Theatre production; a lovely occasion where we reminisced and toasted those no longer with us, vowing to meet again in 100 years' time!

It is clear that my life was busy and fun, but no longer with many professional engagements, except for the audio books. In the absence of a Scottish agent, I sometimes felt a little cheated when I heard through the grapevine about various exciting castings after they had been cast, but actors are an unusual breed, and however disillusioned, we tend to remain optimistic.

Terry and I with our audiobooks.

It kind of sums up how blinkered we had become about the lack of regular work and the reasons for it, when I decided, after many years with my lovely London agent, to look at her website, and discovered that she didn't have one! Most agents have websites where casting directors can access the photos, audio files and show-reels of their clients, but my agent was of the old school and a bit of a dinosaur, which she freely admitted.

But things can suddenly happen which make you realise that nothing is impossible! Spring 2019 was jogging along with the occasional audio book until the arrival of an audition for the role of Mrs Bug in *Outlander*. After my initial horror at the amount to learn, I set about it, and my audition went rather splendidly. I was told I was 'in the pot', which is where I stayed in some trepidation until I reached a short list of three. From then on the stress was enormous, though exciting when I learned that the job would last for two series. Two weeks from the starting date they came back to ask if I was still available; I was down to the last two. For another day I was on pins, but alas – it 'went the other way'. I think this was a final turning point for me; I didn't really want to pursue much else after that, I'd proven I could still do it, although confirming that the odds are always stacked against you. When I was going through it all I read the 'Quote of the Week' in *The Stage*: *A three-month process of auditions for a life-changing job and you wait, knowing you've been short listed. Today I get the call saying the role is on offer to someone else. This is what makes us actors – we cope with rejection. Onwards, upwards.*

When I read my story, I'm aware that it often sounds as if life in the business has been a constant struggle, but I guess I haven't mentioned all the easy straightforward jobs, as a story is usually more compelling if it's full of angst, uncertainty and turmoil. Terry used to write a Christmas letter, and if we had a rocky year, his letter was always more entertaining. I lost count of the times when the going got rough, and I said, "Well, at least you've got material for next year's Christmas letter!"

As 2019 ended, we were still smarting from the endless Brexit furore. Could the nation ever begin to heal? People were 'unfriending' others on Facebook as a result of the dissension caused by the whole sorry affair. There were, apparently, still many who wanted Brexit, Deal or No Deal, whatever the cost. But if we thought this was traumatic, little did we know what 2020 held in store.

Here in Croft Court, our year began positively as we took a step forward with Terry's long-awaited memoirs, *Pretending to Be Somebody Else*. There were a few hurdles to overcome, the main issue being the length; having been written over the past 25 years and covering his life and career from child actor back in the '50s right through to his recent retirement, it was a large tome. I took on the job of proofreading and editing, with little conception of how long it would take. We began in January, and it went on for over nine months, with a prolonged exhausting labour and eventual birth in October. I spent hours on the computer daily: checking punctuation, spelling, factual accuracy (especially after I made my entrance on page 326!), and scanning photos old and new. There was dissent over certain aspects, and times when we doubted the wisdom of having ever embarked on it as we contemplated possible litigation! Terry didn't seem to think it was of any consequence that he referred to one producer as 'an unprincipled shit' and to a theatre director as the 'Wicked Witch of the North'. "But they were!", he said.

Brexit finally happened at the end of January, but was quickly forgotten as the world changed for everyone with the arrival of the coronavirus. As Europe virtually collapsed under the strain, millions ailed and many died with this new 'plague', and we all began a new way of life: shielding, self-isolation, social distancing, and wearing masks. At one stage, some people only emerged once a week to 'Clap for our Carers'! And it went on and on. People dealt with it in many ways: some acquired a new language, renovated their homes, transformed their gardens or became kitchen goddesses - not to mention dealing with a deluge of cartoons, video clips, songs, and home-made entertainment until we all reached saturation point.

I started with many resolutions, but most fell by the wayside as I worked on Terry's memoirs. As friends told of how many books they had read during 'lock-down' I was saying that I had read one lengthy book five times! As Terry was 'shielding' – and not the most obedient shielded man – I had to keep a close eye on his antics as he kept slipping out to the Co-op, and on a couple of occasions had falls on the way back. We saw little of the kids and missed them dreadfully, but we had an online family life, and our diaries were full of Zoom meetings with them and with our publisher. There were phone calls to folk who weren't so comfortable online but needed to keep in touch. In order to get my daily exercise, I had to combine walking with making calls, otherwise I'd never have left my chair. The downside was that if I crossed paths with anyone I knew, I always had a phone strapped to my right ear!

Strangely, we felt busier than before the lock down, although not with any paid work. Medical roleplay was put on hold, and just when I had begun a new role as a Funeral Celebrant, many people were having private ceremonies with memorials planned for some day in the distant future. Work felt less important in the Covid years, which brought everything to a standstill and isolated us all. As for theatre, I could only feel regret for all the young talented people who were just starting out and hanging onto every glimmer of hope. *Soundings*, the audio book company we had both worked with for many years, closed in March, although another avenue opened for me at Isis Books in Oxford, and we went down later in the year to record a book, the only traumatic part being that we got caught up in the second English lock down; having been told that we had to vacate our room by midnight, we only avoided sleeping in the car or driving through the night by persuading the Premier Inn that I was a 'key worker'! 'Lockdown' was named Word of the Year by Collins Dictionary because it encapsulated the shared experience of billions around the world.

As long ago as 2010 I'd been drawn to the idea of becoming a civil celebrant, but I discovered very early on that it was almost as difficult to get a foot in the door of a Funeral Director as get an audition for an acting job! A few years later, and after an email from a friend in Dundee, bemoaning the quality of funeral services at the crematorium because of the constant use of the same few celebrants, I decided to have another go. Since my father's death in 2013 I'd continued visiting Dr John Scott, the psychiatrist who helped dad after his time in Burma during WW2. John was convinced that he wasn't long for this world; with deteriorating health and eyesight, he was tiring of 'waiting for the last bus'. Things were accelerated by a casual conversation on one of my regular visits; because of his lack of faith, he'd decided that he wanted no service, but I felt that he might be denying his family the chance to put him centre stage for the last time. After much thought he asked if I would be willing to conduct his service and he wanted to plan it with me. Having checked that his sons were happy with this turn of events, I agreed; this might be my training.

Dr John Scott

We loved the planning: the eulogy, the choosing of music – and the photograph session! John was a most interesting man with definite ideas about what he wanted said – including how much he had loved every cigarette he had ever smoked! I even went to his undertaker of choice to do a bit of pre-planning. John had asked me to be ready by Jan 4th, 2017, his 90th birthday, a milestone he wanted to reach, but January 4th passed, and I came to realise that John had a new lease of life – and partly because of the funeral planning; he was loving it. I attended funerals when possible, and did a lot of reading on the subject, having procured notes and other materials from a very good course, so having completed the preparation as far as I could, I put everything on hold. I was in a state of limbo, not knowing whether to forge out on my own, or wait until I conducted John's funeral, unless he outlived me!

In the meantime, another friend asked me if I would conduct proceedings for a friend of hers who was bedridden in a care home in Perth. I went for a few meetings with the lady who suffered from extreme mental and physical health issues, which she'd had throughout her life. A strange moment of black comedy came one day when she said that she'd never seen my face, so bowed over was she with her condition. After a couple of attempts to get my face below hers, I finally threw myself on the floor, and as she looked over her bed she said, "Oh, you're a younger person than I thought you were!" I joked that she was seeing me in a great position with my face pulled back at its best angle, and we laughed – but there weren't too many laughs as her suffering was great. Whereas John's eulogy was going to be lengthy, hers would be fairly brief. It would be a burial, with a short eulogy at the graveside and a rendering of *Amazing Grace.*

My two clients soldiered on for a couple of years and died within a few weeks of each other in the winter of 2019. I was more than ready and got tremendous satisfaction from conducting the funerals and went on to conduct several more. I had just got into my stride when Covid struck.

Looking back, the first half of my career had a semblance of a shape, and I can see the development and achievements along the road to winning the Olivier Award. At the time there were many who saw the award as the beginning of a new life and a kind of guarantee that I would go on in the same vein for the foreseeable future, but the best laid plans 'gang aft agley'. Actors are rarely in charge of their own destiny. There are many parts I'd like to have played and many companies with whom I'd love to have had the opportunity to work; there were times when I just missed a particular role by a hair's breadth – or indeed was offered a lovely part but wasn't free to do it, and of course there were times when there was no work around at all, particularly after I returned to Scotland.

I recall the couple who ran our local Post Office asking, "What made you move back? You're never so appreciated if you live round the corner." And when I got involved with a group of actors doing medical roleplay at Ninewells Hospital in Dundee, I arrived one morning at the Mackenzie Building, gave my name, and the receptionist said, "Are you the actress, Lesley Mackie?". "Indeed I am", I responded. She quipped: "Is this a step up or a step down?", which I found very amusing.

Although the opportunities were no longer coming my way, I put a great price on local fame, and being surrounded by those who have followed my career from my childhood made me feel welcome back in my home country, and still gives me pleasure today. My cousin, Susan, was a nurse in a care home and one day while entertaining the residents with a music quiz, they played Judy Garland singing *Over the Rainbow*. "Who is the star singing that song?" was the question put to the residents. An elderly lady shouted out "Lesley Mackie". That made my day!

Over the years when things were quiet, I came to realise how much it meant to me to have the Olivier Award, but it hit home on the occasion when Bernie Lloyd came to visit in 2015. He was clearly unhappy with the way things were going for him. His tetchiness and intolerance were extreme, and we finally had a bit of a showdown when I asked him why he seemed so angry all the time.

He suddenly broke down and admitted how hard it had been for him not to have achieved the success of his contemporaries. He said he carried a kind of resentment around with him but we'd never realised that. Over all the years we'd known him, we'd marvelled at the way he seemed to cope with the fact that he had worked alongside and formed deep friendships with Patrick Stewart, David Suchet and Ben Kingsley, all of whom had been knighted and had incredible success in the business but it hadn't happened for him. He was a fine actor, but hadn't had the luck and opportunities afforded to a few. That aside, he always spoke of his old friends with tremendous warmth and kept in touch with Patrick and David throughout his life. When Terry sympathised and compared my own situation, and the oft frustrating times I'd had since moving back north, Bernie suddenly became quite impassioned, and pointing to my Olivier Award on the top of a small bookcase, emoted "But she's got one of those!"

To anyone who thinks that awards are not important, I'll never forget that visit when Bernie brought home to me that whatever has or has not occurred in my life, they can't take that away from me. I've got 'one of those'!

Epilogue

I can't finish without saying that we managed to get Terry's book published in October 2020, and despite the work and stress involved, I am glad that we spent so much time on the project, as he was thrilled to have completed the book.

By the time we returned to my memoirs, Terry was not a well man, and 2021 became a bit of a blur as his health deteriorated with lung cancer, atrial fibrillation and cognitive decline. We nursed him at home, and unable to attend Katy and Dickie's wedding on October 30th; he went into care during the time we were away, which still hurts me to contemplate.

At the end of November, I went to Oxford to record an audio book, and after an urgent call from Ollie, who stayed with Terry in my absence, Katy, Dickie, baby Teddy and I drove through the night and reached home in time to be with my darling husband as he died on December 1st .

Apart from conducting his funeral, I succeeded in getting him a spacious obituary in *The Stage*, and his name in the *Equity Magazine* memorial section – both on his wish list. We managed to watch last year's Olivier Awards late one night on the telly, and imagine our joy when we realised during the memorial section, that the massive board onstage, listing all the dear departed who had not been singled out for individual mention, included Terry Wale as the first name in the last line on that board. He would have been thrilled.

The last happy occasion he attended was a small celebration for my 70th birthday with a few friends at my brother's house in Dundee.

No one can prepare you for widowhood or being without your buddy of 44 years, but for the past year I've thrown myself into completing this memoir, a project he would have loved to have shared; it has been a consolation and something to focus on during the raw grieving time.

And just when I think it's all over, I'm reminded that this year is the 50th anniversary of the release of *The Wicker Man,* and being one of the few people who was part of the film so many years ago, life has become a succession of Zoom meetings, and sharing Wicker tales, of which I have many, with aficionados planning Wicker documentaries, books, and May Day celebrations in some of the film locations. I plan to be there on the Isle of Whithorn, lustily singing *Summer is a cumin in*, along with Ian, Fergal and many more Wicker enthusiasts. I hope to participate in an anniversary concert on June 24th at the Barbican Theatre in London.

70th birthday celebrations

Printed in Great Britain
by Amazon